FASHIONING THE CROWN

FASHIONING THE CROWN

A STORY OF POWER, CONFLICT, AND COUTURE

JUSTINE PICARDIE

PEGASUS BOOKS
NEW YORK LONDON

FASHIONING THE CROWN

Pegasus Books, Ltd.
148 West 37th Street, 13th Floor
New York, NY 10018

First Pegasus Books cloth edition February 2026

Frontispiece image: Postcard of Queen Elizabeth II.
Photograph by Dorothy Wilding, 1954.

Library of Congress Cataloging-in-Publication Data is available.

ISBN: 979-8-89710-013-2

10 9 8 7 6 5 4 3 2 1

Printed in the United States of America
Distributed by Simon & Schuster
www.pegasusbooks.com

For my husband, Philip Astor

CONTENTS

'I HAVE TO BE SEEN TO BE BELIEVED'

The first time I met Queen Elizabeth II – who will always be 'the Queen' for me – I was lost for words, as so many people were in those circumstances. She was accustomed to this; indeed, my husband, who had known her since childhood, said that even the most sophisticated individuals often 'talked gibberish' when they were introduced to the Queen. As a consequence, she tended to ask simple questions, but on this occasion, her generic opener – 'Have you come far?' – would not help, given that she already knew the answer. We had been invited to dinner at Balmoral, just a few miles from my husband's family home in the Scottish Highlands, and when the Queen greeted me, I somehow managed to curtsey without falling over, while feeling utterly awestruck by the power of her presence. Awe is not conducive to conversation; like countless others before me, I became tongue-tied and inept.

I had not grown up in a monarchist household – on the contrary, my father espoused Marxism during my 1960s childhood; nor had I become an ardent royalist in adulthood. Insofar as I ever thought about the Queen, it was as a reassuringly consistent, grandmotherly figure in the background of our national life, although marginal to my own day-to-day existence. Yet suddenly here she was before me, dazzling in an array of diamond jewellery and an exquisitely embroidered silver evening gown, the magnificent manifestation of her own adage, 'I have to be

Princess Elizabeth, July 1951. Photograph by Yousuf Karsh.

seen to be believed.' The Queen was in her early eighties at the time, but her age seemed immaterial. Instead, I was struck by the glamour and grace of her appearance; by her fine, pale skin and the sparkling blue of her eyes that matched her sapphire earrings; and by the way she looked patiently at me while I stumbled through an attempt at small talk. At the end of that memorable evening, I felt that the Queen was possessed of her own unique style, embodying majesty, mystery and myth. If these are the fundamental qualities of a successful monarch, then our limited conversation was almost irrelevant: her sartorial splendour and superb jewels did the talking.

Our second meeting also took place at Balmoral, this time in a remote mountain bothy on the estate. My husband was shooting with a royal party that day, and the Queen and two or three others, including me, joined them for lunch. She was surrounded by her favourite corgis; fortunately, I am fond of dogs, and such was their steadying influence that I was able to speak in complete sentences, although still rather stilted by shyness. By this point, I had published a biography of Coco Chanel, and had become intrigued by the little-known story of Sir Hardy Amies, one of the Queen's former couturiers, who had risen to the rank of lieutenant colonel during the Second World War. I mentioned to her that my mother had known him, and that I had met him several times before his death in 2003, while I was working at *Vogue*. And then I plucked up courage to ask her about Amies's role as a senior intelligence officer for the Special Operations Executive, liaising with the Belgian Resistance as an undercover agent. The Queen looked at me, with the merest hint of a raised eyebrow, and said, 'Ah yes, those rumours that he was very good at garrotting Nazis.' I had not, in fact, heard any such tales, but tried to mirror her exemplary composure, as a brief silence fell between us. 'Of course, it was excellent cover for a spy, to be a couturier,' she continued; an observation that implied some knowledge of the ways in which clothes can be used to conceal, rather than reveal, the secrets of those who make and wear them.

Before I could ask another question, she deftly changed the subject, steering the conversation towards a less startling anecdote, connected to

The Queen walking at Balmoral, 1967.

my position as the editor of *Harper's Bazaar*. A former wartime editor of the magazine, remarked the Queen, had subsequently married the Scottish laird of a neighbouring estate to Balmoral, and astonished the locals with her flamboyant hats and shocking pink Schiaparelli outfits. 'It caused quite a stir at church,' she said, and smiled wryly, adding that the editor's handwriting was utterly illegible. 'One simply couldn't make any sense of it, whichever way one looked at it.' And here the matter ended, as if in tacit acknowledgement that there would be no further discussion of fashion (let alone espionage) or those who engaged in its obscure and arcane practice.

Needless to say, the Queen was more traditionally dressed than her erstwhile neighbour; at ease in her customary countrywoman's attire of a tartan skirt and leaf-green cardigan, woollen stockings and durable brown leather shoes. It has often been observed that the Queen felt most at home at Balmoral; certainly, this was the place where she could relax into the quiet rural life that she might have enjoyed, in other circumstances, had it not been for her uncle's dramatic abdication in 1936, which made her heir presumptive to the throne. I caught a glimpse of an alternate reality that day, after lunch had finished and the shooting party set off again; for she donned a pair of yellow rubber gloves, and together we cleared away the plates, glasses and cutlery. 'Make sure you don't miss any crumbs,' said the Queen, while I wiped down the table; and then I followed her lead in putting everything back in its proper place, including packing the leftover food into neat Tupperware containers.

This peaceful interlude of domesticity seemed to please the Queen more than our previous conversation, and called to mind the description given of her as a little girl by her Scottish governess, Marion Crawford, who wrote in her memoir: 'Lilibet [as Elizabeth was known affectionately by her family] was a very neat child. She kept her books and all her belongings immaculately tidy. But though no one tried harder or persevered more painstakingly, she never was any good with her needles. This I always felt was a disappointment to her grandmother, that indefatigable knitter, Queen Mary.' Instead, Lilibet preferred playing with her most treasured possessions: thirty or so toy horses, lined up outside the nursery, whose saddles she carefully cleaned and polished every evening. At five, she started riding lessons, which she loved, and her passion for horses was reflected in her reading material; one of her favourite books was *Black Beauty*. Lilibet would also pretend to be a horse herself – 'making convincing little whinnying noises' – or harnessed her governess with a pair of red reins, in a long-running game that involved the delivery of groceries to make-believe customers.

Miss Crawford frequently worried that the young princess was 'almost too methodical and tidy. She would hop out of bed several times a night to get her shoes quite straight, her clothes arranged just so.' Only once did the conscientious little girl behave out of character, her discipline slipping during a French lesson 'taught by a certain Mademoiselle', whose 'methods consisted mainly in the writing out of endless columns of verbs . . . Lilibet, rebelling all of a sudden, and goaded by boredom to violent measures, had picked up the big ornamental silver inkpot and placed it without any warning upside down on her head. She sat there, with ink trickling down her face and slowly dyeing her golden curls blue.'

By the time I met the Queen, her golden curls had turned to silver, and Lilibet's rebellious streak had long since been quelled by decades of rigorous self-control. Yet she retained her childhood love of horses, still riding every morning, wearing a silk Hermès headscarf instead of a protective helmet, much to the dismay of those responsible for her safety. When questioned about her refusal to wear a riding hat, she would say that she didn't want to 'squash' her hair. Perhaps she found pleasure in that small but significant episode of unsquashed recklessness, in her otherwise unimpeachable daily routine. To be a good horsewoman – and she was an outstanding one – is to understand the fine balance between freedom and discipline, wildness and restraint. Her cherished horses, like her adored dogs, did not know she was a queen; they behaved as naturally with her as she did with them. They saw her for who she was; or rather, who she was free to be in their company.

Once, after another shooting lunch with the Queen at Balmoral, I went for a long walk with her daughter-in-law Camilla, who was then the Duchess of Cornwall. We had a surprisingly candid conversation – mostly about books, where Camilla's shrewd and subtle intelligence was clear, but also about the intense pressures on women who marry into the royal family. I remember that we spoke about Daphne du Maurier's gothic novels, and the haunting quality of *Rebecca*, with its nameless narrator; and the lingering presence of the dead first wife in that disquieting story. As we talked, I was reminded that Daphne du Maurier herself (whose life I have written about in a previous book) had stayed at Balmoral for a week in 1953, when her husband was a senior courtier to Prince Philip. Du Maurier found the experience almost unbearably stressful, partly due to the anxiety-inducing protocol that involved dressing up every evening, and because she could never think of anything to say to the Queen. She found Prince Philip only slightly less terrifying, telling a friend: 'I heard sounds coming out of my mouth I did not recognise.' I can relate to this, too, for I was always rather frightened of Prince Philip, with his piercing, hawk-like eyes that saw through any attempt to disguise one's sense of alarm.

At the time, and over the following days, I was struck by the continuing insistence on duty and decorum: the endless requirements that royal women, in particular, must always be polite and perfectly dressed; the strict regime that governs their lives, as they smile and shake hands and wave to the public. Even in private, it seemed, the unwritten rules prevailed: never complain, never explain; keep calm and carry on. I wondered, too, if the ghostly memory of Camilla's predecessor, Princess Diana, was our invisible companion as we walked down that mountain track, along a stony path that she had doubtless trod before us. Beautiful Diana, who refused to stay silent; glorious Diana, who danced and raged and wept; defiant Diana, who in her own way tipped the ink pot over her golden hair in her rebellious reaction to journalists; maddened and maddening Diana, who sought to tell her story, to make her feelings known, instead of keeping her exquisite lips sealed.

Now that Camilla is queen, I find myself thinking again of our conversation on that faraway summer's afternoon. Camilla has not faltered;

she has followed in the steady footsteps of previous queens, almost from the moment the crown was placed on her head at the coronation of King Charles III. Then, she gave only the briefest sign of nervousness, touching her hair, adjusting it beneath the heavy weight of the crown – the same one worn by Queen Mary, Charles's great-grandmother, at George V's coronation in 1911. This is an extraordinary achievement, given the sequence of events that led to Camilla becoming queen – betrayal, heartbreak, divorce, death; a fearful saga of human anguish exposed to the world's merciless judgement.

Bereavement (and with it, intense scrutiny) is, of necessity, an unavoidable accompaniment to the succession of monarchs – the stress of which might explain Charles's occasional irascibility soon after his mother's death made him king. The first signs of irritation were apparent at his accession ceremony at St James's Palace, where he was filmed grimacing at aides and gesturing for a tray of pens to be removed from his desk. Then came the leaking pen incident when he signed a visitors' book at Hillsborough Castle in Northern Ireland. 'Oh God, I *hate* this!' he said, presumably unaware that cameras were still running. 'I can't bear this bloody thing . . . every *stinking* time.' There was no pot of ink to hand, but if there had been, the King looked sufficiently exasperated to have poured it over someone else's head, if not his own. Camilla, admirably cool and composed in her black mourning outfit, took the offending pen from her husband, as he wiped the ink from his fingers, and then signed her own name for posterity.

The King's brief lapses were understandable, on a human level, although disconcerting in comparison to his mother's self-control, which she had learned from her mother and grandmother. Her father and grandfather, however, were prone to equally explosive fits of bad temper during their respective reigns. As an adult, Charles would complain to friends that his mother still treated him 'like a child'; but when he finally acceded to the throne at the age of seventy-three (the oldest monarch in British history), the child in him became visible, if only for a few seconds, before being tucked away beneath the layers of his perfectly tailored suits.

As for my own irrational behaviour when the Queen's death was announced, I burst into tears. The news should not have come as a surprise – she was ninety-six, and visibly frail the last time I had seen her, a few months previously, at the memorial service for Prince Philip. Despite that, I was unexpectedly shocked by her death, and shaken by the feeling that we had lost a crucial symbol of constancy, certainty and continuity. I did not join the immense queue of mourners who waited in turn to file past the Queen's coffin as she lay in state at Westminster Hall, but I watched the news coverage, as an estimated 250,000 people stood patiently for hours, in miles of snaking lines, to pay their last respects to their monarch. In death, her body was finally invisible, hidden from view within the lead-lined oak coffin, which was itself draped with the Royal Standard. Yet her presence, in that liminal space, was made manifest in the Imperial State Crown resting on top of the coffin, alongside the sovereign's orb and sceptre. The mourners wept and bowed their heads before the coffin, raised above them on a crimson catafalque, guarded by soldiers standing vigil in the thousand-year-old hall. This was the place where she, too, had come as a solemn black-veiled mourner for previous generations of her family: first at the age of nine, in 1936, for the lying-in-state of her grandfather, George V; then for her father, George VI, in 1952; her grandmother, Queen Mary, in 1953; and her mother, Queen Elizabeth the Queen Mother, in 2002.

'We shall never see her like again,' said various commentators during the strange, dreamlike period between the announcement of the Queen's death on 8 September 2022 and the state funeral eleven days later; and the phrase circled in my mind, like the interminable queue beside the River Thames, winding towards Westminster Hall. At the same time, we *did* go on seeing the Queen in the media: over and over again, in an endless loop of pictures spinning through her long life. The early black-and-white photographs of her as a newborn baby in 1926 evolved into highly controlled royal portraits that marked the milestones of her reign, and culminated in the digital images of the contemporary era, shared around the world in an instant. In those myriad representations, who was it that we were really

Queen Elizabeth II, Queen Mary and Queen Elizabeth the Queen Mother, in mourning, after the death of George VI, February 1952.

looking at? She was revered by some as a shining symbol of all that made Britain great and reviled by others as a disgraceful relic of an oppressive and cruel colonial past: whatever one's point of view, the Queen's face appeared as familiar as if she were a member of our own family.

Prince Philip had in fact been my husband's godfather, and the royal family were part of the rhythm of his life from infancy: Christmas parties at Buckingham Palace, shooting lunches at Balmoral, summer holidays with the Queen Mother at the Castle of Mey in Caithness. He was certainly capable of making the Queen laugh if he sat next to her at dinner, and she showed many personal kindnesses to him: embracing him in relief when he returned later than expected one evening from a stalking expedition, and writing a sensitive letter when his beloved cocker spaniel went missing. Even so, he remained forever in awe of the Queen, and scrupulously adhered to etiquette, just as his parents had done in the past, and their courtly parents and grandparents before them.

Aside from her closest family and a handful of trusted friends and advisers, very few people could ever claim to have really known the heart of the Queen, for her reticence was inherent to her constitutional position as monarch. Ever since parliamentary supremacy was established in the late seventeenth century, the role of the sovereign has evolved to become ceremonial – to reign, rather than rule – and as such, diplomatic skills are required, along with complete discretion. As a figurehead on the world stage, she was uniquely placed to survey international affairs, and the perpetual machinations behind the scenes. If, as the Queen had so perceptively observed of Hardy Amies, his work as a royal couturier provided a seamless cover story for his activities as a spy, then she too had an understanding of espionage, and the complex ways in which secret statecraft is entwined with diplomacy. Certainly, her regular access to intelligence briefings and confidential documents, delivered in her daily 'red boxes' for seven decades, gave her a more complete overview of the British security services than anyone else in her realm.

As the symbolic head of state, the Queen was obliged to follow the will of her government, at the same time as remaining politically neutral, combining impartiality with loyalty to the Crown. This balancing act was conducted with the utmost secrecy in the weekly meetings she held with her prime minister, where their conversations were entirely confidential. In public, she knew when to remain silent, how to listen, where to tread carefully, why she should avoid saying anything controversial, all the while maintaining an inscrutable appearance, her intentions hidden by the glittering façade of her gowns and jewels. Transparency – that quality so often called for in governance nowadays – was in her case to be avoided, in colloquy and in clothing. For the enigmatic Queen had been educated to believe in the concept of monarchy as described in 1867 by Walter Bagehot in his canonical book *The English Constitution*: 'Above all things our royalty is to be reverenced, and if you begin to poke about it you cannot reverence it . . . Its mystery is its life. We must not let in daylight upon magic.'

Republicans ask why we should continue with the pretence, expense and nonsense of an obsolete monarchy, particularly when it has been besmirched by grubby scandals involving the King's younger brother Andrew. How can such excessive privilege and absurd entitlement be tolerated in a modern democracy? Campaigners for decolonialisation have added their voices to the debate, calling for the Crown to offer reparations for its historic complicity in British imperialism. These are perfectly valid points, and questions that I have asked myself while writing this book. Then another question presents itself, not as an answer, but as a partial explanation for my own curiosity: why is it that so many people in an increasingly secular society remain faithful to the magic and mystery of the Crown? Its vast empire is long gone; its kingdom quarrelsome and disunited; its church declining in significance; its colonial inheritance tainted and stained with blood. And still the British monarchy continues to fascinate a vast global audience. Almost 12 million households in the United States tuned in live to television coverage of the King's coronation (despite the fact that the time difference meant that they were watching in the early hours of the morning). In the UK, viewing peaked at 20.4 million, rather less than for Elizabeth II's funeral (which reached 29.2 million viewers), or for the funeral of Princess Diana

(31 million); but even so, an immense number have chosen to observe these ceremonial religious occasions.

The risk of disruption is always present – perhaps now more than ever, given the speed with which royal mishaps and missteps, vices and vicissitudes, can be circulated and denounced on social media. Yet history suggests that the Crown has never existed in a realm of absolute security, that deference for royalty has always been matched by defiance, and that the ancient robes and rituals associated with the past only survive if they are refreshed and reinvented in response to new dangers. After all, long before the current threats posed by falling approval ratings and rising disenchantment, the monarchy had been confronted by real jeopardy. Consider the tumultuous period between the birth of the house of Windsor in 1917 and the coronation of Elizabeth II in 1953. Her parents and grandparents experienced the horrors of the First World War, where royal cousins were on opposing sides of the conflict; and their kin were murdered during the Russian Revolution. She herself lived through the rise of fascism and the mortal dangers of the Second World War, when her parents narrowly escaped injury or death as Buckingham Palace was bombed in German air raids. Her father's younger brother, the Duke of Kent, was killed in a plane crash on military duty in August 1942. And their older brother, the former King Edward VIII, openly consorted with Nazi leaders, who regarded him as a potential puppet monarch, to be reinstalled on the throne following Germany's planned invasion and subjugation of Britain.

All of which brings me back to my conversation with the Queen about her couturier, Hardy Amies, and why it makes sense that she should rely on a man who understood the menace of Nazism, and the recent perils that she and her family had endured. Unlike her distant ancestors, she was not shielded from enemies by suits of armour. But she had been educated by her closest relatives in the sartorial art of royalty, and the ways in which visual iconography could safeguard the sovereign, even if their reign seemed to be hanging by a thread.

Thus, one cannot begin to fathom the Queen without exploring the turmoil that had engulfed her immediate predecessors on the throne, when, in her father's words, 'the whole fabric' of monarchy was in danger of being torn apart. As such, the royal family came to be protected by its own distinctive uniforms – some overtly military, others relaying coded messages or offering a form of disguise, yet all integral to its identity. Accordingly, from her childhood onwards, the Queen was taught to dress with confidence and conviction. Her clothes, and those of her mother and grandmother before her, thereby represent an intricate pattern of soft power, deployed during a violent era of crisis, both for their family and their realm. And if the garments and jewels of these successive generations of royalty are considered together, they offer tangible clues to trace the Crown's secret history, and how it survived the existential threat of two world wars.

On the day the Queen died, people saw magical signs in the sky: rainbows arching over Buckingham Palace, Windsor Castle and Balmoral. The rainbows vanished, but her royal raiments live on to tell a tale that future generations may learn from, as the monarchy reshapes itself, as it so often has before, to face the challenges ahead.

THE HOUSE OF WINDSOR

If the Queen's heart lay in the Scottish hills of Balmoral, where she died, her final resting place was at Windsor Castle, her ancestral home. This has long been a place of fortification, from its early origins in the eleventh century, when William the Conqueror built it as a strategic stronghold that could be used to defend the monarchy against attack. Hence the decision at the beginning of the Second World War that Lilibet and her younger sister, Margaret Rose, should live within the castle's protective walls and ramparts, attended by Miss Crawford and a company of Grenadier Guards, while their parents were seen to be doing their patriotic duty in London. 'Windsor Castle was a fortress, not a home,' wrote Miss Crawford in her memoir, and recalled their restless nights in the dungeons, which had been converted into a bomb shelter. 'There lingered about it always the memory of others who had probably been incarcerated there, and left some of their unhappiness behind them. The atmosphere was gloomy, and there were beetles.'

More than seventy years later, I went to Windsor Castle for the first time, having been invited by the Queen to stay with my husband, Philip. It was June – we would be attending the races at Royal Ascot – and there were no obvious signs of beetles, nor any imminent threat of bombs. But red-coated guardsmen still paraded, and armed police officers were on patrol. We had been issued in advance with a schedule and dress code for

Soldiers at Windsor Castle, 1948.

formal day and evening wear; I was obliged to bring a surprising number of outfits, hats and accessories, and to change at least twice before lunch. The sartorial requirements were stricter than any I had encountered at the Paris couture shows as the editor of *Harper's Bazaar*, and despite my long experience of the demanding formalities of French fashion houses, a visit to Windsor Castle was infinitely more nerve-racking.

The Queen appeared to be entirely herself in this imposing setting; by which I mean there was never any sense of her performing, in the way that a modern celebrity might do. She was without doubt the most famous woman in the world, but her apparent modesty seemed to me as natural as her dignity. She was not flirtatious, unlike her mother or her mercurial sister; nor did she deploy her regal status as a weapon against others. She embodied the power of pageantry but avoided pomposity, for she held true to her heartfelt belief that she was the servant of the people. And for all her consummate ability to look impassive and unruffled, the rare moments that I witnessed when her face lit up with emotion – as she watched her prized racehorses at Ascot, for example – were wonderfully engaging. The previous year, during her Diamond Jubilee, she had allowed the world to catch a glimpse of her charm and wit, enacting a meeting with James Bond for the spectacular opening of the London Olympics, when it appeared that she was parachuting into the stadium wearing a crystal-embellished peach satin dress. A decade later, she would enchant her public again with another film to mark her Platinum Jubilee – on this occasion a sweet conversation with Paddington Bear (he wore his familiar duffle coat, she a floral print dress; he retrieved a marmalade sandwich from beneath his felt hat, while she took hers from inside her leather handbag). These scripted scenes relied on the Queen's peerless talent for keeping a straight face and playing her part to perfection: as the personification of a quintessential, idealised Britishness.

She did not require much in the way of entertainment, and unlike several other members of her family, she was wholly immune to flattery. Her smile, when it came, was delightful because it was natural, rather than forced. Even so, I felt an acute sense of failure in my inability to amuse her, as my husband apparently could, in our encounters in the majestic state rooms of Windsor Castle. Once, after returning from the races at Ascot, I saw her sitting alone on a crimson damask-upholstered chair by the bay window overlooking the castle grounds. An equerry gave me a polite nudge, and suggested I go and speak to her; I walked over to the chair, feeling self-conscious, and curtseyed. The Queen made a courteous gesture that I should sit down. I murmured something complimentary about her racehorses, and she nodded, kindly, apparently untroubled by my conversational limitations. We talked about the weather, and the beauty of the roses in the Windsor gardens; we returned, again, to the safe and reassuring subject of her dogs. Eventually, she asked if I would like to accompany Philip to see the library. I thanked her, and withdrew, wondering if the correct protocol was to walk backwards, but decided against this, in case I tripped over a precious piece of furniture or delicate porcelain. (Hence the flash of recognition I felt when watching the Queen's cameo with Paddington Bear, which was filmed in the same room; and my childish delight at seeing him drinking out of the spout of a teapot, then spraying a solemn footman with cream from a chocolate éclair.)

After retreating from the Crimson Drawing Room, I found Philip nearby, and we were guided to the Royal Library, following a maze of long corridors, down a flight of steps overseen by a larger-than-life marble statue of Queen Victoria, who looked exceedingly disapproving, and finally arriving at our destination. The library is housed in a series of double-height rooms, each lined with thousands of volumes from floor to ceiling, a set of narrow spiral steps leading to the second level, altogether forming an immense gallery of books. These include a priceless edition of Shakespeare's First Folio (a collection of his plays published in 1623, just seven years after his death), and the Second Folio (from 1632), containing the handwriting of Charles I, who read it while he was imprisoned at Windsor Castle in the days before he was put on trial and executed in 1649. Inside the manuscript the King wrote in Latin, '*Dum spiro Spero*' ('While I breathe, I hope'). The blood-stained linen shirt said to have been worn by Charles at his beheading is amongst the revered artefacts held at Windsor Castle; material evidence that a monarch can lose a kingdom, as well as his head. A former Royal Librarian, Sir Owen Morshead, who gave the young Lilibet occasional history lessons during even the most perilous months of the Second World War, showed the shirt to her as a vivid illustration of past trials that had beset the Crown.

This macabre garment was nowhere to be seen on our visit to the Royal Library, but there were many other treasures to be viewed: drawings by Raphael and Leonardo da Vinci; rare miniature cameos; jewelled chivalric insignia bestowed by previous sovereigns upon their favoured knights; and a piece of rock brought back from the moon. At the far end was a bust of Elizabeth I, who had used these rooms as an indoor walking gallery. I wondered if her namesake had ever run along the red-carpeted floors as a small child, before she had known that she, too, would follow in the footsteps of the first Queen Elizabeth.

The restless ghost of Elizabeth I is said to haunt the Royal Library, while at least a dozen other phantoms and wraiths are purported to walk the corridors or appear at windows, their spectral forms looming in the shadows, their whispers rustling through the night. Miss Crawford reported that it was so dark during the blackout of the war years that at first she became disorientated, 'and for some time I wandered around like one of the Castle's ghosts'.

I have never seen or heard a ghost on any of my visits, but it is an eerie place when the crowds leave, although one never feels alone. Forty sovereigns have inhabited Windsor Castle over the last 1,000 years – representing a near unbroken line of monarchy – and their presence is palpable in the fabric of the building. Only once has the Crown toppled, when England became a republic in the wake of Charles I's execution. After this indignity, the restoration of the monarchy in 1660 saw the transformation of Windsor Castle from a medieval castle into a majestic symbol of royal authority, adorned with an ever-expanding collection of riches. 'It is replete with every kind of historical trophy,' wrote Miss Crawford of her wartime years at Windsor with Lilibet and Margaret, identifying 'the bullet that came out of Nelson's heart, and Bonnie Prince

The Royal Library at Windsor Castle, *c.*1940.

A lace evening gown designed by Hardy Amies in 1952 for Princess Elizabeth to wear on a royal tour of Australia (postponed because of the death of George VI).

Charlie's sword as well as King Henry VIII's armour . . . I personally found them somewhat sinister things to share a shelter with.'

Many of the monarchy's greatest works of art can be viewed at Windsor: portraits by Anthony van Dyck (including a monumental one of Charles I astride a white horse, and his famous painting showing the same king from three viewpoints); masterpieces by Rubens, Titian, Bruegel and Holbein. Magnificence and wealth are everywhere: superb silver and gilded furniture, quantities of valuable porcelain, countless marble busts, umpteen golden candelabra and crystal chandeliers. But aside from these visible exhibitions of power and privilege, dating back to the time when the Crown claimed its divine right to rule, a hidden history is kept safe at Windsor Castle, in the form of the vast Royal Archives amassed within its walls. A few records lie deep in the network of basements that form an underground labyrinth; the vast majority are stored high up in the twelfth-century Round Tower.

The Queen's clothes, however, are now preserved in the care of a textile conservator, who works with a small team in a modern building in Windsor Great Park. It took some months after the Queen's death for her surviving clothing to be assembled there, alongside her mother's, and even longer for the process of cataloguing to commence. My request to see the most significant of the Queen's gowns designed for her by Hardy Amies has therefore taken a year to be granted. But at last I am returning to Windsor on a rainy day in February, when the grey skies are dour and glowering, and the morning is as dark as twilight. The security is strict: two different forms of ID are required, following a previous online screening process, and I must enter via a gate guarded by armed police. Their grave faces seem to reflect the sense of occasion; heightening my own, slightly uneasy feeling that in coming here, I am disobeying Walter Bagehot's warning against poking around and destroying the mystique of the monarchy.

The surroundings are not in the least magical; the building is utilitarian and anonymous, in a small complex of workshops and warehouses. The contents, however, are remarkable: on my way to the textile studio, I pass a restorer at work on a red satin-covered chair that looks very much like the one I saw the Queen sitting on when I encountered her, more than a decade ago, in the Crimson Drawing Room of the nearby castle. There is a treasure trove of royal clothes, too, forming as compelling a historical collection as the annals contained within the Round Tower. Like a handwritten letter or diary that survives long after the death of its author, these corporeal garments are testaments to a past life.

The Amies dresses that I am here to see today are stored in grey boxes, like coffins, to keep them safe from daylight, fluctuations in temperature, and the fatal depredations of clothes moths (whose larvae spin tunnels of silk and feed off the materials that they inhabit, and eventually destroy). The conservator and one of her colleagues open the first box, removing the layers of tissue paper that shroud the garment, and then they don special gloves to lift it onto a display table. It is a strapless red velvet evening gown, with a tiny waist – only 23 inches – and identified by the curators as having been worn by Princess Elizabeth in the late 1940s.

Hardy Amies opened his couture house in January 1946. This gown appears to be strikingly similar in style to Christian Dior's debut New Look collection, launched in February 1947, which introduced long, extravagantly full skirts, in marked contrast to wartime rationing and austerity. A small yet distinctive label – consisting of Amies's own handwritten signature and address (14 Savile Row) – is neatly stitched inside a seam within the black satin lining, hidden by the folds of the floor-length skirt. The crimson is an undeniably regal colour, but this is a party dress for a princess to dance in, rather than stand to attention in her formal regalia. The velvet feels soft to the touch, almost warm in its intimacy, as if it has only just been shrugged off by Lilibet, the laughing girl who wore it in her youth.

There are no official photographs of Princess Elizabeth wearing the dress; but looking at it, I am reminded of the portrait of her great-great-grandmother, Queen Victoria, painted in 1843 by the German artist Franz Xaver Winterhalter. Victoria was just twenty-four at the time, and she had commissioned it as a birthday gift for her beloved husband Albert, who hung it in his Writing Room at Windsor. This is not one of the many formal Winterhalter pictures of the royal family that were created for public display; rather, Victoria is seen in privacy, with her hair half undone, leaning against a red cushion, her lips open in an alluring pose, her shoulders exposed, a heart-shaped pendant on a gold chain dangling from her naked neck.

The Winterhalter portrait hints only briefly at what Victoria is wearing – her lack of clothing is perhaps the point – with the merest dash of white material visible. But another of Victoria's youthful dresses is part of the textile collection at Windsor, and I have asked to see it alongside the Hardy Amies gown. The resemblance is intriguing: Victoria's dress is also made of red velvet, with a tiny waist, a low-cut bodice, and a long, very full skirt. There are differences: the nineteenth-century gown is more elaborate, the fabric tartan rather than plain, trimmed with lace, ribbons and bows. Yet the parallels seem to me to be intentional on Hardy Amies's part, at least in the way in which his design summons up a romanticised version of Victoriana, and a fairy-tale world where a beautiful princess could waltz with her handsome prince. In doing so, Amies was both shaping and reflecting the prevailing mood in post-war fashion; a nostalgic emotion expressed by Christian Dior in the final page of his memoir. 'The maintenance of the tradition of fashion is in the nature of an act of faith,' wrote Dior in 1956. 'In a century which attempts to tear the heart out of every mystery, fashion still guards its secret well, and is the best possible proof that there is still magic abroad.'

Hardy Amies had drawn a comparable conclusion in his own first memoir, published two years previously in 1954; although he cited the tradition of the British monarchy, for by then his most famous client was the young queen. 'The Court and its ceremonies, its Presentation Garden Parties, its Balls, its Royal Enclosures, are still the corner stones of the social edifice . . . I see everywhere a strong, if subconscious, desire to cling to the old order, and even to fight for it. This is the atmosphere which influences fashion.'

Both Dior and Amies knew the brutality of war. Dior had lived through the Nazi occupation of Paris; his sister, a member of the French Resistance, had been captured and tortured by the Gestapo, then deported to a German concentration camp. Amies joined forces with the Belgian

Resistance, many of whom were betrayed by collaborators, executed, or died in imprisonment. Both were influenced by the past – Dior by his mother's wardrobe during the Belle Époque, before the horrors of the First World War, Amies by his mother's work for a court dressmaker in the Edwardian era. Both admired what Amies described as 'the satisfying full curves of the mid-nineteenth century brought right up to date'. Dior designed dresses for the young Princess Margaret; Amies for her older sister, who as heir apparent could not be seen to wear French couture, and as queen remained stalwart in her loyalty to British designers. And both men were homosexual, growing up during a time of widespread prejudice, when being openly queer was to risk persecution and punishment.

These are the associations in my mind, as I search for clues in the two dresses spread out before me; a pair made for princesses before they became queens, and before they were clad in the chain mail of majesty. The threads that link Lilibet and Victoria are naturally relevant in other ways. Neither was born to rule – both came to the throne as a result of a succession crisis – but each proved this to be an excellent qualification for a monarch. So, too, do the examples of Victoria's grandson, George V, a second son whose older brother died at the age of twenty-eight, and in turn his second son, George VI, who was obliged to become king after the abdication of the firstborn son and heir, Edward VIII.

The red velvet gowns are separated by a century, although they have a more immediate connection; not simply as tactile objects that offer clues to the women who wore them, but also as physical vestiges of their relationship, through the bloodline of monarchy. Lilibet was born on 21 April 1926, a quarter of a century after Victoria's death on 22 January 1901. Amidst the ancient surroundings of Windsor Castle, twenty-five years seems very little time indeed. And yet the intervening years were cataclysmic; the suffering and savagery of the First World War and the Russian Revolution ripped apart Victoria's royal dynasty, in ways that would reshape the reigns of successive sovereigns, while destroying others. The battle lines of the Great War saw Victoria's grandchildren become enemies, their realms divided and devastated.

In order to understand how and why involves lengthy expeditions to the Royal Archives in the Round Tower, to trace the warp and weft of the British monarchy. One could devote an entire career to examining just a small section of the hundreds of thousands of documents that are stored there, or the half a million photographs that are also part of the collection. I have spent days reading through the records relating to the clothes worn by several generations of royal women. Time flies as I become immersed in photograph albums, studying the details of family resemblances, which are heightened by their habit of wearing matching tartan kilts, or dressing their children in identical sailor suits. Hours pass in the Round Tower, and then I descend the stone steps again, retracing my path past St George's Chapel, where the dead royalties lie side by side in the crypt. Finally, emerging from a castle gate, I am shaken from my reverie, and wonder if I have somehow lost the thread.

But what I always return to is this: if one is to appreciate the great achievement of Queen Elizabeth II in serving the Crown, as well as her people, then an understanding of her Victorian inheritance is vital. The two queens, Victoria and Elizabeth II, have come to represent the British monarchy at its most successful and enduring. And yet their lineage is far more Germanic than English; a reminder, too, of how the principle of hereditary succession was manipulated by Parliament to accommodate their Protestant ancestor George I, who would have been only fifty-second in line to the throne were it not for the 1701 Act of Settlement. Thanks to this legislation, he became the first of Britain's Hanoverian monarchs. Throughout the eighteenth century, the Hanoverian kings married German brides, and their family heritage was consolidated by subsequent generations. Victoria's mother was a German princess and her father was the fourth son of George III; she was therefore a direct descendant of George I, who was born, died and buried in what is now Germany. The author William Thackeray spoke for many when he wrote of George I that 'we laughed at his uncouth German ways, and sneered at him'.

After her accession, Victoria reinforced the royal relationship with Germany by marrying her first cousin, Albert (Victoria's mother was sister to

Albert's father, the Duke of Saxe-Coburg and Gotha). These ties were further strengthened when Victoria and Albert's eldest daughter married the heir to the Prussian throne – the first of six of their children who would marry into German royal houses. Victoria's matchmaking continued thereafter, as she attempted to ensure that her nine children and several dozen grandchildren made a series of strategic marriages, in an interrelated web of dynastic relationships that stretched beyond Germany, from Scandinavia to Spain, Belgium to the Balkans, Bulgaria, Greece and Russia. Before his death in 1861, Albert believed that these royal unions would be the key to creating European peace and prosperity, and a bulwark against the threat of republicanism. Victoria remained true to her husband's vision, seeing each of the tactical marriages as integral to the power and influence of the monarchy, and to orchestrating good diplomatic relations. As such, she became known as 'the grandmother of Europe', while embodying her role as the matriarch of the mother country.

Yet Victoria's dynasty was fraught with family tensions, irredeemable rifts, and constant dangers. Marriages between cousins had led to an increased risk of the hereditary bleeding disorder of haemophilia (then known as the 'royal disease'), passing down like a curse through the generations, afflicting one of Victoria's sons, two of her grandsons, and six of her great-grandsons. Aside from this calamitous genetic legacy, none of Victoria's descendants was immune to revolution, ruin or regicide. Victoria herself survived seven assassination attempts, and a significant number of her relatives were also targeted, including her sons Bertie and Alfred. That two of her grandsons, George V and Kaiser Wilhelm II, were on opposing sides during the First World War, led to irrevocable consequences. As hundreds of thousands of soldiers died in the killing fields of Flanders, men and their horses shot or poisoned by gas or drowning in the mud, George V was acutely aware that for the British monarchy to survive, it could no longer bear the surname of his German grandparents. Hence the

Three heirs to the throne: Queen Victoria at the christening of her great-grandson (the future Edward VIII), with her grandson (the future George V) and son (the future Edward VII), July 1894.

calculated decision in 1917 that the house of Saxe-Coburg-Gotha should be rebranded in order to sound more English.

There had been widespread anti-German rhetoric and propaganda in England since the start of the war, and confidential discussions about renaming the royal dynasty were already underway in the spring of 1917. But the timing of the public announcement came after increasing public outrage at air raids, in particular the destruction of a school in Poplar, East London, on 13 June in a daylight attack by German Gotha bombers in which eighteen children were killed. The following week, news of a proposed name change appeared in the Court Circular on 19 June, announcing that two of the King's cousins would stop using the suffix 'of Schleswig-Holstein'. There was also an official notice that 'the King has deemed it desirable, in the conditions brought about by the present war, that those Princes of his family who are his subjects and bear German names and titles, should relinquish these titles and henceforth adopt British surnames.' Members of the Teck and Battenberg families were expressly identified in the accompanying article in *The Times*.

This would have a direct effect on his wife's siblings, as well as her children and future grandchildren. Queen Mary had been born Princess May of Teck, the daughter of an Austrian nobleman; her mother was a cousin of Queen Victoria, and herself a Hanoverian. As a result of the new edict, Queen Mary's two brothers were both obliged to renounce their German titles: Prince Alexander of Teck took the new title of the Earl of Athlone, while Prince Adolphus, the Duke of Teck, became instead the Marquess of Cambridge.

As for the problematic name of Saxe-Coburg-Gotha: there was some private debate between a small group of royal advisers about suitably British replacements, including a suggestion of Tudor-Stewart (rejected by the former prime ministers Lord Rosebery and H. H. Asquith as having 'inauspicious associations'). Other names that were considered but swiftly dismissed were Plantagenet, York, Lancaster and England. It was the King's private secretary Lord Stamfordham (a loyal servant to Queen Victoria during the final years of her reign) who came up with the name

Windsor, and a proclamation announcing the change was issued from Buckingham Palace on 17 July 1917.

The house of Windsor was born just days after the King and Queen had made a trip to the Western Front in France. While George set off to inspect the troops, Mary went to see a series of field hospitals, accompanied by her friend and lady-in-waiting Mabell, Countess of Airlie, who would subsequently write about the episode in her memoir. Over the course of their tour, from 3–14 July, Lady Airlie described their encounters with thousands of soldiers, 'covered with mud, bleary-eyed and haggard with fatigue'. Wherever they went, the royal visitors were confronted with the visceral realities of the war. Lady Airlie recorded the many casualties that they saw in makeshift first-aid stations: 'British, Australian, French, Belgian – the endless succession of beds had a terrible sameness of young faces and broken bodies.' She recalled 'the indescribable stench of death and sickness hanging in the air', and the 'harrowing sight' of a battlefield: 'a vast stretch of land that had once been fertile and smiling, covered with crops, but was now only a tumbled mass of blackened earth.' The fields of Flanders were 'pitted with deep craters that had swallowed up farms and villages'; and at a certain point, they found themselves standing on a mass grave, 'a devil's charnel house' of corpses. 'We climbed over a mound composed of German dead, buried by their comrades – all that was left of a whole regiment who had died in wrestling this strip of land from our troops, only to lose it again . . .

'Scattered everywhere in the ineffable desolation were the pathetic reminders of human life – rifles fallen from dead hands, old water bottles, iron helmets. And in the distance the guns boomed relentlessly . . . We stood there speechless. It was impossible to find words. The Queen's face was ashen and her lips were tightly compressed. I felt that like me she was afraid of breaking down.'

News of the royal tour was not made public until after it had finished – for as the King told Lady Airlie, 'I do things because they're my duty; not as propaganda.' Nevertheless, George and Mary were filmed for a silent newsreel (commissioned and produced by the government's official 'War Office Cinematograph Committee'), which still survives in the archives of the Imperial War Museum. George V is seen in uniform at all times, meeting the troops and reviewing tanks and aircraft; while Queen Mary wears her usual full-length dresses and floral trimmed hats, even when watching a fearsome demonstration of flame-throwers and explosives. Several newspaper reports of their visit also appeared after their return ('The King and Queen Visit the Scenes of the British Army's Triumphs' declared the patriotic headline in the *Daily Record* on 16 July). But perhaps the most significant was the official photograph of the King that appeared on the front page of the *Illustrated London News* on 21 July 1917, with the caption: 'Helmeted: The Head of the Royal House of Windsor at the Front'. The full-page portrait showed the King in his field marshal's uniform and a steel helmet, standing resolute amidst the desolation and debris of the Battle of Messines (which had been fought the previous month, at the cost of thousands of lives). Beneath was a short article hailing 'the great victory' of Messines and the courage of the King in visiting the front line, within range of German shells; and announcing that the King and his family had adopted the name of Windsor.

By then, it had become clear that the house of Windsor would have no room for George V's first cousins, Tsar Nicholas II and his German-born wife Alexandra, who was one of Queen Victoria's favourite granddaughters. The King had already declined to grant them asylum earlier that year, fearing that the rising threat of Bolshevism might spread from Russia to Britain. The Tsar – who bore such a marked facial resemblance to George V that they looked more like twin brothers than cousins, and were even mistaken for one another when they spent time together – had led his country into the devastating war against Germany in 1914, as an ally of Britain; a decision that almost certainly contributed to the Revolution in February 1917, and the Tsar's abdication on 2 March. George had always claimed to be devoted to his cousin ('dear Nicky'), describing him as 'the best, straightest, most clear and decided man I know'. But his first loyalty was to the Crown, and the need to protect it against the risk of radical republicanism. The King was ruthless about this objective, as evinced in Lord Stamfordham's letter to the Foreign Secretary, Arthur Balfour, at

REGISTERED AS A NEWSPAPER FOR TRANSMISSION IN THE UNITED KINGDOM, AND TO CANADA AND NEWFOUNDLAND BY MAGAZINE POST.

No. 4083. – VOL. CLI — SATURDAY, JULY 21, 1917. — SEVENPENCE.

The Copyright of all the Editorial Matter, both Engravings and Letterpress, is Strictly Reserved in Great Britain, the Colonies, Europe, and the United States of America.

HELMETED: THE HEAD OF THE ROYAL HOUSE OF WINDSOR—THE KING AT THE FRONT, ON WYTSCHAETE RIDGE.

It was announced on July 17 that the King had adopted for his house and family the name of Windsor. The "Court Circular" of July 14 stated: "During the past fortnight his Majesty has visited General Headquarters and all the different Army and Lines of Communication Areas. The Queen, during the same period, has visited a large number of hospitals and institutions in the Lines of Communication Area." Their Majesties landed in France on July 3, and the King spent the following day with General Sir Herbert Plumer's Army on the scene of its great victory at Messines Ridge and Wytschaete Ridge. His Majesty wore Field-Marshal's service uniform and a steel helmet—a necessary precaution in view of the fact that he was frequently within range of German shells. Some, indeed, fell not very far away, but the King was indifferent to danger. He walked over the battlefield for more than a mile, while Sir Herbert Plumer pointed out localities and explained events.

OFFICIAL PHOTOGRAPH.

the end of March 1917. 'The King has been thinking much about the Government's proposal that the Emperor and his Family should come to England . . . His Majesty cannot help doubting, on general grounds of expediency, whether it is advisable that the Imperial Family should take up their residence in this country.'

The King's strength of feeling increased the following month, when a letter from the influential author H. G. Wells was published in *The Times* on 21 April, calling for the formation of a Republican Society. Wells wrote that such a step would be patriotic in a time of war, and 'agreeable to our friends and Allies, the Republican democracies of France, Russia, the United States, and Portugal, to give some clear expression to the great volume of Republican feeling that has always existed in the British community'. An accompanying editorial in *The Times* hastened to offer its readers the following assurance: 'We prize and reverence the Monarchy because it is the thread which runs through the wonderful story of a national life . . . It binds the whole of the vast fabric together as no other institution does or can do.' The editorial also stated that the British constitutional monarchy had nothing in common with the 'autocracy of the Tsardom' and the 'militarist kingships of the Continent, except that the Crown is hereditary in both'. What remained unspoken, or perhaps implicit between the lines, was that this very inheritance *was* an undeniable link, given that the Tsar, the Kaiser and the King were all first cousins.

Wells's letter received widespread attention, and its contents were reported in other newspapers, including the *Manchester Guardian* and the *New York Times*. As Lord Derby, the Secretary of State for War, observed, 'the revolution in Russia has given all monarchies a knock. Wells's letter to *The Times* would not have been printed a year ago, but now it undoubtedly represents the view held by a very considerable class.' A second salvo by Wells was published in the popular *Penny Pictorial* in May 1917, under the headline 'The Future of the Monarchy'. The author proclaimed that 'the European dynastic system, based upon intermarriage by a group of minority German Royal Families, is dead today'. If the British monarchy were to survive, continued Wells, it must sever itself 'definitively from the German dynastic system with which it is so fatally entangled by marriage and descent'. Nor was this the first time that Wells had taken aim at the sovereign; the previous year, in his widely read wartime novel *Mr Britling Sees It Through*, he had declared that British life was 'corrupted by the fictions of loyalty to an uninspiring and alien Court'. The King, in one of his rarely recorded jokes, apparently quipped in return: 'I may be uninspiring, but I'll be damned if I'm alien.' However, the Liberal politician David Lloyd George would almost certainly have sided with Wells, at least in private; in January 1915, when he was Chancellor of the Exchequer, he was summoned to a meeting with the King at Buckingham Palace and remarked to his mistress, 'I wonder what my little German friend has got to say to me!'

As the war continued to grind onwards, with both sides suffering crushing losses, legislation was passed by Parliament in November 1917 to ensure that George V's relatives who had served in the German army, or remained living in Germany, were stripped of their British titles. Two years previously, in May 1915, the King had struck the names of eight German and Austrian royals – seven of whom were directly related to him or his wife – from the roll of Knights of the Most Noble Order of the Garter, and ordered the removal of their heraldic banners from St George's Chapel in Windsor Castle. Yet, as would become all too evident, the family ties could not be completely erased by the forfeiture of honours.

These momentous events were still recent family history when Princess Elizabeth was born in 1926; not that anyone expected the baby to become a future monarch, given that she was the daughter of George V's second son, Prince Albert. But when I examine pictures of her as a baby, in the archives of the Round Tower, it is impossible not to think of the violence and anguish that had wracked so many of her relatives less than a decade previously. Here they still are, the family groups in leather-bound albums, caught by the camera at gatherings for christenings, weddings, funerals and memorials. In these pages, they are preserved forever; a royal caste united at Windsor Castle and Ehrenburg Palace, in celebration and mourning, all related by their shared origins within the house of Saxe-Coburg-Gotha.

The men are sometimes hard to tell apart, given their habit of wearing the military uniforms of each other's realms. On one page, cousin Wilhelm is sporting a grand outfit at Cowes in August 1889, having just been made an honorary admiral in the Royal Navy by his grandmother. The following year, cousin George is with Wilhelm in Berlin, as a newly appointed colonel of a Prussian dragoon regiment. In September 1896, cousin Nicholas is staying at Balmoral with Queen Victoria, and photographed in his uniform of colonel-in-chief of the Royal Scots Greys. He is accompanied by his wife and their baby daughter, while George and May also join the family reunion.

Perhaps the most haunting of the photographs shows the English and Russian royal relatives holidaying together on the Isle of Wight in August 1909. George and Nicholas are dressed identically in naval style, their wives in similar white gowns, as are their daughters. One of the quartet of Romanov girls, ten-year-old Maria, is sharing a chair with George; his own daughter, Mary, stands close to Tatiana, who at twelve is the same age as her; they all bear an uncanny family resemblance. On the day the photograph was taken, George referred fondly in his diary to the 'delightful' Russian children.

These are the children who will die in July 1918, alongside their parents. They are slaughtered in a basement in a chaotic barrage of bullets and bayonets, as the Bolshevik revolutionaries set about piercing the layers of precious jewels that have been sewn into the girls' underwear for safekeeping. It would be the subsequent discovery of the fragments of these jewels, as well as remnants of shoe buckles and corset ribs, amidst a heap of charred bones in a nearby mineshaft, that led to the identification of the mutilated remains of the dead family.

Within a few months of those murders came the abdication of their cousin, Kaiser Wilhelm II, following Germany's crushing defeat in the First World War. Soon after the Armistice in November 1918, Lloyd

Top: Tsar Nicholas (left) and his first cousin, the future George V.
Below: A royal family gathering on the Isle of Wight in 1909: Edward VII sits in the middle, beside his nephew Tsar Nicholas II, his niece, the Tsarina, and their five children.

George (by then prime minister), declared that the former kaiser should be put on trial at Westminster Hall, and sentenced to death. Wilhelm had already fled Germany, and sought refuge in the Netherlands, where he lived for the rest of his life. Having lost his empire, he set aside his wardrobe of military uniforms, and adopted civilian dress: blue serge suits, loden capes, and a tiepin embellished with a miniature of his grandmother, Queen Victoria.

King George, too, found some comfort in the past. He wore the buttoned boots and stiff collars associated with the pre-war era, and at court he insisted on the same attire that had been *de rigueur* in Victorian times, including frock coats for men and long trains for women. He also ensured that his sons followed his lead in wearing the traditional 'Windsor uniform' whenever they were with him at the castle: a dark blue tailcoat trimmed with red collar and cuffs, breeches and a white waistcoat. The King himself continued to appear in the full dress uniform of an admiral of the fleet or a field marshal on ceremonial occasions; Queen Mary looked even more stately, adorned in crown jewels and floor-length gowns.

Thus the house of Windsor came to represent stability and old-fashioned values, while reinventing itself as thoroughly and reliably British. After the war, George refused to have any further contact with Wilhelm; but their shared history, and that of their Russian cousins, continued to haunt him and his heirs. In my mind's eye, I see the royal family tree embroidered into an elaborate tapestry, torn and threadbare in places, fragile and faded in the areas where daylight has shone too brightly, yet its delicate needlepoint surviving, against all the odds. And I imagine the tapestry still hidden somewhere within Windsor Castle, kept safe in one of the thousand rooms of the ancient fortress. How could it be otherwise, in a family for whom ancestry is destiny?

Queen Mary and George V in Berlin in May 1913, for the wedding of the daughter of Kaiser Wilhelm II (George's first cousin). The King is wearing his German military uniform for the occasion.

'SHE HAS SET THE BABE FASHION FOR YELLOW'

Whenever I find myself walking through the moneyed streets of Mayfair, which are now the exclusive preserve of hedge funds and the headquarters of luxury brands, I often pause just beyond Berkeley Square, to look at a pair of commemorative plaques that are placed opposite each other on Bruton Street. They seem to me to be mementoes of a lost Mayfair that existed between the two world wars: a landscape summoned up by the songs of Noël Coward and the novels of Evelyn Waugh, when (to quote a romantic song title of the era), 'A Nightingale Sang in Berkeley Square'.

Many of Mayfair's historic residential mansions have vanished, demolished by property developers or bombed to extinction in the Blitz. Even so, the past is alive in the immense London plane trees of Berkeley Square, planted in the eighteenth century and towering like the flying buttresses of a leafy green cathedral. Less obvious, but still evocative, are the nearby plaques recording former residents, which might serve as a map for anyone who dreams of slipping through a wrinkle in time. On the north side of Bruton Street, at number 26, a blue circular English Heritage plaque notes that 'Sir Norman Hartnell, 1901–1979, Court Dressmaker,

The Duke and Duchess of York at the christening of their daughter Elizabeth in May 1926. She is wearing the same robe that had been used for all royal christenings since the birth of Queen Victoria's first child in 1841.

lived and worked here, 1935–1979'. On the south side is another plaque, set high into the wall of a modern corporate edifice, marking an event that would prove to be momentous for Hartnell's future, and for that of the entire nation. It reads: 'On this site at 17 Bruton Street stood the townhouse of the Earl of Strathmore and Kinghorne where Elizabeth Alexandra Mary Windsor, later to become Her Majesty Queen Elizabeth II, was born on 21 April 1926.' And so it was that Lilibet's birthplace was just across the road from Hartnell's couture house; a reminder of the uncommon thread that linked them, for he would begin dressing her when she was a child of nine, and continued to do so until his death forty-four years later.

The baby girl was the first in the royal family to bear the surname of Windsor from the outset; she was also given the same first name as her mother, and her middle names were those of her father's grandmother and mother. Lilibet's arrival in the London home of her maternal grandparents reflected an important change in the house of Windsor. Her father, the King's second son, Prince Albert, the Duke of York (known to his family and friends as Bertie), had married the daughter of a Scottish aristocrat rather than a European royal princess, as would have been expected of previous generations. But the war had changed everything, including the lives of Bertie and his bride, Lady Elizabeth Bowes-Lyon. Bertie had served as a junior officer in the British Navy at the Battle of Jutland in 1916, where twenty ships were sunk and the death toll was close to 10,000 sailors. Elizabeth saw four of her older brothers join the Armed Forces when war was declared. One of them died on the battlefield in 1915 at the age of twenty-six, leaving a young widow and a two-month-old baby daughter; three other brothers suffered from a combination of physical injuries and psychological trauma. And when Elizabeth's Scottish home, Glamis Castle, was temporarily converted into a convalescent hospital for wounded and disabled soldiers, she helped to care for the patients.

Despite the long shadow cast by the war, Elizabeth was widely admired by her contemporaries for her vivacity and charm, and Bertie fell in love with her at first sight as they danced together at a ball held at the Ritz

The Duke and Duchess of York on honeymoon in 1923.

Lady Elizabeth Bowes-Lyon in her bridal gown, leaving home for her wedding to the Duke of York.

in the summer of 1920. His courtship was lengthy and assiduous; but when their engagement was finally announced in January 1923, the socialite and diarist Henry 'Chips' Channon declared Bertie to be 'the luckiest of men', and Elizabeth 'more gentle, lovely and exquisite than any other woman alive'. They were married at Westminster Abbey on 26 April 1923; Elizabeth wore an ivory chiffon wedding dress designed by Madame Handley-Seymour, an English court dressmaker patronised by Queen Mary, although its slim, straight silhouette reflected that of Jeanne Lanvin, a Paris couturière favoured by the bride. Elizabeth was an admirer of French fashion, and already a client of Chanel by 1922, but her bridal gown needed to represent her new role as the Duchess of York, and above all, as a royal woman. Her veil was made of antique lace, given to her by Queen Mary; the medieval-looking gown was embellished with another strip of lace, a Strathmore family heirloom, and embroidered with pearls. Her tulle train was edged with Nottingham lace; white roses of York appeared on either side of the circlet of myrtle leaves that she wore in place of a tiara.

On the morning of the wedding, Elizabeth set off with her father from 17 Bruton Street, travelling in a horse-drawn state coach, along a route lined with guardsmen to the Abbey. There, she stopped at the tomb of the Unknown Warrior, commemorating the multitudes of soldiers who had died in the Great War, and laid her bouquet of white roses on the grave. The groom wore his Royal Air Force uniform (he had trained as a pilot in 1919); his older brother, the Prince of Wales, was in a red Grenadier Guards tunic, and his father in the uniform of Admiral of the Fleet. The monarchy's close connection with their military forces was further signified when the newly-weds paused, having left the Abbey, and the Duke saluted the Cenotaph war memorial on Whitehall.

The early years of the Yorks' married life, before the birth of their first daughter, were relatively leisurely, though Bertie continued his round of official duties. In August 1923, Elizabeth accompanied her husband on a day trip to the annual Duke of York's Camp that he had set up two years earlier, which brought together privately educated schoolboys with young factory workers of the same age. Photographs and silent film footage of the Duchess's visit show her dressed in the height of fashion, in a Chanel jersey ensemble and cloche hat; she looks more like a youthful flapper than a regal duchess, smiling gaily as she waves and shakes hands.

Bertie had previously been made president of the Industrial Welfare Society – an organisation that sought, in his words, to 'promote good will between all classes in industry', and in this role, he toured factories and coal mines throughout the country. As such, he was emulating his parents, who expressed their stalwart devotion to duty and service via a succession of engagements with their people. During the four years of war, George V undertook 450 visits to troops, 300 to hospitals, and almost as many to factories and shipyards; and these missions continued in peacetime, too, with the mournful addition of commemorations for the war dead, and solemn pilgrimages to the war graves in France and Belgium.

But unlike his father, Bertie struggled with public speaking due to a debilitating stammer developed in childhood; and even though this improved thanks to speech therapy encouraged by his wife, he preferred to remain in the background at official royal functions. Bertie was always dutiful, yet far less confident in public than his dashing older brother Edward, Prince of Wales (known in the family as David). The heir to the throne, however, showed little interest in marriage or his accession; as Chips Channon, an astute observer, recorded in his diary in 1925, 'The P of W would not raise his finger to save his future sceptre, many of his intimate friends think he would be only too happy to renounce it.'

The Prince of Wales himself complained about his parents' traditionalism, which was rooted in the Victorian epoch; he preferred the trappings of the Jazz Age, with its fast cars, glitzy nightclubs and adulterous affairs. 'I always feel as if I were working, not for the next King of England, but for the son of the latest American millionaire,' grumbled his assistant private secretary, Tommy Lascelles, with some exasperation. By 1927, Lascelles was so enraged at his master's louche behaviour that he told the prime minister, Stanley Baldwin, that the heir to the throne was 'going rapidly to the devil' and 'would soon become no fit wearer of the British

Crown'. Baldwin agreed with him, and then Lascelles went even further, confessing that when the Prince was out riding at point-to-points, 'I can't help thinking that the best thing that could happen to him, and to the country, would be for him to break his neck.' The prime minister replied: 'God forgive me, I have often thought the same.'

That the King did not share these extreme views is evident in his repeated requests to his heir to give up riding in steeplechases. Nevertheless, stories abound of George losing faith in his eldest son in the later years of his reign. 'After I am dead the boy will ruin himself within twelve months,' he is reputed to have said to Baldwin; and to Cosmo Lang, the Archbishop of Canterbury, 'I know my son is going to let it [the monarchy] down.' The King's disapproval of what he saw as his son's dissolute way of life, not least his scandalous preference for mistresses rather than a suitable wife, was most often expressed in complaints about the Prince's refusal to adhere to the customary royal dress codes. Hence the King's bitter accusations that his heir had worn a kilt jacket of too light a grey for church, or failed to don gloves at a ball. In retaliation, the Prince rebelled even further, starting a popular fashion for two-tone shoes and loud check suits, so that the King (according to the Countess of Airlie) 'hauled him over the coals for being the "worst dressed man in London"'.

In contrast, George thoroughly approved of his second son's choice of wife, and their domestic rectitude; for despite Elizabeth's gaiety, she was, in the words of Lady Airlie, 'very unlike the cocktail-drinking, chain-smoking girls who came to be regarded as typical of the nineteen-twenties'. As it happens, Elizabeth did enjoy cocktails and dancing, but she was able to handle her father-in-law from the start. True, when they first met, the King voiced some dismay about her fashionably fringed hairstyle, but soon after the Yorks' marriage, he wrote to his son in the fondest terms: 'The better I know & the more I see of your dear little wife, the more charming I think she is.'

Yet for all the King's innate conservatism, he proved himself able to adapt to the changing political landscape when, in January 1924, Ramsay MacDonald became the first Labour prime minister. MacDonald led a short-lived minority government, relying on the tacit support of the Liberals, with the result that his reforms were less radical than might have been expected; but his role as a working-class representative leading the country was unprecedented. 'The King plays the game straight,' wrote MacDonald in his diary on the day of their first meeting at Buckingham Palace, 'though I feel he is apprehensive. It would be a miracle were he not.' George V himself appeared to be surprisingly philosophical about the new prime minister, who was the illegitimate son of a Scottish maidservant and a farm labourer. 'He impressed me very much, he wishes to do the right thing,' recorded the King in his diary on the same day, 22 January, the anniversary of Queen Victoria's death. 'Today 23 years ago dear Grandmama died. I wonder what she would have thought of a Labour government!'

In the ensuing days, George met MacDonald's ministers, and considered them to be 'very intelligent'; uncharacteristically, he set aside the formal court dress code for their attendance at Buckingham Palace, rather than insisting on frock coats, white breeches and stockings, which many in the Labour Cabinet didn't possess and couldn't afford. One of them, J. R. Clynes, a former millhand and newly appointed Lord Privy Seal, arrived at the palace wearing what the press reported to be 'a black soft hat and a muffler of indeterminate hue beneath his dark tweed overcoat'. Another, John Wheatley, an Irish-born miner and the incoming Minister of Health, wore 'a ten-year-old lounge suit'.

In most regards, the King was scrupulous in adhering to the role of constitutional monarch, as set out by Walter Bagehot in 1867: 'The Sovereign has . . . the right to be consulted, the right to encourage, the right to warn.' It is also worth reminding ourselves of Bagehot's point that a British monarch has no legislative power, and no right of veto over Parliament; and would therefore have to sign their 'own death-warrant', if Parliament passed a law requiring the sovereign to do so. Within this relatively limited framework of influence, George V established a good relationship with the Labour government, and with Ramsay MacDonald in particular, who later wrote that the King 'has been considerate, cordially correct, human and friendly. [He] has never seen me as a Minister without making me feel that he was also seeing me as a friend.'

According to the memoir of Lady Cynthia Colville, a royal courtier and confidante, 'George V once told me that he found Mr Ramsay MacDonald and his colleagues easier to get on with and far readier to listen to the King's advice (which was, after all, based on a good deal of experience) than ever Mr Baldwin and his Cabinet had been.' But the King did make one request of the new prime minister. As MacDonald noted in his diary, the King said that if the Labour government resumed diplomatic relations with Russia, he 'hoped I would do nothing to compel him to shake hands with the murderers of his relatives'. This point was followed up by the King's private secretary, Lord Stamfordham, in a memo to the new Lord Chancellor: 'It would be indescribably abhorrent to HM to have to shake hands with anyone who was, directly or indirectly, concerned with the brutal murder of his cousins, the Emperor and Empress of Russia and their children.' In the event, Moscow dispatched a chargé d'affaires to London, a less senior diplomat than an ambassador, and the King was not obliged to receive him.

MacDonald's government survived only nine months, and Stanley Baldwin was returned as Conservative prime minister by the end of 1924. This was presumably a relief to the Duchess of York, who had declared herself to be 'extremely anti-Labour' in a letter to a friend earlier that year, on the curious grounds that, 'They are so apart from fairies and owls and bluebells and Americans & all the things I like. If they agree with me, I know they are pretending.'

Regardless of her mother's political preferences, Princess Elizabeth was born into a world in flux, when modernism was emerging from an era of bloodshed and revolution; and at a time when the royal family – and her grandfather, in particular – sought to preserve the illusion of graceful continuity, while adjusting to rapidly shifting circumstances. Her birth coincided with the threat of disruptive industrial action, as government negotiations with the miners broke down. On 28 April 1926, the King expressed his frustration in a letter to his wife: '[It] will cost the country many millions & cause a lot of bad blood & give great pleasure to our communists & the Russian Soviet.'

The following week, on 4 May, the Trades Union Congress called the General Strike, and the guards at Buckingham Palace exchanged their ceremonial red tunics and bearskin hats for khaki uniforms and caps. Three days later, Lord Stamfordham wrote to Baldwin, anticipating the introduction of martial law; although the King showed some sympathy for the poorly paid miners, whose employers were intent on cutting their wages while extending their working hours. As Lady Airlie recalled in her memoir, the sovereign had 'a heated dispute' with Lord Durham, a coal magnate, during an encounter at the Newmarket Races, a few days before the strike commenced. 'When the King said he was sorry for the miners Lord Durham replied that they were "a damned lot of revolutionaries". At that His Majesty exploded – "Try living on their wages before you judge them."'

When the General Strike ended on 12 May, George wrote an unusually cheerful entry in his diary: 'Our old country can well be proud of itself, as during the last 9 days there has been a strike in which 4 million men have been affected, not a shot has been fired & no one has been killed, it shows what wonderful people we are.' The King's optimism was not altogether realistic – social unrest would continue, driven by rising unemployment, falling wages and widespread deprivation. But he appears to have been in a hopeful mood, thanks to the birth of his granddaughter, who was now third in line to the throne, after her uncle and her father. Princess Elizabeth was christened in the chapel at Buckingham Palace on 29 May, wearing the Honiton lace royal christening robe that had originally been commissioned by Queen Victoria for the baptism of her first baby in 1841 (and subsequently used for each of her children, as well as those of Edward VII and George V). Lady Airlie attended the ceremony, and described it as 'a happy interlude' in 'those grim weeks following the General Strike'. She also noted, after paying a visit to 17 Bruton Street, that large groups were gathering in the hope of catching a glimpse of the royal baby. The Duke of York was surprised by the assembled throng, but Lady Airlie remarked, 'I knew the reason as I looked at the crowd made up of people of all ages and all classes. Here, in this country which only yesterday had been in the throes of strife and bitterness, was something of continuity and hope in the future.

'The King, I believe, unconsciously shared this feeling, for his pleasure in his little grand-daughter was touching . . . Lilibet always came first in his affections. He used to play with her – a thing I never saw him do with his own children – and loved to have her with him.'

At the beginning of 1927, when Lilibet was just eight months old, she was left in the care of her grandparents, while her parents set off on an official state visit to Australia and New Zealand. (The royal tour had been requested by the Australian prime minister, Stanley Bruce, for the opening of the new Commonwealth Parliament House at Canberra, recently created as Australia's capital city.) They would be away for six months, and on the morning of their departure (6 January), the Duchess of York recorded in her diary that she was feeling 'very miserable at leaving the baby . . . Luckily she doesn't realize anything . . . I had on a grey lamb coat with fox collar & grey everything else. I drank some champagne & tried not to weep.' Several days later, she displayed a similar attention to sartorial detail in the wistful letter she wrote to Queen Mary after they had set sail from Portsmouth on board the battleship *Renown*: 'I felt very much leaving on Thursday, and the baby was so sweet playing with the buttons on Bertie's uniform that it quite broke me up!'

During the Yorks' lengthy absence on their royal tour, the King often referred affectionately in his diary to 'our sweet little grandchild'. After a few weeks spent with her maternal grandparents in February, the baby joined the King and Queen at Buckingham Palace. There she was installed in a nursery with her nanny, Clara Knight (known as 'Allah', and originally employed to look after the youngest Strathmore children) and her Scottish nursery maid, Margaret MacDonald ('Bobo'), who had joined the household when Lilibet was six weeks old, and remained with her as a dresser for more than six decades. Every afternoon, Lilibet was taken to her grandparents, and would be greeted by the Queen's delighted cry of 'Here comes the Bambino!' Her first birthday was celebrated

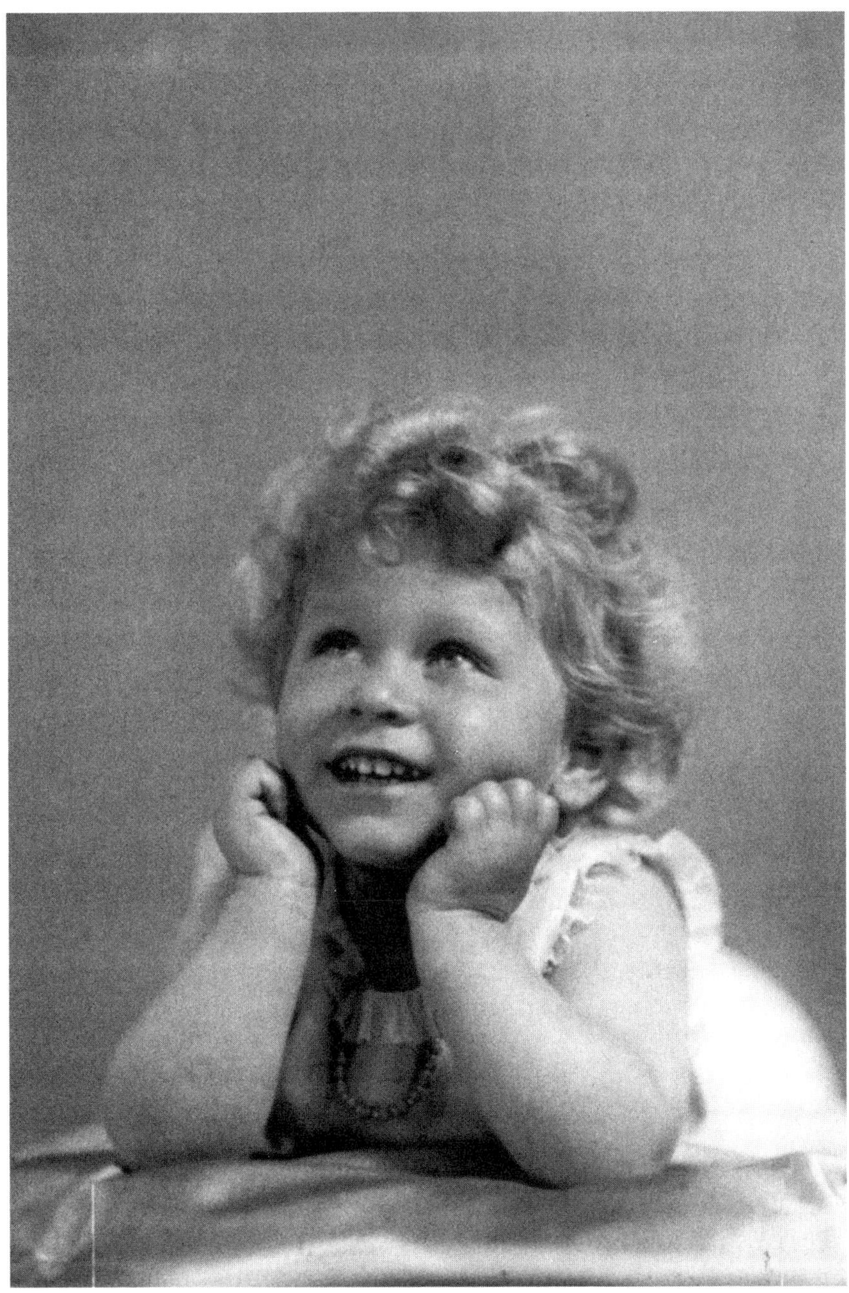

Princess Elizabeth as a child: (opposite, clockwise from top left) with her parents and grandparents, 1927; with her grandparents George V and Queen Mary in Bognor; with Queen Mary and her aunt, the Princess Royal, 1933; and (above) 1928. Photograph by Marcus Adams.

with the King and Queen at Windsor Castle; legend has it that when she learned to talk, she called him 'Grandpapa England'. Unlike his own children, Lilibet seems not to have been frightened of him, nor of his parrot Charlotte, the King's constant companion who ate breakfast with the family every morning. Queen Mary described in a letter to Bertie how the baby 'watched the bird eating pips with an air of absorption', and uttered 'shrieks of delight at each dog she saw'. Just before her birthday, she was photographed in the arms of the Queen; the portrait remains in the royal collection, and reveals a sturdy baby girl in a white dress and sash, looking directly into the camera, while her grandmother holds her up so that their heads are close together. Despite the age difference, they are clearly related; both have an air of determination, a firm jaw, and stiff upper lips.

The bond between Lilibet and her paternal grandparents appears to have deepened throughout her earliest childhood. She was not their first grandchild; their daughter, Princess Mary, had married Viscount Lascelles in 1922, and gave birth to two sons in swift succession. Nevertheless, the King and Queen tended to devote more time to Lilibet than her male cousins, and clearly derived great pleasure from doing so. In her diary, the Queen wrote that the arrival of their first granddaughter was 'such a relief and joy' and described the baby girl as 'a little darling with lovely complexion and pretty fair hair'. This was in marked contrast to Queen Mary's earlier attitude to her own newborn babies, as her official biographer, James Pope-Hennessy, subsequently discovered in the course of his research. According to his friend and source Lady Juliet Duff, the Queen rarely displayed any overt sign of maternal instinct, and once, when showing Juliet one of her babies in its cot, had remarked: 'I wonder what it's thinking? Nothing at all, of course, stupid little thing.'

After the King suffered a serious lung infection at the end of 1928, his doctors advised that he would benefit from the bracing sea air of the South Coast; he agreed to spend three months at Bognor, on condition that Lilibet should come and visit him. When she duly did so, both of her grandparents were equally pleased to see her. Perhaps most unlikely of all, the stately queen noted in her diary her enjoyment of outdoor games with her granddaughter: 'I played with Lilibet in the garden making sandpies!'

From the start, there was intense press interest in the princess's clothes. Indeed, even before the Duchess of York gave birth, journalists were sharing the news that the mother-to-be, along with Queen Mary and Lady Strathmore, had personally sewn some of the baby's layette, while also revealing a charitable aspect to these preparations. 'Many poor gentlewomen', it was reported, 'have profited by the Duchess's order for fine lawn and muslin frocks, little bonnets and jackets.' The following month, readers of the *Westminster Gazette* were informed that the Duchess of York preferred to see babies in cotton, rather than wool; she thought that infants wearing wool 'looked rather like little gnomes' and that her own choice was for 'frilly babies'.

At the time of Lilibet's third birthday, her cherubic portrait was featured on the cover of *Time* magazine, with the caption: 'She has set the babe fashion for yellow.' This coincided with a number of excitable articles in the British press about how the princess had started 'the vogue for yellow'; and declaring that 'she is already a definite leader of fashion, and in no way is her influence more felt than with the "primrose babies"'. The following year, newspapers reported that she had celebrated her fourth birthday at Windsor Castle, where the King had given her a Shetland pony. Afterwards, the little princess was spotted walking across the castle quadrangle in a yellow coat; a large crowd had gathered to see her at the nearest gate, and when she waved to them, they surged forward and almost knocked over an unwary police officer.

In August 1930, the Yorks' second daughter was born, and Miss Crawford joined the household when Princess Margaret Rose was two years old. At this point, the family was living between Royal Lodge in Windsor Great Park and a London townhouse at 145 Piccadilly, close to Hyde Park Corner. As soon as Margaret was old enough, the two sisters were dressed in identical outfits, chosen by their mother. According to Miss Crawford, 'They wore cotton frocks, mostly blue with a flower pattern, and little cardigan coats to match when it was cool. Blue of a certain misty shade was always the Duchess's favourite colour.' Lilibet, however, 'had a passion for cherry red, and a red coat she was particularly attached to'. Crawfie also reported that their nanny, the faithful Allah, believed that 'little princesses should be little princesses always . . . She never quite approved of their plain tweed coats, business-like berets and stout walking shoes.' When the girls were invited to parties, Allah would 'come into her own and produce two dear little figures like dolls, all organdie frills and ribbons and bows'. (It is noteworthy that two of the most consistent caregivers in Lilibet's life were Allah and Bobo, whose intimate relationships with her from infancy onwards were inextricably linked with the daily routines of dressing and undressing her.)

The royal sisters were featured together in *Vogue* in March 1933, with a photograph of them wearing demure white dresses, ankle socks and sandals. The accompanying article confidently revealed that 'the two children never wear low-waisted styles' and that 'their ordinary afternoon frocks remain surprisingly simple: *broderie anglaise* in the summer style with a scalloped cross-over its only decoration for Elizabeth; a simpler frock of cotton for Margaret with smocked yoke and wide scalloped hem-line'.

At eight, Lilibet appeared as a couture-clad bridesmaid at one of the most fashionable weddings of the decade, when her uncle, Prince George, the Duke of Kent, married his second cousin, Princess Marina of Greece and Denmark. The bride's family history was a reminder of the tribulations of European royals: her grandfather, King George I of Greece, had been assassinated in 1913 when Marina was six years old; her mother was a Russian grand duchess, and both of her parents were first cousins of Tsar Nicholas II. The revolutionary turmoil that had engulfed Russia and Greece drove Marina's family into exile in Paris; there, she developed a reputation for style, and often appeared in outfits by the French couturier Jean Patou.

When it came to her wedding gown, however, Marina was expected to share the sartorial patriotism of her future mother-in-law, and therefore turned to the London-born Edward Molyneux, who would also design her trousseau and the bridesmaids' dresses. In his youth, Molyneux had trained at the Edwardian court dressmaker Maison Lucile, owned by

Lady Duff-Gordon, which had included Queen Mary amongst its royal clients. Soon, the prodigiously talented young man became a key designer for Lucile, and accompanied Lady Duff-Gordon as she expanded beyond her original Mayfair premises to establish businesses in Paris in 1910, and in New York the following year.

At the outbreak of the First World War, Molyneux signed up to join the army, serving with distinction in the Duke of Wellington's Regiment, where he became a captain. He was wounded twice: first in July 1916 and then in April 1917, and awarded the Military Cross for leading his company under fire. An injury to one of his eyes meant that Molyneux was unable to return to the front line, and he joined the British Admiralty's naval intelligence unit in London, known informally as Room 40, which used cryptanalysis to decode enemy signals.

In April 1919, Captain Molyneux opened his first Paris couture salon on the prestigious Rue Royale. Funding for this ambitious venture had come in part from Alfred Harmsworth, Viscount Northcliffe, the proprietor of several newspapers including the *Daily Mail* and *The Times*. It is possible that their paths crossed during the war, when Harmsworth was appointed as the government's director of propaganda, or via his wife, Viscountess Northcliffe, who volunteered for the Red Cross. At any rate, by November 1919, the *Daily Mail* was celebrating Molyneux as 'one of the great Paris dressmakers', whose designs were 'taking the city by storm'. Molyneux also received considerable support from Edward Stanley, seventeenth Earl of Derby, Secretary of State for War from 1916 to 1918, and subsequently the British ambassador in Paris until 1920. His third influential ally was Harold Nicolson, at the time a Foreign Office diplomat, with whom the discreetly homosexual Molyneux had an affair. 'I have got such a funny new friend – a dressmaker,' Nicolson wrote to his wife, Vita Sackville-West, on 15 September 1919, 'with a large shop on the Rue Royale, a charming flat at the Rond Point (where I spent the *whole* of Saturday night – sleeping on the balcony) and about 10 mannequins of surpassing beauty. I am lunching at the shop today. My dressmaker is only 27 – and it is rather sporting to launch out into so elaborate an adventure at that age.' Nicolson went on to describe Molyneux as 'very attractive', and told Vita that he was planning to stay with him in his flat, whenever he was in Paris. Like Nicolson, Molyneux would marry; but unlike Nicolson, his marriage – in 1923, to the daughter of a rich Canadian industrialist and former premier of British Columbia – lasted only a year.

Such was the range of Captain Molyneux's diplomatic connections that some in his family believed that he continued to aid British intelligence in the interwar period; certainly, he would go on to provide invaluable help to the secret services during the Second World War, and may well have played a part in the recruiting of Hardy Amies, who regarded Molyneux as a mentor and role model. None of these clandestine activities would have succeeded were it not for the fact that he was a superb couturier, with an international clientele. Soon after the opening of his salon, Molyneux's clients included Lady Diana Cooper (whose husband Duff would become the British ambassador in Paris in 1944) and Lady Cynthia Curzon, the daughter of the then Foreign Secretary, who wore a Molyneux bridal gown when she married the politician Oswald Mosley in May 1920. Their wedding took place in the Chapel Royal at St James's Palace, and amongst the guests were George V and Queen Mary, who remembered Molyneux as 'the clever young man from Lucile'.

In 1932, Molyneux opened a London salon on Grosvenor Street in Mayfair, in response to a royal directive that ladies attending court should 'wear dresses of British design, and from London dressmakers'. This would be crucial for his selection as the designer of choice for Princess Marina and her bridesmaids; and his reputation as the pre-eminent British couturier soared to even greater heights. Marina was photographed in her Molyneux trousseau for the British edition of *Vogue* and appeared on the front cover of the magazine in the same week as her wedding on 29 November 1934. The wedding dress itself, and the bridesmaids' outfits, were widely praised; the *Yorkshire Post* was amongst the many newspapers to devote an entire page to the descriptions, reporting that Princess Marina's gown was made in London by Molyneux, 'of white and silver lamé, brocaded in an

English rose design. Although it is practically all silver, except for the white gauze background which hardly shows, the brocade is unusually supple and quite uncrushable.' The two youngest bridesmaids, meanwhile, Princess Elizabeth and Lady Mary Cambridge, wore 'short high-waisted frocks of stiffened white tulle with full double-tiered skirts. These are mounted on white crêpe embroidered in silver pin spots which shine through the tulle and renew the general silvery effect.' The *Yorkshire Evening Post* had already run a story in advance of the wedding, announcing that 'Princess Elizabeth has naturally been very interested in the fitting of her fairy-like bridesmaid's frock which has two tiers on the skirt and a half wreath of silver roses outlining the neck. She has been busy rehearsing in the nursery at 145 Piccadilly, how she will carry her little bouquet of white "York" roses. The frock suits her fair colouring to perfection.'

No mention was made of the scandals in which the bridegroom had previously been embroiled, when he enjoyed various bisexual liaisons and dangerously large quantities of morphine and cocaine, supplied to him by his socialite paramour, Kiki Preston, otherwise known as 'the girl with the silver syringe'. In café society, Prince George was nicknamed 'Babe', and rumours circulated that his lovers included the performer and playwright Noël Coward (who was, incidentally, a close friend of Molyneux; the couturier designed the costumes for all of Coward's leading ladies on stage). George was also easy prey for blackmailers; on one occasion, paying money to a young man in Paris to whom he had written sexually compromising letters. But the newspapers remained scrupulously deferential in their reporting of his wedding, while *Vogue* emphasised the sophistication of the newly married couple: 'The Duke and Duchess of Kent represent, in the idiom of this age, the spirit of gaiety, international culture and elegance.'

It was Noël Coward who captured something of the dissonance of the era, in a satirical revue that he staged at the Adelphi Theatre in London in 1932. Besides introducing several of his most popular songs, including 'Mad About the Boy' (which inevitably drew speculation as to the identity of the adored boy), Coward lamented the 'Children of the Ritz', wearing Molyneux gowns while the world came tumbling down around them.

Lilibet and her family, who lived along the street from the Ritz in their Piccadilly townhouse, seemed to represent something rather more secure than the decadent Duke of Kent or the daring Prince of Wales, with his penchant for other men's wives. The Yorks ('we four', as they called themselves) had become the role models for a wholesome and close-knit family life. If the monarchy was supposed to set a good example to the nation, then traditional family values needed to be upheld. What would be the point of the royal family if they did not play their parts to perfection? At the very least, they had to be a family writ large.

In this sense, it is understandable that the King and Queen felt such affection for the Yorks, and Lilibet in particular. Their bond was remarked upon by the sharp-eyed American journalist Janet Flanner in a profile of Queen Mary for the *New Yorker* in May 1935. The article was timed to coincide with celebrations to mark the Silver Jubilee of George V's reign, and Flanner noted that while the Prince of Wales and Duke of Kent were the 'most modernizing, modifying filial influences', Lilibet held a special place in Queen Mary's heart. 'Princess Elizabeth looks exactly like her grandmother,' observed Flanner, and added with some prescience that the little girl was 'presumptive Queen of England'. She was not the first to speculate on this subject. On the day of Lilibet's birth, Chips Channon had written in his diary: 'I have a feeling the child will be Queen of England'; although the accuracy of this prediction was undermined by the rest of his sentence – 'and perhaps the last sovereign'.

In retrospect, Janet Flanner's portrait of Queen Mary could equally well be applied to her granddaughter in later life; she described her 'priceless stateliness' and 'her fine photogenic façade, a splendid surface . . . on which nothing private now shows'. Flanner remarked on Queen Mary's antipathy to wearing black and her preferred choice of 'hydrangea-colored town suits', and hats 'worn high on the head like a crown'. The readers of the *New Yorker* were also informed that in the matter of Queen Mary's wardrobe, 'The King has a big word to say. On the whole he likes ladies' clothes as they were and is on the conservative side; both of them are what dressmakers call "anti-fashion" in their taste.'

'We Four': the Yorks (top), 1934. Photograph by Marcus Adams; and (above) with their dogs at Royal Lodge, their home in Windsor Great Park, 1936. Photograph by Lisa Sheridan.

Flanner's description of Queen Mary as being 'anti-fashion' may not be entirely accurate; Lady Airlie certainly believed otherwise, recording in her memoir that it was the King who tended to impose his conventional tastes. 'Her style of dressing was dictated by his conservative prejudices; she was much more interested in fashion than most people imagined, and sometimes I think she longed in secret to get away from the hats and dresses which were always associated with her.'

Unfortunately for Queen Mary, this wish for freedom remained unfulfilled; for as Lady Airlie wrote, she never contradicted the King, being 'almost early Victorian in her attitude to her husband'. Even the most cautious attempts at experimentation were apparently thwarted, as the following extract from Lady Airlie's memoir makes clear. 'Having been gifted with perfect legs, she once tentatively suggested to me in the nineteen-twenties that we might both shorten our skirts by a modest two or three inches but we lacked the courage to do it until eventually I volunteered to be the guinea pig. I appeared at Windsor one day in a slightly shorter dress than usual, the plan being that if His Majesty made no unfavourable comment the Queen would follow my example.'

The next morning, the two women had to accept defeat, when the King had stated decisively that he disliked Lady Airlie's dress, and regarded it as being far too short. 'So I had my hem let down with all speed and the Queen remained faithful to her long full skirts.'

Some small progress appears to have been made by the early 1930s, when Queen Mary was reported in the press as having 'expressed interest and delight' in Coco Chanel's use of British textiles, and was even said to have chosen one of these fabrics to be made into a dress. The appreciation was mutual: in 1931, Chanel described Queen Mary as 'the only regally dressed queen still alive'. And according to her daughter-in-law Elizabeth (speaking to James Pope-Hennessy in 1957), '*Everything* interested her – *Dior* or *whatever* it was.'

Nevertheless, Janet Flanner's profile captured the ways in which Queen Mary transcended the fashions of the day, thereby achieving an unusually timeless quality in her appearance, and creating a template for queenliness that held sway over future generations of Windsor women. Skirts might rise or fall with the stock markets, but Queen Mary stayed steady, maintaining her equilibrium, poise and composure. As Chips Channon noted in his diary on the Jubilee procession: 'All eyes were on the Queen in her white and silvery splendour! Never had she looked so serene, so royally majestic . . . she has become the best-dressed woman in the world.'

Queen Mary's influence would be apparent again in the wedding of her third son, Prince Henry, the Duke of Gloucester, to Lady Alice Montagu-Douglas-Scott in November 1935. Lady Alice was the daughter of a Scottish aristocrat, the Duke of Buccleuch, and was described in *Vogue* as being 'very much of an outdoors person [who] does not like towns, crowds or publicity'. Her wedding day did indeed turn out to be relatively private: as her father had died just a few weeks earlier, the ceremony was transferred from Westminster Abbey to the chapel in Buckingham Palace. But there was still intense public curiosity about the bridal gown, and even more regarding the bridesmaid dresses to be worn by Princesses Elizabeth and Margaret.

Another British couturier was chosen on this occasion: Norman Hartnell, who had opened his first salon at 10 Bruton Street in 1923 when he was still only twenty-two. Unlike Molyneux, Hartnell had little training as a couturier; instead, he began designing stage costumes during his time as a Cambridge undergraduate, for student productions by the Footlights dramatic club. He also appeared in these revues – most often playing the female lead, dressed in his own flamboyant creations and attempting to pass as an alluring woman, rather than the parody of a pantomime dame. His sensual pleasure in cross-dressing was part of his private life, too, and would continue to be so for many years, although as a closely guarded secret. When Hartnell left Cambridge, after failing his exams, he searched in vain for employment either in the London theatre world or at a well-established couture salon. He did manage to find a job for a court dressmaker on the fringes of Mayfair, but was fired after three months. Undaunted, he set up his own business with the help of his sister and a modest family inheritance.

Hartnell's first notable clients included the four beautiful daughters of William Lygon, seventh Earl Beauchamp; the eldest, Lady Lettice, ordered a romantic silvery gown from one of his early collections. In 1925, Lord Beauchamp visited Hartnell's salon to buy dresses for his wife and daughters as Christmas presents. The following summer, Lettice appeared at the Duchess of Sutherland's costume ball in Mayfair wearing another of Hartnell's designs, described in the press as 'a marvellous 18th-century frock of Romney blue taffeta', hand-painted with 'bouquets of lilac, roses, cornflowers and daisies', and a 'lace underdress' that had 'pink ribbon bows and roses'. This extravagantly ornate gown was made in the same year that Chanel's iconic little black dress had been hailed as the embodiment of contemporary chic by American *Vogue*. Hartnell's nostalgic romanticism was entirely at odds with Chanel's vision of sleek, streamlined style; in private, he admitted to loathing the prevailing modernist fashions of the 1920s, and what he described as the 'dreary creations of Mlle Chanel'.

Such fantastical designs appealed to the Lygon sisters in their roles as Bright Young People, a much-publicised social circle who appeared at an endless parade of fancy-dress parties satirised by their friend Evelyn Waugh in his novel *Vile Bodies*. By 1928, British *Vogue* had explicitly linked Hartnell with this glamorous group: 'His clothes express the vagaries . . . of a wayward smart generation.' Indeed, when two of the quixotic Lygon sisters, Sibell and Mary, inspired what would later become a comic set piece in *Vile Bodies*, they were wearing Hartnell party frocks. Intoxicated and disorientated after a lengthy evening of revelry, they turned up at 10 Downing Street, occupied at the time by their father's friend Stanley Baldwin, and having startled the prime minister, they fell asleep and departed the following morning.

Hartnell himself held a circus-themed party at a similarly exalted address: 17 Bruton Street – the famous birthplace of Princess Elizabeth. This event took place in the first week of July 1929, when the Strathmores had moved out, and their former home was standing empty. The enterprising Hartnell leased the building for the evening – it was

Norman Hartnell outside his Mayfair premises, 1938. Photograph by Felix Man.

A model wearing a Norman Hartnell gown, *c*.1929. Photograph by Sasha.

conveniently situated across the road from his salon – and hundreds of fashionable guests turned up, many of them wearing outrageous costumes designed by the host, who was posing in a circus ringmaster's outfit.

The festivities were staged less than a month after Ramsay MacDonald had returned to Downing Street as Labour prime minister, following the so-called 'flapper election', where women over the age of twenty-one were allowed to vote for the first time. There were already signs of financial turbulence, and in October that year the Wall Street Crash would force the roaring twenties to a juddering halt. But the frenzied antics of the Bright Young People were still newsworthy in the last summer of the decade, and Hartnell's party made the headlines: 'The Lions of Mayfair: Queer Menagerie Party', proclaimed the *Daily News and Westminster Gazette*. According to the *Sunday Pictorial*, 'It was a night of surprises, beginning with the sounds of a street organ issuing from the stately house in which the Earl and Countess of Strathmore lived until a short time ago . . . The drawing room had been turned into a real circus ring with tiny performing bears and a wee pony which walked upstairs.' A columnist for *Tatler* observed: 'The old-fashioned house in Bruton Street, where the party was given, must have been horribly shocked at finding itself dressed up in the most garish spangles and plush,' and described the circus side-shows of 'houp-la, fortune-telling, and coconut shies'. One of the female guests wore 'live snakes coiling around her person'; the exploding flashlights of photographers briefly set fire to the decorations; and the buffet was adorned with 'pale green ice animals'. Sibell Lygon and her friend Nancy Mitford were entertained by Siberian wolf cubs, and there was some dispute in the press as to whether the notoriously wild Ruthven twins were disguised as monkeys or bears. Nancy's newly married sister Diana arrived hand-in-hand with her husband Bryan Guinness (they were the couple to whom Evelyn Waugh dedicated *Vile Bodies*); while the bridesmaids at another recent society wedding (including Lady Honor Guinness, soon to marry Chips Channon) came in their matching gold gauze dresses designed by Hartnell.

Yet for all the frivolity of his fancy-dress costumes, Hartnell was also receiving commissions for the formal white gowns that debutantes wore to be presented at court for the first time; and, in due course, they returned to him for their wedding dresses. It even seemed possible that Hartnell's loyal clients, the Lygon sisters, might become royal brides themselves. Chips Channon, in his diary entry for 2 February 1928, described seeing the Prince of Wales after a society wedding: '[He] slunk vulgarly in. I watched his old-young face, so lined by dissipation, late hours . . . I have had a sudden brainwave – shall we marry him to Lettice Lygon?' Nothing came of this plan, but Lettice's younger sister Mary did become romantically involved with Prince George. The great beauty of the family, she had first met George when she was presented to his parents at Buckingham Palace in May 1928, wearing a Hartnell gown of white silk tulle, embroidered with silver thread, and a silvery lace and tulle train.

For several months the following year, George had temporarily withdrawn from the social whirl, in an endeavour to cure his drug addiction. George's oldest brother played some part in this attempt at rehabilitation. (In a letter to his married mistress, Freda Dudley Ward, the Prince of Wales reported that while keeping watch over George, he was doing needlework to soothe his nerves: 'It would make you laugh and maybe cry a little too.') The King and Queen had been kept informed of their youngest son's dependency on cocaine and morphine – the King noted in his diary (in November 1929) that George's psychiatrist had said he 'was not at all an easy case'. It remains uncertain, however, as to whether they were aware of his bisexual affairs. As for Lady Mary's family, who had entertained Prince George at their ancestral home, Madresfield: they hoped that the romance would lead to an engagement, despite George's reputation for debauchery. But it was the scandal that engulfed Lord Beauchamp in 1931, which ultimately ended any possibility of a royal marriage.

Beauchamp was denounced as being homosexual by his brother-in-law Hugh 'Bendor' Grosvenor, the second Duke of Westminster (who by then was married to his third wife, as well as continuing a longstanding affair with Coco Chanel). It is unclear why, exactly, Bendor was so intent on bringing about the downfall of his sister's husband; but he employed private detectives to spy on Beauchamp, and gathered incriminating evidence that the Earl had sexual relationships with his manservants, amongst others. Westminster proceeded to arrange a meeting with the King, and informed him that Beauchamp – a knight of the Garter and former Lord Steward of the Royal Household who had carried the sword of state at the King's coronation in 1911 – was breaking the laws against homosexuality. The monarch's response – repeated in society gossip, but possibly apocryphal, was: 'I thought men like that shot themselves.' Another version had the King saying that he was under the impression that people 'only did such things abroad'. It seems unlikely that the King was ignorant of 'such things' taking place closer to home: his older brother, the hapless Prince Eddy who died in 1892, had been previously linked with what was known as 'the Cleveland Street scandal', involving a homosexual brothel in London.

Meanwhile, the unfortunate Lady Beauchamp, a pious and unworldly woman who was bullied by her brother into filing for divorce, was allegedly confused about the meaning of the accusations against her husband: 'Bendor tells me that Beauchamp is a bugler.' Westminster himself was more explicit when he sent a note to Beauchamp after denouncing him to the King: 'Dear Bugger-in-law, you got what you deserved.' Further gossip came courtesy of Harold Nicolson, who recalled a dinner at Madresfield when he was asked by a fellow guest, 'Did I hear Beauchamp whisper to the butler, "Je t'adore"?' Nicolson covered for their host by replying that Beauchamp had said, 'Shut the door.'

Amidst the froth of mischievous chatter, a family tragedy unfolded: Beauchamp resigned from his position as leader of the Liberal peers in the House of Lords, and in June 1931 he was forced into exile on the Continent, under the threat of criminal prosecution. No mention appeared in the British newspapers about the true reason for Beauchamp's sudden departure; he was simply reported to have been unwell, and leaving for the German spa resort of Bad Nauheim, 'to take the cure'. His children never forgave their uncle and became estranged from their mother, who had a nervous breakdown and died in 1936. Tellingly, when Waugh fictionalised the family saga in his masterpiece *Brideshead Revisited*, he gave the disgraced peer a female rather than a male lover; homosexuality was still illegal when the novel was published in 1945. For a gay man such as Norman Hartnell, who was born in 1901, secrecy continued to be imperative, and the danger of blackmail was as menacing as criminal prosecution. If a privileged aristocrat such as Lord Beauchamp could fall from grace, how much more perilous was it for Hartnell, who was also intent on concealing his true origins? His birthplace was a Streatham pub, the aptly named Crown & Sceptre; his father an enterprising publican whose financial acumen paid for Norman to be sent to a private school, Mill Hill, and then to Magdalene College, Cambridge.

Hartnell's autobiography, *Silver and Gold* (published in 1955), makes no mention of his family background, nor of his cross-dressing performances at Cambridge. Instead, it reveals his passion for creating fantasy through the medium of costume, with all the detail omitted from his private life transferred to his vivid description of clothes. Here, for example, is Hartnell's account of his first collection, presented in February 1924: 'A foaming feather band of shaded blue-grey was stitched on to the hem of periwinkle blue velvet, rose ostrich fronds to pale pink lace and one outrageous garment of crimson was emblazoned with a gilt thread dragon.' When his sister suggested that his collection might include 'a simple little dress of black wool or brown tweed', Hartnell retorted, 'I despise simplicity. It is the negation of all that is beautiful.'

And yet by the time of his first royal commission, Hartnell had proved that he was capable of restraining his natural preference to decorate everything with sequins, spangles and glitter. This more nuanced approach – along with his personal understanding of the importance of discretion – was vital in his evolution from a fancy-dress costumier for the Bright Young People to trusted royal couturier for the house of Windsor. Queen Mary played a discreet role in approving Hartnell's designs for Lady Alice's bridal gown and trousseau, while the King made his own intervention regarding the attire for the youngest bridesmaids, Princesses

Elizabeth and Margaret. As Hartnell recorded in his memoir, George V required 'that the little ones should wear girlish dresses', so they were shortened from the original full-length designs. 'They were of palest pink satin; short skirts bordered with three graduating bands of ruched pink tulle, tiny sleeves and a tulle-bordered bodice.'

Hartnell's memoir gives only the briefest description of Lady Alice's ivory satin wedding dress – it was of 'strictest simplicity', in 'a soft tone with something of the glimmer of pearl', and worn with a tulle veil. (The *Sketch* hailed it as 'a masterpiece of British design', noting that the satin had 'a wonderful pink pearl tinge' and was 'specially woven for the bride'.) But he lovingly recounted the visit to his salon of the York sisters, to be fitted for their bridesmaids' dresses, accompanied by their mother: 'My first sight of them was a truly enchanting vision and one which I shall never forget . . . the Duchess of York was in silver grey georgette, clouded with the palest grey fox, and her jewels were dewdrop diamonds and aquamarines. The young princesses, on each side of her, as she led them by the hand, wore little blue jackets, silver buttoned, and tiny grey hats wreathed in blue forget-me-nots, making a symphony of silver and blue.'

Soon afterwards, Hartnell was asked to be in attendance at Buckingham Palace for the photographs of the newly-weds (who would now be known as the Duke and Duchess of Gloucester), which took place in the throne room. Again, he described the scene in reverent terms in his memoir. '"Would you please go forward and arrange the Duchess's veil?" a page murmured to me. I walked forward, made a bow and knelt to disentangle the bride's veil from the spur of the Duke who towered above me, resplendent in the blue, damson and gold of the Tenth Hussars.

'As I stood up a deep voice said to me: "We are very pleased. We think everything is very, very pretty." It was the voice of Queen Mary.'

As far as Hartnell was concerned, this might as well have been the voice of God, calling upon him to fulfil a divine mission.

'THAT WOMAN IN MY OWN HOUSE!'

When the royal family gathered for the wedding celebrations of the Duke and Duchess of Gloucester on 6 November 1935, there was one figure conspicuous by her absence, but very much on the minds of those present. By then, the Prince of Wales was passionately in love with Wallis Simpson, a twice-married American who was the subject of feverish gossip in London society. The King and Queen could not bring themselves to utter her name, and the Yorks did their best to avoid meeting her, as did the Gloucesters. Such was the controversy surrounding the notorious Mrs Simpson that Norman Hartnell would not even mention her in his memoir, despite the fact that she had been a prominent client as the mistress of the Prince of Wales.

Hartnell's discretion did not prevent his seamstresses from discussing Mrs Simpson amongst themselves in their Bruton Street workrooms, and wondering whether she might become the future queen. One of Hartnell's assistants, Muriel Monson, would later remember Mrs Simpson as an 'immaculate and well-groomed person, who gave the most praise of anyone who came and ordered clothes' (her gracious appearance marred only by her 'very grating voice').

Nevertheless, when Wallis first appeared on the fringes of café society in 1931, as a friend of the Prince of Wales's then lover, Thelma Furness, she was regarded as insignificant by most who met her. 'Mrs Simpson

Wallis Simpson, *c.*1937, wearing her Cartier ring and bracelets. Photograph by George Hoyningen-Huene.

seemed somewhat brawny and raw-boned in her sapphire-blue velvet,' recalled the young photographer Cecil Beaton of their initial encounter at an Arts Club ball. 'Her voice had a high nasal twang.' This is the version that appears in Beaton's published edition of his diary; the unexpurgated original was far more brutal: he called her 'a brawny great cow or bullock . . . Her voice was raucous and appalling. I thought her awful, common, vulgar, strident, a second-rate American with no charm.'

Beaton would change his mind four years later, when it was clear that the heir to the throne had become utterly devoted to Wallis: 'I found her bright and witty, improved in looks and chic.' Having had the opportunity to study her, in photographic sittings and sketches, Beaton described her as 'soignée and fresh as a young girl. Her skin was as bright and smooth as the inside of a shell, her hair so sleek she might have been Chinese.' At the same time, however, 'Mrs Simpson proved an exceptionally difficult woman to draw. I found nothing facile to catch hold of and soon discovered that even the slightest impression was devilishly difficult.' Beaton judged her to be 'alluring', yet even he, with his abundant creative gifts, struggled to convey Mrs Simpson's appeal in words or illustrations. Nor was he alone in these difficulties. Indeed, very few of those who met Wallis could understand why she had captured the heart of the most eligible bachelor in the world, a popular Prince Charming whose good looks made him more famous than any Hollywood film star.

Certainly, Chips Channon, who was first introduced to Mrs Simpson in January 1935, appears to have been baffled by her ascent to royal favourite, as is evident in his diary: 'She is a nice, quiet, well-bred, mouse of a woman with large startled eyes and a huge, huge mole. I think she is surprised . . . and rather conscience-stricken by her present position and the limelight, which subsequently falls upon her.' Three months afterwards, Channon invited Mrs Simpson to lunch at his home in Belgrave Square, but her attractions remain stubbornly opaque in his diary entry for 4 April. 'She is a jolly, plain, intelligent, quiet little woman, both unpretentious and unprepossessing.' Her only notable feature, remarked Channon (aside from her facial mole, 'a carbuncle on her chin' that continued to preoccupy him), was her newfound confidence. Wallis now had 'the air of a personage and walks into the room as if she almost expected to be curtsied to: at least she would not be surprised. She has complete power over the Prince of Wales.'

As far as the Prince's family was concerned, Wallis was simply unspeakable. The Duchess of York knew of her brother-in-law's association with Mrs Simpson by the summer of 1933, and so, it would seem, did his parents. On 1 August, in a tactful letter to Queen Mary, the Duchess wrote that the King had 'mentioned to me that he had heard a certain person had been at the Fort [Fort Belvedere, the Prince's home in Windsor Great Park] when Bertie & I had been there, & he said that he had a very good mind to speak to David about it. I never had a chance to reopen the subject, but I hope he won't do this . . . relations are already a little difficult when naughty ladies are brought in.' Wallis was not yet the lover of the Prince (their affair began at the beginning of 1934); but as a divorcee with two living husbands, she was regarded as unsuitable company for royalty.

According to the Prince of Wales himself, his mother never once mentioned Wallis's name. 'Instead, she was silent,' he told his American ghostwriter Charles Murphy when they were working together on his memoir, *A King's Story*, published in 1951. 'Her silence, coupled with inflexible opposition to divorce, meant she disapproved.'

Initially, the King and Queen appeared to follow their daughter-in-law's advice to tacitly ignore 'a certain person', but the Prince wanted more from his parents. In November 1934, he ensured that the Simpsons were guests at his younger brother George's wedding to Princess Marina at Westminster Abbey, and also included their names on the list of people to be invited to an evening reception at Buckingham Palace to celebrate the marriage. The King deleted the Simpsons from the guest list, but the Prince of Wales somehow reinstated them; and Wallis made her entrance in a violet lamé gown with a vivid green sash. This audacious outfit had been designed for the occasion by Eva Lutyens, a Russian émigré to London (and daughter-in-law of the eminent architect Sir Edwin Lutyens), who was known for her bold colour combinations and avant-garde aesthetic. The unusual dress made an emphatic statement, setting Wallis apart from the more conventionally dressed guests, and drawing attention to her otherness, in ways that might be construed as challenging. Certainly, the bravado of her appearance highlighted her marked difference to the royal wives, with their formal gowns and traditional tiaras. Wallis herself judged the dress to be 'outstanding', referring to it in her own account of what happened that evening: 'The Prince of Wales brought Prince Paul, Regent of Yugoslavia, and also brother-in-law of the bride, over to talk with us. "Mrs Simpson," said Prince Paul, "there is no question about it – you are wearing the most striking gown in the room."'

Wallis's memoir (*The Heart Has Its Reasons*, published in 1956, and written in collaboration with Charles Murphy) states that the Buckingham Palace reception was 'truly memorable' because 'it was the only time I ever met David's father and mother. After Prince Paul had left us, David led me over to where they were standing and introduced me. It was the briefest of encounters – a few words of perfunctory greeting, an exchange of meaningless pleasantries, and we moved away. But I was impressed with Their Majesties' great gift for making everyone they met, however casually, feel at ease in their presence.'

Her description is presumably laced with irony, given that it is diametrically opposed to those in the royal household who were shocked at the sight of Mrs Simpson. According to the Prince of Wales's equerry, John Aird, who wrote about the tense encounter in his diary that night, the Prince introduced Wallis to Queen Mary, and then tried to present her to his father, but was 'cut off'. The King was outraged. 'That woman in my own house!' he complained furiously to another guest at the reception, his friend and kinsman Count Albert Mensdorff (a former Austro-Hungarian ambassador to London). As a consequence, George V issued strict orders that Mrs Simpson was to be banned from attending the Silver Jubilee celebrations and the Royal Enclosure at Ascot.

The Prince was undeterred, and managed to persuade his father to invite the Simpsons to a court ball in May 1935, by swearing that Wallis was not his mistress. 'It is rather a shock to think of the Prince of Wales lying,' wrote Aird in his diary; while Tommy Lascelles thought the Prince's claim of a platonic relationship with Wallis to be 'as credible as . . . a herd of unicorns grazing in Hyde Park and a shoal of mermaids swimming in the Serpentine'.

When the Silver Jubilee ball commenced at Buckingham Palace on 14 May, the Prince of Wales led Wallis onto the dance floor where, as she subsequently recalled in a florid passage in her memoir, 'I felt the King's eyes rest searchingly on me. Something in his look made me feel that all this graciousness and pageantry were but the glittering tip of an iceberg that extended down into unseen depths I could never plumb, depths filled with an icy menace for such as me.'

At the time, however, Wallis appeared to be enjoying the attention. On 17 May, Chips Channon noted in his diary that she was 'madly Americanly anxious to storm society', and being received with open arms by those (including himself) who recognised Wallis's newfound power. 'The royal romance surpasses all else in interest . . . she has somehow completely subjugated him. Never has he been so in love.' A week later, Channon and his wife accepted an invitation to 'Mrs Simpson's little flat in Bryanston Court'. There, they found the Prince of Wales mixing and passing the cocktails, as if he were the '*jeune homme de la maison*' (the young man of the house), while 'his voice is more American than ever'.

Throughout this period, the Prince's relationship with Mrs Simpson was kept out of the British press, with a deferential tact that is impossible to imagine now, when every salacious detail relating to royal affairs is shared avidly on social media. Even so, by the summer of 1935, as Cecil Beaton wrote in his diary in August, 'her name seems never to be off people's lips. For those who enjoy gossip she is a particular treat. The sound of her name implies secrecy, royalty, and being in-the-know. As a topic she has become a mania.'

Much of the tittle-tattle revolved around the mystery of her hold over the Prince of Wales. Was it her sexual expertise, supposedly learned in the brothels of China in the 1920s? Hence Beaton's knowing reference to her sleek 'Chinese' hair, and the sly caption beneath a portrait of her that appeared in the US edition of *Harper's Bazaar* in May 1936: 'Mrs Ernest Simpson, the most famous American in London, wears a Chinese dinner dress.' As if to emphasise the point, the portrait itself – by the Surrealist photographer Man Ray – places Wallis beside a Chinese sculpture, a glazed ceramic god-like figure from the Ming dynasty.

Those who observed the couple together speculated as to whether she was the dominant partner in a sadomasochistic relationship. John Aird confided his concerns to his diary, when accompanying Wallis and the Prince of Wales on a Mediterranean cruise in August 1934, noting that his master's submissive adoration was 'awful and most embarrassing for others', and that he 'follows W around like a dog'. The following year, in May 1935, after discussing the matter with another courtier, Aird wrote that the Prince was possessed by 'the sexual perversion of self-abasement'. Similarly, the journalist Robert Bruce Lockhart – a friend of the Prince (and a former British spy) – believed that he was 'suffering from dementia erotica'. Chips Channon also sensed that 'this infatuation for Wallis is almost dementia', but wondered, with the authority of someone who was himself bisexual, whether the Prince 'suffers from sexual repression of another nature. His horror of anything even savouring of homosexuality was exaggerated, especially in a world where it is *far* from unknown; and at the same time there are tales (I have heard them all my life and some I believe to be half true), which reveal him in *quite* another light. Certainly, too, he has *always* surrounded himself with extremely attractive men.'

Some believed that the Prince was attracted to Wallis precisely because of her masculine looks, a theory that has led several contemporary biographers to postulate that she may have had a chromosomal abnormality, or what is sometimes referred to as 'intersexuality'. An intrusive curiosity about Wallis's body – as if a medical or physiological approach might offer a way to penetrate her mysterious sexual allure – is not simply a prurient modern obsession. 'This is one of the oddest women I have ever seen,' wrote James Pope-Hennessy in his journal, after spending time with Wallis (by then the Duchess of Windsor), in the course of researching his

Wallis Simpson with Chinese figure, 1936. Photograph by Man Ray.

biography of Queen Mary. 'I should be tempted to classify her simply as An American Woman *par excellence*, were it not for the suspicion that she is not a woman at all. She is, to look at, phenomenal. She is flat and angular and could have been designed for a medieval playing-card. The shoulders are small and high; the head very, very large, almost monumental; the expression is either anticipatory . . . or appreciative – the great giglamp smile, the wide, wide open eyes, which are so very large and pale and veined, the painted lips and cannibal teeth.'

Nor was the conjecture simply confined to the pages of private diaries: Lady Cynthia Colville, for example, the eminently respectable lady-in-waiting to Queen Mary, discussed the matter with a well-known psychologist, Dr William Brown. She suggested to Dr Brown that Mrs Simpson had hypnotised the Prince; he thought it more likely that the Prince's sex life had hitherto been unsatisfactory, and that Mrs Simpson had resolved any previous difficulties. When Dr Brown's views were brought to the attention of Clive Wigram, George V's private secretary, Wigram noted in a confidential memo that the Prince 'had a weak spot in his mental equipment which Mrs S by foul and unfair means has exploited for her own advantage. As long as HRH is under this spell it would be useless to try to get him to go to a doctor to dispel this evil influence. She has him too tight in her grasp and is like a vampire.'

If Wigram believed that Wallis was a wicked mistress of the dark arts, he increasingly came to see the Prince of Wales as a lunatic, and was overheard by Tommy Lascelles complaining: 'He's mad – he's mad. We shall have to lock him up.' Lascelles himself regarded their master as ever more wilful and destructive, citing the story of how he ordered a gardener at Windsor to cut all the spring blossom from lovingly nurtured peach trees – thereby destroying the summer harvest of fruit – and send it to Wallis, as a short-lived bouquet to decorate her London drawing room. 'Caligula himself can never have done anything more wanton,' observed Lascelles in his diary.

Whatever the ultimately unfathomable secrets of their relationship, the Prince of Wales had not immediately fallen in love with Wallis when they first met at Lady Furness's country house in January 1931. Thelma was the American wife of Marmaduke Furness, an immensely wealthy British shipping magnate; it was a second marriage for both of them. The Simpsons had far less money than Lord and Lady Furness – Ernest Simpson worked for his family's firm of shipbrokers, which had suffered substantial financial losses in the wake of the Wall Street Crash – but Wallis was socially ambitious, and equipped with what Thelma would later describe as 'a distinct charm and a sharp sense of humour'. Three years later, a few days before Thelma embarked on a trip to America, she had lunch with Wallis at the Ritz. In Thelma's version of their conversation (which appears in her memoir), Wallis 'said suddenly, "Oh, Thelma, the little man is going to be so lonely." "Well, dear," I answered, "you look after him for me while I'm away. See that he does not get into any mischief."' In Wallis's memoir, it was Thelma who said, 'laughingly', 'I'm afraid the Prince is going to be lonely. Wallis, won't you look after him?' By the time Thelma returned to England in March 1934, Wallis had completely supplanted her in the Prince's affections. Thelma realised this when she joined them for dinner at Fort Belvedere, and 'I noticed that the Prince and Wallis seemed to have little private jokes. Once he picked up a piece of salad with his fingers; Wallis playfully slapped his hand.' As soon as she saw the slap, Thelma knew that Wallis was now in control of the situation. 'Wallis looked straight at me . . . Wallis, of all people. And this was the friend I had asked, jokingly, to look after the Prince for me while I was away . . . I knew then she had looked after him exceedingly well. That one, cold defiant glance had told me the entire story.'

If Wallis was indeed cold and defiant, then these attributes were as necessary to her protective armour as the hard-edged chic that she later made famous in her role as the supremely stylish Duchess of Windsor. Born Bessie Wallis Warfield on 19 June 1896, she had grown up a poor relation of prominent Baltimore families. Her father died of tuberculosis when she was a baby, and she and her mother were dependent on the inconsistent charity of wealthier relatives. Added to her childhood insecurity was the perception that she was not a natural beauty. 'Nobody ever

The Duchess of Windsor in Paris, 1937. Photographs by Horst P. Horst.

called me beautiful or even pretty,' she wrote in her memoir. 'My jaw was clearly too big and too pointed to be classic. My hair was straight when the laws of compensation might at least have provided curls.' This may explain why she developed a highly attuned sense of style, a ruthlessly maintained whip-thin figure, and a wisecracking wit that some found alarming. 'Wallis was vivacious with a *bite*,' said one of the men who had known her in her youth. That visceral undercurrent of danger – the cannibal teeth observed by Pope-Hennessy – is also evident in an account by the German-born actress Lilli Palmer of Wallis's 'voracious vitality'. 'If she had happened to be hungry, she might have taken a bite out of you. Whenever I looked at her I was reminded of the nutcracker we used for cracking walnuts when we were children. It was made of polished wood in the form of a woman's head which could open its mouth very wide and *c-rr-ack*, the nut disintegrated.'

The threat of Wallis's bite was combined with her powerful desire for male admiration, solicited through a combination of bold flirtation and a distinctive dress sense. As she declared on the opening page of her memoir, 'The person who knows me best, my Aunt Bessie . . . insists that I have always had a plan germinating in the back of my mind.' By way of proof, Aunt Bessie cited Wallis's choice of outfit at her 'first young people's party . . . On that occasion, according to my ever-truthful aunt, I am supposed to have persuaded my mother, after a foot-stamping scene, to substitute for the blue sash she wanted me to wear with my white dress a bright red one. "I remember exactly what you said," my aunt now insists. "You told your mother you wanted a red sash so that the boys would notice you."'

A red sash seems trivial, and yet it takes on significance in Wallis's telling, because she – and her ghostwriter – selected it as a meaningful introduction to understanding a misunderstood woman. In this and other instances in her memoir, Wallis's clothes are one of the few tangible clues to her true identity. We can never be altogether sure how accurately Charles Murphy captured her tone of voice and personality. He relied on recordings of their conversations, as well as handwritten notes, and after reading an early draft, Wallis broke off the partnership for a time, telling him: 'I do not feel myself in the pages. That is no fault of yours; it is most likely the fashion in which I have tried to put myself over to you.' After a failed attempt to collaborate with another ghostwriter, Wallis returned to Murphy, and was sufficiently satisfied with the results to allow the book to be published as 'her personal testament'. The end result is as polished as the Duchess of Windsor herself, although it also brings to mind Harold Nicolson's comment about his official biography of George V: 'I have created a pure tailor's dummy,' he wrote in his diary (on 26 July 1951, shortly before finishing the book), 'and have not tried to make him live at all, since if he did so he would appear as a stupid old bore.' Nicolson accepted this as inevitable, given his job as an authorised biographer: 'I quite see that the Royal Family feel their myth is a piece of gossamer and must not be blown apart.' As a ghostwriter, Murphy was even more constrained, with the invidious task of breathing life into the brittle figure of Wallis, while restoring her tattered dignity. It is therefore unsurprising that the persona in her memoir so often appears masked.

Murphy's true feelings about his subjects are apparent in his later book, *A Windsor Story* (published in 1979), where he described being in their company as akin to 'watching a brisk comedy of manners, with a famous actor and actress playing the roles in which their fateful love affair had cast them'. The longer he looked on, 'the more revealing and – on that account – the more unreal and pathetic it all came to seem.' The couple's celebrated romance appeared to be 'fraying' before his eyes, as Wallis grew visibly irritated by the man who still adored her. This emotional unravelling may explain why they both paid such close attention to the minutiae of their clothes, in a vain attempt to keep up appearances. Besides, their shared interest in fashion was, at the very least, a mutual source of satisfaction.

All of which means that it is worth taking note of the sartorial details in Wallis's memoir, from the red sash onwards. A key scene describes her debut in Baltimore society, at the age of eighteen, when she was intent on choosing clothes that made her the centre of attention at a ball in 1914. 'My choice was white satin combined with chiffon,' she recalled, 'in a

Wallis (clockwise from top left) during her first marriage to Earl Winfield Spencer; on her first wedding day, 1916; in 1927; at school, 1910.

knee-length tunic banded with pearl embroidery – a style borrowed shamelessly from a ballroom gown in which Irene Castle was at that time dancing to spectacular success on Broadway.' Although Irene Castle's name is now far less renowned than that of Wallis Simpson, the reference is intriguing. As it happens, Cecil Beaton devotes a dozen pages to Irene Castle in his book, *The Glass of Fashion* (published in 1954), while Wallis receives only a passing mention: rather cruelly, she is reduced to nothing more than a hostess with a 'fetishistic concern for trivialities' who organises 'her entertainments for café society with an equal unction and determination'.

By contrast, in Beaton's view, the American dancer Irene Castle 'introduced a completely fresh note' in the years just before and during the First World War. 'It is no accident that Stravinsky's early music and Picasso's Cubist period coincided with the success of a woman who was to be one of the most remarkable fashion figures the world has known. Mrs Castle was as important an embodiment of the "modern", in the social and fashion sense, as these artists were in the world of art.' She cut her hair short, wore boyish clothes, popularised the foxtrot and the tango, and heralded the emancipation of the Jazz Age.

If Wallis hoped to emulate Irene Castle – and her dedication to dancing, along with an early photograph of her sporting a monocle, suggests she might have done – her next step proved to be the opposite of liberation. In April 1916, two months before her twentieth birthday, she met Earl Winfield Spencer, a US Navy pilot who was eight years older than her; they were engaged in September, and married in November that year. Wallis applied the same perfectionism to the design of her bridal gown as she had to her debutante's dress, and offers a loving description of it in her memoir. It was made of white velvet, 'with a court train and pointed bodice elaborately embroidered with pearls. My skirt fell over a petticoat of heirloom lace. I carried a bouquet of white orchids and lilies of the valley, and I had a spray of orange blossom arranged in coronet fashion around a veil of tulle, which was also edged with white lace.'

Yet for all the fairy-tale romance of Wallis's outfit, the marriage foundered due to the ugly reality of her husband's alcoholic rages, when he would accuse her of flirting with other men. She left him in the summer of 1921, and then attempted a reconciliation when he was posted to Hong Kong, where she joined him in September 1924. After what she described as a brief 'second honeymoon', their relationship broke down again. 'To his already formidable repertory of taunts and humiliations he now added some Oriental variations,' she revealed in her memoir. 'I gathered that during our long absence he had spent a considerable amount of his time ashore in the local singsong houses. In any event, he now insisted on my accompanying him to his favourite haunts, where he would ostentatiously make a fuss over the girls.'

Wallis's surprisingly candid reference to the 'singsong houses' – bordellos offering erotic entertainments, as well as opium and gambling – represents a partial response to the rumours about her supposed sexual exploits in China. The transcripts of Charles Murphy's interviews with Wallis reveal that their conversations touched on this contentious subject. When Murphy asked her about the 'outrageous things being said about you', she replied that 'friends of mine told me that fantastic stories about me came back from China. There was nothing fantastic about my life in China . . . I would see every possible story of invention simply made by venom, feminine venom.'

Her choice of words suggests that it was only malicious women who created what she called the 'terrific propaganda' about her past, when in fact men were just as likely to be scandal-mongering. Murphy came to believe that Wallis was unable or unwilling to be honest with him or even with herself. 'It is extremely difficult,' he wrote in his diary on 21 November 1954, 'almost impossible to penetrate her caution. Her life, I suspect, frightens her.'

And yet whatever the truth of the matter, Wallis displayed a remarkably intrepid spirit in China, leaving her husband for good and setting off from Hong Kong on an expedition to Shanghai and Peking. There, she made new friends in the expatriate community, became an accomplished poker player, and enjoyed the freedom of what she would call 'my lotus year' with a series of adventures. One of these, if gossip is to be believed, was an affair with a glamorous Italian aristocrat named Count Galeazzo Ciano, who would subsequently marry Mussolini's daughter and serve as Italy's foreign minister in the Fascist government. Later, when Wallis became involved with the Prince of Wales, rumours swirled that a so-called 'China Dossier' had been compiled on the orders of the King and the prime minister, Stanley Baldwin, investigating her alleged immorality and nefarious activities during her travels in the Far East. When Charles Murphy asked Wallis to address this story, she said: 'Lady Astor goes around talking about some dossier of mine. We've never been able to trace some dossier . . . Well, if anyone put out a dossier it must have been the British.' It is possible that the 'feminine venom' that Wallis referred to was linked in her mind to Nancy Astor, the first woman to sit as a Member of Parliament, who did indeed possess a formidable capacity for mischief and malice. However, the only hard evidence that I can find about Nancy's antipathy to Wallis appears in a diary entry by Harold Nicolson, by then an MP himself, who was friendly with both women. He reported that Nancy (an American divorcee who had emigrated to England from Virginia and married, incidentally, my husband's great-uncle) was 'terribly indignant' about Mrs Simpson appearing at court. Only 'the best Virginian families should be received at Court', she told Nicolson, and added that any mention of Mrs Simpson in the Court Circular would have a 'deplorable' effect in Canada and America.

Nor have I – or anyone else – found convincing evidence that Wallis had even the slightest contact with Ciano, and although she did have a liaison with an Italian naval officer in Peking, the existence of a 'China Dossier' seems unlikely. But still the wild conjecture spread that Wallis became pregnant by Ciano, and had an abortion that left her infertile; and that she subsequently had a secret affair with Joachim von Ribbentrop, the Nazi diplomat who supposedly sent her seventeen carnations every day, one for each night they had spent together. These and other dubious accusations continue to circulate today, which presents a conundrum for those attempting to write about her. As the historian Philip Ziegler observed in his official biography of Edward VIII, 'The career and personality of

Wallis Simpson have been the subject of so much speculation, so much lurid and unbridled fantasy, that it seems ungenerous to the reader to resort to established truth.' Ziegler notes the allegations that Wallis learned her sexual techniques in the brothels of Hong Kong or Shanghai, and became Ribbentrop's mistress and a spy for the Nazis, while admitting that these charges are almost as challenging to disprove as to prove.

Ziegler's magisterial biography was published in 1990, and draws extensively on the Royal Archives; yet what he calls 'the established truth' about Wallis has become more veiled with the passing of time, however conscientiously one tries to establish the facts. This is partly because the precise details about Wallis's life before meeting the Prince of Wales remain difficult to ascertain. According to her own memoir, she decided to return to America in the summer of 1925, 'in the mood of a female Ulysses'. On the voyage home, she suffered what she described as 'an obscure internal ailment', which required her to be admitted to hospital for surgery when the ship docked in Seattle. After recovering from this ordeal, Wallis set off to stay with her mother (who was by then living in Washington, DC) and applied for a divorce. She made some half-hearted attempts to get a job, but instead found a second husband, perhaps in pursuit of the security that had so far eluded her. But there was an element of impropriety in this new relationship, too: for when she first met Ernest Simpson in New York at the end of 1926, he was still married and had a young daughter. Wallis's autobiography suggests that Ernest's marriage was already 'in difficulties'; but his wife remembered it differently, and later declared, with some bitterness, that she had been ailing in hospital at the time, when Wallis 'moved in and helped herself to my house and my clothes and, finally, to everything'.

At any rate, Ernest left his first wife and child in New York, and married Wallis in London in July 1928. 'I wore a yellow dress and a blue coat that I had had made in Paris', recalled Wallis in her memoir, adding that the municipal setting, Chelsea Register Office, 'was more appropriate for a trial than for the culmination of a romance.' (Is this a hint that she might have felt some subconscious guilt for her role in the end of Ernest's marriage?) Ernest began working for his firm's London branch, and the couple set up home together in a smart new block of flats, Bryanston Court, on George Street in Marylebone. Wallis had just turned thirty-two, and threw herself into the business of cultivating social contacts in London, initially with the help of Ernest's older sister, Maud Kerr-Smiley, who had married an MP and lived in a large house in Belgravia.

By an odd coincidence, it was at Maud's home that the Prince of Wales had first met Freda Dudley Ward, in February 1918, the final year of the war. She took shelter in the doorway when an air-raid warning sounded, and having been invited inside to join the party that evening, Freda made a great impression on the royal guest of honour. This would mark the beginning of a longstanding relationship that only ended with the ascent of Wallis Simpson; although Freda later admitted that she had never been truly in love with the Prince because he was 'too slavish'.

The Prince's letters to Freda – the wife of William Dudley Ward, a Liberal MP and vice chamberlain of the royal household – give some indication of his emotional immaturity. Many are in baby talk; others address her as 'mummie'. (She was actually the same age as him, and the mother of two young daughters.) He was often filled with self-pity, but not always sympathetic to the suffering of others. In October 1918, as the war slowly ground to a close, he wrote to Freda, enclosing a gift that he had acquired for her while accompanying the British troops as they advanced through northern France into Douai: 'a city of the dead . . . we didn't stay long; I went into the cathedral & the only decent piece of loot I could find was a rosary in the "sacristie" which I took for my darling little girl & which I enclose merely to amuse her!!'

In early 1919, two days after the death of his youngest brother John on 18 January, he described his sibling in a letter to Freda 'as more of an animal than anything else & only a brother in flesh & nothing else!!' John's death, at the age of thirteen, from epilepsy, was in his words, 'the greatest relief imaginable', but also a severe inconvenience: being 'plunged into mourning for this is the limit just as the war is over which cuts parties etc. right out!!'

The Prince of Wales's discontent is threaded throughout the correspondence, particularly when he was parted from Freda during his royal tours: the 'long separation is absolute cruelty to a child', he wrote in August 1919 from Ottawa. 'I'm a vewy depwessed & despondent little boy tonight,' he continued in a similar vein on the train to Calgary on 14 September. The following month, as the Canadian tour progressed to Manitoba, his mood had not improved: 'Christ I am fed up with the job of P. of W. It's such a hopelessly thankless one.' Christmas Day was spent with his family at Sandringham, their country retreat in Norfolk, but brought no relief: 'I'm sure I'll end in a madhouse soon as my brain really is going & I feel so hopelessly & utterly lost.' On 14 January 1920, still at Sandringham, he wrote: 'You know you ought to be really foul to me sometimes sweetie & curse & be cruel; it would do me worlds of good & bring me to my right senses!! I think I'm the kind of man who needs a certain amount of cruelty without which he gets abominably spoilt and soft!!'

If his love letters imply a desire to be dominated, as well as mothered, these urges were perhaps connected to the Prince's early experiences with his first nanny. In his memoir, he said that she would 'pinch and twist my arm' before bringing him to see his parents. As a result of her sadism, he would cry and be banished back to the nursery: 'to demonstrate, according to some perverse reasoning, that her power over me was greater than that of my parents'.

What also becomes evident from the letters is that the heir to the throne was already ambivalent about becoming king – long before his abdication. In April 1920, for example, while the Prince was on a royal tour of New Zealand, he wrote to Freda: 'I long more & more to chuck this job & be out of it & free for YOU, sweetie; the more I think of it all the more certain I am that really . . . the day for Kings & Princes is past, monarchies are out-of-date, though I know it is a rotten thing for me to say and sounds Bolshevik.' The following month, when the Prince was greeted by cheering crowds in Melbourne (more than half a million people came out to welcome him to Australia), he wrote: 'This ghastly existence of mine really seems to get more intolerably strenuous & difficult each day . . . I just don't see how I'm going to avoid a nervous breakdown . . . & what makes me more unhappy than anything else is that I know this eternal strain is aging me prematurely.' To grow old, he added, was the very last thing he wanted; for 'keeping young is my only weapon or tool'.

The Prince's desire not to grow up might explain his anorexic regime of dieting and exercise, which ensured he was so thin that his parents worried about him. 'Do smoke less, take less exercise, *eat more* and rest more,' wrote his father in 1913, as the Prince approached his nineteenth birthday (when he was a reluctant student at Magdalen College, Oxford). 'You are just at the critical age from now till you are 21 and it is most necessary that you should develop properly, both in mind and body. It all depends . . . whether you develop into a strong, healthy man or remain a sort of puny, half grown boy.' Queen Mary expressed her concerns in a slightly more sympathetic manner, encouraging her unhappy son 'to do your best to get strong & well for I feel sure that the depression you unluckily suffer from is due principally to your brain not being properly nourished & this must be put to an end or you will get worse'. Courtiers were also aware of his eating disorder; the Duchess of Devonshire, for example, observed in May 1913 that the Prince's weight had fallen to seven stone four pounds. 'The poor boy is evidently suffering from hysteria and I am sure they don't manage him well,' she wrote to her husband. 'He was given a big scolding yesterday and threatened with a rest cure and forcible feeding . . . I thought he looked even more miserable than usual.' The Prince's obsessional behaviour was not improved by the King's insistence on recording his children's weights at regular intervals, long after their infancy. Thus the King's admonishments to his eldest son to eat more were accompanied by these details in the winter of 1913: 'I see by the weighing book here that on December 22, 1910, you weighed 7st. 13lbs., and when I weighed you at Balmoral you were 7st. 8lbs., so instead of increasing you have lost 5 lbs. in nearly three years, that is certainly not as it should be.'

When war broke out the following year, the Prince of Wales was still just as slight; and although at only five foot seven he was well below the regulation height of six foot, he nevertheless joined the Grenadier

The Prince of Wales in the uniform of the Grenadier Guards during the First World War.

Guards. Much to his disappointment, he was kept away from the front line of the battlefields in France, and confined to administrative duties at General Headquarters. 'It's a pretty rotten life for me,' he complained to his equerry, Godfrey Thomas, in February 1915. 'I am but an onlooker in uniform, and become less like an officer every day.' The following month, when so many of his contemporaries were dying in the trenches, he told Thomas: 'I hate being a prince and not allowed to fight!!' His grievances continued when he was sent to Egypt in 1916 to visit the Anzac troops, the surviving veterans of the brutal Gallipoli campaign. 'Oh!! to be out here privately and not as the P of W,' he grumbled to Thomas. 'That's what ruins my life and ever will!!!!'

Little wonder that those around the Prince of Wales came to believe that he had never really grown up. Tommy Lascelles thought 'that for some hereditary or physiological reason his normal mental development stopped dead when he reached adolescence . . . There was one curious outward symptom of this; I saw him constantly at all hours of day and night, yet I never observed on his face the faintest indication of the bristles which normally appear, even in men as fair as he was.' Lascelles also noted in his diary that when he 'mentioned this peculiarity' to the royal physician, Lord Dawson, the doctor replied that 'it was a common phenomenon in cases of arrested development'. If Dawson's theory were true, continued Lascelles, 'it would account for many of [the Prince's] vagaries of conduct, and for his often childish outlook on life.'

Even the Prince's choice of home, Fort Belvedere (originally built in the eighteenth century as a royal folly for the youngest son of George II), appeared to reflect his juvenile tendencies. It was 'a child's idea of a fort', wrote his friend, Lady Diana Cooper in her memoir, 'and the sentries, one thought, must be made of tin'. While staying there in July 1935, she gave an evocative account of her surroundings in a letter to another friend. 'I am in a pink bedroom, pink-sheeted, pink Venetian-blinded, pink-soaped . . . The house is an enchanting folly and only needs fifty red soldiers stood between the battlements to make it into a Walt Disney coloured symphony toy.'

There, the Prince gardened enthusiastically, played the bagpipes and ukulele, frolicked in a newly installed swimming pool, sewed needlepoint tapestries (a hobby he had learned in childhood, taught by his mother), practised standing on his head, and amused himself and his guests with card games, dancing and jigsaw puzzles. Yet despite all these distractions, he was rarely content or carefree.

According to Wallis's memoir, when she first met the Prince of Wales she was initially surprised 'to discover how small he was'. As she studied his face, she noticed 'the slightly wind-rumpled golden hair, the turned-up nose, and a strange, wistful, almost sad look about the eyes when his expression was in repose'. Soon afterwards, she found herself 'fascinated by the odd and indefinable melancholy that seemed to haunt the Prince of Wales's countenance; his quick smile momentarily illuminated but never quite dispelled this look of sadness'.

The Prince, for his part, would subsequently recall what he described as the 'mocking look' that came into Wallis's eyes during their first conversation. She was 'plainly in misery from a bad cold in the head,' he recalled in his memoir, 'and having been informed that she was an American, I was prompted to observe that she must miss central heating'. Her reply was swift and scornful: 'You have disappointed me . . . Every American woman who comes to your country is always asked that same question. I had hoped for something more original from the Prince of Wales.'

Wallis was equally challenging when they met again that summer, in June 1931, after she had been presented at court wearing a formal gown with a train, ostrich-feathered headdress and fan borrowed from Thelma Furness. She had overheard the Prince muttering to his uncle, the Duke of Connaught, that 'something ought to be done about the lights. They make all the women look ghastly.' Following the ceremonials at Buckingham Palace, Thelma had invited the Simpsons to a drinks party at her London home, where the Prince joined them, and complimented Wallis on her outfit. As she recounted in her memoir, 'I responded with a straight face, "I understood that you thought we all looked ghastly". He was startled. Then he smiled.'

Wallis Simpson when she was presented at court, June 1931.

In his own memoir, he would identify Wallis's bold 'forthrightness' as a trait that 'enchanted me'. Wallis's autobiography suggests the same, while admitting her initial disbelief that the Prince was in love with her. 'I could find no good reason why this most glamorous of men should be seriously attracted to me. I certainly was no beauty, and he had the pick of the beautiful women of the world. I was certainly no longer very young.' In time, she became aware that he responded to her 'American independence of spirit' and 'directness', but she also sensed that she was able 'to penetrate the heart of his inner loneliness'.

The candour of the paragraph that follows in her memoir is, again, surprisingly revealing of her own motives in embarking on an affair with the Prince: 'Over and beyond the charm of his personality and the warmth of his manner, he was the open sesame to a new and glittering world that excited me as nothing in my life had ever done before.' She was impressed by the speed with which his slightest wish was granted – 'trains were held; yachts materialised; the best suites in the finest hotels were flung open; aeroplanes stood waiting' – and by his 'calm assumption that this was the natural order of things, that nothing could ever possibly go awry'.

When Wallis returned from a sybaritic Mediterranean cruise with the Prince in September 1934, her endlessly patient husband was waiting at Southampton to meet his errant wife. As she recalled in her memoir, she replied to Ernest's questions about the trip by saying, 'It was like being in Wallis in Wonderland.' 'Ernest looked at me quizzically. "It sounds to me," he said thoughtfully, "indeed like a trip behind the 'Looking Glass'. Or, better yet, an excursion into the realm of Peter Pan's Never-Never Land."' From then on, she and Ernest referred in private to the Prince as Peter Pan.

If the Prince was the lost boy who wouldn't grow up, continually in flight from adulthood, could Wallis play the role of Wendy Darling, the girl who nurtures Peter Pan like a little mother? In J. M. Barrie's original story, Wendy leaves Peter Pan to return to reality, and becomes a fully grown, adult woman with a daughter of her own. Wallis and her prince would never have children; but their letters to each other – in the words of the editor of their correspondence, Michael Bloch – suggest 'a mother–son relationship. His letters to her are infantile, adoring . . . they plead for affection and protection. Hers to him are sensible, affectionate, admonishing, possessive.' Thus while the Prince was declaring his undying love, and promising that nothing could separate them – 'not even the stars' – Wallis would respond with practical notes about domestic arrangements and menus for the entertaining of guests. 'I like everyone to think you do things well. Perhaps I'm quite fond of you.' 'I think it would be nice to have the drinks . . . on the porch outside the drawing room. I also think you are a very nice boy.'

In an undated letter to 'David dear' (which Bloch believes was written in the summer of 1935, when Wallis turned thirty-nine), she explicitly refers to him as Peter Pan. 'Sometimes I think you haven't grown up where love is concerned and perhaps it's only a boyish passion for surely it lacks the thought of me that a man's love is capable of . . . I have lost something noble for a boy who may always remain Peter Pan.'

It remains unclear who, or what, constituted the nobility that Wallis felt she had lost. (Her reputation? The stability of her marriage to Ernest? The self-sacrificing nature of Ernest himself?) But she had gained the eternal adoration of a future king who would give up his throne for her, and remain forever beguiled by her mysterious ability to hold him close, while keeping her distance. As he wrote in his memoir, 'In character, Wallis was, and still remains, complex and elusive; and from the first I looked upon her as the most independent woman I had ever met.' The same adjectives appear on his list of Wallis's characteristics that he prepared for Charles Murphy, while they were working together, along with 'proud', 'strict' and 'exacting'.

Perhaps there the matter should end, except that Wallis's elusiveness continued to baffle onlookers, as if her life was akin to a mystery without a clarifying conclusion. Even the most psychologically astute of observers found her difficult to interpret. 'It is impossible to assess what makes her function or why,' wrote James Pope-Hennessy in his notes of their second encounter in 1957. (He was visiting the Duke and Duchess of Windsor at their French country home, following Wallis's suggestion that he could help her husband write some articles on men's fashion.) 'I should say she was on the whole a stupid woman, with a small petty brain,' concluded Pope-Hennessy, while professing to find her 'good-natured and friendly', and enjoying the luxurious indulgence of her hospitality. But his description of Wallis turns her into a strange marionette, as he observed her 'settling herself on a low wide day-bed by the wall, her legs tucked up; she does not curl up; but somehow dismantles herself, so that she looks like a puppet lying in the wings of a toy theatre'.

Where the marionette does come to life, in Pope-Hennessy's account, is on the subject of fashion, when he asked her about her favoured Parisian couturiers, Christian Dior and Cristóbal Balenciaga. 'The Duchess became very intelligently informative about Dior's gifts, Balenciaga, the ways their clothes are made and worn, her conversations with them . . . how, with some very grand dresses, garnets go better than rubies – and so on. Controversial topics were evaded, and the conversation became imperceptibly flirtatious and slightly intimate.'

By talking about clothes, Wallis seemed to skirt around the subject of her enmity with her royal sister-in-law, Queen Elizabeth the Queen Mother. She confided to Pope-Hennessy (in his words, 'with seeming irrelevance'), that she had dismissed her English maid, Irene, who had previously worked for Queen Elizabeth for five years. 'I had to get rid of her: I had a Balenciaga dress with a crinoline. Well, Irene ironed that crinoline so that you couldn't see what it was by the time she'd finished. I took it back, but even Mr Balenciaga himself couldn't decide just *what* she had done to that crinoline. And she just *burned up* five more of my dresses. Well, that surprised me, because I thought that, after all those years with the Queen Mother, if she hadn't learnt to iron a crinoline, what *had* she learned? And you know, whenever I see pictures of those poor girls, with their suits all screwed up under the arms, I think of Irene. I'd like to take those girls' clothes apart and loosen them up.'

Pope-Hennessy did not venture to question Wallis any further about 'those girls', but presumably she was referring to the Queen Mother's daughters, Elizabeth and Margaret, and implying that, like their mother, they did not understand the niceties of Parisian haute couture. Wallis herself showed no inclination to 'loosen up' in her own choice of outfit, as Pope-Hennessy witnessed in her entrance before dinner: 'presently a tapping of high heels and the creak of stiff silk announced the Duchess, who wound her way down the staircase sheathed in a red-orange very tight, almost hobbled, dress.' This makes me wonder whether her allusion to taking 'those girls' clothes apart' is an oddly intimate glimpse of aggression; a variation, perhaps, of the hostility that Pope-Hennessy witnessed in Wallis's 'facial contortion, reserved for speaking of the Queen Mother, which is very unpleasant to behold, and seemed to *me* akin to frenzy'.

When the conversation returned to the topic of Pope-Hennessy's researches into Queen Mary, Wallis remarked that it must be 'a very difficult book to write'. Pope-Hennessy replied, 'Yes, it is, both because of Queen Mary's reticence, and because royal psychology is hard to grasp, if you know what I mean.'

Wallis's response again seemed to be tangential, and yet somehow revealing. 'I certainly do know,' she replied, recalling the early stages of her relationship with the Prince of Wales. 'I was very confused. Becoming a public figure in almost middle age was no joke. If I went out shopping to buy a length of scarlet ribbon, people would collect to watch me, and I got, well, just so confused I'd buy green ribbon instead and go running out of the shop.' The Prince, in contrast, retained his royal composure: 'If we went to a shop together, he'd just go right on choosing as if there was no-one there at all.'

What neither of them knew was that in 1935 they were being carefully watched in shops, and elsewhere, by the Special Branch of the Metropolitan Police. This is one of the strangest chapters of their story – and several aspects of the undercover operation remain ambiguous. According to the British academics Richard J. Aldrich and Rory Cormac (whose authoritative book *Spying and the Crown* includes a section on the surveillance of Wallis and the Prince of Wales), the investigation was commissioned by the King himself in 1935, when he discovered that his son had recently given Mrs Simpson £110,000 worth of jewels, as well as a substantial allowance (estimated by John Aird to be £6,000 per annum). The astonishing price of the jewels – roughly equivalent to £7 million today – was already the subject of fervid discussion at the time. For example, the author Marie Belloc Lowndes, a successful writer of detective fiction, recorded in her diary her impression of meeting Mrs Simpson at a country house dinner party in January that year: 'She wore a very great deal of jewellery, which I thought must be what is called "dressmaker's" jewels, so large were the emeralds in her bracelets and so striking and peculiar a necklace.' Later, several of her fellow guests asked Mrs Belloc Lowndes – who was much admired for her insights into female psychology – what she had thought of the Prince's mistress. Her answer suggests that she was unable to see beyond Wallis's shimmering carapace, which sought attention while also keeping enemies at arm's length. 'I said what had struck me most were her perfect clothes and that I had been surprised, considering that she dressed so simply, to see that she wore such a mass of dressmakers' jewels. At that they all screamed with laughter, explaining that all the jewels were real, that the Prince of Wales had given her fifty thousand pounds' worth at Christmas, following it up with sixty thousand pounds' worth of jewels a week later at the New Year. They explained that his latest gift was a marvellous necklace which he had bought from a Paris jeweller.'

Aldrich and Cormac (both experts on intelligence history) state that the King was so alarmed by the Prince's reckless behaviour that he 'took the remarkable step of putting his son and heir under Special Branch surveillance'. In order to do so, he enlisted the support of his prime minister, Stanley Baldwin, and together they met the head of the Metropolitan Police, Philip Game. A decision was made that the operation should be led by Superintendent Albert Canning, a highly regarded senior officer at Special Branch who knew the Prince, having travelled with him to France as a personal detective in the summer of 1924. Canning had at his disposal a substantial team of detectives to trace Mrs Simpson's movements, monitor her phone calls and analyse her motives. Aldrich and Cormac believe that an additional cause of concern was the suspicion that Wallis was a security risk, given her supposed closeness to Ribbentrop, Hitler's special envoy to London. (Canning had previously been tasked with collecting intelligence on fascist activities in Britain.)

In her memoir, Wallis claimed that she had only met Ribbentrop twice, on both occasions at the home of Emerald Cunard, an American-born society hostess who entertained lavishly in London. Cunard's role in introducing Ribbentrop to Wallis and the Prince, and their shared pro-German sympathies, had been noted by other attentive observers, quite aside from those at Special Branch. 'Much gossip about the Prince of Wales's Nazi leanings,' wrote Chips Channon in his diary on 9 June 1935; 'he is alleged to have been influenced by Emerald (who is rather éprise [in love] with Herr Ribbentrop) through Mrs Simpson.' Two days later, on 11 June, the Prince made a controversial public statement at the Annual Conference of the British Legion, when he suggested that a delegation should visit Germany: 'I feel that there could be no more suitable body or organisation of men to stretch forth the hand of friendship to the Germans than we ex-servicemen, who fought them and have now forgotten all about it and the Great War.' A British Legion party duly set off for Germany, where their itinerary included a trip to Dachau concentration camp. The prisoners were locked away underground, out of sight of the visitors, while their places were taken by well-fed SS guards dressed up in the inmates' uniforms.

As soon as word reached the Palace of the Prince's speech, he was summoned by his father, who sternly reminded him not to get involved in politics, particularly foreign affairs. The King also told the Prince that his remarks about Germany were contrary to Foreign Office policy. The effect of the Prince's intervention was instantaneous: it was widely reported in German newspapers, and Chips Channon referred to it in his diary as 'extraordinary'. Although the Prince's public remarks might seem harmless enough, he was talking favourably about the Nazis in private. Count Mensdorff, a retired diplomat, gave a judicious account of his conversation with the Prince in November 1933: 'It is remarkable how he expressed his sympathies for the Nazis in Germany. "Of course it is the only thing to do, we will have to come to it, as we are in great danger from the Communists here, too." . . . I was very surprised. I also asked him how he imagined that one got out of the National Socialist dictatorship . . . He seemed not to have thought very much about all these questions. It is, however, interesting and significant that he shows so much sympathy for Germany and the Nazis.'

The Prince had shared a similarly positive stance on Hitler a few months previously, in July 1933, when he told the former kaiser's grandson, Prince Louis Ferdinand of Prussia, that 'it was no business of ours to interfere in Germany's internal affairs either *re* Jews or *re* anything else, and added that dictators were very popular these days and that we might want one in England before long'. (Hitler had seized power earlier that year, and the Nazis were enforcing vicious anti-Semitic measures as part of their increasingly repressive regime.)

In comparison to these disturbing views, the Special Branch findings seem almost laughably trivial: for example, Canning reported that Wallis and the Prince had been watched as they visited an antiques shop in South Kensington, where they called each other 'darling'. Afterwards, when questioned, the proprietor of the shop said that Mrs Simpson had the Prince 'completely under her thumb'. Another report described Ernest Simpson as 'the bounder type', who hoped that he would be rewarded with 'high honours' – possibly a baronetcy – when the Prince of Wales became king.

Thus far, there was nothing particularly revelatory. More than a year earlier, John Aird had described Ernest as 'a very unattractive and common Englishman'. In fact, Ernest had been born in New York, the grandson of a Jewish émigré named Leon Solomon, who had left his home in Warsaw for London. One of Leon's sons emigrated to America in 1873, changed his surname to Simpson, and set up a shipping brokerage firm in 1880. In turn, his only son Ernest chose to leave the US in 1917, after studying at Harvard, and served during the latter part of the First World War as an officer in the Coldstream Guards. He became a British citizen, and apparently never again mentioned his Jewish heritage (although it was included in one of the Special Branch reports).

In a codified, class-conscious milieu, Ernest Simpson was an outsider, despite his Guards' tie and stiff upper lip. Tommy Lascelles referred to him as 'nothing worse than a nincompoop'; few observers seemed to have any sympathy for Ernest, and his self-respect was stifled by his reverence for royalty. Indeed, when the Prince of Wales gave Ernest the gift of a length of brown and beige houndstooth tweed, it was made up by the Prince's tailor into an overcoat as an exact replica of the one that the Prince himself wore, which Ernest had admired. This gave rise to the jibe in his own family that Ernest was the man who sold his wife for a bolt of cloth.

Back at Special Branch, the team ferreted out further details, and on 3 July 1935 Canning reported: 'The identity of Mrs Simpson's secret lover has now been definitely ascertained. He is Guy Marcus TRUNDLE, now living at 18 Bruton Street.' He was 'a very charming adventurer, very good looking, well bred and an excellent dancer', according to Canning. 'He is said to boast that every woman falls for him. He meets Mrs Simpson quite openly at informal social gatherings as a personal friend, but secret meetings are made by appointment when intimate relations take place.'

Canning's men had established that Trundle was born in York in April 1899, the son of a respectable vicar, and served as a pilot in the Royal Flying Corps from 1917 until the 1920s. In 1932, he had married the daughter of a retired army general, and was currently working as 'a motor engineer and salesman' for the Ford Motor Company. Special Branch had not discovered his salary, but Trundle had admitted receiving 'money from Mrs Simpson as well as expensive presents'. Furthermore, continued Canning, 'Mrs Simpson has said that her husband is now suspicious of her association with other men as he thinks this will eventually cause trouble with P.O.W. Mrs Simpson has also alleged that her husband is having her watched for this reason and in consequence she is very careful for the double purpose of keeping both P.O.W. and her husband in ignorance of her surreptitious love affairs.'

There is much that remains bewildering about the Trundle affair, but it was taken seriously at the time, presumably as a means to undermine the ascendancy of Mrs Simpson. If the Special Branch report is to be believed, Trundle had already been unfaithful to his wife with a Mrs Fearnley-Whittingstall, 'prior to his association with Mrs Simpson'. It is of course possible that Trundle was a fantasist who enjoyed boasting about his 'intimate' encounters with Wallis, or that someone else invented the entire story. Certainly, her more sympathetic biographers do not accept that any such affair took place, citing her letters to her Aunt Bessie in 1935, which describe such a busy social life that it would have been difficult to schedule secret assignations with Guy Trundle. And yet these same letters can themselves be unreliable: on 31 July, for example, Wallis wrote to her aunt that Ernest 'is still the man of my dreams', despite the fact that they were spending the summer apart, allowing Wallis to go on holiday with the Prince.

One intriguing detail of the Special Branch report is Mr Trundle's Mayfair address: 18 Bruton Street, next door to Princess Elizabeth's birthplace, and across the road from Norman Hartnell's premises at number 26, where Wallis was a client (at least until she switched her allegiance to Parisian couture). Recently, in an attempt to make some sense of this puzzling matter, I returned to Bruton Street on a sultry afternoon in late July, when the summer heat was rising from the pavements, and the traffic idled at a standstill. Like the spying Special Branch detectives who had stationed themselves nearby, I could see that Trundle would have had a good view of Hartnell's establishment from his home. As with the Strathmores' townhouse, the original property at number 18 has long since been demolished and replaced with a modern block, currently the London offices of Bugatti, the luxury car manufacturer. This seems somehow appropriate, given Trundle's own career as a car salesman. It is also a pleasing reminder of Norman Hartnell's observation, when the Duchess of York first brought her daughters to be fitted for their bridesmaids' dresses in 1935, that the two little princesses 'seemed more interested in the scintillating cars that purred . . . outside the window, than in their frocks'.

Hartnell's splendid building is still standing, and his name is embossed on the frontage, although nowadays there is an elegant antique shop on the ground floor, while the storey above is occupied by a bespoke jewellery designer whose sophisticated creations would doubtless have appealed to Wallis. Venturing inside, I discover that Hartnell's original interiors have been carefully preserved, and look as graceful as when he unveiled his new premises in September 1934, to fulsome praise from *Harper's Bazaar*: 'At 26 Bruton Street women can choose Hartnell gowns against a background as glamorous as any in England and see artistic achievement rounded to perfection.'

His royal warrant remains etched on a bevelled mirror, and vast crystal chandeliers cast their gleaming light over the former couture salon on the first floor, where faceted glass columns rise up to the high ceilings. To one side are mirrored alcoves, edged with concealed lights, designed to display Hartnell's hats, and reminiscent of a Hollywood film star's dressing room. As I gaze out of the tall windows towards the street, I can also see my own watchful reflection in the looking-glass walls that enclose the room. I imagine Mrs Simpson standing here, surrounded by luxury, her jewels refracted and multiplying in the mirrors, feeling herself to be Wallis in Wonderland. And just for an instant she seems to come alive; no longer a mere puppet, to be manipulated in a royal drama, but a self-made woman; a bold adventuress, her bright eyes seeking new conquests. For a fleeting moment, the improbable seems possible in the curious world through the looking glass. If only these walls could talk.

SANDRINGHAM TIME

In the burnished glow of a glorious autumn day, beneath the bright blue skies of north Norfolk, it is easy to understand why George V felt such affection for the country retreat originally built by his father in 1870. 'Dear old Sandringham,' wrote George affectionately, 'the place I love better than anywhere else in the world.' The sprawling mansion is, at least by royal standards, unexpectedly intimate: the Saloon, just beyond the main entrance, is furnished with comfortable sofas and armchairs; a jigsaw puzzle laid out on a side table, as if in readiness for a convivial family gathering. Beyond the Saloon is the light and airy White Drawing Room, its large bow windows overlooking the beautifully tended gardens, where late roses are still in bloom. A full-length portrait of George V's mother, Queen Alexandra, hangs over the fireplace; she wears a pearl choker and a corseted dove grey dress trimmed with swathes of intricate lace, the decorous effect made curiously suggestive by the way she lifts the swathes of material at the front of her long gown to reveal the golden fabric beneath.

The prettily painted ceiling panels are adorned with fluffy clouds, brightly feathered pheasants and partridges (the game birds that populate the grounds of this sporting estate). Through a door lies Queen Alexandra's smaller drawing room, with floral silk-lined walls and a Dresden porcelain chandelier and matching mirror (housewarming gifts from the

Sandringham House in Norfolk, January 1936.

Kaiser). Glass vitrines are filled with Queen Alexandra's jade and amber knick-knacks and Fabergé figurines. Many of the latter had been commissioned by Alexandra's husband, Edward VII, at the suggestion of Alice Keppel, his mistress (and by coincidence the great-grandmother of the present Queen Camilla).

Sandringham's architecture – featuring a plethora of ornamental cupolas, parapets, gables, balustrades and towers – has been scorned by some commentators as an absurd hotchpotch of late Victoriana. James Pope-Hennessy, for example, visiting in 1956 in the course of researching his biography of Queen Mary, described it as 'a preposterous, long, brick-and-stone building . . . tremendously vulgar and emphatically, almost defiantly hideous'. Yet despite its outward exuberance, as befits a royal residence famed for its Edwardian house parties and lavish entertainments, Pope-Hennessy found the interiors of Sandringham 'rather ominous and charged with implications of past unhappiness which one could sense, but not grasp'. He was particularly struck by the gloom of a small bedroom where George's elder brother, known within the family as Eddy, had died. It was 'a dim and cheerless hole', and the adjoining chamber was 'the most sinister little room of them all . . . very narrow, very poky . . . I should not like to be alone in that room at night'. By the end of his tour of Sandringham, he was glad to escape this 'horrible' house filled with portraits of dead royalties: 'It was like a visit to a morgue, and everywhere were their faces, painted, drawn or photographed . . . ringed in by their own family and their own likenesses.'

Unlike James Pope-Hennessy, I did not feel the atmosphere to be troubling, although it would be impossible to ignore the spirit of history that pervades the place. For it was here that Queen Mary came first as a child – when she was still Princess May of Teck – to stay with her mother's cousins; and here, too, that she arrived as the fiancée of Prince Eddy (an engagement that had been arranged by Queen Victoria), to celebrate his twenty-eighth birthday on 8 January 1892. But then Eddy caught influenza, and within a week, May joined the family at his deathbed. She returned to Sandringham later that year, and was taken into the dead

Prince's bedroom, which had been kept exactly as if he were still alive, his clothes and hairbrushes preserved like religious relics. The following spring – again at the firm prompting of Queen Victoria – George embarked on his own courtship of May. They were married in July 1893, and spent their honeymoon at Sandringham; a destination that Queen Victoria thought ill-advised in the circumstances ('rather unlucky and sad', she wrote to her eldest daughter). Even so, George and May became devoted to one another; and unlike his notoriously philandering father, who had earned the nickname 'Edward the Caresser', or his reputedly louche older brother, George remained unwaveringly faithful to his wife. All things considered, May was fortunate to have been spared marriage to Prince Eddy, who, as James Pope-Hennessy discovered during the course of his research, was rumoured to have contracted syphilis, possibly as a result of his visits to a male brothel. Pope-Hennessy did not reveal this in his official biography of Queen Mary, but instead described Eddy as 'wayward and self-indulgent', with 'variable' emotions.

Mementoes of Prince Eddy are still visible at Sandringham today: his face appears in a cameo clasped in his mother's hand, in the life-size painting of Alexandra that dominates the drawing room; and again in the entrance hall, in a portrait with George, depicting the brothers as young naval cadets wearing matching uniforms. Elsewhere, there are traces of other family tragedies: a photograph of the doomed Tsar Nicholas II, for example, stands on the desk in the Saloon. Were it not for the handwritten signature ('Nicky'), one would be forgiven for thinking that it was his cousin George's doppelgänger.

George V's eldest son recalled his childhood days at Sandringham as being brightened by the arrival of his indulgent grandparents, especially at Christmas, which he described in his memoir as 'Dickens in a Cartier setting'. But he grew to dread annual festivities there as an adult, and in 1935 he brought little in the way of good cheer to an already

George V's Christmas radio broadcast from Sandringham, 1934.

diminished party. The Duchess of York was suffering from pneumonia, and too ill to join the gathering in Norfolk; her husband remained by her bedside at their Windsor home. The King was equally unwell, and grieving for his favourite sister, Victoria, who had died on 3 December. The young princesses, Lilibet and Margaret, were sent to Sandringham, however, providing some solace for their doting grandparents; and the newly-wed Gloucesters came too, together with the Kents and their firstborn baby son.

The Prince of Wales arrived late, thereby upsetting his mother, as the family had already started opening presents; and he was clearly miserable to be separated from Wallis, who stayed with her husband in London. On Boxing Day, the Prince wrote to Wallis: 'It really is terrible here and so much the worse Xmas I've ever had to spend with the family, far worse than last year, and that was bad enough.' His peculiar attitude to food, and its weird influence on their relationship, was also evident in his letter: 'Please don't over eat until we can again together or I'm there to say stop or you'll be quite ill I know.'

In his memoir, he appeared to have forgotten about the absence of the Duke and Duchess of York at Sandringham, but remembered his own wretched feelings of apprehension and isolation: 'In this closely-knit fabric of family ties I felt detached and lonely. My brothers were secure in their private lives; whereas I was caught up in an inner conflict and would have no peace of mind until I had resolved it. But this was hardly the time or the place.'

By then, the ailing king was too weak to go out shooting; instead, he would ride his favourite white pony, Jock, accompanied by his beloved Lilibet. Despite his worsening cough, George V was able to make his annual Christmas broadcast from Sandringham (his fourth such message since the popular practice was instituted in 1932): he spoke of the 'personal link between me and my people, which I value more than I can say. It binds us together in all our common joys and sorrows.' A quarter of a century after his accession to the throne, the King still fulfilled his stalwart public role as a reassuring father figure during 'this family festival of

Christmas', even at a time of rising political uncertainty. 'In Europe and many parts of the world, anxieties surround us. It is good to think that our own family of peoples is at peace in itself and united in one desire to be at peace with other nations.'

For all George's comforting words, and his public invocation of 'the spirit of goodwill and mutual helpfulness', in private he was profoundly concerned about the future. 'A few weeks before his death,' wrote Lady Airlie in her autobiography, 'King George had said passionately, "I pray to God that my eldest son will never marry and have children, and nothing will come between Bertie and Lilibet and the throne."' But so deep was the rift between George V and his heir that neither raised the contentious subject of Mrs Simpson, nor resolved any of the difficulties that beset their fractured relationship. To King George, who had made such a success of a Victorian arranged marriage, his son's obsession with Wallis remained incomprehensible. Yet for the Prince, Wallis was infinitely more important than a royal mistress, such as those kept by his grandfather. 'Oh! my Wallis I know we'll have *Viel Glück* [good luck] to make us *one* this year,' he wrote to her on New Year's Day; and in another letter declared: 'You are all and everything I have in life.'

On 18 January, it became evident that the King's heart was failing, as he drifted in and out of consciousness. Bertie had already been summoned to Sandringham, while Lilibet and Margaret were sent home with their nanny to Royal Lodge, where their mother was still recuperating. The Prince of Wales returned by aeroplane, thereby inspiring the final line of John Betjeman's evocative poem, 'The Death of King George V': 'a young man lands hatless from the air.'

'When a King starts to die,' he recalled, with some bitterness, in his memoir, 'the whole world crowds in for the death-watch, to follow with morbid curiosity every detail in the pathetic process of mortality . . . Of the shadowy figures that slipped in and out of my father's room as the end approached I particularly remember two. One was the doctor, Lord Dawson, as much courtier as physician . . . the other was the Archbishop of Canterbury, a noiseless spectre in black gaiters.'

It was Dawson who wrote the statement that would be broadcast by the BBC on the evening of 20 January: 'The King's life is drawing peacefully to its close.' And it was Dawson, too, who made the decision (unknown at the time, but revealed in his private diary half a century later) to hasten George V's death with a fatal injection of morphine and cocaine. This was to ensure that the news would appear 'in the morning papers rather than the less appropriate evening journals'; hence the bulletin announcing the King's death at 11.55 p.m. came just before the deadline for *The Times*.

Hardly had the King been pronounced dead than Queen Mary took the hand of her eldest son and kissed it in a customary act of fealty. He responded with an outpouring of grief that was, according to George V's private secretary Clive Wigram, far more demonstrative than that of his mother and siblings, all of whom were present at the deathbed. 'The Prince of Wales became hysterical, cried loudly, and kept on embracing the Queen,' noted Wigram, disapprovingly, in a private memorandum that night.

The new king's first act as monarch was one that traditionalists in the royal household found as shocking as his excessive weeping. Ever since the days of his grandfather Edward VII, the 180 or so clocks at Sandringham had been kept half an hour forward, to provide additional daylight for shooting and perhaps as a remedy for Queen Alexandra's incorrigible tardiness. As Edward VIII, he immediately ordered that all the clocks should be altered from 'Sandringham Time' to Greenwich Mean Time, an action that seemed to him (as he wrote in his memoir) entirely 'innocent and logical', yet even so 'produced a shaking of old heads and a muttering in the beards over my presumption in tampering with an old family idiosyncrasy'.

The news of the abolition of 'Sandringham Time' travelled far beyond the inner circles of royalty, reaching the intellectual heights of the Bloomsbury Group. Virginia Woolf, writing to her nephew Julian Bell, remarked on the matter soon afterwards: 'I am told on the very best authority that the new King is a cheap second rate little bounder . . . and was daily so insulted by the [former] King that when the King died the only thing Edward could do to show his feelings was to have all the clocks put back half an hour.' Woolf's letter is similarly eloquent on the subject of the nation's response to the death and funeral of George V: 'We have been . . . deluged in tears and muffled in crape for the past ten days. The British public has had a fit of grief which surpasses all ever known. It was a curious survival of barbarism, emotionalism, heraldry, ecclesiasticism, sheer sentimentality, snobbery, and some feeling for the very commonplace man who was so like ourselves.'

Chips Channon was more sympathetic to the predicament of his friend. As George V lay dying, he wrote in his diary, 'My heart goes out to the P of W tonight, as he will mind so terribly being King. His loneliness, his seclusion, his isolation will be more than his highly strung . . . nature can bear.' Channon's keen attention to detail was in evidence again when he attended the dead King's lying-in-state at Westminster Hall, and observed 'the boyish' new king, 'so young and seemingly frail'. Beside him were 'a cluster of royal ladies, all in heaviest black . . . Princess Marina, as ever, was infinitely more elegant than the others: she wore violets under her veil, and her stockings, if not flesh-coloured, were of a black so thin, that they seemed so. She is always chic, glamorous and romantic and makes the other royalties, except the magnificent Queen, look dowdy . . . The Duchess [of] York, and Duchess of Gloucester, both looked very like partridges.'

Lilibet accompanied her mother to Westminster Hall, and witnessed the solemn sight of her father and three uncles in full dress uniform, standing guard at each corner of the catafalque. Her governess, Miss Crawford, had watched Lilibet's departure, 'in her black coat and black velvet tammy, looking small and, I thought, rather scared.' Afterwards, the nine-year-old princess said that she had seen 'great heaps of flowers' as they filed past the coffin on the raised dais, and noticed the stillness of her father and his brothers. '"Uncle David was there," she told me, "and he never moved at all, Crawfie. Not even an eyelid. It was wonderful. And everyone was so quiet. As if the King was asleep."' She also attended her grandfather's funeral on 28 January, a 'small, forlorn-looking figure in its

Edward VIII and his brother the Duke of York follow their father's coffin in the procession to Westminster Hall, January 1936.

inky black', according to her governess. 'Lilibet in her sensitive fashion felt it all deeply,' continued Miss Crawford. 'It was very touching to see how hard she tried to do what she felt was expected of her. I remember her pausing doubtfully as she groomed one of the toy horses and looking up at me for a moment. "Oh, Crawfie . . . ought we to play?" she asked.' Miss Crawford assured her that yes, they should, but admitted in her memoir that it was not easy to keep the little Princesses cheerful 'in that suddenly muted house'.

Yet there were many who felt hopeful about the new king's reign. At forty-one, he still had an appealing air of youthful vigour; as *The Times* declared in a leader, 'his laughter-loving boyishness' and 'delightful sense of humour' had 'won the hearts' of his people. Others, however, were rather less confident about the future. Sir John Simon, the Home Secretary, noted that Edward VIII had 'no sense of royalty', while Alec Hardinge (previously George V's assistant private secretary, and soon to be promoted in the court hierarchy to principal private secretary), wrote that the new monarch 'appeared to be entirely ignorant of the powers of a constitutional sovereign, and of the lines on which the King's business should be carried on'.

It is possible that their misgivings may even have been shared by Edward VIII himself. In his memoir, he described following his father's coffin in the solemn procession through London to Westminster Hall. The coffin was draped in the Royal Standard, surmounted by the priceless Imperial State Crown; unfortunately, the jolting of the heavy gun carriage carrying the coffin had caused the Maltese cross on top of the crown – set with an immense sapphire and 200 diamonds – to come loose. To his horror, 'suddenly, out of the corner of my eye, I caught a flash of light dancing along the pavement. My natural instinct was to bend down and retrieve the jewels, lest the equivalent of a king's ransom be lost forever. Then a sense of dignity restrained me, and I resolutely marched on.' Fortunately, the falling Maltese cross was spotted by a sergeant-major of the Grenadier Guards flanking the gun carriage, who scooped it up with swift efficiency. Despite the safeguarding of the jewels, the new king was startled: 'It seemed a strange thing to happen; and, although not superstitious, I wondered whether it was a bad omen.'

Harold Nicolson certainly thought so. 'A most terrible omen,' he wrote in his diary that day. Two of his fellow MPs, Walter Elliot and Robert Boothby, also happened to witness the incident as they watched the procession go past, and heard the King say: 'Christ! What will happen next?' 'A fitting motto', remarked Elliot to Boothby, 'for the coming reign.'

Edward VIII and Wallis Simpson during their Mediterranean cruise aboard the *Nahlin* yacht in the summer of 1936.

'MY STRIPTEASE ACT'

If senior politicians and courtiers had their doubts about the new king, so too did the woman he loved, who knew him better than even his closest advisers. As Wallis tried to adjust to their change in circumstances, her ambivalence about her lover's overwhelming neediness is implicit in the letter she wrote to her Aunt Bessie on 30 January 1936: 'I have had to be at the new King's beck and call, being the only person he has to really talk things over with normally, and it has all been a great strain.' She had witnessed his Accession ceremony at St James's Palace, and the brief description that she gave to her aunt has an air of unreality about it: 'The proclamation of Edward XVIII [sic] the most picturesque thing – such costumes from the Middle Ages, the heralds looking like a pack of cards.' Her next sentence returns to the more prosaic yet (for them) continually absorbing subject of weight: 'The King has lost six pounds.' And then comes the guarded affection that is so characteristic of Wallis's attitude to their relationship, to the point of damning him with faint praise: 'I am very fond of him and proud and want him to do his job well and he is so lonely and needs companionship and affection, otherwise he goes wrong. Ernest of course has been marvellous about it all. He has the make-up of a saint.'

Duff Cooper, Secretary of State for War, who had sat next to Wallis at a dinner party three days previously, was in no doubt about her lukewarm feelings. 'She talked to me a great deal about the King,' Cooper wrote in his diary, 'and even suggested that it would be better if she were to go away altogether. I think she is a nice woman and a sensible woman – but she is as hard as nails and she doesn't love him.'

Although Wallis felt conflicted about her role in the King's life, she did at least continue to take pleasure in her elevated social status in smart London society, as she admitted to Aunt Bessie: 'I am up to my neck in people all wanting more than ever to be friends . . . Isn't it all funny and strange too? I'm just the same however and enjoying it all as a huge game – laughing a lot inside and controlling my tongue and sense of humour on the outside.'

There were occasions, nonetheless, when Wallis did not attempt to hide her amusement. On 12 February, Chips Channon noted her lively animation at the home of the King's friend and equerry Lord Brownlow, where she was the wisecracking centre of attention of what Channon referred to as 'the New Court'. 'Mrs Simpson very charming and gay and vivacious,' he wrote in his diary. 'She said she had given up wearing black stockings before she began to do the "can-can" – a remark typical of her breezy gay humour, quick, American and not profound.'

For all Wallis's air of gaiety, several other concerns become apparent in her correspondence with her Aunt Bessie. Writing from Fort Belvedere on 9 February, she expressed her belief that her lover would 'make a great King of a new era – and I believe that the country thinks the same. Actually the old regime was a little bit behind the times but very dearly loved. The late King was not sociable nor the Queen and I'm sure this one will entertain more at the Palace.' Despite her pre-eminent position, Wallis did not appear to take it for granted that she would become queen, nor even that her marriage to Ernest would end. Indeed, she seems to suggest that the new king would be better off, if only he could find a more suitable wife. 'It's a very lonely job – and it's a tragedy that he can't bring himself to marry without loving. The English would prefer that he marry a Duke's daughter to one of the mangy foreign princesses left. However only the years and himself can arrange that for him.' She continued the letter with a reference to the period of official mourning for George V: 'London is dull naturally. We all look like black birds. As I always wear so much black for economy I got into mourning with no expense.'

Wallis was already receiving a handsome income from the King, as well as his extravagant gifts of expensive jewellery. (The ever-observant Chips Channon noted her new pair of 'breathtaking pear-shaped diamond clips', worth £22,000.) But she still remained obsessively focused on money, as if intent on proving her own adage: 'You can never be too rich or too thin'. In the same letter, she told her aunt that she was selling her old clothes, and planning to go to Paris the following month, to order some new outfits from the couture house of Mainbocher at a substantial discount. This discreet financial arrangement was mutually beneficial, with Mainbocher receiving useful publicity for dressing the King's favourite.

A fortnight later, in another letter to Aunt Bessie, Wallis reported, with some satisfaction, that the King had secured her a cut-price rate to stay at Le Meurice, the luxurious Paris hotel of her choice. 'I can hardly wait to go,' wrote Wallis. 'I am *so tired* of it all here and really terribly worn out.' But her mood did not improve when she arrived in Paris at the beginning of March, and complained to her aunt of the 'exhaustion, rage and despair' that she felt while staying there. In a letter to Bessie written on 8 March 1936 – the day after Hitler had ordered his armies into the Rhineland, in contravention of the Versailles Treaty – Wallis said that she hoped 'the Germans will slap all the French couturiers, modistes etc.' Wallis's oddly displaced aggression was perhaps more to do with her lover's exasperating demands than her dealings with the Parisian fashion houses (or indeed any affinity she felt for the Nazis); for her letter continues, petulantly, 'the little King insists I return and I might as well'. So incessant were his telephone calls to her in Paris ('about 4 times daily') that she grumbled about being unable to rest.

In marked contrast to his vigilant attentiveness towards Wallis, and her travel arrangements, the King seemed to have rather less concern for his constitutional duties, in particular those regarding the government papers that he was expected to read and sign in his role as head of state. Both Wigram and Hardinge became increasingly concerned about the King's irresponsibility regarding the official red boxes dispatched from Downing Street. Unlike his punctilious father, he was slow to attend to them, and worse still, left their contents scattered around Fort Belvedere for anyone to see, so that when several files disappeared, it was unclear if they had been lost or stolen. The courtiers were not alone in these anxieties. In February, Wigram had been summoned to a meeting with the highest-ranking civil servants, including Robert Vansittart (Permanent Under-Secretary for Foreign Affairs). Together, they expressed their disquiet that Mrs Simpson had access to confidential documents and secret intelligence reports. Vansittart also told Wigram that French and Swiss agents in London had informed their governments that 'Mrs Simpson is one of the key points in this country as the King discusses everything with her. The Foreign Secretary is very anxious lest the FO Cypher may be compromised, as Mrs S is said to be in the pocket of the German ambassador.'

Quite aside from the contentious issue of Wallis's supposed relationship with Ribbentrop, she was a client of a Russian-born fashion designer named Anna Wolkoff, whose fanatically pro-Nazi sympathies brought her to the attention both of the Foreign Office and British Intelligence. Anna's father, Admiral Nikolai Wolkoff, was a former aide-de-camp to Tsar Nicholas II and had been posted to London as a naval diplomatic attaché in 1913. In the wake of the Bolshevik revolution in 1917, Admiral Wolkoff and his family were never again able to return to Russia; Anna (the oldest of four children) was fifteen at the time, and remained in London, where her parents opened the Russian Tea Rooms in South Kensington.

Like her father, Anna was virulently anti-Semitic, believing that Bolshevism was the result of a Jewish plot. She was creatively ambitious, too, and after leaving school, she had been one of the first female students to enrol at the Architectural Association. Having failed to complete her studies there, she honed her talent for needlework and became a dressmaker, with high-profile clients including Princess Marina (whose mother was a friend of Anna's mother). In 1935, she established a couture salon at 37 Conduit Street in Mayfair, a short stroll from Norman Hartnell's premises, and later used her dressmaking business as cover for her subversive work on behalf of a secretive fascist organisation, the Right Club. She engaged in enthusiastic propaganda on its behalf, and took to signing her letters 'PJ' (Perish Judah). An undercover MI5 agent recorded Wolkoff as declaring that 'Hitler is a god . . . it would be wonderful if he could govern England'. Naturally, she chose to holiday in Austria and Germany, where she was delighted to meet Rudolf Hess, amongst a number of other prominent Nazis.

Wolkoff was equally proud of her association with Mrs Simpson, and boasted that the Prince of Wales had first fallen in love with Wallis because of the elegance of the clothes she had made for her. While never reaching the same level of fame as Norman Hartnell, Wolkoff's designs nevertheless appeared in the British edition of *Vogue*; and *The Times* praised her collection in September 1935. 'She uses striking materials in simple styles, and gives to each suit and frock some individual touch,' reported the newspaper's fashion correspondent, drawing attention to a 'complete travelling outfit in a novel tweed' and a velvet lined coat in 'mellow mulberry tones'. Wolkoff receives no mention in Wallis's memoir, but that is hardly surprising: she was arrested in May 1940, after handling stolen documents from the US Embassy and passing coded messages to Germany, at least one of which reached the notorious traitor William Joyce ('Lord Haw-Haw'). Having been found guilty of espionage, Wolkoff was sentenced to ten years of penal servitude at Holloway, where she taught her fellow prisoners to sew.

Whether or not Vansittart's suspicions about Wallis's links with Ribbentrop were justified, the King's own actions suggested that he was a potential security risk. Apart from his alarmingly lax approach to the red boxes, he also gave the continuing impression of being pro-German, at a time when Hitler's regime was becoming ever more repressive. Take, for example, the report of the Duke of Saxe-Coburg and Gotha, a grandson of Queen Victoria who came to London in January 1936 and appeared in a Nazi uniform at the funeral procession of his cousin George V. An ardent follower of Hitler since 1922, with the rank of *Obergruppenführer* in the Storm Troopers, Coburg spoke to Edward VIII on three separate occasions in January, and sent a detailed account of their conversations to Berlin, for the confidential attention of the Führer himself. According to Coburg (who had originally befriended Edward when he was still the young Prince of Wales, visiting his German relatives in 1913), the new king regarded an alliance with Germany as 'an urgent necessity and a guiding principle for British foreign policy'. When Coburg asked him if a discussion between Baldwin and Hitler would be desirable, 'he replied in the following words: "Who is King here? Baldwin or I? I myself wish to talk to Hitler, and will do so here or in Germany. Tell him that please."' King Edward, concluded Coburg, 'is resolved to concentrate the business of government on himself. For England, not too easy. The general political situation, especially the situation of England herself, will perhaps give him a chance.'

As an unofficial envoy for Hitler, Coburg took full advantage of his royal connections – most often via his sister Alice, who was married to Queen Mary's brother, Lord Athlone. Hence Duff Cooper's reference in his diary to an invitation from the Athlones to Kensington Palace on 25 January 1936: 'I was tactfully left alone with the Duke of Coburg after luncheon in order that he might explain to me the present situation in Germany and assure me of Hitler's pacific intentions.' Coburg was not an altogether reliable witness – another of his self-serving reports, concerning his meeting with Neville Chamberlain (then the Chancellor of the Exchequer), contains the erroneous claim that he was 'an Eton schoolfellow of mine'. Nevertheless, Coburg was far from being the only Nazi to believe that the new king's views aligned with his own: Ribbentrop, for instance, was convinced that Edward was 'a kind of English National Socialist', while Hitler was said to regard him 'as a man after his own heart and one who understood the *Führerprinzip* [the leader principle] and was ready to introduce it into this country'. Nor was it simply the Nazis who saw him as a potential fascistic monarch. Chips Channon, who was himself an admirer of 'the new vigorous civilisation of the Nazis', wrote in his diary later that year that the King 'is going the dictator way; he is pro-German and against Russia and too much slipshod democracy. I shouldn't be surprised if he aimed at making himself a mild dictator, a difficult task for an English king.'

Yet any authoritarian streak in his character was more often submerged by his abject desire to please Wallis. During a weekend at Fort Belvedere in February 1936, Lady Diana Cooper noted in a letter: 'Wallis tore her nail and said "Oh!" and forgot about it, but he needs must disappear and arrive back in two minutes, panting, with two little emery-boards for her to file the offending nail.'

If, as Diana Cooper implied, his actions were lacking in the dignity required of a sovereign, then this compulsion was also in keeping with his rebellion against the regal traditions embodied by his parents, both of whom regarded the Crown as representing a sacred vocation. As was the case when his father was still alive, the filial mutiny was most often expressed through the medium of clothes. His second book, *A Family Album* (published in 1960) is almost entirely concerned with reminiscences about royal fashion, and yet reveals far more about his innermost feelings than his earlier, carefully constructed and often opaque autobiography. 'Constriction was the order of our schoolroom costume,' he recalled. 'We had a buttoned-up childhood, in every sense of the word.' Nor, to his dismay, did the restraints lessen for royalty in adulthood: 'My father . . . remained imprisoned in frock-coats and boiled shirts.' As the Prince of Wales, he had sought to break 'the bonds of sartorial tradition. But always, in doing so, I incurred reprimands from that frock-coated enclave, the Palace. It is therefore hardly surprising that, on my Accession to the Throne, one of my first actions was to abolish the frock-coat for wear at Court.'

Diana Cooper's own keen understanding of the nuances of style is one of the reasons that her observations of her friend (as prince, king, and exiled Duke of Windsor) are so perceptive. During the same weekend that she saw him dancing attendance on Wallis, and entertaining guests less than a month after his father's death, Lady Diana gave a detailed description of his choice of outfit at dinner. 'His Majesty's evening kilt was better than ever,' she wrote to her friend Conrad Russell from Fort Belvedere on 17 February. 'I think it was a mourning one, although he denied it – anyway, it was pale dove grey with black lines, and his exquisitely-fitting jacket rather Tyrolled-up, I thought, in shape and buttons.' Here was the new king in a dandified costume, beautifully dressed and yet in danger of veering towards the absurd, at least in Diana's waspish view, as he 'donned his wee bonnet and marched round the table, his stalwart piper behind him, playing "Over the sea to Skye"'.

By wearing a kilt at Fort Belvedere, the new king was both maintaining and breaking a family tradition; for while both his grandfather and father had regularly worn Highland dress, as had their sons from childhood onwards, this was only when they were in Scotland. At Windsor and Buckingham Palace, they would have been attired in the requisite formal uniforms. George V's standards were as strict in these matters as in all others; indeed, by way of illustration in *A Family Album*, Edward quoted letters that he had received from his father. One contained a set of instructions on what the nine-year-old prince should wear at Balmoral: 'I hope your kilts fit well. Take care and don't spoil them at once as they are new. Wear the Balmoral kilt and grey jacket on weekdays and green kilt and black jacket on Sundays. Do not wear the red kilt until I come.' An equally stern letter was dispatched by George to his son as he approached his eighteenth birthday in 1912, informing him that he 'must have tights [knee breeches] and a Windsor coat and white waistcoat made by the time you arrive at Windsor'. To George V, like his father and grandfather before him, this was no mere formality; rather, a solemn sign of respect for the dignity of the Crown.

In the months that followed King George's death, his heir's desire for liberty went far beyond an urge to jettison frock coats or wear kilts outside Scotland. 'All my life,' he declared in *A Family Album*, 'I had been fretting against those constrictions of dress which reflected my family's world of rigid social convention. It was my impulse, whenever I found

The future George V with three of his sons (left to right, Prince Henry, Prince Edward and Prince George) at Balmoral, *c.*1906.

Edward VIII and Wallis Simpson during their cruise in 1936.

myself alone, to remove my coat, rip off my tie, loosen my collar and roll up my sleeves – a gesture aspiring not merely to comfort but, in a more symbolic sense, to freedom.' Wallis, he continued, 'likes to describe this process as "my striptease act".'

Duff and Diana Cooper would have front-row seats at the King's most overt striptease performance in the summer of 1936, when he invited them on a Mediterranean cruise aboard a luxurious chartered yacht, the *Nahlin*. Diana described the scene (in another letter to Conrad Russell) as they joined the royal party on the Dalmatian Coast, to be greeted by their bare-chested host: 'The young King naked but for little straw sandals, little grey flannel shorts and two crucifixes on a gold chain round his neck.' Wallis was beside him, wearing matching diamond crosses on a Cartier bracelet around her wrist, and according to Diana, looked 'a figure of fun, in a child's piqué dress and a ridiculous baby's bonnet. As her face is an adult's face *par excellence*, the silly bonnet really was grotesque.' When the *Nahlin* was anchored, and they went ashore, crowds of local people would gather to stare, astonished, at the King; although Diana was surprised that they recognised the 'naked-ish' figure before them: 'no hat (the child's hair gleaming), espadrilles, the same little shorts and a tiny blue-and-white singlet'. She gave a similar description in a letter to her mother, the Duchess of Rutland, adding that despite his moments of dejection ('the little face looks gloomy and apologetic . . . How he spoils everyone's fun'), the scantily-clad king also gave the impression of being 'utterly unselfconscious – just now in the middle of a long walk, two girls throwing flowers and shrieks of "Edwaaaard", he stooped to tie up his shoe – taking three minutes over it so we are all left staring at his bottom.'

According to Wallis's memoir, at one point on the cruise it became evident to her that both Diana and the royal equerry, John Aird, 'were appalled at the spectacle of their King on public exhibition without a shirt'. This incident occurred when the yacht was passing through the narrow straits of the Corinth Canal, on the way to Athens. On either side, the banks 'were swarming with Greeks, all cheering, some snapping cameras, and others waving gaily-coloured kerchiefs . . . It seemed as if the spectators had only to reach out to touch the King. The bucolic charm of this scene entertained me.' When Diana asked Wallis if she could persuade the King to put on some more clothes, Wallis simply replied, disingenuously, 'After you, my dear Diana. If this were my President, I might. But you have had more experience in dealing with kings.'

On Corfu, Wallis exhibited her own inimitable way of handling royalty, when the party dined with the recently restored King George II of Greece (Edward's second cousin) and his English mistress. Diana described to Conrad Russell how Wallis entertained the King of Greece, 'her voice rasping out, the wisecracks following in quick succession'. After they had returned to the yacht, 'Wallis was very lit up, successful in all things, her frock was pretty, she'd done well with the foreign king. She talked everyone's head off.'

But then the mood soured; Wallis asked why the Greek monarch didn't simply marry his mistress, and another guest replied that this would be impossible, as she was already married to another man. Presumably the response rankled with Wallis, yet she directed her annoyance at her devoted lover, rather than anyone else. Diana watched the King, in his typically obeisant attitude to Wallis, 'fussing over her proudly, gone down on hands & knees to pull her dress from under the chair feet. She stared at him as one would at a freak [saying], "Well, that's the *maust* extraordinary performance I've ever seen." Then she started picking on him . . . on and on she went.' Diana, embarrassed by Wallis's continuing verbal assault on the King, went to bed, but guessed that the unhappy scene would continue for hours. The following day, Wallis was still sulky, and Diana confided to Conrad that 'the sooner the trip ended for us, the better . . . Wallis is wearing very, very badly. Her commonness and Becky Sharpishness irritate.' Diana also believed that Wallis was rapidly tiring of her lover. 'The truth is she's bored stiff by him, and her picking on him and her coldness towards him, far from policy, are irritation and boredom.'

Wallis's smoothly ghostwritten memoir gives no indication that anything was awry; she described the final episode of their holiday as an idyllic sojourn in Vienna, where 'in this ancient and urbane capital on the

Danube, with its long tradition of royalty and sympathy for romance, our happy summer reached its high noon'. In reality, the King continued to throw caution – and his clothes – to the wind, as became evident in the account written by Alec Hardinge's wife Helen: 'In Vienna, they booked in at the Hotel Bristol. Visiting a public bath there with his chauffeur and six detectives in attendance, the King stripped down and wandered round the steam-room naked, to the astonishment of the rather proper Austrian bathers who were there.' Meanwhile, the American press redoubled their reporting on the love affair between Edward and Mrs Simpson; *Time* magazine, for example, informed its readers that the couple were together day and night in Vienna, just as they had been on the *Nahlin* cruise.

But as Diana Cooper had suspected, Wallis was having serious doubts; and after the King had returned to London, and she was once again installed at her favoured Parisian hotel, Le Meurice, she wrote to him on 16 September 1936. The letter begins with the news that she has a cold (and – perhaps more provocatively – has eaten a 'trout and 2 ears of delicious corn'). Wallis then switches abruptly to her desire to end their relationship and return to her husband. She and Ernest, she explains, 'are so awfully congenial and understand getting on together *very* well – which is really an art in marriage. We have no small irritations one for the other. I have confidence in his being able to take care of me and himself. In other words I feel secure with him.'

Her letter goes on to acknowledge, with unusual honesty, that she will miss the luxury and privileges that accompanied her affair with the King. 'True we are poor and unable to do the attractive amusing things in life which I must confess I do love and enjoy – also the possession of beautiful things is thrilling to me and much appreciated but weighed against a calm congenial life I choose the latter . . . I know Ernest and have the deepest affection and respect for him. I feel I am better with him than with you – and so you must understand . . . in a few months your life will run again as it did before and without my nagging . . . [I] know that you will go on with your job doing it better and in a more dignified manner each year. That would please me so. I am sure you and I would only create disaster together.'

If Wallis can sometimes give the impression of being a sphinx without a riddle, this letter at least is admirably clear. And its effect on her lover was dramatic: according to Tommy Lascelles, the King threatened to cut his throat if Wallis left him. She evidently yielded to his emotional blackmail, and set off to join him at Balmoral (having first seen her solicitor in London, and instructed him to continue with her divorce proceedings against Ernest, which had commenced at the end of July).

From then on, Edward VIII's reign quickly unravelled. He had previously been asked to open a new hospital in Aberdeen, but refused on the dubious grounds that he was in mourning for his father, and instead delegated the obligation to the Duke and Duchess of York. To make matters worse, on the day of the opening ceremony, he drove himself to Aberdeen to meet Wallis at the train station, and despite wearing motoring goggles in an attempt at disguise, was recognised and photographed. A local evening newspaper published the photograph, beneath the headline 'His Majesty in Aberdeen. Surprise visit in car to meet guests'; beside it was another image of the ever-dutiful Yorks at the hospital.

The story of the snub quickly spread – and although Wallis's name was still kept out of the British press, *Time* updated its readers with the news that the 'embittered' citizens of Aberdeen had 'chalked [the] streets with the John Knoxian exhortation: "Down with the American Harlot!"' The magazine also reported that the Home Secretary, Sir John Simon, 'intimated that His Majesty's conduct is fairly disgraceful'. Chips Channon was clearly aware of the disapproving tone of this and other overseas journalism when he noted in his diary that the King 'has been foolish, indeed almost brazen. The Mediterranean cruise was a press disaster; the visit to Balmoral was a calamity . . . Aberdeen will never forgive him.'

The diarist Marie Belloc Lowndes was similarly attuned to the growing sense of impropriety, particularly at Balmoral. 'In the castle Mrs Simpson was given the rooms which had been in turn inhabited by Queen Victoria, Queen Alexandra and Queen Mary; from there she used to issue forth late each morning, in shorts. She and the King, both wearing

Edward VIII and Wallis Simpson at Balmoral, September 1936.

shorts, would go about the village of Crathie, exciting horror and disapproval by their appearance.' But perhaps the most vivid description of all came from Cecil Beaton, when he was shown a home movie (by Wallis herself) of what he called in his diary the 'fatal' visit to Balmoral. It was, he wrote, even more revealing than the previous film footage he had seen of 'the *Nahlin* adventures, the King almost naked'. The mere act of allowing a camera into Balmoral, exposing the King to be there with Wallis, was 'most startling, most obscenely intimate, like looking at people making love'.

Meanwhile, there was growing tension between the Yorks and Wallis and the King. Gossip spread that Wallis referred to Elizabeth as 'the dowdy Duchess', and mocked her as having the appearance of a fat Scottish cook. As has continued to be the case in the royal family's bitter schisms, each side blamed the other. Earlier in the year, the two couples had met at Royal Lodge in Windsor Great Park; Wallis's version, given in her memoir, says that the King had taken the opportunity to show Bertie his new American station wagon. Afterwards, they had walked around the garden together, making polite conversation, before having tea in the drawing room, where 'the two little Princesses joined us . . . They were both so blonde, so beautifully mannered, so brightly scrubbed, that they might have stepped straight from the pages of a picture book.' Wallis was equally complimentary about the Duchess of York: 'Her justly famous charm was highly evident. I was also aware of the beauty of her complexion and the almost startling blueness of her eyes.' At the same time, Wallis suggested that she was the victim of unwarranted hostility: 'I left with a distinct impression that while the Duke of York was sold on the American station wagon, the Duchess was not sold on David's other American interest.'

The Duchess of York, in contrast, held her brother-in-law responsible for the ill feeling, along with Wallis, whom she still could not bring herself to name. In a letter sent to Queen Mary from Birkhall (the home occupied by the Yorks on the Balmoral estate), she described the uneasy atmosphere during the King's visit to Scotland in September 1936. 'David does not seem to possess the faculty of making others feel wanted.

It is very sad, and I feel that the whole difficulty is a certain person. I do not feel that I can make advances to her & ask her to our house, as I imagine would be liked, and this fact is bound to make relations a little difficult . . . The whole situation is so complicated & horrible, and I feel so unhappy about it.'

In the vain hope of avoiding publicity, Wallis's lawyers had arranged for her divorce proceedings to be heard at a court outside London, at Ipswich in Suffolk. The date was set for 27 October, and in order to qualify for the jurisdiction of the Ipswich tribunal, she had to be resident in the county for the preceding two weeks. Wallis duly moved into a rented house in the coastal resort of Felixstowe, from where she wrote an apprehensive letter to the King: 'Do you feel you still want me to go ahead as I feel it will hurt your popularity in the country . . . isn't it best for me to steal quietly away . . . I can't help but feel you will have trouble in the House of Commons etc. and may be forced to go. I can't put you in that position . . . I'm sorry to bother you my darling – but I feel like an animal in a trap.'

Wallis's anxiety was understandable, not least because of the legal difficulties of getting divorced at the time; indeed, it was only since 1923 that a woman had been allowed to petition for divorce on the grounds of her husband's adultery. The complex and costly process was in two stages, and involved demonstrating the 'guilt' of the respondent (in this case Ernest Simpson, who obligingly provided the necessary proof by agreeing to check into a hotel with another woman), as well as the 'innocence' of the petitioner. If the judge agreed, a decree nisi would be granted, followed by a decree absolute six months later. Any evidence of collusion or connivance would lead to the failure of the divorce petition, as would the disclosure that Wallis herself was guilty of adultery, which may explain why in the same letter to Edward, she admitted, 'I'm terrified that this judge here will lose his nerve – and then what?'

In the end, the judge in Ipswich did grant the decree nisi. 'I suppose I must find adultery in this case', said Mr Justice Hawke, after hearing Wallis's evidence, in which she claimed that Ernest had started neglecting her in the autumn of 1934, and the testimony of hotel staff that they had seen Ernest in bed with a woman who was not Mrs Simpson. Robert Egerton, a junior member of the team of solicitors representing Mrs Simpson, subsequently recalled that the judge 'would have liked to find a way out of presiding over what was palpably a judicial farce'. Egerton himself, who went on to have a long and distinguished legal career, observed (in his private account of the case): 'It will surprise many people that Mrs Simpson should have, in effect, denied that she had committed adultery with the King . . . He was passionately in love with Mrs Simpson and, with reckless disregard of the consequences, had secured her company on a cruise and at Balmoral. Who could be blamed for assuming that there had been sexual intercourse?'

Yet Edward VIII was undeterred by any potential legal problems, including the very real threat of an investigation into the truth of the allegations made in the divorce petition, led by a government official known as the King's Proctor. This judicial process could be initiated after the decree nisi; and if the King's Proctor were to find any evidence of collusion or lying, then the divorce would be rescinded. Perhaps inevitably, a number of outraged members of the public did call for the intervention of the King's Proctor in the case of Mrs Simpson's divorce, on the grounds that she had committed adultery with Edward, and that the law was therefore being subverted.

In the midst of the furore, the monarch remained determined that nothing would prevent him marrying Wallis, and he was no more receptive to the attempts of the prime minister, Stanley Baldwin, to dissuade him from this risky course of action than he had been to Wallis's concerns. It is quite possible that, as his father had predicted, he was already planning to abdicate. Certainly, his own memoir hints as much, as he describes moving into Buckingham Palace at the beginning of October, after his return from Scotland. 'I took up residence in that vast building without pleasure; the dank musty smell I had always associated with the building assailed me afresh the instant I set foot inside.' Rather than inhabiting his father's apartment on the second floor, he moved into the

'Belgian suite' on the first floor (named after Queen Victoria's uncle, Leopold I), which had previously been used as guestrooms for visiting foreign monarchs. Nor did he make changes to this suite, other than adding a private telephone line to Fort Belvedere. 'One never tinkers much with palaces; like museums, they seem to resist change,' he wrote. 'Besides, a curious presentiment induced me to leave the rooms as they were. Somehow I had the feeling that I might not be there very long . . . During the two months I lived at Buckingham Palace, I never got over the feeling of not quite belonging there. I felt lost in its regal immensity.'

A similar sense of alienation is apparent in the description in his memoir of delivering the King's Speech at his first – and only – state opening of Parliament, on 3 November 1936. As it was raining that morning, he cancelled the ceremonial procession from Buckingham Palace, on the grounds that 'pageantry needs sunshine. There are few sadder spectacles than that presented by a dripping cortège splashing down a half-empty street, its finery bedraggled, its once resplendent participants soaked to the bone.' So instead of travelling in a gold coach escorted by members of the Household Cavalry, along streets lined with troops from the Brigade of Guards, the King arrived at the House of Lords by car. Once inside, he looked out over the assembled audience of peers and parliamentarians, and felt sickened 'by an almost suffocating smell of moth-balls given off by the colourful robes removed from storage for this formal airing. It was nauseating.'

Chips Channon, there in his role as a Conservative MP, noted in his diary that the King looked as young as he had at his original investiture as Prince of Wales in 1911, a 'happy Prince Charming'. Others were appalled by the presence of Wallis, watching the ceremony from the Royal Gallery. 'She must be a brazen-faced woman to appear thus . . . within a week of the divorce which has set everyone talking,' wrote the Reverend Alan Don, chaplain to George V and also to the Archbishop of Canterbury, in his diary. Don was no less scathing about the King: 'His Majesty protests that Mrs Simpson is not his mistress – but he spends immense sums of money on her – is he quite normal?' After discussing the matter further with an eminent psychologist, Don concluded that 'His Majesty is sexually abnormal which may account for the hold Mrs Simpson has on him'.

Two days later, on 5 November, Harold Nicolson was at the House of Commons, and told his wife Vita: 'All the talk as usual was about Mrs Simpson. The extreme view is that the Cabinet should employ a gangster to murder her. I regard that view as too extreme. But there is no doubt that they fear his marriage, and that there will almost be a revolution if it occurs. The main feeling is one of fury that this empty-headed American who has twice been divorced should bring this great Empire to the brink of a very great crisis. My own view is that I am sorry for her and blame him . . . What a mess!'

Even Channon, who remained loyal to the King and Mrs Simpson, acknowledged that the situation could not continue indefinitely. On 10 November, he was alarmed by the scene inside the Chamber of the Commons, when one MP asked 'an innocuous question about the coming Coronation' and another (John McGovern, a left-wing Glasgow MP) jumped up and declared, 'Why bother, in view of the gambling at Lloyd's that this Coronation will never take place?' As Channon wrote, 'There were roars of "Shame! Shame!" and [McGovern] called out, "*Yes, Mrs Simpson.*" This was the first time her name has been used in the H of Commons proper, although the Smoking Room and Lobbies have long buzzed with it. I was shocked: but the terrible truth is that the monarchy has lost ground in a frightening manner since last January. Edward Charming charms his people no more.'

The final weeks of Edward VIII's reign included a brief visit to South Wales, where he saw the derelict steelworks and crowds of suffering people, and on 19 November made his famous declaration that 'something must be done to find them work'. He then raced back to London, in time to dine at Chips Channon's grand home in Belgrave Square. 'I saw that the King was in a gay mood,' reported Channon in his diary that night; 'no doubt a reaction from his depressing Welsh tour . . . and felt elated, as I do after two or three days in my constituency.' The King remarked to Channon's wife Honor that 'he approved of splendour', and there was much on display that night, including the jewels worn by Wallis, which rivalled those of Princess Marina and her sister Olga, who were guests at the party. 'Tiaras nodded, diamonds sparkled,' rejoiced Channon; 'the atmosphere had been terrific, so many royalties, so many jewels.'

Channon continued to be dazzled by Wallis's precious gems – the following week, at another dinner party, he sat next to her and noticed that she 'was wearing yet more new jewels: the King must give her new ones every day'. He also recorded that a source at Cartier had revealed they were 'resetting magnificent, indeed fabulous jewels for Wallis – and for what purpose if she is not to be Queen?' One of the most spectacular was the emerald ring that the King gave to Wallis after her court appearance in Ipswich, engraved with the date and the message: 'We are ours now'. He had paid £10,000 for the flawless emerald from Cartier, and was a prodigious customer at Van Cleef & Arpels, too, buying Wallis a superb ruby and diamond bracelet (inscribed 'Hold Tight') and a matching tassel necklace (the latter a present for her fortieth birthday on 19 June). 'Mrs S was smothered in rubies,' remarked Channon after dining with her that summer.

The King's contradictory attitude to the trappings of royalty – dispensing with ceremonial regalia when it did not please him, while lavishing majestic jewellery on Wallis – seemed to reflect his own ambivalence about his constitutional obligations. As the titular head of the Church of England, he could not marry Wallis, given that the church did not allow the marriage of divorced people if their former spouses were still alive; but he remained determined to do so, against the advice of the prime minister, Stanley Baldwin, and other senior government figures. As the crisis accelerated, Baldwin made the extraordinary request that Edward VIII's telephone lines should be tapped, in the interests of national security; and in early December, MI5 dispatched one of its most enterprising intelligence officers (Thomas Argyll Robertson, known as 'TAR') on this undercover mission. The instructions were to 'arrange for the interception of telephone conversations between Fort Belvedere and

Buckingham Palace on the one hand and the Continent of Europe and various addresses in London on the other'. Thus it was that Robertson and his colleagues were among the first to hear the momentous news that Edward VIII intended to abdicate, to be replaced by his brother Bertie, who would reign as George VI. This was in marked contrast to the ten-year-old Princess Elizabeth, who only became aware of the drama that would change her life forever when she happened to see a headline on the front page of the *Evening Standard*.

The formal announcement was made on 10 December, much to the dismay of Ribbentrop, who reported to Berlin: 'The abdication of King Edward is the result of the machinations of dark Bolshevist powers against the Führer-will of the young King.' Oswald Mosley's British Union of Fascists remained loyal to Edward VIII, with several thousand Blackshirts rallying to demonstrate outside Buckingham Palace, the Houses of Parliament and 10 Downing Street, chanting: 'One, two, three, four, five, we want Baldwin, dead or alive!', and waving placards that read, 'Stand by the King!' Mosley himself proclaimed the King's right to marry whoever he wished; but it would be wrong to assume that the majority of Edward's supporters were fascists. Winston Churchill tried to encourage Edward not to abdicate (while hoping that he would eventually tire of Wallis); and David Lloyd George took a similar view.

After months of self-imposed silence about the King's relationship with Mrs Simpson, when the British press finally broke the story in early December the newspapers were divided in their editorial opinions. The *Daily Telegraph*, *The Times* and the *Morning Post* were critical of the King, but the *Express*, the *Mail*, the *Mirror*, the *Sketch*, the *News Chronicle* and the *Evening Standard* were more sympathetic. According to the journalist Robert Bruce Lockhart, those who disapproved of the conduct of Edward and Mrs Simpson tended to be traditionalists; or in his words, 'Mrs Rector and Mrs Town Councillor'. As he noted in his diary, abdication was also regarded as a preferable outcome by 'serious people' in Whitehall, the City, and Parliament, although not necessarily on moral grounds, but because of what they perceived as the King's 'irresponsibility'. Hence

The former king making his abdication speech, broadcast by the BBC on 11 December 1936.

their relief at his decision to step down from the throne; for in the words of the former Labour prime minister, Ramsay MacDonald, Edward VIII's departure 'was all for the good', and the country could be 'thankful for the tools of Providence'.

Naturally, Chips Channon did not align himself with his colleagues in the House of Commons (deeming them to be 'hopelessly middle-class'); and mourned the abdication in his diary on 11 December. 'Edward, the beautiful boy King with his gaiety, honesty, his American accent and nervous twitching, his flair and glamour . . . was no more.' Despite his youthful enthusiasm for Elizabeth Bowes-Lyon before her marriage, Channon was not a fan of the Yorks, whom he regarded as dreary and dull. '[They] will do their best, but it is a reactionary move and they will remain the puppets of the Tory Party forever. Will the monarchy survive this blow?' In one sense, Channon answered his own question, in his description of listening to Edward's abdication speech on the radio after dinner at a friend's house: 'I wept . . . we rose, played bridge, and I murmured a prayer for King Edward VIII of glorious memory. Now we must settle about our business and support the Yorks loyally.' And yet Channon continued to feel depressed at the prospect of the new king, George VI, describing him as 'completely uninteresting, undistinguished and a godawful bore'.

On 12 December, Chips and Honor went to stay with the Duke of Norfolk at Arundel, and arrived to find 'a large party of frumps'. Chips, who confessed to having been 'in tears all day', recovered sufficiently to examine 'some relics of Mary, Queen of Scots' that were in the possession of the Catholic Duke of Norfolk. 'Will people a hundred years hence treasure belongings of Edward VIII? The Operetta reign is over, ten months of fun and splendour and indiscretion . . . convention will triumph, and gaiety will lie dead.'

Channon was once again partly prophetic – although it would be Wallis's belongings that proved most valuable, at least in financial terms, after her death in 1986. Many of her famous jewels were auctioned by Sotheby's in Geneva the following year, fetching more than $50 million (a record-breaking sum at the time). In 2010, another Sotheby's jewellery sale showcased twenty pieces, which sold for a total of £8 million. These included Wallis's Cartier panther bracelet of onyx and diamonds that went for £4.5 million (the highest price ever paid for a bracelet at auction). A Sotheby's executive described the jewels as telling 'the story of perhaps the greatest love story of the twentieth century, the romance that led Edward VIII to abdicate the throne of Great Britain'.

Few of those who knew Edward and Wallis well would have agreed with that assessment. Harold Nicolson, who had initially liked Wallis, came to believe that she was either 'a fool or a minx'. Four days after the abdication, Nicolson had lunch with his old friend Tommy Lascelles, who appeared to be relieved at the fall of his erstwhile master, and by the fact that the Duke of Windsor (as Edward was now known) had left the country to find sanctuary in Austria. In a letter to Vita, Harold reported Tommy's view 'that some disaster was certain to arrive sooner or later . . . He says the [ex-] King is like the child in the fairy stories who was given every gift except a soul . . . "He was without a soul," he kept on saying, "and this made him a trifle mad. He will probably be quite happy in Austria. He will get a small *schloss*; play golf in the park; go to night-clubs in Vienna; and in the summer bathe in the Adriatic. There is no need to be sorry for him. He will be quite happy wearing his silly Tyrolese costumes . . . and he never cared for England or the English."'

In contrast, Lascelles offered encouraging words about Edward's replacement, his more conscientious younger brother: 'The new King will be first class – no doubt about it.' As for Lascelles' predictions about the future life of the Duke of Windsor: he eventually settled with Wallis in France, rather than Austria, but did continue to enjoy playing golf, going to nightclubs, and bathing in the sea and swimming pools of the Riviera. He retained his status as a leader of fashion in café society, and was, in the words of James Pope-Hennessy, 'very silken and natty and well-arranged'.

The royal family's rupture was never fully healed, setting a precedent for fraternal and generational estrangement that has cursed successive generations to this day. And the Duke of Windsor remained understandably hurt that his family refused to welcome Wallis into their midst, even after their marriage. But he had his revenge, in a small yet pointed way, having inherited his father's treasured collection of diamond and platinum tiepins. George V 'would have felt undressed without a pin in his tie,' recalled his eldest son in *A Family Album*. 'Since I hardly ever wear a pin in my tie, I had the tops of them mounted on [Wallis's] various gold accessories, which she carries in her handbag: a jewelled horseshoe, for example, on a compact; [the King's] monogram on a case for her comb.'

How George V would have hated it: his royal tiepins mutilated, the jewels added as adornments to Wallis's make-up kit (for he loathed seeing women wearing lipstick or nail varnish or powdering their faces), and tucked into the intimate recesses of her handbag. Yet Wallis, too, faced her own indignities. Soon after the abdication, Madame Tussaud's commissioned a waxwork model of the notorious Mrs Simpson, to add to its gallery of prominent figures (both dead and alive). The American writer Janet Flanner visited the exhibition for the *New Yorker*, and discovered that the effigy of Wallis was ostracised on the second floor. 'It is the only unnumbered, uncatalogued, and isolated item in the whole show,' she wrote. 'Mrs Simpson merely has her name on a card.' The lonely figure was clad in a scarlet evening gown that had been copied from one of 'her actual gowns', and equipped with 'a Continental-looking handbag that bears her initials in rhinestones'. Beyond her, and 'defended from her by a group of Famous Soldiers in uniform, is the Royal Family. Two steps lead up to a dais on which King George VI and Queen Elizabeth are posed beneath a red velvet canopy. On the top step stand all the royal relatives – all, that is, except the Duke of Windsor. The morning after his abdication, his effigy, in its gold-frogged scarlet tunic, was removed from beneath the canopy and taken down two steps. It now stands on the floor, well over toward Mrs Simpson.' On a pedestal above the former Edward VIII stood the figure of the Duke of Wellington, 'whose boot is even with the former ruler's neck.'

Wallis, exiled in France, was mortified by the news of her waxwork at Madame Tussaud's, and wrote to the Duke of Windsor's lawyer, Walter Monckton, asking him to do something about the humiliating spectacle: 'It really is too indecent and so awful to be there.' Monckton was, of course, powerless in this regard. So there the effigy remained, a captive scarlet woman; while Wallis contemplated her future with a man whose overwhelming love for her had led to such indignity. In the same week that Janet Flanner's piece was published in the *New Yorker*, Wallis sent a tender letter to her ex-husband Ernest (who was by then involved in a relationship with their mutual friend, Mary Kirk). 'It should never have been like it is now,' Wallis confessed, and spoke of being 'illogical and so groomed by my pride'. Yet again, she referred to Edward by the nickname that she and Ernest had used for him in the past: 'I think Peter Pan should have written [to] you too, but then you see he doesn't understand.'

Only the most hard-hearted could fail to feel some sympathy for Wallis at this point; and she certainly felt extremely sorry for herself, as she made clear in a letter to Edward (undated, but believed to be contemporaneous with her letter to Ernest, which she wrote on 16 February 1937). 'I really can't continue to carry on with all of England taking cracks at me and no decent society speaking to me. What have I done to deserve this treatment? . . . I do feel utterly down. It has been such a lone game against the world for me and a woman always pays the most – and you my sweet haven't been able to protect me.'

But for all her anguish and apprehension, Wallis was nothing if not a survivor. While she awaited the decree absolute of her divorce (which was finally granted in early May, following a somewhat selective investigation by the King's Proctor), Wallis prepared for her third wedding, and ordered a trousseau of eighteen couture outfits from Elsa Schiaparelli's latest collection in Paris. By doing so, she would place herself at the forefront of modernist fashion – in an entirely different league to her days as a client of Anna Wolkoff and Norman Hartnell. No longer would she be demeaned or chastened, but instead she dressed to kill, in direct opposition to the traditional garb of royal women, and one woman in particular: her nemesis, the new royal consort, Queen Elizabeth.

HARD CHIC

In the springtime of 1937, when Wallis Simpson went shopping for her wedding trousseau, Elsa Schiaparelli was regarded as the most outrageous designer in the world, not least for her signature colour, a violent puce that she dubbed 'shocking pink'. Yves Saint Laurent would later describe this vivid tone as having 'the nerve of red . . . an aggressive, brawling, warrior pink'; while Schiaparelli saw it as 'bright, impossible, impudent . . . like all the light and the birds and the fish in the world put together'. By the time she died in 1973, her legend had long since been eclipsed by that of her great rival, Coco Chanel. But in her 1930s heyday, Schiaparelli was the embodiment of the 'hard chic' that she had made fashionable, for as Cecil Beaton observed, her genius lay in 'inventing her own particular form of ugliness'.

Born in Rome in 1890, the daughter of a distinguished academic and niece of a renowned astronomer, Schiaparelli had been made to feel that she was an unattractive child. Her memoir, *Shocking Life*, in which she refers to herself in the third person as 'Schiap', describes her earliest attempts to beautify herself as 'her first surreal act of decoration'. After gathering seeds of nasturtiums, daisies and morning glories, she planted these 'in her throat, ears, mouth . . .' Much to her disappointment, no flowers emerged; but the theme of metamorphosis would recur throughout her career as a couturière. Schiaparelli's ingenuity made her a leader

Wallis Simpson in *Vogue*, wearing a Schiaparelli dress 'lightly scattered with matchstick motifs' and a black 'Circassian cap', July 1935. Photograph by Cecil Beaton.

of avant-garde style in Paris, renowned for her collaborations with Salvador Dalí and Jean Cocteau, and her mischievous hats (fashioned in the form of a lamb cutlet, for instance, or an upturned high-heeled shoe).

Janet Flanner, writing in the *New Yorker* in June 1932, remarked that 'a frock from Schiaparelli ranks like a modern canvas', while acknowledging her talent for three-dimensional fashion: 'Inclined to see women as something built rather than something born, she used costumes like fine veneer, the dovetailed angles, corners, and metal trim making her seem not so much merely a dressmaker as a cunning carpenter of clothes.' Schiaparelli herself wrote that clothes should be architectural, insisting that 'the body must never be forgotten and it must be used as a frame is used in a building . . . the more the body is respected, the better the dress acquires vitality.' Ever the contrarian, she also proclaimed: 'Never fit the dress to the body, but train the body to fit the dress.' This approach reached its apogee with her 'Bureau-Drawer Suit', inspired by a Dalí drawing of a female figure shaped as a mobile chest of drawers. Schiaparelli's sartorial version of the Dalí sketch appeared in her 1936 autumn–winter couture collection, when she presented suits and coats embellished with drawer pockets and decorative handles. Presumably it was these that Cecil Beaton had in mind when he wrote, after sketching Wallis Simpson in November 1936, 'She reminds one of the neatest, newest luggage and is as compact as a Vuitton travelling case.'

At first glance, Wallis's preference for 'hard chic' might seem entirely at odds with Edward's choice (in his own words) to 'dress soft'; although perhaps it was her very hardness that most attracted him. He yearned for the two of them to be made one – forming the 'WE' that he often referred to in his love letters, and the jewellery he commissioned which combined their initials (hers always coming first). She was less certain; as she had already made clear when she wrote to him from Paris on 16 September 1936: 'I am sure you and I would only create disaster together.' His response was plaintive – 'Why do you say such hard things?' – and yet he remained certain that they could not be divided, ending his letter: 'God bless WE.'

Their union certainly caused a stir in the world of fashionable Paris; for having fled from what Edward deemed the stiff 'starchiness' of the British court, Wallis flirted with the free-for-all of surrealist style. Despite its apparent playfulness, this could also be perilous territory, as is evident in Cecil Beaton's photograph of Schiaparelli's 'Bureau-Drawer' ensembles (published in the September 1936 issue of *Vogue*). A trio of models stands in a studio, separated from each other by the painted forms of faintly sinister Dalí-esque rocks. One of the models covers her face with a neatly gloved hand, as if she cannot bear to be seen, or to see what might lie ahead of her. Another model is holding aloft a copy of the surrealist magazine *Minotaure*, featuring a Dalí cover that shows a woman with a ferocious bull's head, an open drawer in place of her breasts, her thighs revealing compartments for a bottle and cocktail glass, her blood-red nails sharp as talons, and a lobster emerging out of her abdomen, its claws waving over her pudendum.

Wallis Simpson may not have subscribed to *Minotaure*, but she was certainly an avid reader of *Vogue* and *Harper's Bazaar*, both of which were enthusiastic champions of Schiaparelli and Dalí. *Bazaar* had already started publishing fashion illustrations by Dalí in 1935, and hailed Schiaparelli for her 'volcanic energy and a fantastically fecund sense of modern invention'. The magazine's owner, William Randolph Hearst, was less impressed, however, and particularly objected to an image that appeared in *Bazaar* towards the end of 1936 of 'Schiaparelli's black wool ball-shaped cape'. This, he complained in a memorandum to the editor Carmel Snow, 'is to my mind awful . . . like a picture of the "Iron Virgin" . . . which closed on its victim with iron spikes, and which is exhibited merely to produce a shudder'.

In retrospect, *Vogue*'s fashion editor Bettina Ballard reflected (in her 1960 memoir): 'A Schiaparelli customer did not have to worry as to whether she was beautiful or not . . . She was noticed wherever she went, protected by an armour of amusing conversation-making smartness. Her clothes belonged to Schiaparelli more than they belonged to her – it was like borrowing someone else's chic and, along with it, their assurance.' Schiaparelli believed precisely the opposite: 'A dress has no life of its own unless it is worn, and as soon as this happens another personality takes over from you and animates it, or tries to, glorifies or destroys it, or makes it into a song of beauty. More often it becomes an indifferent object, or even a painful caricature of what you wanted it to be – a dream or an expression.'

Wallis's own autobiography does not mention Schiaparelli, nor Dalí, nor Beaton, which seem to me notable omissions. Perhaps by the time it was published in 1956, she no longer wished to be associated with the extremes of surrealist fashion. After all, Schiaparelli had gone bankrupt and closed her couture house in 1954 (and was, moreover, monitored by the FBI as a potential spy during the war, while also arousing the suspicions of the Germans). Yet Cecil Beaton's memorable pictures of Wallis wearing the most notorious garment from her Schiaparelli trousseau – a white organza dress with a crimson waistband, beneath which is positioned a larger-than-life lobster painted by Salvador Dalí – are more revealing than much of her memoir. The shoot was staged in France, at Château de Candé in the Loire Valley, where Wallis had been staying since March 1937, at the invitation of its shady millionaire owner, Charles Bedaux and his wife Fern. Beaton arrived the weekend before Wallis's divorce was finally granted (the announcement of her decree absolute was made on 3 May). The coronation of George VI and Queen Elizabeth was scheduled for 12 May, the same date that had originally been set for Edward VIII to be crowned. If Wallis had ever believed that she might once have taken her place as queen beside Edward, the humiliation of the past months had proved otherwise. As she told Beaton, in a frank late-night conversation at Château de Candé that he recorded in his diary, 'it had been difficult for her not to give way and hang herself on one of the many pairs of antlers in the room in which we sat. But her control has been very firm. She is very like a man in many ways, and said she has few woman friends.'

Beaton does not refer to the iconoclastic lobster dress in his diary; he simply writes that the 'camera session started with "romantic" pictures in the shade of sunlit trees, where the thick grass was covered by daisies . . . The photography went on for many hours. Birds sang; conditions and settings and organdie dresses were ideal . . . Wallis, helpful

Wallis Simpson wearing her Schiaparelli lobster dress, May 1937.
Photograph by Cecil Beaton.

and serious, purposely dropped her usual badinage.' Given that Wallis approached fashion and photography with utmost dedication, her choice to wear such a provocative dress is significant. Beaton's images are black-and-white, but even without being able to see that the lobster is bright red, it is hard to ignore Dalí's insistence on the creature's sexual connotations, given its suggestive position between Wallis's thighs. Such was Dalí's fame by this point that Wallis was presumably aware of his fetish for crustaceans; certainly, the erotic symbolism of the dress reflected the artist's *Lobster Telephone*, created in 1936, where the phallic tail is placed over the mouthpiece.

At the time, Wallis's Schiaparelli trousseau received widespread coverage in the American press, where she was celebrated as being far more fashionable than those within the British elite who had scorned her. The New York *Daily News*, for example, ran a full-page article on 16 May 1937 beneath the headline 'Absent Wally Outshines Folk at Coronation', accompanied by illustrations of her Schiaparelli purchases, the lobster dress being the most prominent. The fashion correspondent declared that 'Wally' (as she was impertinently nicknamed in the US), 'took an easy first place against all contenders' in the 'feminine world of rich and titled folk . . . [She] has been chic for a long time. But this year she has taken her Old Masters degree in dress, as it were.' Having made this bold claim, the reporter did not attempt an artistic critique of the lobster dress, saying simply that Wallis would be waltzing in it ('she is a marvellous dancer, you know'), and that the lobster looked 'realistic'. Readers were informed that Wallis's other choices from Schiaparelli included a 'smart frock for afternoon . . . of black silk crêpe printed here and there with white turtles'; a fitted black suit with buttons in the form of 'patent leather chessmen', plus a co-ordinating white blouse printed with black chessmen; a 'glorious sky blue and silver negligee'; 'a hyacinth blue tweed jacket with three black jet butterflies embroidered on each lapel'; and a dramatic midnight navy evening coat, also adorned with butterflies.

It is a measure of Wallis's self-control, combined with Beaton's consummate expertise, that she looks so composed in the photographs he took of her in the lobster dress, which would be published by *Vogue* the following month. In spite of Dalí's best efforts to heighten the absurdity (during its creation he had to be dissuaded from smearing mayonnaise on the gown, but did add several sprigs of green parsley to the design), Wallis rises above the lobster, and makes the dress her own. Beaton's portrait could easily have looked ridiculous or clumsy – a clownish distortion of Leonardo da Vinci's enigmatic masterpiece, *Lady with an Ermine* (in which a beautiful young woman cradles a wild creature close to her breast, its claws visible against her velvet dress). The photograph of Wallis makes no claim to be art: it represents a fleeting moment in time, intended only for the flimsy pages of an ephemeral magazine, but it nevertheless holds one's attention long after the fashion itself has dated.

Wallis maintains her dignity in another of Beaton's portraits from the same shoot, wearing a Schiaparelli black evening dress, its matching jacket appliquéd with bold baroque scrolls of white patent leather. There she stands in a panelled room at the Château de Candé, her face watchful, her taut figure as slender as Schiaparelli's mannequins in Paris, yet still very much her own woman.

Beaton captured a similar air of self-sufficiency when he returned to the Château to take the official wedding photographs on 3 June 1937. In the event, Wallis had chosen not to wear a Schiaparelli bridal gown; instead, she selected Mainbocher, the sartorial equivalent of deciding that discretion is the greater part of valour. This Paris couture house had been founded by her fellow American, Main Rousseau Bocher (who, like his peer Edward Molyneux, had served in intelligence during the First World War). Mainbocher, as he came to be known, shared a similarly discreet approach to design as Molyneux, which represented the antithesis to Schiaparelli's audacious aesthetic. Bettina Ballard, who knew Mainbocher and admired his work, quoted him as saying: 'I instinctively veer away from exaggeration, which always tends to be tiresome and dates very quickly. To me subtlety has quite another and more lasting message. So I try to blend mystery rather than to rave and rant with my shears.'

Wallis modelling a Schiaparelli outfit from her trousseau, May 1937.
Photograph by Cecil Beaton.

An official wedding portrait of the Duke and Duchess of Windsor, June 1937.

Wallis's wedding dress was an exemplary expression of Mainbocher's ethos: a column of blue silk crêpe with long sleeves and a high neck, a line of small buttons emphasising her pin-thin midriff; the silhouette fitted, yet altogether more demure and irreproachable than a Schiaparelli fantasy. Beaton described the material as 'a hard blue', worn with a matching tulle and feathered hat that gave a 'halo effect'. However, his choice of adjective to describe the colour – soon to be called 'Wallis blue' in fashion magazines – may have been influenced by other factors. In his diary, he wrote that Wallis 'seemed especially unlovable, hard and calculating and showing an anxiety but no feeling of emotion'. Beaton, in turn, became harsh in his private comments about Wallis ('her face broken out in spots'); and behind-the-scenes in her bathroom, where she prepared for the photographs, he noted, with distaste, a towel 'crumpled in the corner, and on the side of the bath a Gillette razor'.

Beaton also recorded that the Duke of Windsor 'looked like a wizened little ten year old boy . . . home from school for the holidays'. But for all his child-like air, the Duke knew how to pose for the camera, and 'would not allow himself to be photographed on the right side of his face, preferring the left'. His expression, continued Beaton, was 'essentially sad', his 'tragic eyes overruling the impertinent tilt of his nose'. At one point, his face suddenly looked 'tortured like a German gargoyle, contorted and frowning'. Wallis, too, seemed harassed, and Beaton, camera still in hand, heard the bridegroom complaining about his family. 'The Duke swore, "What the bloody hell do they mean by that . . . what the hell has it got to do with my brother . . . my brother's got houses and palaces, what the hell . . ."'

It would not be surprising if the Duke's joy at marrying Wallis was mingled with a streak of rage: none of his relatives had accepted the invitation to the wedding, and nearly all of his friends had found excuses not to be there. To add insult to injury, the Duke was informed the day before his long-awaited marriage that Wallis would not receive the title 'Her Royal Highness'; a decision taken by George VI that ended any possibility of reconciliation between the two brothers. Wallis had suspected that this would be the case. In December 1936 she had written to her lover from France, blaming Queen Mary, as well as the new king: 'It is plain that York [George VI] guided by her would not give us the extra chic of creating me HRH.' Nevertheless, the Duke of Windsor was devastated, and believed that his family had betrayed him and insulted the woman he loved. 'The family he is through with,' wrote one of the few wedding guests, Lady Alexandra ('Baba') Metcalfe, whose husband Major Edward ('Fruity') Metcalfe stepped in as best man after the Duke's brothers had refused to attend. Baba also noted in her diary that Wallis pretended not to care about the royal title being denied to her, 'but she minds a great deal really'.

This was far from being the glamorous rival coronation anticipated by the American press. 'It was hard not to cry & in fact I did,' confessed Baba after the ceremony. 'It could be nothing but pitiable & tragic to see a King of England of only 6 months ago, an idolized King, married under such circumstances.' Even so, when she saw that Edward was crying, she believed his tears to be those of happiness, while witnessing no such emotion in Wallis. 'We shook hands with them in the salon. I realised I should have kissed her but I just couldn't . . . her attitude is so correct. The effect is of an older woman unmoved by the infatuated love of a younger man.'

Cecil Beaton was more philosophical, believing that Wallis was 'determined to love' her third husband, though she was clearly 'not in love with him'. And despite the lack of a royal title, observed Beaton, 'for Mrs Simpson, events might have been worse. If she has not been fated to wear a crown, she is still loved by an abdicated King . . . It won't be so bad to be called the Duchess of Windsor.' When he left the Château, Beaton impulsively 'kissed Wallis goodbye – not because she encouraged me to – she seemed so unlike a bride . . . metallic and hard – it was like kissing a stone – but I felt moved by all that had happened.'

If the bride's steeliness and the groom's melancholy were apparent in several of Beaton's wedding portraits, it was even more pronounced in the photographs published by the British press, where the newly married couple looked strangely ill at ease. In general, the English newspapers' coverage of the wedding expressed less wholehearted enthusiasm than their American counterparts. The *Daily Mirror* ran a photograph of the Windsors on the front page, accompanied by a report from its 'special correspondent' in France, who said that the Duke had remained 'unsmiling' during the ceremony at the Château de Candé, while Wallis's 'long oval face, her dull cream skin and deep red mouth were shadowed as the clouds passed across the brilliant sun, which filled the salon first with sunlight, then with shade'. A brief article appeared in *The Times*, with no mention of the bridal gown, but noting that the couple had been married in a French civil ceremony, followed by a Church of England marriage ceremony conducted by a Darlington vicar, the Reverend Robert Anderson Jardine. The *Daily Express* secured an interview with the vicar's wife, who explained that the previous week her husband had written to the Duke of Windsor offering his services, and had been gratefully accepted. (Inevitably, Jardine's superiors disapproved of his enterprise, and dismissed him from his post. After seeking a fresh start with a lecture tour of America, Jardine had a short-lived career in Hollywood, officiating at a disused church that he renamed 'the Windsor Cathedral'.) The *Express* also informed its readers that Wallis had ordered sixty-six dresses for her wedding trousseau, and although neither Mainbocher nor Schiaparelli were named, the lobster gown was listed as being among the 'unusual dress decorations' chosen by the bride, alongside mermaids and glass flowers.

The Windsors spent their lengthy honeymoon at an Austrian castle owned by Count Paul Munster, who was already known to the British security services as an associate of Oswald Mosley, the leader of the British Union of Fascists. They travelled there via Venice, where Mussolini's authorities had arranged an impressive display of flowers and gondolas to greet the newly-weds. In October 1937, they embarked on their infamous tour of Nazi Germany as honoured guests of the Third Reich; an initiative originally suggested by their new friend Charles Bedaux, who had substantial business interests there. By this point, Bedaux – who was born in France and made his fortune as a time-and-motion tycoon in the United States – was regarded with suspicion by the British, French and US intelligence services. (He would be arrested by the Americans in Algeria in 1943, and charged with treason, but killed himself before he could face trial.)

The Duke of Windsor's admiration for Hitler's regime was by no means unusual amongst the British establishment of the era; David Lloyd George, the former Liberal prime minister, became a keen advocate for the Nazi leader after meeting him in Germany in September 1936. 'He is a born leader of men,' he declared to the readers of the *Daily Express*. 'A magnetic, dynamic personality with a single-minded purpose, a resolute will and a dauntless heart . . . He is the George Washington of Germany – the man who won for his country independence from all her oppressors.' Thanks to Hitler, proclaimed Lloyd George, the German people 'are more cheerful. There is a greater sense of general gaiety of spirit throughout the land. It is a happier Germany.'

Several prominent peers were equally impressed by Hitler: so much so that they joined the Right Club, the pro-Nazi group whose members ranged from Anna Wolkoff to the fifth Duke of Wellington. Lord Redesdale, one of the so-called 'wardens' of the Right Club, had visited Germany in 1936 at the urging of his daughters Diana and Unity Mitford, who by then were part of Hitler's inner circle. (When Diana married Oswald Mosley in October that year, the secret ceremony took place at the Berlin home of their friends Joseph and Magda Goebbels, with Hitler and Unity as guests.) Such was Lord Redesdale's own high regard for the Nazi regime that he wrote a letter to *The Times* in March 1936 commending Hitler as 'a right-thinking man of irreproachable sincerity and honesty', who set an excellent example 'in the life he leads and in all that he does'.

Chips Channon was similarly fulsome in his praise. 'One felt one was in the presence of some semi-divine creature,' he wrote in his diary after seeing Hitler in the Olympic stadium in August 1936, and declared that the Games had made Berlin 'the rallying point . . . of the grand and chic of the earth'. At the same time, the questionable notion that Nazism was glamorous briefly occurred to Diana Vreeland, the American fashion editor of *Harper's Bazaar,* who wrote in her column: 'Why don't you wear bare knees and long white knitted socks as Unity Mitford does when she takes tea with Hitler at the Carlton in Munich?' (Although Vreeland's flirtation with fascist chic was short-lived, she remained an ardent admirer of the Duke of Windsor's fashion sense, declaring that he 'had style in every buckle on his kilt, every check of his country suits'.)

In the summer of 1937, Channon and his wife returned to Nazi Germany, revelling in 'the joys' of holidaying there, thanks to 'the orderly arrangements, the polite people, the friendly atmosphere, the amazing architecture and startlingly good roads'. In Berlin, they had tea with the British ambassador, Sir Nevile Henderson. 'He is pro-German, anti-French, anti-Jew, pro-Italian, and, indeed, thinks along the lines that I do,' noted Channon with satisfaction in his diary. Channon was equally confident that these views were shared by Lord Halifax (soon to be appointed Foreign Secretary, in which role he would be key to the policy of appeasement). After Halifax travelled to Germany in November 1937 to meet Hitler and Hermann Göring, Channon was gratified to hear his impressions: '[Halifax] described Hitler's appearance, his khaki shirt, black trousers and patent leather evening shoes! And, he said, he liked all the Nazi leaders, even Goebbels! . . . He was much impressed, interested and amused by the visit.'

Halifax's trip took place soon after the Windsors', who were entertained by Göring at Carinhall, his immense country estate in the forests north of Berlin. The Duke's memoir makes no mention of their adventures in Germany (it ends with his abdication); but the Duchess does provide an account, including a detailed description of their time with Göring and his wife Emmy. Most of Wallis's observations were concerned with the attractive surface of things: Göring greeting them 'in an immaculate white uniform, with rows of medal ribbons across his tunic'; Frau Göring's bedroom, which 'was spacious and sunny and decorated with bright chintzes'; the 'fine quarters' provided for the large staff of housemaids, whose rooms had 'gay cretonne curtains', and whose dresses 'were of peasant designs, with pleated skirts and smocked blouses'. Their tour of the Görings' magnificent home provided an opportunity to view the impressive gymnasium in the basement, 'equipped with weight-lifting apparatus, an electric exercising horse, horizontal bars, and a massage apparatus bearing the Elizabeth Arden trademark'. (Göring had an unlikely penchant for Elizabeth Arden products, and enjoyed wearing bright red varnish on his toenails.)

Then they went up to the attic, where Wallis surveyed 'the most elaborate toy railway I have ever seen – yards and yards of intricately connected tracks, dozens of switches, coal tipples, charming little stations, and any number of locomotives'. Both couples appeared to enjoy the friendly encounter: the Duke and the commander-in-chief of the Luftwaffe playing happily together with a toy aeroplane that released wooden bombs onto the train set, while Frau Göring confided in Wallis 'that she was expecting her first child'.

The Windsors' itinerary also included meetings with Heinrich Himmler, whose menacing reputation as the head of the SS does not emerge in Wallis's depiction of his 'bespectacled meekness . . . a clerk caught up in politics'. Himmler had, in fact, been responsible for establishing Buchenwald concentration camp three months previously, and Dachau in 1933, and devised and implemented the sadistic methods of the Gestapo. She regarded Hitler's deputy, Rudolf Hess, as 'charming of manner and good-looking', while the Nazi propagandist, Joseph Goebbels, 'impressed me as the cleverest of the lot – a tiny, wispy gnome with an enormous skull. His wife was the prettiest woman I saw in Germany, a blonde with enormous blue eyes and a flair for clothes.'

Wallis's own style remains visible to a limited extent in the surviving photographs and film of her time in Germany. On their arrival at Berlin station, for example, she is wearing an impeccably tailored blue suit and a sizeable jewelled brooch that shines alongside the gleaming insignia of the men in Nazi uniforms who flank her husband and herself. Frau Göring would subsequently write that the Duchess was extremely well dressed: 'I could not help thinking that this woman would certainly have cut a good figure on the throne of England.' Unfortunately, there are no images of Wallis in evening dress at the galas held in the Windsors'

The Duke and Duchess of Windsor during their visit to Hitler's Bavarian mountain retreat, on their tour of Germany in October 1937.

honour, including a large dinner hosted by Edward's cousin, the Duke of Saxe-Coburg and Gotha.

Perhaps the most fitting choice of designer for the tour was Anna Wolkoff, the pro-Nazi dressmaker who had also taken full advantage of German hospitality. Schiaparelli's surrealist style would have been too controversial – Hitler had declared in 1933 that he was banning the 'incomprehensible eccentricity' of avant-garde art, which far from being modern, in his view, looked as primitive as if produced in the Stone Age by 'cultural Neanderthals'. Such overt hostility seemed only to increase Dalí's fascination with the Führer, expressed in his 1939 painting, *The Enigma of Hitler*. This depicts a telephone, a viscous substance dripping from one end, the other shaped like lobster claws, hovering over a photograph of Hitler that lies on a plate, alongside a few dried beans or maggots. A translucent furled umbrella hangs limply on a leafless branch: a symbol of the impotence of appeasement, given that the British prime minister, Neville Chamberlain, was carrying his trademark umbrella when he returned from meeting Hitler in Munich in September 1938. In the background is a barren shoreline; a female figure can be glimpsed, her clothing providing the only colour in Dalí's picture – a faded pink jacket that has none of the bravura of his collaborations with Schiaparelli.

Wallis herself gives no details in her memoir of what she wore on their tour of Nazi Germany, nor of her husband's inspection of a training camp for Hitler's elite SS division, where the Duke was seen to give the Nazi salute. She does, however, provide a description of their visit to Hitler at Berghof, his Bavarian mountain retreat. The Windsors travelled to the nearest town, Berchtesgaden, on the Führer's private train, escorted by his deputy, Rudolf Hess, and were met at the station by his interpreter, Paul Schmidt, who accompanied them to the meeting. The Duke spoke fluent German, and insisted he had no need for Schmidt, who nevertheless remained present throughout the private meeting with Hitler, which lasted over an hour; Wallis, meanwhile, stayed with Hess. The party then had tea together in front of the fire in the drawing room, the Duke and Hitler continuing to speak in German, which meant that Wallis was unable to understand their conversation. Instead, she studied the Nazi leader. 'I could not take my eyes off Hitler,' she recalled. 'He was dressed in his brown Party uniform . . . at close quarters he gave one the feeling of great inner force. His hands were long and slim, a musician's hands, and his eyes were truly extraordinary – intense, unblinking, magnetic . . . Once or twice I felt those eyes turned in my direction. But when I tried to meet their gaze, the lids dropped, and I found myself confronted by a mask.'

If the Duchess of Windsor felt any disquiet in the presence of Hitler, it is certainly not apparent in the photograph of them together. He is bowing and clasping her hand, the swastika on his sleeve prominent in the eye of the camera. Wallis's gaze is directed at his face, and the warmth of her smile is striking. Despite her dark hat and coat, she looks radiant. To one side, her husband is also smiling; although it is impossible to know whether this was because he genuinely liked Hitler, or because the Führer pointedly called the Duchess 'Your Royal Highness' (as did every other Nazi they met in Germany). An eyewitness report in the *New York Times* suggests that they parted on excellent terms: 'The Duchess was visibly impressed with the Führer's personality, and he apparently indicated they had become fast friends by giving her an affectionate farewell. He took both their hands in his saying a long goodbye, after which he stiffened to a rigid Nazi salute that the Duke returned.'

The Duke remained quite unabashed by their dealings with the Nazis, who had financed the Windsors' visit, long after the full horrors of the Third Reich had been exposed. 'I never thought Hitler was such a bad chap,' he later remarked to his friend Lord Kinross (with whom the Duke collaborated on the writing of his book about royal fashion, *A Family Album*). And at a dinner party given by the Windsors after the war, where the guests included their unrepentantly fascist friends Oswald and Diana Mosley, the Duke turned to Sir Oswald and said, 'It was the Jews who brought us into the war.' Even Mosley, when repeating this remark to the author Kenneth Rose, commented that having been 'interned for three and a half years for maintaining just that, I had had enough and declined to discuss the matter with the Duke'.

As to what Hitler felt about the Windsors, the only official narrative comes from his interpreter, Paul Schmidt, who included the episode in his autobiography (published in English in 1951). Schmidt wrote that the Führer was 'evidently making an effort to be as amiable as possible towards the Duke, whom he regarded as Germany's friend . . . [The Duchess] was simply and appropriately dressed and made a lasting impression on Hitler. "She would have made a good Queen," he said when they had gone.' If the interpreter's memory is to be trusted (and Schmidt prided himself on his powers of recall, although his memoir does not allude to the Holocaust), the conversation was principally concerned with 'social progress in Germany'. The Duke 'expressed his admiration for the industrial welfare arrangements he had seen, especially at the Krupp works in Essen' (where tanks and U-boats were already in production in the weapons factory), and 'was frank and friendly with Hitler'. Yet ambiguity is not altogether absent from Schmidt's recollections: 'There was, so far as I could see, nothing whatever to indicate whether the Duke really sympathised with the ideology and practices of the Third Reich, as Hitler seemed to assume he did.' That the Führer's assumption was shared by other senior figures in the Third Reich became apparent to the British Foreign Office, who were briefed by their intelligence agents and consular staff there. The British consul in Dresden, for example, related that the Nazis' belief in 'the Duke's supposed strong pro-Fascist sympathies' had been 'strengthened' during the tour, thanks to his praise for the regime's 'great achievements'. The Windsors' police protection officer, Philip Attfield, a detective assigned to them by Special Branch, also reported back to British Intelligence, both on this trip and during their time in France. Thus, it was with some authority that the shrewd former diplomat Robert Bruce Lockhart noted in his diary on 22 November 1937: 'Germans still believe [the Duke of Windsor] will inaugurate [an] English form of Fascism and alliance with Germany.'

The day after the Windsors' meeting with Hitler, the *New York Times* commented: 'The Duke's decision to see for himself the Third Reich's industries and social institutions and his gestures and remarks during the

last two weeks have demonstrated adequately that the Abdication did rob Germany of a firm friend, if not a devoted admirer, on the British throne. He has lent himself, perhaps unconsciously but easily, to National Socialist propaganda . . . [The Duke] is reported as declaring that the British ministers of today and their possible successors are no match for the German or Italian dictators.'

If the Duke of Windsor did find Nazism alluring, could it have been as much a personal compulsion as a political choice? As the critic Susan Sontag observed in her 1974 essay, 'Fascinating Fascism', Nazi aesthetics endorsed 'two seemingly opposite states, egomania and servitude', creating what she regarded as 'a natural link' between sadomasochism and fascism. Needless to say, the Duke himself never explored this subject in his own writing. But for all his advocacy of 'soft dressing' as a form of freedom from the rigidity of his royal childhood, and the unyielding formality of the court, his demeanour in Germany suggested that the strict Nazi uniforms, shiny black leather boots and death's head skulls on SS regalia might prove rather too seductive for him to resist.

The Duke of Windsor with the Nazi politician Robert Ley, head of the German Labour Front, during a visit to a factory in Berlin, October 1937.

ROYAL COMMAND PERFORMANCE

It was with a profound sense of dread that George VI came to the throne: an accession he had never sought, and for which he felt ill-suited and wholly unprepared. As he wrote to Godfrey Thomas (Edward VIII's assistant private secretary) on 25 November 1936: 'If the worst happens & I have to take over, you can rest assured that I will do my best to clear up the inevitable mess, if the whole fabric does not crumble under the shock and strain of it.'

When the worst did happen, the new king went to see his mother; and as he confessed in his own private chronicle of the abdication crisis, 'I broke down and sobbed like a child'. Queen Mary herself would later recall her son's despair, telling Harold Nicolson he had cried on her shoulder 'for a whole hour'. The new queen took to her bed with influenza, admitting to a close friend that 'everything seems like a bad dream'. Soon afterwards, in a letter to the Archbishop of Canterbury, she described the shock of the abdication as akin to 'a heavy blow to the head . . . literally stunning'. She told another correspondent (the author Osbert Sitwell) that 'gossip and ill-natured stories are rife' – suggesting she was aware of the malicious rumours that her husband suffered from epilepsy or was mentally incapacitated – and added, 'I fully expect that we may be unpopular for some time'.

The distress extended far beyond the royal family. Janet Flanner reported in her column for the *New Yorker* on what she perceived as a widespread

George VI delivers a live radio broadcast to the British Empire on the evening of his coronation, 12 May 1937.

mood of mourning: 'King Edward's abdication was very much like a funeral.' He had been 'adored', she continued, and his popularity was of a particularly modern kind: 'He is the most contemporary man England has known: his charm is cinematographic.' As such, Edward's sudden departure left a void in the kingdom, at a time of increasing uncertainty in the wider world, with the violent outbreak of the Spanish Civil War, widespread totalitarianism, and the growing threat of European despots and dictators. But in Flanner's view, the British people had not lost 'that miracle-loving element . . . which tends toward iconography, kings, prophets, and special beings in strange, lovely garments. This element in other lands has recently found its less monarchic element in Nazi trappings, Fascist fanfares, a Communism which makes a shrine of Lenin's tomb, and in America, a worship of cinema stars.'

The shy, stuttering George VI was clearly not possessed of his older brother's charisma; and gloom seemed to spread across the country at the beginning of the new reign. Queen Mary's friend, Mabell Airlie, wrote about this unhappy period in her memoir: 'There was an indescribable flatness and dreariness in the atmosphere of those early months of 1937. The whole nation was feeling the after effects of the shock caused by the Abdication with all its bitterness and disillusion.' The melancholy extended to Stanley Baldwin, with whom Lady Airlie spent a day in January. The prime minister, she wrote, 'looked tired and discouraged', and 'thought that the new King would have a great deal to contend with'. Baldwin then told her: 'There's a lot of prejudice against him. He's had no chance to capture the popular imagination as his brother did. I'm afraid he won't find it easy going for the first year or two.' Lady Airlie's loyal response was to quote George V: 'Bertie has more guts than the rest of his brothers put together.'

He had certainly faced challenges as a stammering child, often lapsing into silence when the exhausting struggle to express himself became too humiliating. At the age of eight, the sensitive little boy was also forced to wear painful splints on his legs (at night in bed and during the day), as a supposed cure for his knock-knees. A loving marriage helped him grow in confidence, as did the encouraging support of Lionel Logue, the speech therapist he had first consulted in October 1926, before the royal tour of Australia and New Zealand, and to whom he turned again in preparation for the coronation. Nevertheless, he would never be altogether free of his fear of speaking in public, and those frustrations occasionally flared up into a sudden outburst of bad temper: a state that Tommy Lascelles referred to as 'Nashville', because of the actual 'gnashing of his teeth'.

Perhaps as a consequence of his speech impediment, the new king was more attuned than his older brother to the visual imagery of monarchy: the robes and regalia that spoke louder than words. And unlike Edward VIII, who was often impatient with what he regarded as pointless pomp or pageantry, he also grasped the silent yet significant power of royal symbolism. By choosing to become King George VI – rather than using his first name, Albert – he signalled that he would be following in his father's measured footsteps to the throne, thereby restoring continuity after the disruption of the abdication. Similarly, in a marked contrast to Edward VIII, who could never fully bring himself to inhabit Buckingham Palace, George VI moved there with his family in February 1937, as if to prove their absolute commitment to their new roles, and a return to the stability represented by previous generations.

Although the palace had originally been designed in the eighteenth century as a private retreat for George III and Queen Charlotte (fourteen of their fifteen children were born there), it more than doubled in size during the reign of George IV, and was further extended by Queen Victoria and Prince Albert. It was at Albert's suggestion that the public-facing east wing was added, with a handsome façade from which the royal family could step out onto a central balcony, making themselves visible to their subjects. These iconic appearances on the balcony began in 1851, when Queen Victoria acknowledged the crowds that had gathered in front of the palace to celebrate the opening of the Great Exhibition. In doing so, the sovereign herself became the star attraction on a purpose-built stage, thereby establishing a tradition that still endures to this day.

For Miss Crawford, who had become accustomed to life in the family home of 145 Piccadilly, the change in circumstances was not altogether welcome. The palatial gilded state rooms, she wrote in her memoir, 'resembled the setting of a luxurious pantomime', but the atmosphere felt 'oddly dead'; while the electrical wiring was eccentric: 'My bedroom light could be turned on and off only by a switch some two yards outside my doorway in the passage.' She felt it was 'all far too big', and disliked the 'interminable corridors' that linked the hundreds of rooms (775 in total). Mice were everywhere, despite the daily battles waged against them by a full-time employee known as the Vermin Man. 'I still recall with a shudder that first night spent in the Palace,' recalled Miss Crawford. 'The wind moaned in the chimneys like a thousand ghosts.'

I thought of her words recently, when visiting Buckingham Palace to give a talk about an exhibition of royal photographs that was being staged in the King's Gallery. This area of the palace was previously a private chapel for Queen Victoria, but after being bombed during a wartime air raid, it was redeveloped as a gallery for the Royal Collection. On previous visits to the palace, I have entered through the main gates from the Mall, overlooked by the monumental memorial to Queen Victoria. But on this occasion, I came in via a side door, and was led along a labyrinth of passages that looked like the backstage of an immense theatre or opera house. Industrial metal piping and skeins of electrical cables were visible, and if a dusty grey mouse had scuttled across the floor, it would not have been surprising. Here was the utilitarian yet vital behind-the-scenes operation that allowed the palace pantomime to continue unabated; here lay the inner workings of the endless royal performance.

If the brief reign of Edward VIII had descended into a scandalous striptease act, then George VI gave every appearance of intending to restore the seamless decorum of the monarchy. In March 1937, Harold Nicolson was invited to dinner at Buckingham Palace, and noted 'the mass of gold candelabra and scarlet tulips', which provided a fitting setting for the royal couple. He was particularly struck by the poise of the new queen. 'Nothing could exceed the charm or dignity which she displays,' he wrote in his diary, 'and I cannot help feeling what a mess poor Mrs Simpson would have made of such an occasion.'

The new king also revived the tradition that the royal family should entertain at Windsor Castle – in marked contrast to Edward VIII, who preferred long weekends at Fort Belvedere – and Duff and Diana Cooper were amongst the guests who spent a night there in April (Duff having been invited on the strength of his role as a government minister). The couple were delighted, as both were worried that their previous closeness to Edward and Wallis might lead to their exclusion from the new court. As Diana reported in a letter to her friend Conrad Russell, the shifts in style soon became apparent: Duff had been advised by a courtier in advance of their visit that 'knee-breeches would be worn', but when they arrived at Windsor, she heard an 'impatient voice bawling "Trousers, trousers, I've said trousers four times."' Evidently, 'the King had changed his mind' about the breeches – fortunately, Duff had packed trousers, too – and Diana dressed for dinner in an evening gown of the 'Queen's own blue'. Even so, she fretted that her dress might be regarded as too redolent of Edward VIII's raffish reign: 'It's high-cut and modest in design, but I'm not sure that it isn't worse than "strip-tease" because for some reason it shows the minutest details of anatomy through its draping.' Later that night, Diana resumed her missive, recording that the Queen, who wore a glossy satin gown, looked like 'a lily and rose in one'. Much to her annoyance, however, Duff disappeared after dinner, and 'I had the humiliation of being taken to my rooms through the meandering mazes of the Castle by a red-liveried man.' When Duff finally reappeared, well after midnight, he told Diana that he had been 'drinking tea with the Queen. She put her feet up on a sofa and talked of Kingship and "the intolerable honour" but not of the [abdication] crisis.' 'Duff so happy,' remarked Diana; 'me rather piqued.'

Having returned to London the next day, Diana rang to update her friend Chips Channon (who was anxious that he had been 'black-listed' by the new king and queen). 'It was all v different from the Fort and the late regime,' he wrote in his diary on 17 April. '"That was an operetta, this is an institution," she said.' The following morning, Channon noted: 'Thousands got up early to see the rehearsal of the Coronation procession, which took place in the early dawn and drew crowds.'

Meanwhile, at Buckingham Palace, the little princesses were having their final dress fittings for the coronation. 'The King had taken immense interest in the children's outfits,' recounted Miss Crawford in her memoir. 'We had had one scene when Margaret found Lilibet was to wear a little train, while she had none! They both wore lace frocks with little silver bows, and cloaks edged with ermine. The King had special coronets made for them, very light.'

On the morning of the coronation, Miss Crawford saw the children after they were dressed. 'They came to me very shyly, a little overawed by their own splendour and their first long dresses. "Do you like my slippers?" Lilibet said, lifting her skirt to show me her silver sandals. I also saw that she was wearing short socks that revealed a length of honest scratched brown leg!'

Crawford's indiscretion – literally, raising the skirts of royalty – both here and elsewhere in her memoir would cause her subsequent excommunication by the family she had served for sixteen years. Lilibet's own handwritten essay about the coronation – neatly inscribed with red crayon 'To Mummy and Papa, From Lilibet, By Herself' – gives an exact description of the ceremonial garments that she and Margaret wore. Their dresses were 'white silk with old cream lace and had little gold bows all the way down the middle. They had puffed sleeves with one little bow in the centre. Then there were the robes of purple velvet with gold on the edge . . . Papa was dressed in a white shirt, breeches and stockings, and over this he wore a crimson satin coat.'

It so happens that Lilibet's account of their outfits – written just after the coronation – is more accurate than that of her governess. When I checked with the Royal Archives, the bows on the princesses' dresses were indeed made of gold fabric, rather than silver (and both she and her sister had trains). At eleven years old, Lilibet was already mindful that sartorial niceties were no trifling matters; an understanding she had learned from her parents and grandparents.

From her vantage point in the royal box at Westminster Abbey, where she sat with her sister and grandmother, Queen Mary (who 'looked too beautiful in a gold dress patterned with gold flowers'), Lilibet watched the coronation. 'I thought it all very, very wonderful and I expect the Abbey did, too,' she wrote. 'The arches and beams at the top were covered with a sort of haze of wonder as Papa was crowned . . . When Mummy was crowned and all the peeresses put on their coronets it looked wonderful to see arms and coronets hovering in the air and then the arms disappear as if by magic.'

Her essay also hints at the unique predicament in which she now found herself as heiress to the throne: there was no one else who could truly understand what it felt like. Lilibet was entirely alone in this position – 'By Herself' – because the only person still alive to have shared this experience was her uncle, who had fled the country and escaped his own coronation. Evidently, she had questioned her grandmother at some point during the ceremony, but the dowager Queen Mary could offer little insight. As Lilibet observed in her essay, 'What struck me as rather odd was that Grannie did not remember much of her own Coronation. I should have thought it would have stayed in her mind for ever.'

Towards the end, she admitted, 'the service got rather boring as it was all prayers. Grannie and I were looking to see how many more pages to the end, and we turned one more and then I pointed to the word at the bottom of the page and it said "Finis". We both smiled at each other and turned back to the service.' Afterwards, 'we were all shivering, because there was a most awful draught coming from somewhere, so we were glad to get out of the box . . . When we got back to our dressing room we had some sandwiches, stuffed rolls, orangeade and lemonade. Then we left for our long drive . . . we went along the Embankment, Northumberland Avenue, through Trafalgar [Square], St James's St., Piccadilly, Regent St, Oxford St with Selfridge's lovely figures, through Marble Arch, through

The royal family on the day of George VI's coronation: (top) on the balcony of Buckingham Palace; (above, left to right) the Duchess of Kent, Duchess of Gloucester, Countess of Strathmore, Queen Mary, Princess Elizabeth, Princess Margaret and the Princess Royal, in Westminster Abbey; (opposite) the newly crowned king and queen with their daughters in their coronation robes.

Hyde Park, Hyde Park Corner, Constitution Hill, round the Memorial and into the courtyard . . . Then we all went on to the Balcony where millions of people were waiting below. After that we all went to be photographed in front of those awful lights.'

A decade previously, in June 1927, Lilibet had appeared on this balcony as a baby in her mother's arms, flanked by her father and grandparents, when her parents came back from their six-month tour of Australia and New Zealand. On that occasion too, large crowds had gathered outside on the Mall to witness the family reunion. She returned to the balcony in her supporting role as a bridesmaid to Princess Marina following the wedding of the Duke and Duchess of Kent in November 1934, and for her grandparents' Silver Jubilee celebrations in May 1935. For these and other events, both inside and outside Buckingham Palace, Lilibet would become accustomed to the process and paraphernalia of the cameras. So if she did feel unsettled by the lighting on the day of the coronation, her solemn face in the official portraits does not betray any emotion as she stands to attention between her newly crowned parents, her head held high in a coronet of her own.

Janet Flanner, reporting again from London for the *New Yorker*, regarded the coronation as a triumphant restoration of the monarchy's prestige. 'It was composed of remarkable relics and innovations – costumes, coaches, soldiery, and a royal family, all brought up to date in the person of an ermine-caped young King whose sacred, ancient oaths [were] broadcast through loudspeakers to the whole world.' She also took this opportunity to introduce the youthful Norman Hartnell to the readers of the *New Yorker*, explaining that although the new queen's coronation robe was made by the court dressmaker Madame Handley-Seymour, 'about three dozen of her spring and summer costumes are being done in Bruton Street by Norman Hartnell'.

Hartnell had already begun designing for Elizabeth the previous year, when she was still the Duchess of York: her initial orders were made in January 1936, shortly after the death of George V, for black ensembles suitable for formal court mourning. Early in 1937, Hartnell was invited to Buckingham Palace, and commissioned to create the coronation gowns that would be worn by Queen Elizabeth's six maids of honour. In his autobiography, Hartnell recalled his first visit to the palace, where he had a meeting with the royal couple, and learned of their plans to draw on nineteenth-century references: 'Both the King and the Queen had been studying the historic picture of the Coronation of Queen Victoria painted by Sir George Hayter, and had been impressed by the charming appearance of the Maids of Honour. Their Majesties pointed out the head-wreaths of gilded wheat which the trainbearers wore. Using this as the *leit-motif* of the accompanying dress, I drew a design of stiff ivory satin with a high corsage and short sleeves, the dress embroidered with a wheat-ear motif in pearls, crystal and gold.'

It was on the same afternoon that George VI made another significant suggestion, which would come to define the look of his wife as queen, and in due course, their firstborn daughter. 'The King invited me to inspect some of the decorative pictures which portrayed many beautiful dresses of the Victorian period,' wrote Hartnell. 'Cigarette in hand, he led me off to one of the picture galleries and many other of the State Apartments to view the paintings by Winterhalter who endowed his women . . . with such regal and elegant grace and truly captured the very spirit of the mid-century decades. His Majesty made it clear in his quiet way that I should attempt to capture this picturesque grace in the dresses I was to design for the Queen. Thus it is to the King and Winterhalter that are owed the fine praises I later received for the regal renaissance of the romantic crinoline.'

As an idea, this was a masterstroke – a superb visual riposte to the angular modernism embodied by Wallis Simpson. For as Janet Flanner observed in her article about Norman Hartnell (published on 5 May 1937, the week before the coronation, and a month before the wedding of the Duke and Duchess of Windsor), the new queen needed to convey elegance, without being 'too Frenchily chic'.

A show of patriotism was threaded into every stitch of the Queen's coronation gown, which had been embroidered with emblems of the British Isles and Empire by the Royal School of Needlework (including the rose of England, thistle of Scotland, maple leaf of Canada and mimosa of Australia). Nor were Handley-Seymour and Hartnell the only British dressmakers represented at the coronation: the Anglo-Irish Edward Molyneux was commissioned to create the dresses for the four canopy bearers of the Queen, the duchesses of Norfolk, Roxburghe, Buccleuch and Rutland. Molyneux designed their gowns in white and gold faille with a pattern of roses, and he also made a golden brocade dress for Princess Marina and another embellished with gilded embroidery for Lady Diana Cooper.

But it was Hartnell who emerged as the clear favourite, particularly when Queen Mary bestowed her own patronage upon him and ordered three evening gowns. Much to his surprise, as he reminisced in his memoir, her first choice of dress from his latest couture collection seemed highly unlikely: 'a sheath-like affair of glittering soft green mother-of-pearl, called "Fish Out of Water" . . . I could not imagine how the dress could possibly transform itself suitably to become the *grande dame* figure of the Queen.' However, her dresser, Miss Weller, assured him that this could be done, 'with a few adroit adjustments', and selected a different fabric for Queen Mary's consideration: 'a lovely shade of aquamarine blue, to be embroidered with aquamarine sparkles'. Hartnell then submitted illustrations of this and two other dresses, in silver brocade and mauve lace, all of which met with royal approval.

He was far too discreet to publish the details of Queen Mary's subsequent fittings that he attended at her London home of Marlborough House. Fortunately, Hartnell kept a private record of their first encounter there, his words brimming with delight. 'The upholstery and curtains of Queen Mary's bedroom were of carnation-pink satin brocade. Soft pink net curtains flapped and fluttered in the morning breeze and all the windows were wide open. Pink carnations and roses of every pinkish hue leaned their heads out of silver vases . . . There she stood, with diamonds a-glitter at her ears and throat, her silver hair immaculately coiffed . . . in a gown of shimmering blue paillettes, the first gown I had made for her.' He watched, awestruck, as Miss Weller attached Queen Mary's chivalric

Order of the Garter to her gown: 'the brilliant blue ribbon of peacock blue and the circlet of embroidery with "*honi soit qui mal y pense*" in flashing diamonds.'

Next came the fitting of the silver brocade dress, 'with its pattern of magnolias, marguerites and ferns strengthened by pearl and rhinestone embroideries'; and finally the mauve lace dress. Hartnell was thrilled by the effect: 'from each arabesque of Nottingham thread cascaded a fall of mauve crystal. Each pendant fragment of threaded crystal fringe sewn on in varying lengths – short round the corsage and graduating longer and longer upon the skirt, like fronds of wisteria twinkling with dew.'

As Queen Mary examined her reflection in the looking glasses of her dressing table, she asked Hartnell to open her wardrobe, so that she could see herself in profile in its long mirrored doors. Inside he spied serried rows of her famous toques, including one 'of palest pink and silver', trimmed, like many of the others, with 'a downy plume of pink ostrich'. This he recognised as having 'graced Queen Mary's noble head' when, with King George V, she had driven through the streets of London for the Silver Jubilee celebrations of 1935.

Queen Mary's example would underpin the regal style of her daughter-in-law Elizabeth; and she also provided advice on the coronation crowns. 'To Garrard's to see the jewellers working on the resetting of Bertie's & Elizabeth's crowns,' she noted in her diary on 9 April 1937. 'Most interesting.' Elizabeth's crown reflected the continuity of the monarchy, the majority of its 2,800 diamonds sourced from Queen Victoria's Regal Circlet, including the spectacular Koh-i-Noor diamond that had been successively mounted in the crowns of Queen Alexandra and Queen Mary. For Hartnell – who described himself in his memoir as 'more than partial to the jolly glitter of sequins' – the opportunity to create sparkling gowns that would complement the dazzling royal jewels was a godsend; and his theatrical gifts were ideally suited to creating costumes for the coming reign. His sense of drama was not at odds with the new king and queen's profound reverence for the monarchy; indeed, the central area of Westminster Abbey that was originally built for the crowning of

sovereigns has always been known as the Theatre (the word even appears in Lilibet's youthful account of the coronation).

Harold Nicolson, who was watching the ceremony as a member of the congregation at the Abbey, observed afterwards: 'There is no doubt that they have embarked on this task with a real religious sense.' Both George and Elizabeth were deeply committed to their vows of faith, yet the spiritual element of the coronation was expressed through material means, as well as prayer. The Reverend Alan Don, an active participant in his role as chaplain to the King and to the Archbishop of Canterbury, witnessed this aspect at first hand, and wrote in his diary about the sacred act of anointing the King with holy oil. 'This was really most moving – to see him sitting in St Edward's throne, stripped of all his beautiful robes, waiting in simple white garments – a mere man, unadorned – for his hallowing – and then the canopy, almost concealing him from the sight of man, and the Archbishop entering beneath it as into a tabernacle with the holy oil – and then, what a change! – the Kingly vestments and all the emblems of his royal estate, betokening his new status as the Anointed of the Lord – here indeed was the essence of the whole matter, the consecration of our King.' (In 2020, a fragment of the fabric dipped in the holy oil was sold at auction for £820, the envelope containing it inscribed: 'Wool used at the anointing of King George VI, Westminster Abbey, May 12 '37', and signed with the initials of the Dean of Westminster.)

For some in the audience, the figures of Edward and Wallis were absent but not forgotten. Winston Churchill, who had initially argued strongly against the abdication, whispered to his wife Clementine: 'You were right. I see now the "other one" wouldn't have done.' Chips Channon expressed a more regretful note in his diary: 'The sun shone through the windows and the King, abashed, looking young . . . almost boyish, suddenly reminded me of his brother "over the water"; and I thought, as many others, too, must have been thinking, of that sad, more glamorous wistful Edward VIII alone with Wallis . . . no doubt listening in

The coronation procession in Westminster Abbey, May 1937.

on the radio to the Coronation service of his brother, which ought to have been his own had he not reached the acme of folly and infatuation.' Channon observed that Queen Elizabeth appeared 'dignified', although he could not restrain himself from criticism: 'She is fatter, and much more bosomy.' He mused, too, about what was in Queen Mary's mind, as 'she swept out' of the Abbey, and added that 'she and the Court group hate Wallis Simpson to the point of hysteria . . . why persecute her now, when all is over? Why not let the Duke of Windsor, who has given up so much, be happy?' And yet Channon had already expressed his own doubts about their impending marriage: 'Will she seem older, less seductive? And he, less dazzling? They are left now with only themselves, gone are their crowns, shattered their schemes, vanished their Empire.'

According to reports in *Time* magazine and the *New York Times*, the Duke of Windsor had indeed heard the radio broadcast of the coronation at the Château de Candé. Journalists were briefed by Herman Rogers (Wallis's faithful friend and unofficial press spokesman) that the Duke listened while 'quietly knitting a dark blue sweater for his fiancée'. As for Wallis, sitting beside him, she subsequently admitted in her memoir: 'The words of the service rolled over me like an engulfing wave; I fought to suppress every thought, but all the while the mental image of what might have been and should have been kept forming, disintegrating, and re-forming in my mind.'

One of the most perceptive observations about the coronation, and the associated family dynamics, was made by Cecil Beaton, who had photographed Wallis in France in early May (and would return to the Château de Candé to photograph the wedding of the Windsors in June). On the day of the coronation, Beaton watched the arrivals from a vantage point outside Westminster Abbey; and after listening to the King's speech on the radio later that evening, he wrote in his diary: 'It is interesting to note how as soon as someone becomes loved they blossom. Since the King has become so universally loved & his duties of kingship have been taken up with such devotion, he has acquired an added beauty & nobility. It is the same metamorphosis that comes to a cinema star.

As with his beauty, so with his speech. The technical difficulties have been overcome & his voice is solemn, deep & emotional. It is psychologically interesting, the fluke that is never a fluke, the only word over which he stumbled was "distress".'

The King's speech therapist, Lionel Logue, had been integral to the coronation rehearsals, and he remained a reassuring presence at Westminster Abbey, and afterwards at Buckingham Palace, for the final hurdle of the day: the live BBC broadcast at 8 p.m. The carefully scripted words of the radio speech referred to 'the honour and integrity' of the Crown, as well as stressing the unity of the audience, including 'the free peoples of the Commonwealth', who were listening around the world. 'Never before has a newly crowned King been able to talk to all of his peoples in their own homes on the day of his Coronation,' intoned the sovereign. 'Never has the ceremony itself had so wide a significance, for the Dominions are now free and equal partners with this ancient kingdom, and I felt this morning that the whole Empire was in very truth gathered within the walls of Westminster Abbey.' Those inhabitants of the Empire who were still campaigning for their liberation from the shackles of colonial rule would doubtless have been unconvinced by the King's utterance of the word 'free'; not least because he also reigned as the Emperor of India, and would continue to do so until India gained independence in 1947. (The presence of the Koh-i-Noor diamond in Queen Elizabeth's coronation crown was equally contentious, given that the legendary gem was a spoil of war, having been seized by the British East India Company from the last Maharaja of the Sikh Empire in 1849, and presented to Queen Victoria the following year.)

Nevertheless, the King himself had no hesitation in pronouncing that his peoples were free. As Cecil Beaton observed, the only faltering in the sonorous speech came at the end of the fourth sentence: 'The Queen and I wish health and happiness to you all, and we do not forget at this time of celebration those who are living under the shadow of sickness or distress.' Robert Wood, a kindly BBC sound engineer who was present at this and future broadcasts by the King, revealed in his autobiography that

George continued to have problems with the double s sound in words such as 'oppression' and 'suppression' (both of which were unfortunately unavoidable during the war). 'The King struggled without let-up,' wrote Wood. 'I was full of admiration for his perseverance, his resolution.'

We can never fully know why saying 'distress' caused particular difficulties for the King on the day of his coronation. Even so, Beaton believed that when George fought to articulate the word, 'the dramatic effect could not have been better produced by a Reinhardt [Max Reinhardt, the Austrian film and theatre director]. He has become King now.' Beaton also noted that his friend, the author Osbert Sitwell – who was in the audience at the Abbey – had told him that when the King was crowned, he displayed 'the simplicity of movement & gesture of a great actor'.

These interpretations are not, of course, the full story; and although Lionel Logue was himself an amateur actor, this does not necessarily mean that he taught the King to perform as if on stage. Nevertheless, Robert Wood's account of the transmission of the coronation – which he oversaw as the BBC's chief engineer in charge of external broadcasting – reveals that the occasion was as much a public spectacle as a devout religious ceremony. It was, wrote Wood, 'the most complicated broadcast the BBC had ever attempted . . . we used 472 miles of wire and 12 tons of equipment'. Less than six months after MI5 had secretly wiretapped the telephone lines of Edward VIII and his brother (in a clandestine surveillance operation that involved the discreet support of the head of the General Post Office), an entirely new system of wiring was required for the coronation broadcast, again with the help of GPO engineers. 'I had to think of all sorts of details, even down to the hiring of full morning dress for the engineers working inside the Abbey,' recalled Wood, 'complete with top hats and grey gloves.' In addition to the commentaries for the English-speaking audiences, 'the service was also covered in Czech, Danish, Dutch, Finnish, Flemish, French, German, Hungarian, Japanese, Norwegian, Spanish, Swedish and Serbo-Croat'. Wood set up fifty-eight microphones, including thirty-two concealed within Westminster Abbey: 'we did a nice little job of camouflage, hiding them in chinks of masonry, under prayer stools, in chandeliers and lecterns. We even managed to tuck one into each arm of Edward the Confessor's chair, which would be used for the actual enthronement, and put a third on its carved back. The results more than rewarded us.'

Despite Wood's meticulous preparations, and the careful rehearsals with clerics, George VI's own diary of the coronation reveals that there were moments of muddle, as those around him stumbled or fumbled with the props. When the solemn moment came for the monarch to take his sacred oath, the Archbishop held out the Order of Service for him to read, 'but horror of horrors his thumb covered the words of the Oath.' Another bishop stood on the King's ceremonial robe, and nearly tripped him up. ('I had to tell him to get off it pretty sharpish as I nearly fell down.') And the actual placing of the crown on the King's head was equally fraught: 'I had taken every precaution as I thought to see that the Crown was put on the right way round, but the Dean & the Archbishop had been juggling with it so much that I never did know whether it was right or not.'

Fortunately, none of the bungling, nor the broadcasting, appeared to detract from the emotional resonance of the ceremony. Queen Mary, who had witnessed the coronation of her husband's parents, Edward VII and Queen Alexandra, as well as being crowned alongside her husband in 1911, wrote in her diary approvingly: 'Bertie & E. looked so well when they came in & did it all too beautifully. The Service was wonderful & impressive – we were all much moved.' If Queen Mary's clipped diction was a subtle reminder of emotional repression – or suppression – then her son's stammer might have prompted a more profound understanding of the meaning of distress. And at a time when Hitler's endless torrent of speeches was an indication of the fluency of fascism, George VI's hesitancy suggested that the meaning of each word truly mattered. (The American author John Updike, who addressed his speech impediment in his memoir, *Self-consciousness*, has written movingly that 'those who stutter win, in the painful pauses of their demonstration that speech isn't entirely natural, a respectful attention, a tender alertness. Words are, we are reassured, precious.')

Thus George VI rose to the challenge of wearing the crown, while those around him found their own ways to adjust to the shifting circumstances. As the Duke of Windsor knitted, and Wallis fretted, Lilibet watched from the sidelines. Owen Morshead, the Royal Librarian, described her arrival at the coronation in a letter to his aunt: 'the two darling little Princesses in their full kit, their embryo trains looking as if they would grow with their wearers . . . little Princess Margaret very sweetly lifted up the front of her dress in ascending the steps, looking across surreptitiously to observe how her bigger sister was tackling it.'

The eleven-year-old Lilibet did not stumble or trip on the steps to the Abbey; but no one (including herself) could have predicted how she would tackle the path that lay ahead. In his diary, Cecil Beaton wrote – without any context or explanation – a list of what he described as 'three Coronation nightmares'. Two are mildly comic: the Archbishop of Canterbury dreamt that he had to crown Mrs Simpson; and the Duchess of Kent dreamt that she had to wear her mother-in-law Queen Mary's hat. The third is more enigmatic, and has long remained in my mind: 'Princess Elizabeth dreamt that she was invisible.' For Beaton – an ambitious social climber and fashion photographer for whom visibility was everything – to be hidden would indeed be nightmarish. But for a little princess in an embryo train, a cloak conferring invisibility might very well have been the magical stuff of dreams.

Princess Elizabeth arriving at Westminster Abbey for the coronation.

Queen Elizabeth arriving in Paris, wearing a white ensemble by Norman Hartnell, to be greeted by the French president, Albert Lebrun, July 1938.

THE WHITE WARDROBE

On 19 July 1938 the King and Queen departed from Buckingham Palace to undertake the first state visit of their reign: a trip to France, which had been delayed for three weeks after the death of the Queen's mother, Lady Strathmore. The tour was a vital one, intended to show the unity of the French and British democracies in the face of the rising threat from the fascist dictatorships of Germany and Italy. While there could be no question of cancelling the royal journey, the Queen's clothes needed to be redesigned, to reflect the fact that she was now in mourning.

Norman Hartnell had already been commissioned, earlier that year, to create her entire wardrobe for the visit; as he recalled in his memoir, he had designed thirty 'grand dresses to be worn from morning to midnight under the most critical eyes in the world'. These had originally been made in what he described as 'many lovely colourings which were now unwearable'. Summoned to the palace for an urgent meeting with the Queen to discuss whether she should don funereal black in Paris, Hartnell 'ventured my own solution to the problem. "Is not white a Royal prerogative for mourning, Your Majesty?"' His suggestion was accepted – it formed an appropriate way to honour the medieval tradition of French queens wearing white mourning (*en deuil blanc*) – and Hartnell immediately set to work. 'It was settled that I was to pass, as it were, a magic wand over the whole collection and transform all the dresses into white in the fortnight that was left to us.' At least no specialist dyeing of matching colours would be required, but nevertheless the task was immense for Hartnell and his seamstresses, and the Queen needed to have new fittings. Six days before the departure for Paris, she wrote to her mother-in-law Queen Mary: 'I am nearly demented with rushing up & down & trying to order & try on all my white things for Paris!'

In the midst of these frantic preparations, the King succumbed to gastric influenza, and was confined to bed for several days. Tensions were increased due to intelligence reports of a potential assassination plot by Spanish anarchists, while the French government feared the possibility of an attack on the King and Queen by the Gestapo. These risks were taken seriously: only four years previously, King Alexander of Yugoslavia had been assassinated in France by a Bulgarian revolutionary (and the French foreign minister died in the same attack).

The outlook for Europe as a whole was even darker as the King and Queen readied themselves for their departure. Hitler had invaded Austria in March that year, and was showing every sign of seizing Czechoslovakia. As the Nazi troops were marching into Vienna, the British prime minister, Neville Chamberlain, was negotiating with the Italian dictator Benito Mussolini, attempting to reach a diplomatic agreement between their two countries. Chamberlain had also made it clear that he was not prepared to stand in the way of Hitler's ambitions by embarking on what he regarded as an unwinnable war. ('You have only to look at the map,' Chamberlain wrote to his sister on 20 March 1938, 'to see that nothing that France or we could do could possibly save Czechoslovakia from being overrun by the Germans . . . I have therefore abandoned any idea of giving guarantees to Czechoslovakia, or to the French in connection with their obligations to that country.') The French premier Édouard Daladier hastened to London the following month, and was not reassured by his conversations there, nor when he dined at Windsor Castle. According to William Bullitt, the well-connected American ambassador in Paris who reported directly to President Roosevelt, Daladier now believed 'Chamberlain [to be] a desiccated stick; the King a moron; and the Queen an excessively ambitious woman who would be ready to sacrifice every other country in the world in order that she might remain Queen Elizabeth of England . . . He felt that England had become so feeble and senile that the British would give away every possession of their friends rather than stand up to Germany and Italy.' Although the ambassador attributed these views to Daladier, the comments about the King and Queen in his letter to Roosevelt sound as if they came directly from the Duchess of Windsor, whose company Bullitt enjoyed – so much so that he and Wallis were rumoured to be having an affair. The Duke of Windsor, for his part, was still said to be 'very pro-German', and greatly irked that he and Wallis were not going to be invited to any of the royal banquets in Paris, nor received by the King and Queen while they were in France.

Against this troubled and turbulent background, and a fraying Entente Cordiale, did it really matter which colour or style the Queen might wear in Paris? What use were white lace crinolines against the dark forces of fascism that had recently paraded during Hitler's triumphant visit to Italy in May, when legions of Mussolini's Blackshirts goose-stepped in their polished jackboots, raising their arms in the Nazi salute? The Rome correspondent for *The Times* reported at the beginning of May that the preparations for Hitler's arrival were 'stupendous', costing between £3 million to £4 million. 'A new railway station and a new road (the Viale Adolf Hitler) have been built for the Führer's arrival in Rome . . . acres of grandstands for spectators have been set up. Grandiose effects of decoration and illumination have been devised, not only in Rome but in Florence and Naples as well.' The Italian police chief was liaising with Himmler himself, continued the correspondent, to ensure the safety of Hitler, with 4,000 additional men on duty. Meanwhile, the largest stage in the world had been built for a production of Wagner's *Lohengrin*, and the opera would be performed 'by a giant orchestra' of musicians from 'all the principal opera houses of Italy'.

When Hitler arrived by train in Rome on 3 May 1938, he was greeted by both Mussolini and the diminutive king of Italy, Victor Emmanuel III. Victor was only five foot – hence his nickname of 'Il Piccolo' ('the little one') – but perhaps by way of compensation, he had a very large moustache and a rather tall wife; not that women were much in evidence during Hitler's time in Italy. The Führer's secret girlfriend, Eva Braun, had accompanied him to Rome on his private train, but stayed in a separate hotel to him. Nor were they seen in public together (instead she amused herself by going shopping for crocodile handbags and fashionable shoes from her favourite designer, Salvatore Ferragamo). Mussolini's military demonstrations were a gigantic expression of bombastic masculinity: as *The Times* testified, these were vast spectacles 'on a scale to impress even German imaginations'. Almost the entire Italian naval fleet – including 200 ships and 90 submarines – was assembled in the Bay of Naples, performing exercises 'to demonstrate its power, speed and efficiency'. The Italian Air Force gave another show of strength, with 300 planes bombing targets with real explosives; while 400 tanks were paraded in front of the Führer in Rome, alongside massed ranks of infantrymen. After a week of fascist pomp and fireworks, Hitler returned by train to Berlin, where the station was bedecked in the colours of Germany and Italy; he was greeted by salvos of rockets, and yet more cheering crowds. The Berlin correspondent for *The Times* reported that Hitler had sent a telegram to King Victor Emmanuel, declaring that 'the spirit of German–Italian friendship . . . has been strengthened afresh', and wrote to Mussolini to say that 'the community of ideas between the Fascist and National-Socialist Movements is a sure guarantee that the true comradeship which unites the two of us will be carried on forever by our peoples'.

Hence the crucial importance of the British state visit to France, which was conducted with a powerful sense of pageantry, as if to prove that democracy would not be outshone by fascism. The King and Queen sailed from Dover aboard the Royal Navy vessel HMS *Enchantress*, accompanied by eight destroyers and eighteen RAF planes. Midway across the Channel, they were met by seven French naval ships, all flying Union Jacks, and as they entered the port of Boulogne, a statue of Britannia was unveiled as a memorial to the first British troops to land in France in August 1914. The historic military alliance between the two countries had already been heralded in the French press: 'France will never forget that a million soldiers of the British Empire sleep beneath her soil,' declared one newspaper in advance of the royal arrival.

Having departed London clad in black mourning, the Queen changed into a white outfit on the train to Paris. *The Times* reported in unusual detail on this and subsequent outfits, as well as announcing that the designer Norman Hartnell would be 'in attendance during the visit'. Readers were informed that when the Queen arrived in Paris, she was wearing a 'reception gown and coat in white crêpe . . . with softly draped bodice; three-quarter coat luxuriously trimmed with silver fox; Napoleon hat turned off the face with feather mounts of shaded black-and-white Paradise plumes; black velvet handbag and gloves'. The King and Queen were welcomed at a newly decorated train station by the French president, Albert Lebrun, and his wife, and thousands of white doves were released into the skies above Paris. The opulent apartments where they stayed at the Quai d'Orsay, the French Foreign Ministry, had been especially decorated for them, at great cost: new silks were woven and luxurious bathrooms installed; paintings and tapestries were brought from the Louvre; the bed and desk arranged in the King's room were formerly the possessions of Napoleon; and the Queen's bed had belonged to Marie Antoinette. (Disappointingly, history does not relate how Elizabeth felt about sleeping in the bed of the last queen of France, who had lost her head to the revolutionaries' guillotine in 1793.)

Just as the Italians had bedecked Rome with swastikas in honour of Hitler, British flags fluttered everywhere in Paris, including one said to be the largest ever made, flying from the Eiffel Tower. These diplomatic courtesies were returned in the form of the Queen's clothes, for Hartnell had taken great care to incorporate French fabrics and emblems into his designs. Thus, at the state banquet at the Élysée Palace on the evening of their arrival, the Queen wore what *The Times* described as a 'Pompadour dress with crinoline skirt entirely covered with bands of silver Valenciennes lace, mounted on tulle, the lace re-embroidered with paillettes and diamonds'. In his memoir, Hartnell disclosed that the billowing skirt for this gown had used 'hundreds of yards' of French lace, and was 'sprinkled with silver'.

White cloth had already become fashionable in the expert hands of Parisian couturiers such as Madeleine Vionnet and Jeanne Lanvin; for if the little black dress was synonymous with the Jazz Age of the 1920s, the mood had swung in the aftermath of the Wall Street Crash in one of those apparently contradictory yet powerful shifts in style. Coco Chanel, the great proponent of black as an emblem of chic, led the way in designing and wearing long white gowns from 1930 onwards, and described this as the era of 'candid innocence and white satin', creating a counterpoint to the dark days of the Depression. Where Hartnell differed from Chanel was in his choice of a neo-Victorian shape for the elaborate evening gowns, though several of his designs for day dresses reflected the more modern, slim silhouette favoured by the Paris couture houses.

This was evident in the first outfit worn by the Queen on Tuesday, 20 July, when she appeared in a 'chalk-white crêpe morning ensemble', her short coat trimmed with cuffs of 'snow-white fox', and her hat embellished with French lilies of the valley. On the same morning, the King was seen in the full dress uniform of an Admiral of the Fleet when he went to the Arc de Triomphe with a cavalry escort to lay a wreath at the Tomb of the Unknown Soldier. Following lunch at the British Embassy, the royal couple accompanied President and Madame Lebrun to an exhibition of British paintings at the Louvre. Having already changed twice (her second outfit of the day was an 'ensemble in ivory-white lace', worn with a 'little hat of white straw' adorned with ostrich feathers), Queen Elizabeth emerged in yet another new look for an afternoon garden party at the Bagatelle in the Bois de Boulogne. This, said *The Times*, was 'a diaphanous' frock of 'crisp white lace', but Hartnell's account is far more romantic: 'The Queen wore a dress that trailed on the green grass of the lawns . . . It was of the finest cobweb lace and tulle and with it was worn a sweeping hat delicately bordered with white osprey.' Much to Hartnell's delight, while the Queen was watching an outdoor performance of ballet dancers at the garden party, 'she opened a parasol of transparent lace and tulle . . . At a stroke, she resuscitated the art of the parasol makers of Paris and London.'

Although Hartnell had feared the 'critical eyes' of the French press

Queen Elizabeth in a white gown by Norman Hartnell, attending a garden party with George VI during their state visit to France, July 1938.

Hartnell's illustration of a gown for the Queen's white wardrobe.

finding fault with his designs, their praise was fulsome. In fact, the only disparaging remarks were made by Lady Diana Cooper, who had travelled out to Paris to attend several events, including the first night's banquet, where she sat next to the King. As she subsequently revealed in a letter to her friend Conrad Russell, their conversation soon strayed into gossip about the notorious Mitford sisters. When Lady Diana mentioned that Diana Mitford 'lives in sin with Oswald Mosley', the King replied, 'They say her sister lives in sin with Hitler, but I don't believe it'; then added, 'He doesn't do anything like that, does he?' Diana went on to tell Russell that 'the Queen's figure [is] better, I really think', but she was unimpressed by her 'unfortunate dress, hooped in the wrong place, made of silver'. *The Times* found no such fault with Hartnell's shimmering series of evening gowns; amongst the 'loveliest of all' was the one in which Queen Elizabeth attended the Opéra: 'white duchess satin panniered with draperies of white satin and flounced with silver lace entirely embroidered with diamonds and silver paillettes. Clusters of white camellias . . . strewn on the skirt . . . A regal cape of snow-white ermine.' The lines were particularly reminiscent of those that the King had pointed out to Hartnell in the nineteenth-century Winterhalter portraits at Buckingham Palace. Indeed, *The Times* even referred to another of the Queen's crinoline evening gowns as a 'Winterhalter frock of white tulle, lightly embroidered with silver thread tracery and re-embroidered by hand with the finest silver paillettes'.

In his memoir, Hartnell related being invited to the Quai d'Orsay one evening, so that Queen Elizabeth could thank him personally for his creation of the white wardrobe. Hartnell was thrilled to see the royal couple in all their finery: 'The King was in his Field Marshal's full uniform of scarlet and gold and his Orders glittered under the candelabra. The Queen was wearing her white, gold and silver crinoline dress, with the vermillion sash of the Legion of Honour.' Hartnell, too, received an official accolade when he was appointed an Officier d'Académie by the French government the following year for his services to fashion. Equally gratifying, he wrote, were 'the warm congratulations' from Parisian couturiers. These included Christian Dior, who would later tell the British press (after his own 1947 New Look collection had made him world-famous): 'Whenever I try to think of something particularly beautiful, I think always of those lovely dresses that Mr Hartnell made for your beautiful Queen when she visited Paris.'

Rather to everyone's surprise, a mood of royalist gaiety seemed to seize Paris. On 21 July the *Daily Mirror* ran a front-page picture of Queen Elizabeth posing gracefully in her Hartnell garden party outfit, accompanied by the banner headline: SHE IS QUEEN OF TWO NATIONS. Beneath, an unnamed French diplomat was quoted as saying: 'Today France is a monarchy again. We have taken your Queen to our hearts. From now on she rules over two nations.'

In her column from Paris for the *New Yorker*, Janet Flanner observed: 'What was dryly planned as a necessary, expensive, and elaborate diplomatic gesture, a last-minute motion to help preserve European peace, irrationally turned into a wholesale good time for all concerned, as if no one had a care in the world. Paris went on a four-day spree of cheering.' In planning and executing the entertainment, Flanner continued, the republican French showed 'their genius for royal fêtes', and for all the heavy security in place to protect the King and Queen, 'the public had the time of its life'. Synchronised fireworks flared from the Eiffel Tower, multi-coloured fountains played along the Seine, and grand Parisian monuments were floodlit and festooned, draped in cloth of gold, or scarlet tapestries, or giant tricolours. There was even a touch of wit – of the sort that would never appear at a Nazi rally – in the shape of two Loch Ness monsters that bobbed in the Seine to amuse the King and Queen as they travelled by boat down the river.

Nevertheless, as Flanner noted, the military review at Versailles, during which 50,000 French soldiers passed before the King, was 'of course the real point of the visit, despite all the lovely fuss and feathers. For patriots and militarists, it was a splendid and picturesque sight.' And the parading army, she continued, 'did France proud. It looked disciplined, virile, and well-tailored, and it put on a stunning show.'

While the King and President Lebrun inspected the troops, the Queen visited the Hertford British Hospital, of which she had become patron the previous year, wearing on this occasion a cream day dress and matching jacket. She then travelled by train with Madame Lebrun to join their husbands at the Palace of Versailles, and changed yet again, for a luncheon held in the magnificent Galerie des Glaces (or Hall of Mirrors). Hartnell had designed a highly wrought gown for the Queen to wear in this setting: floor-length white silk organdie, entirely hand-embroidered in *broderie anglaise*, its full skirt further embellished with white organza flowers, and worn with a dramatic black velvet sash.

Diana Cooper was also a guest at Versailles, and described the tableau in her memoir, without any of the cutting spite that occasionally flashes like a sharp knife through the pages of her private diaries: 'We lunched in the Galerie des Glaces, with thirteen glasses apiece for the thirteen precious wines, all bottled on the birthdays of presidents and kings.' They were served 'feather-light delicacies' by waiters in formal livery, complete with powdered hair. Afterwards, the guests strolled to the Chapel of Versailles, where a 'heavenly choir sang Monteverdi, and the Roi Soleil flooded the scene with dazzling shafts of light'.

Suddenly, the choir was drowned out by the roar of aeroplanes flying overhead in a military display, 'casting menacing shadows across the serenity of the service.' Later that evening, Diana joined the crowds outside the Quai d'Orsay, cheering as the King and Queen came out onto the balcony to acknowledge them. 'I can never forget it. To the French the Royal Visit seemed a safeguard against the dreaded war. That at least is what they told me but I could see nothing to allay fears.' She was not alone in her premonition of imminent danger. Her husband's political ally, Winston Churchill – who had been invited to Paris with his wife Clementine as guests of the French government – wrote an elegiac article for the *Daily Telegraph* celebrating 'the charm and elegance' of the state visit, while implying that such gentle beauty could not endure. 'The scenes at Bagatelle, at the Opéra, in the chapel of Versailles . . . might well have been devised to show how much there is in human life above and beyond the blare of trumpets or the webs of diplomacy . . . Poor indeed

Queen Elizabeth visiting the Australian National Memorial at the Villers-Bretonneux military cemetery, July 1938.

must be the heart which could not delight in this day-dream amid the mellow sunshine of Freedom and France.'

By then, Churchill's trenchant warnings about the rising menace of the Nazis were being brushed aside by Chamberlain and his Cabinet; and George VI was one of many who hoped that the prime minister was right in pursuing a policy of appeasement rather than aggression. In the wake of the apocalyptic brutality of the First World War, a longing for a lasting peace was understandable. After all, the Treaty of Versailles, which was supposed to promise an end to all conflict with Germany, had been signed in the grand Hall of Mirrors on 28 June 1919, less than two decades previously. Yet Hitler, in railing against the humiliation inflicted on his country by that very peace treaty, was echoing a widely held view, and the prospect of another conflagration seemed ever more threatening.

A grim martial spectre loomed again on the final day of the tour, when the King and Queen visited Villers-Bretonneux in northern France, for the unveiling of a memorial to nearly 11,000 Australian soldiers who died in battle there during the Great War, many of them with no known graves. After the King had laid his official wreath, the Queen spontaneously added a small posy of fragile red poppies that she had been given by a local child, who had gathered them from the surrounding fields. It is said that when Hitler saw the newsreel of the ceremony, he called Queen Elizabeth 'the most dangerous woman in Europe'. Given Hitler's own understanding of the power of visual iconography – evident in the technically brilliant propaganda films he commissioned from Leni Riefenstahl – he was well placed to judge the effect of Queen Elizabeth in action. Unlike Riefenstahl's expertly crafted Nazi documentaries of the Nuremberg rallies and the Berlin Olympics, the film footage of the royal couple in France is flickering and unsteady. It is also monochrome, so if you watch it now, you cannot see the vivid poppies, nor the medals worn by the soldiers and dignitaries gathered for the memorial ceremony. But Queen Elizabeth is instantly recognisable, her Hartnell day dress softly glimmering amidst the dark military uniforms, her upturned hat of white felt trimmed with white feather wings.

Marianne (right, in an ermine cape) and France
(left, in an embroidered Ascot dress), 1938.

THE DOLLS

While the King and Queen were in Paris in July 1938, they were given gifts that manifested the finest French *savoir faire*, and perhaps hinted at the delicacy of diplomacy and fragility of peace: a priceless collection of Lalique glass and a Sèvres porcelain dinner service. Their two daughters, who had not accompanied them, also received presents: a selection of French literature in blue leather-bound books for Princess Elizabeth, and a child-sized florist's shop for Princess Margaret Rose. But it was the gift from 'the children of France' to the English princesses that received most attention in the press: two dolls named Marianne and France, complete with wardrobes of superb Parisian couture, cases of exquisite jewellery, and a pair of sleek Citroën sports cars (one in olive green, the other cornflower blue). When the *Illustrated London News* published a full page of photographs showing the preparations for the royal visit to Paris, the largest image was of Marianne and France seated in their motor cars, with two little girls gazing at them admiringly from the side of the road.

The tradition of sending dolls with fashionable trousseaux to the daughters of European royalty dated back many centuries, particularly as betrothal gifts. The French King Henri IV, for example, gave several such dolls to his bride-to-be, Marie de' Medici, before their wedding in 1600. An even earlier selection of richly dressed dolls accompanied the six-year-old Princess Isabella, daughter of Charles VI, when in 1396 she travelled from her home in France to England as the child bride of Richard II. Isabella had just turned seven when she was crowned at Westminster Abbey in January 1397; she was widowed only three years later, and died aged nineteen; a queen in name, but her life lived as a pawn in the power struggles of the medieval monarchy.

Whereas past royal dolls were adorned in finery made by court dressmakers, Marianne and France displayed the art of contemporary couturiers. Regular reports on the making of their wardrobes appeared in the newspaper *Le Journal* from May 1938 onwards, with special stories for younger readers describing 'the fairy tale' of the dolls. The pair were christened as a result of a poll conducted by *Le Journal*, which announced that Marianne, a brunette, was the elder of the two, and that France was a blonde whose eyes sometimes looked 'a little sad'. In the words of *Le Journal*, their 'godmother' was Madame Georges Bonnet, wife of the French foreign minister, but they were also 'our daughters, the ambassadresses', preparing for a new life in England as 'the best-dressed dolls in the world'.

Their wardrobes were made by many – although not all – of the leading couture houses in Paris, including Jeanne Lanvin, Lucien Lelong, Maggy Rouff, Jeanne Paquin, Jean Patou, Robert Piguet, Marcel Rochas and Madeleine Vionnet. (The notable exceptions were Coco Chanel and Elsa Schiaparelli.) Louis Vuitton supplied their luxurious luggage; Cartier crafted the enchanting coral and lapis lazuli jewellery; Hermès contributed elegant handbags, purses and gloves; precious perfumes in crystal flacons came from Bourjois, Coty, Guerlain and Lancôme. The dolls – along with their sumptuous belongings – were exhibited at the Marigny Theatre in Paris on 16 and 17 July 1938 (the weekend before the royal visit). The following day, *Le Journal* reported: 'an endless procession of admirers had patiently queued to see, at last, the trousseaux, possessions and the two "ambassadresses" about which they had read so much'. So popular proved the exhibition – with adult visitors far outnumbering children – that the opening hours were extended on the Sunday, from eight in the morning until eight at night; all the while, 'impassively, the dolls of France watched the crowds go by with wide-open eyes'.

Marianne and France had been constructed in the famous Jumeau doll workshops; or as *Le Journal* put it, more whimsically, 'a cheerful-looking factory where every day of the year little porcelain girls and boys are born'. But their custom-made wigs were fashioned out of human hair by the coiffeur Valentin, and their eerily spectral gaze was the work of Monsieur Peigne, a manufacturer of artificial eyes for human patients. This may explain why, on the only occasion I saw the dolls in a glass vitrine at Windsor Castle, my thoughts wandered uneasily to 'The Sandman', a macabre short story by the nineteenth-century German author E. T. A. Hoffmann. This nightmarish tale, which describes the sinister Sandman stealing children's eyes, features prominently in Sigmund Freud's influential essay 'The Uncanny' (first published in German as 'Das Unheimliche' in 1919, and in English in 1925). So, too, does a glass-eyed doll that plays a pivotal role in Hoffmann's story. Freud defines uncanniness as a mingling of unease and the oddly familiar: an association suggested by the word *unheimlich*, which derives from *Heim*, meaning home. Therein lies a province of creeping dread, where madmen might appear at the threshold, mutilating children and destroying families as swiftly as smashing glass. Given that Freud was writing his essay soon after the end of the First World War, when a generation of soldiers had been killed or disfigured amidst the mud and misery of no-man's-land, such a realm of gothic horror seemed all too close to home.

Whatever one's feelings about dolls and other tropes of the uncanny – doppelgängers and doubles, puppets or people who look 'dead behind the eyes' – there is another oddly unsettling dimension to Marianne and France. For while the majority of their wardrobe is distinctly adult, their bodies are those of young children (in which sense they are reminiscent of the diminutive Princess Isabella). Each doll is just under three feet tall, with elastic cording threaded through their limbs and torso to allow for movement. Of the few garments that look more appropriate for children, one was supplied by Robert Piguet (where the young Christian Dior was working at the time) – a blue woollen 'school dress' – and the furriers

Jungmann created a girlish grey lamb coat and muff, trimmed with crimson velvet. Jean Patou designed the only outfit to incorporate trousers – a chic yachting ensemble, combined with a blue blazer, white linen shirt and a peaked sailor's cap. The dolls' shoes are flat, worn with socks rather than stockings; but for the most part, Marianne and France were adorned with glamorous gowns or alluring negligées, often replicas of the latest fashions of the season. And yet they also came equipped with prams and monogrammed cots, as if they were still babies.

It took more than a week to pack the dolls and their accoutrements into twenty crates to be shipped to the French Embassy in London. But once they arrived there in August 1938, everything came to a halt. The ambassadresses were sidelined by the all too real diplomatic crisis over Czechoslovakia, where Hitler was clearly determined to annex the predominantly German-speaking Sudeten region. The royal family were relaxing on their Scottish estate as the Nazis finalised their military plans, although Chamberlain (a guest at Balmoral at the time) reassured them that there was no immediate cause for alarm. The violence and venom of Hitler's speech at the Nuremberg Rally on 12 September suggested otherwise. Queen Mary, who listened to this on the radio, wrote to the King to say that she was 'horrified at [Hitler's] voice & shouting & what he said, so theatrical and awful'. But her conclusion reflected Chamberlain's own view: 'God grant we may not have war . . . the Czechs are not worth fighting for.'

Meanwhile, the French prime minister, Édouard Daladier, was under increasing pressure, given his country's position as Czechoslovakia's closest ally. In early September the French ambassador in London, Charles Corbin, had informed the British Foreign Secretary, Lord Halifax, that France 'would have to mobilise and declare war if a German attack was made on Czechoslovakia'. This meant that the British, in turn, should come to the aid of their French allies; yet when Daladier and his foreign minister, Georges Bonnet, arrived in London for talks on 18 September, nothing was resolved. By then, Chamberlain had flown back from the first of his meetings with Hitler, convinced that he had prevented the outbreak of war. He flew to Germany again on 22 September, his famous

The dolls in their sports cars in Paris (top); and (above) displayed at St James's Palace in London, December 1938.

umbrella clasped firmly in his hand; and Daladier and Bonnet travelled to London three days later. The King also returned to Buckingham Palace from Balmoral in mid-September, feeling that he should be close to the prime minister during the emergency, and offered to write personally to Hitler; a suggestion that Chamberlain declined.

George VI was unsurprisingly bewildered by the diplomatic situation. 'Everything is in a maze,' he said to Tommy Lascelles on 17 September. Two days later, writing to his wife (who had remained at Balmoral with their daughters), the King confessed despairingly, 'My brain is getting addled.' On 21 September, Elizabeth came to London to support her husband, and found the city already embarking on preparations for war. Trenches were being dug in the parks; anti-aircraft batteries were erected on Horse Guards Parade and Westminster Bridge; and gas masks were being issued. Mussolini had used poison gas to devastating effect in his war against the Abyssinians in 1935, and there were fears that the Nazis would do the same.

On 27 September, both the Queen and the prime minister made separate speeches, each of which was broadcast by the BBC to an audience of millions. The royal couple were supposed to have travelled together to Clydebank in Scotland, to launch the world's largest passenger liner, *Queen Elizabeth*. Given the gravity of the international situation, the King remained in London, and so the Queen went without him; as she departed by train the evening before, the stations were filled with children being evacuated from the capital. At Glasgow, she was joined by her daughters, who were brought there from Balmoral to witness the ceremony. The Queen had been asked to use the occasion to deliver a special message from her husband (in a speech written by his private secretary Alec Hardinge), and she did so in a clear and confident voice. The King, she declared, 'bids the people of this country to be of good cheer, in spite of the dark clouds hanging over them, and indeed, over the whole world. He knows well that, as ever before in critical times, they will keep cool heads and brave hearts; he knows, too, that they will place entire confidence in their leaders, who, under God's providence, are striving their utmost to find a just and peaceful solution to the grave problems which confront them.' She paid tribute, as well, to the ships that crossed the Atlantic 'like shuttles in a mighty loom, weaving a fabric of friendship and understanding between the people of Britain and the United States'. It was 'altogether fitting', she continued, that 'the noblest vessel ever built in Britain . . . should be dedicated to this service'.

Later that evening, Chamberlain struck a more ominous note in his speech to the nation: 'How horrible, fantastic, incredible it is that we should be digging trenches and trying on gas masks here because of a quarrel in a faraway country between people of whom we know nothing.' Duff Cooper was one of a minority in the Cabinet who spoke out forcefully against appeasement; he told his wife Diana that Chamberlain seemed like 'a man bewitched and bound by Hitler's magnetic spell'. Meanwhile, Diana joined the Women's Voluntary Service, to help assemble gas masks for civilians, 'clamping snouts and schnozzles on to rubber masks . . . and distributing them to queues of men and women. Mothers would ask me for small ones for children. There were none.' The Home Office was forced to issue a statement that there was no 'satisfactory equivalent of a gas mask for babies'. Instead, the official government advice 'in the event of a gas attack' was to wrap the baby 'completely in a blanket', and carry it to the nearest air-raid shelter. As to where that shelter might be, the Home Office provided an illustrated booklet outlining how to construct 'a quick refuge for six' in the back garden, using a 'corrugated iron roof, sandbags or boxes filled with earth, and old boards'. Those taking shelter should nevertheless don their gas masks, 'as the trench would not be gas-proof'.

Meanwhile Chamberlain had returned to Germany once again, to meet Hitler and Mussolini in Munich on 29 September; and the infamous Munich Agreement was signed the following morning, forcing the Czechoslovakians to surrender strategic territory to the Nazis. In the alarming circumstances that prevailed, it is understandable that the royal family, along with a significant majority of the British population, greeted the news with relief. When Neville Chamberlain landed at Heston aerodrome, waving a piece of paper signed by Hitler, and promising that it brought 'peace for our time', he was driven straight to Buckingham

Palace where the King wished to congratulate him personally. Afterwards the royal couple took the prime minister and his wife out onto the balcony overlooking the Mall, to wave to the cheering crowds. 'What an excellent photo of you two with the Chamberlains,' wrote Queen Mary to her son the next day. 'The paper the P.M. & Hitler signed is most interesting, let us hope that at last our 2 countries will come together.'

Queen Elizabeth, for her part, wrote to Chamberlain's wife Annie, saying that she 'must feel so proud & glad that through sheer courage and great wisdom he has been able to achieve so much for us & for the World. Our gratitude is beyond words.' Yet as William Shawcross observes in his official biography of Queen Elizabeth, 'the extent to which the King and the Queen so publicly embraced Chamberlain and his policies, on the balcony of the Palace, was imprudent, if not unconstitutional . . . The monarch must always be above party politics and the Munich agreement was, despite its popularity, controversial and was still subject to a debate and vote in the House of Commons. Indeed Labour and the Liberals voted against it.' Clement Attlee, the leader of the Labour Party, went further, making an impassioned speech in the House of Commons (on 3 October) about what he saw as the betrayal of Czechoslovakia, and of democracy, describing the Munich Agreement as 'one of the greatest diplomatic defeats that this country and France have ever sustained'.

Duff Cooper resigned in protest at the agreement (on the same day as Attlee's speech), and when he made his way to Buckingham Palace to hand in his seals of office, he met with the King. 'He said he could not agree with me,' Cooper wrote in his diary, 'but he respected those who had the courage of their convictions.' Queen Mary, however, was irritated by those politicians, such as Cooper, Attlee and Winston Churchill, who remained vocal opponents of Chamberlain. 'He brought home Peace,' she wrote to the King; 'why can't they be grateful?' For once, the royal family found themselves in accord with the Duke of Windsor, who sent his heartfelt congratulations to Chamberlain. (The Duke had been keen to visit Hitler again, as a mediator, and was therefore full of praise for Chamberlain in taking such 'a bold step'.)

In the days following the Munich Agreement, enterprising shopkeepers offered besuited Chamberlain dolls entitled 'The Peacemaker', which proved to be surprisingly popular purchases, while more than 20,000 letters of thanks poured into Downing Street, along with innumerable gifts of umbrellas, hand-knitted socks, and a silver dinner service. The *Paris-Soir* newspaper even began a campaign to present Chamberlain with a property in France, a 'House of Peace' where he could enjoy his hobby of fishing.

But the euphoria was short-lived. A British diplomat in Berlin reported that soon after Chamberlain's departure from Germany, Hitler had said: 'If ever that silly old man comes interfering here again with his umbrella, I'll kick him downstairs and jump on his stomach in front of photographers.' When several members of the Cabinet argued for rapid rearmament, they were frustrated by Chamberlain's response that this was a 'false emphasis', as there was no need for 'a new arms race'. Their exasperation was shared by Harold Macmillan, a Conservative MP who had provided sanctuary to forty Czech refugees at his country estate in Sussex; and so strong were his feelings that on Guy Fawkes Night he burned an effigy of Chamberlain on the bonfire. The future prime minister revealed that he had 'sacrificed for the purpose a black Homburg hat in quite good repair, as well as a rolled umbrella'.

Far worse was to follow. On 7 November, a junior diplomat at the German Embassy in Paris was shot and mortally wounded by a seventeen-year-old Jewish youth, whose family had just been deported from their home in Hanover and were now enduring terrible conditions, alongside thousands of other Jews, on the Polish border. The following day, the Nazis used the assassination as a pretext for introducing their latest pogrom: all Jewish newspapers and magazines were to immediately cease publication, and Jewish children could no longer attend 'Aryan' state schools. Executions ensued of Jewish prisoners at Buchenwald concentration camp; and on 9 November, a night of terror was unleashed against the Jews of Germany and Austria. Hundreds of synagogues were burned to the ground, thousands of homes looted and destroyed, tens of thousands of Jews were attacked, beaten, arrested and dispatched to concentration camps. The shards of shattered glass that filled the streets outside ransacked Jewish shops and buildings gave the night its name: Kristallnacht. In the immediate aftermath, the Nazi regime issued decrees ordering Jews to pay for the damage to their own property, while also banning them from running businesses or engaging in any other economic activity, and allowing for their assets to be transferred to 'Aryan' ownership.

Shocked condemnation of the violence followed in the British press. 'Racial hatred and hysteria seemed to have taken complete control of otherwise decent people,' wrote the Berlin correspondent of the *Daily Telegraph*; 'I saw fashionably dressed women clapping their hands and screaming with glee, while respectable middle-class mothers held up their babies to see the "fun".' Even *The Times*, whose editorial stance was strongly pro-appeasement, published a disapproving leading article: 'No foreign propagandist bent upon blackening Germany before the world could outdo the tale of burnings and beatings, of blackguardly assaults upon defenceless and innocent people, which disgraced that country yesterday.'

Five days after the devastation of Kristallnacht, a delegation of Jewish and Quaker leaders appealed directly to Chamberlain to permit the temporary admission of unaccompanied children from Germany and Austria to the United Kingdom. Following a parliamentary debate, permission was granted (although the mission would not be funded by the state, but by charitable organisations that had to guarantee £50 for every refugee). The initial group of 196 children arrived in Harwich from Berlin on 2 December, including Jewish orphans who had been left homeless after the savagery of Kristallnacht. The first train from Vienna left on 10 December with 600 children on board, and in the following nine months, almost 10,000 children travelled to England on what became known as the Kindertransport. Each child had been allowed to take only a single small suitcase with them; most of them would never again see their parents or other family members, who were murdered in the Holocaust. The final train, which was due to leave Prague on 1 September 1939, was cancelled by the German authorities. Of the 250 Jewish children who were intended to escape from Czechoslovakia that day, nearly all were sent to the Terezin concentration camp just north of Prague, and from there to the gas chambers of Auschwitz.

✣

On 15 November 1938, the same date that the first appeal was made to save Jewish children from the Nazis, the French dolls suddenly reappeared in the press, following three months of mysterious silence. *The Times* reported that the French ambassador, Charles Corbin, had personally delivered the dolls to the Queen and her daughters at Buckingham Palace on the previous evening. The following week, Princess Elizabeth wrote to her French tutor Georgina Guerin: 'We saw the dolls on the Wednesday after you left. They really are pretty. They are nearly as tall as Margaret and the dresses! Oh! It is almost impossible to say. There are long dresses for evening – one is covered in little frills . . . All the dresses are different and Marianne had a leopard-skin coat . . . The dolls have two beds, two perambulators and two little cars. They are going to be put on public display soon and the money will be given to French children in hospital, I think.'

The exhibition was held in St James's Palace in December 1938, and the proceeds from the entrance tickets were shared between a French charity and a children's hospital in the East End of London, named after the princess herself. A leader appeared in *The Times* on 9 December, welcoming both the dolls and the 'doubly happy' idea of the exhibition, while acknowledging that 'their fame has hitherto been a little overshadowed by the grosser and noisier links' that bound Britain and France together. Elizabeth and Margaret were photographed at the exhibition on 22 December; unlike the dolls, they were dressed identically in children's clothes: matching wool coats, fur gloves, white socks and simple strapped shoes. As in Paris, the attraction proved so popular that thousands queued to see the dolls, and the exhibition was extended into January 1939.

It is tempting, at this point, to cite Hilary Mantel's memorable essay 'Royal Bodies' (published in 2013 in the *London Review of Books*) that drew parallels between dolls and princesses. She described Catherine – the Duchess of Cambridge at the time – as 'becoming a jointed doll'; represented by the press as 'a shop-window mannequin, entirely defined by what she wore'; 'built by craftsmen, with a perfect plastic smile and the spindles of her limbs hand-turned and gloss-varnished.' Mantel died in September 2022, and so did not live to see the dignified manner in which Catherine (by then the Princess of Wales) announced in March 2024 that she was being treated for cancer; or her subsequent decision to withhold specific details of her outfits, in an attempt to prioritise her work, rather than her wardrobe. That said, various newspapers and social media commentators are always swift to identify the designers and prices of everything she wears.

In the more deferential age of the 1930s, no such overt comparisons were made between the French dolls and the English princesses. Instead, Marianne and France were accepted in the same spirit that they were offered: as diplomatic gifts, imbued with all the light-hearted appeal of the diminutive, yet nevertheless expressing a serious commitment to peace.

The princesses themselves never had the opportunity to play with their dolls; a marked contrast to the child-sized thatched cottage that had been a sixth birthday present to Elizabeth from the people of Wales in 1932. This was known as the Little House (Y Bwthyn Bach), and it provided an opportunity for her and her sister to be displayed as homely 'ordinary' children when they were photographed in it, while also emphasising their conventional feminine virtues, as they learned to keep the playhouse clean and tidy, like miniature housewives.

By the time their father became King, however, it was becoming clear that their education should be expanded beyond the domestic sphere, particularly in the case of Princess Elizabeth, given her position as heir to the throne. In 1938 she began rigorous twice-weekly lessons in constitutional history with Henry Marten, the vice provost of Eton College, who would later recall teaching her that the secret of the monarchy's survival for more than a millennium was its ability to adapt. Her tutor devised a challenging curriculum and a daunting reading list that included *The Law and Custom of the Constitution* by Sir William Anson, *The English*

Top: Princess Elizabeth (right, holding a doll) and her sister Margaret (left) in the Little House; and (above) Elizabeth in front of it, 1933.

Constitution by Sir Walter Bagehot, *English Social History* by G. M. Trevelyan and *Imperial Commonwealth* by Lord Elton. Marten also taught the princess about what he considered to be the most important changes that had recently affected the monarchy: firstly, the 1931 Statute of Westminster, which had founded the modern British Commonwealth by making an allegiance to the Crown the only surviving link between the United Kingdom and the self-governing, newly autonomous Dominions. (The Statute applied to Canada, the Irish Free State, South Africa, Australia, New Zealand and Newfoundland.) Secondly, the advent of broadcasting, which allowed the royal family to sustain that link by speaking directly to the millions of members of the Commonwealth around the world.

According to Miss Crawford, both the King and Queen were keen to encourage their daughters to feel that they were part of a wider community – hence the decision in the summer of 1937 to set up a Girl Guides company at Buckingham Palace, where they were schooled in team games, first aid, pitching tents and bird-watching. Even so, as Miss Crawford acknowledged, life in a palace was not conducive to creating a connection with the broader population. 'A glass curtain seems to come down between you and the outer world, between the hard realities of life and those who dwell in a court, and however hard a struggle is made to avoid it, escape is not entirely possible.'

Elizabeth admitted something similar as a young woman, when she was having her portrait painted by Pietro Annigoni in a state room at Buckingham Palace, shortly after her own accession to the throne. In his autobiography, the artist wrote that she had told him about spending hours as a child in the same magnificent drawing room, looking out of the windows. 'I loved watching the people and the cars there in the Mall,' she said. 'They all seemed so busy. I used to wonder what they were doing and where they were all going, and what they thought about outside the Palace.'

As for Marianne and France: in 1940, they were sent on a year-long tour of Canada, to raise funds to support refugees who had managed to flee there from war-torn Europe. The dolls' journey eventually took them to Ottawa, where they were entrusted to the care of Princess Alice, the wife of the Governor General of Canada, the Earl of Athlone, and a great-aunt to Princesses Elizabeth and Margaret. (No mention was made in the accompanying press coverage that Princess Alice's brother, the Duke of Coburg, was still a prominent Nazi in Germany.) The widespread publicity prompted an American publishing company to sell a book of paper dolls with cut-out clothes, reproducing an illustrated selection of the couture trousseaux designed for Marianne and France. But these paper dolls were not named after the French originals; instead, the book was titled: *Cut-Outs from the Dolls of the Royal Princesses of England.* The same company also produced *The Princess Paper Doll Book*, with a picture of Elizabeth and Margaret on the front cover wearing matching frilly dresses. Inside were several pages of 'their' clothes to cut out, and dress them up in, including riding habits, party frocks, coats and hats, all clearly designed for children.

For some unknown reason, two of the French dolls' actual possessions did remain in England: a pair of jewel cases, one in pink leather, another in blue. When the nightly air raids began in 1940, and the princesses took cover with Miss Crawford in the dungeons of Windsor Castle, their governess had already ensured that Elizabeth and Margaret had packed these cases 'with their favourite brooches, the things that they wear every day, which did not need to go into the safe'.

It was not until 1946 that the dolls returned to England as part of the Athlones' luggage, and finally ended up at Windsor Castle, where they were sporadically exhibited in a cabinet along the corridor from Queen Mary's Dolls' House. But whereas the latter – a miniature mansion designed by Sir Edward Lutyens in 1924 – remains a prime attraction for visitors of all ages, Marianne and France appear to have fallen from favour. The last time I looked for the dolls, they were nowhere to be seen; when I asked why, a curator simply sighed, and gave a small shrug. It seems the ageless ambassadresses have now been confined to storage, along with their belongings; but their watchful eyes will still be open, gazing into the darkness of their silent tomb.

FAIRY QUEEN

In May 1939, when the King and Queen embarked on a diplomatic voyage across the Atlantic to Canada and the USA, Elizabeth took with her several dozen ensembles created for the tour by Norman Hartnell, and a copy of Hitler's autobiographical manifesto. 'I am starting to read the unexpurgated version of "Mein Kampf",' she wrote to her mother-in-law, Queen Mary, from aboard ship on 8 May; 'it is very soap-box, but very interesting. Have you read it Mama?'

By this point, it was clear that appeasement had done nothing to diminish Hitler's genocidal ambitions to create a vast Nazi empire. On 15 March, German troops had marched into Prague, and Hitler declared that Czechoslovakia no longer existed. Two weeks later, in response to rumours that Germany planned to attack Poland, Chamberlain told the Polish government that Britain would come to its aid if an invasion ensued. It was in these ominous circumstances that President Roosevelt had invited the royal couple to the United States. The tour was intended as a public display of the strong and enduring links between the British and North American democracies, even though it was the first time that a reigning British sovereign had visited the US or Canada.

But there were also fears of threats to this apparent unity, both from the French Canadian separatist movement, who resented the presence of a British monarch, and the isolationists in the US who did not want to

The King and Queen in Ottawa, May 1939.

be dragged into another European war. And sceptics were already voicing their doubts about the ability of the royal couple to paper over these cracks. Take, for example, an article that appeared in the influential *Scribner's Magazine* in advance of the royal tour, which observed: 'If a public relations counsel had the power to choose from scratch which British personalities he would drop into the American scene for the greatest British profit, they would not have been King George and Queen Elizabeth. The important fact about the United States is that a large part of the country still believes that Edward, Duke of Windsor, is the rightful owner of the British throne, and that King George VI is a colorless, weak personality . . . As for Queen Elizabeth, by Park Avenue standards, she appears to be far too plump of figure, too dowdy in dress, to meet American specifications of a reigning Queen. The living contrasts of Queen Mary (as regal as a woman can be) and the Duchess of Windsor (chic and charmingly American) certainly does not help Elizabeth.'

Meanwhile, on 8 May the Duke of Windsor made what appeared to be an attempt to upstage his brother by broadcasting to the American people directly from the First World War battleground of Verdun, in an appeal for peace. The timing of his speech was unfortunate, given that the King himself had not yet arrived in America; hence Elizabeth's remark, in her letter to Queen Mary (written on the same day as the Duke of Windsor's address), 'how troublesome of him to choose such a moment'.

Equally troublesome was the fact that the royal couple were soon to be delayed by fog on their journey, marooned at sea and surrounded by immense icebergs in the same area that the *Titanic* had sunk. Tommy Lascelles, who was accompanying the King and Queen, wrote to his wife Joan to say that they were confronted by 'a wall of ice, looking like a continent, stretching across the horizon on both sides of us'. When the fog descended, he continued, one of his colleagues said that it was as if they were all dead: 'It *was* rather like that – a strange sensation of being suspended somewhere right outside the world, with no dimensions. Space was limited to the grey wall outside and time was non-existent – we might have been there three days or three months.'

Queen Elizabeth appears not to have had any such metaphysical thoughts, or at least none that she shared in her letters home. To Queen Mary she acknowledged, 'It is rather foggy, and the foghorn moans hoarsely every minute or so – such a melancholy noise.' And to her daughter Lilibet, she said their delayed journey was causing 'anxiety', but 'the little band' aboard their ship had been playing a popular dance song ('The Umbrella Man') 'which helped to cheer *me* up . . . We are all trying to behave like Guides & "smile under difficulties".' She also reminded Lilibet to enjoy her lessons with Mr Marten at Eton, and to 'learn as much as you can from him, & mark how he brings the human element into all his history – of course history *is* made by ordinary humans, & one must not forget that.'

During the six weeks of separation from their parents, Lilibet and her sister were taken on various educational expeditions by Queen Mary (including to the Tower of London and the Bank of England to see the gold in the vaults), and a widely publicised trip to London Zoo, where they were photographed riding on an elephant and meeting a panda. As was the case from her earliest childhood, Lilibet continued to learn the regal art of composure from her grandmother. When George and Elizabeth were departing from Portsmouth harbour, Queen Mary was there with Lilibet and Margaret to bid them farewell. 'The ship left punctually at 3 – it was a fine sight from the jetty – & we waved handkerchiefs,' wrote Queen Mary in her diary later that evening. 'Margaret said "I have my handkerchief" & Lilibet ansd [answered] "To wave, not to cry" – which I thought charming.' Queen Mary's own legendary self-control would be manifested two weeks later, after her stately Daimler was hit by a lorry and overturned with her inside. According to Lord Claud Hamilton, a courtier and fellow passenger who reported on the accident in a letter to Tommy Lascelles, she emerged from the wreckage badly bruised but with her dignity intact, 'as if She might have been walking down the steps at the Coronation. She had not Her hat or one curl out of place . . . The only sign of disorder was a broken hat pin and Her umbrella broken in half.' Such was Hamilton's reverence for Queen Mary that his missives always referred to 'Her' and 'She', as if she were a deity.

Lilibet was also receiving lessons in how to be royal via her mother's regular missives. Writing from Banff on 27 May 1939, the Queen told her daughter 'how important it is that the people here should see their King, & not have him only as a symbol'. She returned to this significant point again in Ontario: 'We have been almost continually "on show" . . . Every hour there are thousands & thousands of people waiting at the various stops. They are so happy to have "the King" with them, & sometimes I have tears in my eyes when one sees the emotion in their faces. It means so much to them to see the Sovereign who they are so loyal to.'

Although Elizabeth emphasised the importance of her husband being visible to the crowds, she, too, played an important role in the tour – as did her wardrobe (providing further material evidence for her daughter's understanding of how a queen must 'be seen to be believed'). Norman Hartnell, in his memoir, reveals his own grasp of what he called the 'dress diplomacy' that was vital to the success of the North American tour. He had been supplied with 'a complete and detailed itinerary' in advance of the visit, and was instructed that on 'each day there would be six or seven occasions demanding a change of costume'. Nor could the same gown be worn in different cities. 'For instance,' wrote Hartnell, 'should Her Majesty wear a magnificent dress of white satin and turquoise in Ottawa, she would not appear, even for an exactly similar occasion, in that same outfit in Montreal. The people of Montreal would expect a new and different dress and might consider it a slight if the Queen wore the Ottawa dress which they would have seen in their morning newspapers. So the task for the designer of a wardrobe for a State Visit is indeed a responsible one.' (Such an extravagant strategy no longer prevails: Catherine, Princess of Wales, is the most valuable ambassador for the contemporary British fashion industry, yet makes a point of recycling certain outfits over the years, to demonstrate her commitment to sustainability and, presumably, fiscal prudence. Even though her wardrobe contains some haute couture, she also wears affordable mass market brands, with the intention of making the monarchy seem more relatable.)

Much of the royal journey traversing Canada and the United States was undertaken by train – and so numerous were Queen Elizabeth's garments that two entire carriages were required for her forty trunks of luggage. As Hartnell wrote, her clothing needed 'to be suitable for every extreme of climate, from the sultry streets of New York in a heat wave, through the damp heat of a garden party at the White House, right up to the icy heights of the Rocky Mountains'. He was particularly pleased with his solution to the issue of what the Queen should wear at four o'clock in the morning when the Royal Train stopped at a station: 'Her Majesty was expected, with the King, to meet and greet the loyal people ranged alongside the platform. Should this be a grand dress as worn at midnight, or a little dress for breakfast? A compromise was found. It was a kind of "hostess dress", as they are known in the United States, a long flowing negligée dress in nectarine velvet touched with a narrow band of sable.'

Despite the reservations previously expressed in *Scribner's*, and the startling concept of the Queen looming into public view in the early hours of the morning wearing a fur-trimmed negligée, her appearance was widely praised. So, too, was her decision to wear a dress made of blue American wool (the fabric had been especially woven in advance by the US National Wool Growers' Association). According to a correspondent for *Time* magazine, onlookers in French-speaking Quebec described her as 'charmante' and 'chic'. 'In point of fact,' continued the reporter, 'the Queen, who has never ranked among Europe's ten best dressed women, had never looked smarter. US fashion experts, noting her clothes from news photographs, were pleasantly surprised at the Queen's style.' The only sour note was struck by a United Press journalist, who claimed that the Queen's wardrobe lacked 'oomph', and that 'several Fifth Avenue stylists' had told him, anonymously, that she seemed 'matronly' in comparison to the 'trimmer' Duchess of Windsor. But even these critics acknowledged that the Queen's 'graciousness' would 'bring back a type of woman who has been obscured by the fashions of recent years – the elegant, graceful, feminine, lady-like woman'.

Of course, it was not simply Queen Elizabeth's clothes that created a positive response, but the apparently spontaneous warmth with which

Queen Elizabeth and Eleanor Roosevelt in Washington, DC, June 1939.

she greeted the crowds – most notably when she and the King mingled with thousands of First World War veterans at the unveiling of a memorial in Ottawa. 'The Queen has a perfect genius for the right kind of publicity,' wrote Lord Tweedsmuir, the Governor General of Canada at the time, having watched her chatting with the ex-soldiers; 'the unrehearsed episodes here were marvellous.'

President Roosevelt and his wife Eleanor were similarly impressed, after the King and Queen arrived in Washington, DC, on 8 June 1939. More than 600,000 people had lined the streets of the nation's capital to welcome them, and both looked the part: George VI in his magnificent Admiral of the Fleet uniform, Elizabeth in a lavender-blue ensemble, long gloves and a feather-trimmed hat. The heat was stifling – 'burning, boiling, sweltering,' wrote the Queen to Lilibet – and as she was riding in an open carriage with Mrs Roosevelt, she unfurled a parasol to shelter from the sun. But she took care to hold it high above her head, so that she remained visible to the crowds, and continuously waved and bowed to the people on the left and right side of the carriage. Eleanor Roosevelt observed the Queen's remarkable ability to give the appearance of connecting with individuals in those vast crowds, so that 'many of them felt that her bow was really for them personally'.

Queen Elizabeth kept smiling throughout the royal visit to America: from diplomatic receptions at the British Embassy to a state dinner at the White House; from greeting hundreds of members of Congress at the Capitol to a parade through Manhattan, where an estimated 3 million people crowded the streets to see the royal couple. By the time they toured the World's Fair in New York, the King was exhausted and clenching his teeth with the strain, but the Queen's smile remained firmly in place.

After leaving Manhattan, they set off to visit the Roosevelts at their country home overlooking the Hudson River in New York State. From there, the Queen wrote to Lilibet again, and described the informal 'picnic luncheon', where they had eaten 'all our food on one plate – a little salmon, some turkey, some ham, lettuce, beans & HOT DOGS too!' During their time together, the King and the president had lengthy and productive conversations about the international crisis, and how America might support Britain should there be war with Germany. Eleanor Roosevelt, an astute observer of character, would subsequently tell a friend: 'Both [the King and Queen] interested me & I think he feels things more than she does & knows more. She is perfect as Queen, gracious, informed, saying the right thing & kind but a little self-consciously regal.'

These qualities made a lasting impression on the people who met the Queen on this historic tour, including the eight-year-old daughter of the president's aide, Harry Hopkins. Mrs Roosevelt had an affectionate relationship with Diana Hopkins, whose mother had died, and asked Queen Elizabeth if she might see her during their stay at the White House. The Queen agreed, and Diana was duly presented to the royal couple, before they left for a dinner at the British Embassy. 'The King was resplendent in his uniform,' recalled Mrs Roosevelt, 'but Diana had eyes only for the Queen, who wore a white spangled dress and a jeweled crown.' Afterwards, Mrs Roosevelt returned the 'starry-eyed little girl' to her father. 'She said: "Oh, Daddy, I have seen the Fairy Queen."'

King George and Queen Elizabeth returned on the liner *Empress of Britain*, arriving in English waters on 22 June, to be joined by their daughters aboard the ship so that the whole family could sail into Southampton together. There they were welcomed by Queen Mary, the Kents and the Gloucesters. The royal family continued onwards by train to Waterloo, where they were greeted by the prime minister, and then travelled in state carriages to Buckingham Palace. The route was lined with cheering throngs, and the MPs gathered in Parliament Square added to the jubilation. 'We lost all our dignity and yelled and yelled and yelled,' wrote Harold Nicolson in his diary. 'The King wore a happy schoolboy grin. The Queen was superb. She really does manage to convey to each individual in the crowd that he or she has had a personal greeting . . . She is in truth one of the most amazing Queens since Cleopatra.'

The ensuing weeks were marked by two significant events: firstly, a family visit to the Royal Naval College at Dartmouth, where the King had studied, and whose current cadets included Prince Philip of Greece. Lilibet had already come across her distant cousin at least once before: they were both great-great-grandchildren of Queen Victoria, and saw each other at the wedding of Princess Marina and Prince George. But according to Miss Crawford, this was the occasion that the thirteen-year-old princess began to pay attention to the handsome older boy, who looked 'rather like a Viking, with a sharp face and piercing blue eyes'.

A few days later, on 28 July, the Queen met Cecil Beaton for the first time, an encounter that would in its own way prove to be fruitful. Beaton recounted the story in his diary: 'The telephone rang. "This is the lady-in-waiting speaking. The Queen wants to know if you will photograph her tomorrow afternoon." At first, I thought it might be a joke . . . But it was no joke. My pleasure and excitement were overwhelming. In choosing me to take her photographs, the Queen made a daring innovation. It is inconceivable that her predecessor would have summoned me – my work was still considered revolutionary and unconventional.'

In fact, Beaton had already photographed several royals: beginning with Queen Victoria's sculptress daughter, Princess Louise, in 1927, and followed by Prince George (later the Duke of Kent) in 1932. In November 1935, he photographed Princess Alice on the occasion of her marriage to the Duke of Gloucester, and her sister-in-law Princess Marina, the Duchess of Kent, in the coronation summer of 1937. ('She looked like a Winterhalter painting,' he recorded in his diary, of Marina.) When Marina's sister Olga came to stay with her husband, Prince Paul of Yugoslavia, at Buckingham Palace in July 1939, Beaton photographed the two women together there; and it seems likely that it was Olga who encouraged Queen Elizabeth to commission him.

What made Beaton a controversial choice at this point in his career was not that he was revolutionary – his idealised royal portraits were supremely romantic – but that he had been fired by Condé Nast in January 1938 for adding anti-Semitic slurs, in tiny handwriting, to his illustrations for a feature on New York society in American *Vogue*. His insults had been aimed at the wives of Jewish film producers, and included references to 'kikes'. These offensive comments were noticed by the widely syndicated newspaper columnist Walter Winchell (the son of Jewish immigrants to New York, and a staunch anti-Nazi campaigner), who immediately brought them to the attention of millions of readers. In response, Condé Nast terminated Beaton's contract, and issued a statement saying, 'I was particularly distressed that these slurring comments should have been printed in *Vogue*, especially during these days of cruel, vicious and unreasoning persecution of Jews.'

Beaton apologised publicly, but privately thought that Nast's statement was 'unduly pompous'. His own analysis of his behaviour does not provide an altogether persuasive explanation. 'I am not anti-Jewish and am violently hostile to Hitler,' he wrote in his diary, 'but if there is any possible explanation these quotes contained my subconscious momentary irritation at having seen so many bad Hollywood films.' Beaton continued to regard his use of abusive language as an 'impertinence' rather than anything more serious, although the ban against his work appearing in *Vogue* was still in force when he received the request to photograph the Queen in July 1939.

Beaton was certainly not alone in his anti-Semitism, which was endemic in the British aristocracy (particularly amongst the pro-German peers who were members of the Right Club). Nor were the cosmopolitan circles in which he moved free of those who professed a facile admiration for Hitler. As Beaton wrote in September 1938, his friend Stephen Tennant (a central figure in the Bright Young People of the 1920s) had declared that he liked 'Hitler's mysticism, the way he parted his hair, and the mad stormy look in his eyes'. The Duke of Windsor, too, whom Beaton continued to photograph after his wedding in 1937, remained unrepentantly anti-Semitic, and more willing to find fault with Jews than Hitler.

Queen Elizabeth, for all her previous support for appeasement, did not espouse these views, but she was still willing to be photographed by Beaton, regardless of the controversy surrounding his departure from

Vogue in New York. Given that Beaton was being offered the opportunity to photograph a reigning Queen for the first time in his career, one might expect that on this occasion he would take care to remain on safe territory. Yet to do so would involve him suppressing the spiteful instincts that had been perceived by his friend Jean Cocteau, who described him as 'Malice in Wonderland' when they spent time together in 1935 (a phrase that Beaton had noted in his diary at the time with apparent satisfaction).

Beaton had not always been a fan of Queen Elizabeth; indeed, his verdict on her wedding photographs in April 1923 was to sneer at her 'sloppy' appearance. By the end of that year, when he saw her dancing at the Ritz, he was more complimentary: 'She is a charming looking little person. She looks horrid from her photographs but she is really delightful with a very fresh complexion and face and charming smile.'

Sixteen years later, when he went to Buckingham Palace to meet Queen Elizabeth on the morning of this all-important royal sitting, Beaton carefully scrutinised her features again, and found them wanting. 'The face looked very dazzling, white & pink,' he recorded in his diary, '& the complexion flawless but as a photographer I was anxious at the lack of definition in it. It is a face I know so well from millions of pictures, but here in reality it seemed so negative.' He deemed her eyes 'pretty but pale' with 'very few eyelashes', her lips 'surprisingly thin', and complained of 'a vast expanse of cheek that might be difficult to light'. Her arms and wrists were 'white & rounded, with diamond bracelets & perfumed with tuberose'. He passed no comment on her legs, but judged her to be 'very short & her heels are very high. I liked her but feared for the camera results. In the glaring light from the garden windows, she looked flat & shadowless.'

Beaton also noticed that the Queen was wearing a dove grey dress with long, fur-trimmed sleeves, which he recognised as having been designed by Norman Hartnell for her recent North American tour. She mentioned to him that Hartnell was already intrigued, having spotted Beaton in the palace. 'I expect he had visions of his lovely dresses appearing again,' she told Beaton. As it happens, the two men were not friends, despite their similar backgrounds and creative concerns, and the secrets they kept about

Queen Elizabeth (opposite) in the Blue Drawing Room at Buckingham Palace; and (above) with a backdrop adapted from Jean-Honoré Fragonard's *The Swing*; July 1939. Photographs by Cecil Beaton.

their private lives as gay men, at a time when homosexuality was still illegal. Both had been students at Cambridge – Beaton at St John's College (from 1922 to 1925), Hartnell at Magdalene (1920 to 1922) – and would have overlapped, had not Hartnell left the university a year early without taking his degree. Both came from upwardly mobile families in London, but hid their parents' working-class origins. Hartnell's parents had run a London pub; Beaton's father was a timber merchant and his mother the daughter of a Cumbrian blacksmith. Both shared a love of performing at school – Hartnell at Mill Hill, Beaton at Harrow – invariably taking female parts, and designing their own costumes and stage sets. Both continued to do so at university, and Beaton was well aware of Hartnell's reputation for artistic talent at Cambridge. For example, when Beaton was asked to illustrate the cover of the university magazine *Granta*, he was shown a previous contribution by Hartnell, which had been deemed by his peers to be a great success. Beaton's response, however, was contemptuous; as he wrote in his diary on 1 June 1923, the illustration 'by that horrid N. B. Hartnell' was 'the worst thing I've ever seen'.

He was no more forthcoming with praise for Hartnell's work as a couturier, either before, during or after photographing Queen Elizabeth in July 1939; and yet the graceful creations she wore unquestionably contributed to the success of Beaton's portraits. Just as Hartnell's gowns mirrored those worn in the original nineteenth-century Winterhalter paintings that the King had suggested as inspiration, so, too, were they integral to Beaton's photographs (in his own words) 'of the fairy Queen in her ponderous Palace'. The first shots were posed inside the opulent Blue Drawing Room, and then against the theatrical backdrops that he had set up for the purpose. One of these was an enlarged late-eighteenth-century Italian engraving of classical ruins. This formed the setting for a picture of the Queen wearing a crinoline embellished with gold and silver embroidery, and magnificent nineteenth-century jewellery, including a superb ruby necklace, diamond bracelet and tiara that had previously belonged to Queen Victoria, and the star and sash of the Order of the Garter.

For the second backdrop, Beaton adapted Jean-Honoré Fragonard's rococo masterpiece, *The Swing*, removing the original pink-clad female figure at the centre of the painting and leaving the verdant setting as a decorative way to frame his own subject. By taking away Fragonard's titillating girl on the swing – and the libertine beneath her, looking up her skirts to see her naked flesh above her gartered stockings, along with an older man pushing the swing – Beaton creates the space for his version of alluring beauty. But his choice also invites questions from the viewer: why choose this painting in particular? Could he be teasing us with the voyeuristic reference? Beaton had retained the statue of Cupid from Fragonard's painting, with his finger raised confidentially to his lips in a gesture calling for silence. Given that Beaton studied art at Cambridge (albeit without passing his final exams), it seems implausible that he was unaware of the potential for mischievous association; just as he must have known the risks of inserting the sly, secretive abuse in his illustration for *Vogue*. His pleasure in risqué double-entendres was evident in a book that he was creating at the time, which would be published a few weeks later, entitled *My Royal Past*. This was a faux-memoir of 'Baroness von Bülop', whose frolicsome reminiscences were illustrated by pictures of Cecil and his friends, cross-dressing as minor royalties. All of the participants in this romp would have doubtless understood the use of 'queen' and 'fairy' as terms for queer men; and the timing of the book's publication, to coincide with the release of his 'Fairy Queen' photographs of Elizabeth, was itself recognised as an in-joke, and further 'proof', in the words of one of Beaton's gay friends, of 'your implacable will to shock. It is in fact a master-stroke even to see the book with its sinister undercurrents of sex, perversions, crass stupidities and general dirt, beaming severely from Maggs Bookshop in Berkeley Square.'

Yet Beaton got away with his suggestive Fragonard setting for the Queen, just as he had done previously when using it as a background for the photographs of Marina and Olga. Perhaps for additional cover, he surrounded Elizabeth with the bouquets he had seen in her rooms earlier ('a pointillist bower of flowers – hydrangeas, sweet peas, carnations'.)

Queen Elizabeth in the gardens of Buckingham Palace, July 1939.
Photograph by Cecil Beaton.

There, posed in her spangled tulle crinoline and another shimmering diamond tiara, the Queen looked 'like a fairy doll', wrote Beaton in his diary. So much effort had gone into his concealment; was this part of the thrill for him? Risking exposure, but not quite hiding in plain sight?

After working for three hours – far longer than the allotted twenty minutes – Beaton suggested that they should move outside, to take advantage of the early evening sunlight in the palace gardens. The Queen agreed, and went to change into a different outfit, to the astonishment of a superintendent, who said to Beaton: 'Do you mean to say she's gone off to change once more? Why, she hasn't had her tea yet, has she? Well, this means the poor King will have to have his tea alone!'

When the Queen reappeared, she was 'smiling and laughing', continued Beaton, and wearing 'a champagne-coloured garden party dress and hat and parasol – and loving it – a delighted porcelain doll'. Yet the strength of her character also shone through; the Queen was 'a shrewd and witty woman', Beaton observed, who told him that the eighteenth-century parasol was 'a symbol of all summer'. At one point, he noted, a courtier remarked of the sylvan setting, 'It's lovely, it's just like a Winterhalter picture.' For Beaton himself, as they crossed the lawns towards the lake, 'the atmosphere felt strange and timeless . . . something outside reality'.

But Elizabeth was well aware that they were working together to create an effect, and of the potential illusions offered by Beaton's expertise. As he recorded in his diary, 'The Queen talked gaily. "I am interested in your photography. You have such a high standard. Can you do a lot afterwards? Can you take out a whole table?" "A table is a bit much, Ma'am. But I can slice people in half."' His expert use of retouching tended to be subtler than that; but any wrinkles were smoothed out, chins tightened and waistlines neatened. Intriguingly, however, such was Elizabeth's astuteness that subsequently she would be the one to request less airbrushing from Beaton. This occurred in 1950, following a sitting to mark her fiftieth birthday; after Beaton had sent the finished proofs to the Palace, he received a telephone call from her private secretary. 'Her Majesty had seen the pictures,' Beaton wrote, 'liked them extremely well, but considered I had been perhaps too kind. Her Majesty felt that, since she had battled through a number of years, she could not have come through them completely unscathed. Would it be possible at this stage to take away the retouching? This is the first time that any of my sitters has suggested that the pictures were too flattering.' She was also alert to Beaton's subliminal sense of spite; as she remarked to his biographer, Hugo Vickers, when he was researching his book in 1981: 'Of course, there was another side to him. Pins going in . . . here . . . there.'

When Beaton's portraits of Queen Elizabeth were included in an exhibition of royal photography at Buckingham Palace in 2024, I had the opportunity to look at them more closely, before they were enclosed again in their glass frames. The staged photographs with the Fragonard background are, for me at least, too contrived to transcend their period; they veer towards the kitsch, rather than achieving immutable elegance. That said, the photographer and sitter did achieve something significant together within the surroundings of the palace. If Queen Mary had bestowed the newly invented house of Windsor with a majestic sense of perpetuity, which had been fractured by her son's abdication and Wallis's razor-sharp chic, then Queen Elizabeth re-established the quality of timelessness. But the best of Beaton's imagery of Elizabeth adds another dimension, of nostalgic romance and idyllic Englishness. These remain tangible in the outdoor portraiture from that halcyon day in 1939, still glowing in the golden hour before twilight; almost as if one might be able to slip into the picture even now, following the gentle sound of laughter, the call of birdsong and the scent of roses, stepping out into the lost Arcadian gardens of the last summer before the war.

Queen Elizabeth in the gardens of Buckingham Palace, July 1939.
Photograph by Cecil Beaton.

BATTLE CAMP

If the role of a British monarch is a performative one, then what should the Queen wear for war? An ethereal fairy-tale gown no longer looked the part, and nor would delicate garden-party dresses or parasols do much to counteract the terrifying prospect of Hitler's stormtroopers marching into Buckingham Palace. And yet, like Queen Mary in the First World War, Elizabeth never showed any inclination to don military uniform. When war was declared against Germany on 3 September 1939, following the Nazi invasion of Poland, the Queen was already colonel-in-chief of several army regiments, and she would be appointed commandant-in-chief of the three women's services: the Auxiliary Territorial Service (ATS), the Women's Royal Naval Service (the Wrens), and the Women's Auxiliary Air Force (WAAF). But these were honorary positions, and in contrast to her husband, who followed his father's example by wearing martial uniform whenever he was seen in public during the war, Elizabeth appeared only in civilian dress, for the specific purpose of boosting morale.

The question of her wartime clothing was addressed by Norman Hartnell in his memoir. As with the Queen's state visit to France in 1938, when she was in mourning for her mother, it was felt that black would not necessarily be appropriate for her public appearances. 'Black does not appear in the rainbow of hope,' Hartnell wrote; nor was white a suitable alternative

George VI and Queen Elizabeth, carrying their gas masks, touring ARP defences in Bermondsey, London, September 1939.

Queen Elizabeth visiting the British Red Cross, September 1939.

Princess Marina in her uniform of the Women's Royal Naval Service, April 1940.

in the face of German aggression. Instead, 'the Queen made a wise decision in adhering to the gentle colours, and even though they became muted into what one might call dusty pink, dusty blue and dusty lilac, she never wore green and she never wore black. She wished to convey the most comforting, encouraging and sympathetic note possible.' There was one notable exception to this rule, as Chips Channon observed in his diary on 28 November 1939: 'At the Opening of Parliament the King was in naval uniform, and the Queen wore trailing black velvet, furs and pearls, and I have never seen her so regal and beautiful. She was dressed to perfection. Everyone remarked on it.' But in general, she tended to be seen in an array of pastel ensembles designed by Hartnell; in contrast to her sister-in-law Marina, who wore a smart Wren uniform (designed for the women's naval service by her favourite couturier, Edward Molyneux), albeit with the addition of high heels and jewellery, which infringed the official regulations.

From the very first days of the war, Elizabeth undertook a constant round of official engagements, often by her husband's side. On 12 September, for example, the *Daily Mirror* reported on the royal couple's 'surprise tour' of South London's air-raid defences: 'The Queen, who was dressed in powder blue, carried her gas mask in a haversack which she wore slung over her arm. The King, in the blue-grey uniform of a marshal of the Royal Air Force, carried a service respirator.' The details of their itinerary revealed that the government's fears of annihilating poison gas attacks were still very much to the forefront: 'The King and Queen visited underground and overground shelters, a gas cleansing station, municipal baths – where they saw decontamination apparatus – and a medical mission.' At this point, the mass evacuation of children from London was already underway, and the public were braced for imminent and cataclysmic bombing. Yet the *Daily Mirror* ran a large picture of the Queen beaming as she met the locals who had gathered to greet her, with a caption that declared: 'The Queen's smile was always infectious, and the whole dashed crowd is smiling with her, as you see.' The propagandist message was spelled out again in the accompanying text: 'And so people smile, and they'll go on smiling, for every smile's a cloud of gloom in Naziland.'

In reality, not everyone in the royal court was maintaining this determinedly cheerful and patriotic attitude. On 11 September 1939, the same day that the royal couple were touring South London, the Duke of Buccleuch, who held the prestigious position of Lord Steward of the Royal Household, was attending a surreptitious meeting with other members of the aristocracy at the Mayfair home of the Duke of Westminster. This secretive cabal, which included anti-Semitic fascist sympathisers, was intent on making peace with Germany, and for all their positions of power and privilege, none was closer to the Crown than Walter Montagu-Douglas-Scott, Duke of Buccleuch since 1935. Walter's sister Alice was married to the Duke of Gloucester, and he had already embarrassed his royal brother-in-law by travelling to Germany for Hitler's birthday celebrations in April 1939, having previously entertained Ribbentrop at his Scottish estate. Buccleuch's dubious position would eventually lead to him being removed as Lord Steward, although not until the following year, in June 1940, when the King wrote in his diary: 'It was rather a painful interview as he has been "dubbed" as being pro-German in his attitude towards the War & has said stupid things, but we parted amicably.'

At the start of what would become known as 'the Phoney War' (because Hitler had not yet invaded Western Europe), the royal couple were more suspicious of the Duke and Duchess of Windsor than they were of Buccleuch. When the Windsors returned from France to England at the outbreak of war, Elizabeth refused to see Wallis, and so the two brothers met each other without their wives at Buckingham Palace on 14 September 1939, for the first time since the abdication nearly three years previously. The King felt that it would be better for his troublesome brother to return to France, where a post as liaison officer had been devised for him at the British Military Mission. Windsor accepted the job, but the King subsequently reported to their younger brother, Prince George, Duke of Kent, that he was 'his usual swaggering self, laying down the law about everything'. The Queen, writing to Prince George on 5 October, went even further, comparing Windsor to the Führer: 'Odd creature, he is exactly like Hitler in thinking that anybody who doesn't agree with him is automatically wrong.' And her antipathy for the Duchess of Windsor continued unabated, as she declared in a letter to Queen Mary on 26 September: 'I haven't heard a word about Mrs Simpson – I trust that she will soon return to France and STAY THERE. I am sure that she hates this dear country, & therefore she should not be here in war time.'

The King and Queen were not alone in their mistrust of the Windsors. When the King met General Sir Edmund Ironside, Chief of the Imperial General Staff, two days after seeing his brother, they discussed the possibility of security breaches. As the King wrote to his mother, General Ironside 'put it very strongly to me' that the Duke of Windsor's military role in France would mean that he 'would get access to the secret plans of the French'. Ironside was concerned that Windsor might pass these on to Wallis, so it was agreed that 'anything really secret' must be kept well away from him. Such caution may have been warranted, given that the Windsors had remained in contact with the mysterious Charles Bedaux – who was suspected of being a spy – and continued to see him in Paris. Certainly, even the Duke's most loyal friend, Fruity Metcalfe (who was serving as his unpaid equerry) felt uneasy about the Windsors' relationship with Bedaux. 'Last night I fixed a dinner in a private room here [the Ritz] for Charles B to meet them,' Fruity wrote to his wife Baba on 4 October. 'He [Bedaux] knows *too* much – about *every* country in Europe . . . It is *terrifying* . . . He has left at dawn for an unknown destination this morning. He hinted at Berlin being one of those places.' Given that Baba's former brother-in-law, and sometime lover, was Oswald Mosley – hence her nickname of 'Baba Blackshirt' – Fruity was well able to form a view of the Windsors' more questionable associates.

However, the initial difficulties concerning the Duke of Windsor tended to be the result of minor matters of protocol, in particular squabbles about uniform and precedence. Irritation ensued on several occasions when Windsor assumed that soldiers were saluting him, rather than a more senior commanding officer. Similarly, a contretemps blew up just before he was due to visit the headquarters of the RAF in France. As king, he had been Marshal of the Royal Air Force; and now presumed that he was an air vice-marshal, so asked that his uniform should be altered accordingly. Churchill (who surely had more urgent matters to attend to, given his role as First Lord of the Admiralty) advised Windsor that this was not possible, and that he should wear the uniform of a major general.

Wallis's bitterness about these apparently petty episodes in the early months of the war is evident in her memoir: 'We had two wars to deal with – the big and still leisurely war, in which everybody was caught up, and the little cold war with the Palace, in which no quarter was given.' She believed that as far as her husband's family was concerned, 'I simply did not exist.' In reality, Wallis loomed large in the minds of the royal family, but Queen Elizabeth still referred to her as 'Mrs S' or 'Mrs Simpson', as if refusing to accept that her sister-in-law was now the Duchess of Windsor. 'The fact that our love had withstood the tests and trials of three difficult years made no difference,' recalled Wallis. 'Nothing was ever said. It was simply a case of our being confronted with a barrier of turned backs, rigid and immovable.'

She responded by volunteering for aid work in Paris, and was photographed looking elegantly trim in her uniform of the Section Sanitaire of the French Red Cross, packing 'comfort kits' of knitwear and cigarettes for the troops, and delivering supplies to military hospitals. 'I was busier and perhaps more useful than I had ever been in my life,' she wrote, while acknowledging the strangely unsettling hiatus of the Phoney War, when France was 'braced for the blow that was mystifyingly held in abeyance'.

Cecil Beaton was also attempting to adapt to the early months of the war, but without much success. 'I feel frustrated and ashamed,' he confessed in his diary in September 1939. 'This war, as far as I can see, is something specifically designed to show up my inadequacy in every possible capacity. I am too incompetent to enlist as a private in the army.' Instead, he signed up to operate the telephones in the event of air raids near his country home in Wiltshire. Nothing ever happened during these ARP shifts, apart from a sporadic false alarm. Occasionally he drove to London, which in the blackout appeared to him to be 'a real town of the dead with rows of empty houses, discarded even by the caretakers and their cats'.

One of Beaton's self-portraits appeared in the *Sketch*, posing as an ARP telephonist on duty, and he photographed a number of small children who had arrived in Wiltshire as evacuees. But he could not help fretting about the fate of his images of Queen Elizabeth, which he feared would not be published in wartime. 'The public is in need of a fillip,' he noted in his journal, 'and these pictures would be a sop if they were allowed, but taken in all the full regalia they are very grand and do not look like wartime pictures as indeed they were not meant to be.' By this point, the portraits were in private circulation: on 2 October, Elizabeth replied to a letter from her friend Prince Paul of Yugoslavia, who had mentioned that he would like one of the prints. She promised to send this, and in doing so, revealed her own view of the photographer: 'Mr Beaton, who is mincing away at some light war work, will execute my order as soon as possible. I believe he is a telephone operator. Can you not imagine him saying, "Number darling? 2305? Oh divine, my dear."'

In the same letter to Prince Paul, Elizabeth again vented her feelings about the Windsors: 'I think that he at last realises that there is no niche for him here – the mass of the people do not forgive quickly the sort of thing that he did to this country, and they HATE her . . . I had taken the precaution to send her a message before they came, saying I was sorry I could not receive her. I thought it more honest to make things quite clear. So she kept away, & nobody saw her. What a curse black sheep are in a family!'

This left Beaton in a potentially uncomfortable position, given that he had again photographed the Windsors in Paris earlier that year (against one of the same backdrops – of classical ruins – as he would use for Queen Elizabeth in the July sitting). He was far from being a go-between for the warring couples, but it seems likely that they all knew his position as the photographer of choice for the opposing sides of a divided family.

In early November, Beaton returned to Buckingham Palace for a meeting with the Queen, to discuss the possible release of the summer photographs. He was scathing about her outfit on this occasion, writing in his diary: 'The Queen was in her pretty blue room, in a granite grey dress, with steel bead embroideries bordering an edging of astrakhan. It was an ugly dress & very dowdy, & her shoes were too elaborate, & too pale a grey felt, & her jewellery was messy, rather too many little bits, three rows of small pearls, two small pearl clips, a very ordinary diamond bracelet.' Then, having found fault with her appearance, he tried to talk himself out of such aggressive criticism: 'Does it matter *what* she wears, or even what she looks like, for her aura is one of such goodness & sympathy, her charm so overwhelming. She seemed to have a slight cold & kept holding a crumpled handkerchief to her nose, but her voice was as plaintive & clear as ever. It is like a sad child's voice, infinitely moving & appealing. She held her head on one side, looked very wistful & yet managed the interview in quite a businesslike way, not in a hurry, willing to linger & gossip, to admire the pictures (for she did like them very much), but also not wishing to be rushed into any commitment.'

Beaton found himself wondering if the Queen was 'camp', as was the view of his gay friends; and although he couldn't quite bring himself to go that far, he decided that 'she certainly has a great sense of humour . . . She sums up people in a brilliant & penetrating way.' A hint of malice returns at this point in his diary: 'Knowing her limitations she makes an asset of them, appealing for protection from her lack of gifts, talents, without compromising herself & pretending to be different from the person she is.' Ultimately, he declared, 'She is ideal as Queen of England for she is the personification of all that is best & a "real" Lady.'

His use of 'real', in quotation marks, is intriguing, given his own love of cross-dressing; but at any rate, Beaton and Queen Elizabeth appeared to reach an agreement on how to proceed. One of his portraits of her – posed against the painted Fragonard backdrop, wearing a Hartnell gown, diamond tiara, Garter riband and star – was chosen to appear as the cover and frontispiece of a fundraising anthology to which she had lent her support: *The Queen's Book of the Red Cross*. This went on sale before Christmas, with a preface written by Elizabeth, in which she praised the volume as 'a tribute to the noble work of the Red Cross, and to the unselfish devotion of those who are carrying it on. My feeling of gratitude and admiration is shared, I am certain, by every other woman in our Empire – especially by the wives and mothers of those who are fighting to defend its liberty.' Everyone who bought the book, she continued, as well as all the authors and artists who had contributed to it, 'are helping forward the great work of mercy on the battlefield; to all of you, I would send this Christmas message – God bless you'.

Another of Beaton's pictures of the Queen was used to illustrate a card sent by the royal couple that Christmas to the soldiers of the British Expeditionary Force. This went some way to rehabilitating Beaton's reputation with *Vogue*, although he would not be published by Condé Nast for another year. He also received permission to sell the approved portraits of the Queen to the press; the *Daily Sketch* duly published these – on 5 December 1939 – beneath the headline 'Pictures that the People of Britain Will Treasure'. (An accompanying caption explained that the Queen's sumptuous gowns had been designed by Norman Hartnell for the royal tour of Canada the previous summer, thereby absolving her of any potential accusations of wartime extravagance.) Quite aside from the financial reward – which Beaton described in his diary as 'a boon and a blessing' – the Queen gave him an extremely useful piece of advice at their meeting in November, suggesting that he should find a role as a propaganda photographer for the Ministry of Information.

In due course, Beaton followed her wise counsel, but not before hurling himself into one final act of high camp frivolity: he wrote, designed and staged a pantomime called *Heil Cinderella*, in aid of the *Daily Sketch* fund to provide cigarettes and other comforts to the Armed Forces. Beaton cast himself as an 'Ugly Sister' (perhaps in an act of contrition, given that he would almost certainly have preferred to appear as a beautiful Fairy Godmother), and wrote in his diary: 'It is like running a war and I cannot think that Hitler feels more unnerved and responsible than I do . . . The Russians bomb Finland and it matters less to us because we have still to find a Dandini.'

Cecil Beaton's portrait of Queen Elizabeth, which was published on the cover of *The Queen's Book of the Red Cross* in December 1939.

Few would agree with Beaton's airy dismissal of the Soviet pact with Nazi Germany, which allowed Stalin to order the invasion of Finland; an episode of war that was anything other than phoney for the Finnish troops who fought back against the Red Army. And yet I cannot bring myself to dismiss, in turn, Beaton's continuing commitment to camp during a time of conflict; if only for the reason that Hitler and Stalin were united in their authoritarian belief that all such 'decadence' should be crushed. Long before Beaton was sashaying across stage in *Heil Cinderella*, the Nazis banned the cross-dressing cabaret acts that had previously flourished in Berlin; and the persecution of gay men in Germany was already well underway, as thousands were arrested and imprisoned in concentration camps, their 'degeneracy' marked by the pink triangles they were forced to wear on their striped uniforms.

As for Beaton's musings about whether Queen Elizabeth might be deemed 'camp': I never knew her, but my husband did, and he would maintain she was not, while acknowledging that she was a popular gay icon. Instead, he describes her as having been refreshing company, with a taste for mischief, and at times even flirtatious. She enjoyed the company of men, whatever their sexual preferences – Noël Coward was a warm friend, for example; and the senior member of her domestic staff was the flamboyantly gay William Tallon, who worked devotedly for her for fifty years, and carried the title of Steward and Page of the Backstairs (itself the source of amusement in the tabloid press). And despite gossip about the illicit homosexual activities of her favourite younger brother, David Bowes-Lyon (who was married), she remained consistently loyal and loving towards him.

But to return to Cecil Beaton, and his portrayal of the Queen in 1939: I am reminded of Susan Sontag's seminal essay, 'Notes on Camp' (published in 1964). Sontag writes that 'Camp is esoteric – something of a private code, a badge of identity', and describes an affinity between 'Camp taste and homosexuality . . . homosexuals, by and large, constitute the vanguard – and the most articulate audience – of Camp'. She sees it as a vision of the world in terms of style, defined by artifice, performance and exaggeration. 'To perceive Camp,' she observes, 'is to understand Being-as-Playing-a-Role. It is the furthest extension, in sensibility, of the metaphor of life as theatre.'

For Sontag, 'Camp is a woman walking around in a dress made of three million feathers'; in which case, Beaton's portrait of the Queen wearing a Hartnell gown covered in thousands of sequins surely satisfies the definition. Indeed, it is tempting to speculate that a camp element remains integral to the façade of the house of Windsor; just as it was for Hartnell's royal creations. But, crucially, Beaton's photographs of Queen Elizabeth could be enjoyed by a wide audience, many of whom would not view them as camp. And for Beaton's images to be compelling, particularly as wartime propaganda, he needed to put aside his own tendency towards spitefulness. As Sontag writes, 'Camp taste is a kind of love, love for human nature. It relishes, rather than judges . . . Camp is a *tender* feeling.'

There could be no tenderness in Hitler's Third Reich, and the word 'camp' had already taken on a sinister meaning in the context of Nazism. Queen Elizabeth, like her husband, had prayed for peace, but unlike the Duke of Buccleuch and his ilk, they were not blind to the threat of the Führer's ambitions. 'I <u>know</u> . . . that we are fighting evil things, and we must face the future bravely,' she wrote to Cosmo Lang, the Archbishop of Canterbury, just five days after the declaration of war. 'I realise clearly, that if one did not love this country & this people with a deep love, then our job would be almost impossible. The only hope for the world is love.'

Her words were echoed by W. H. Auden in the famous line from his poem, 'September 1, 1939': 'We must love one another or die.' Yet the ensuing years of war would prove, as if there were any doubt, that love was not enough in the battle against Hitler. As Winston Churchill declaimed to the House of Commons on 13 May 1940, in his first speech as prime minister, leading an all-party government: 'I have nothing to offer but blood, toil, tears and sweat.' The Phoney War had ended in April with the German invasion of Norway, and, in May, of Belgium, Luxembourg, France and the Netherlands. 'We have before us an ordeal of the most grievous kind,' continued Churchill. 'We have before us many, many long months of struggle and of suffering.'

The royal couple would each play a part in that campaign – not least in giving sanctuary to the Dutch and Norwegian monarchs, forced to flee the German forces. (Queen Wilhelmina of the Netherlands arrived in London on the same day as Churchill's speech, with nothing but the clothes on her back and a tin helmet, given to her by the commander of the British destroyer that had rescued her.) Amidst the destruction and despair, the King called for a national day of prayer to be held across the country on Sunday, 26 May. The royal couple attended the morning service at Westminster Abbey – the King wearing his RAF uniform, the Queen in a demure beige dress and coat, her face clearly visible beneath a matching hat. 'We were all conscious that the British Expeditionary Force are in a position of great peril,' wrote Alan Don, the King's Chaplain, in his diary after the service, 'and that the most momentous battle of all time is about to start – a counterattack, let us hope, with the full strength of a revitalised French army.' In reality, the evacuation from Dunkirk was beginning, in which more than 338,000 Allied soldiers would be rescued over the following nine days. (Among the thousands who were not able to escape was the Queen's nephew, John Elphinstone, who would spend five years in German prisoner-of-war camps, including Colditz.)

Dunkirk has been described as both a miracle and a disastrous defeat; an inspiring embodiment of the British spirit against all the odds, and a tragic loss of lives in the most terrible conditions. On 4 June 1940, Churchill warned the nation that Britain faced imminent invasion, while issuing his legendary declaration: 'We shall fight on the beaches, we shall fight on the landing grounds, we shall fight in the fields and in the streets, we shall fight in the hills; we shall never surrender.' The King took up target practice in the gardens of Buckingham Palace, shooting his rifle where Beaton had photographed Elizabeth less than a year before. The Queen began receiving daily instruction in firing a revolver, as she explained to Harold Nicolson when they lunched together at the palace on 10 July. Nicolson – who had recently been appointed by Churchill as parliamentary secretary to the Ministry of Information, serving Duff Cooper – reported in a letter to his wife that Elizabeth had said that she would fight to the end, telling him: 'I shall not go down like the others.' 'I cannot tell you how superb she was,' continued Nicolson. 'But I had anticipated her charm. What astonished me is how the King has changed. I always thought him rather a foolish loutish boy . . . He was so gay and she was so calm. They did me all the good in the world . . . [They were] sensible and resolute. WE SHALL WIN. I know that. I have no doubts at all.'

What also remained certain was that if the time came for the Queen to put her handgun training into practice, she would not be in uniform; for here stood a woman who could wield her pistol while wearing a pastel-coloured frock, her steely face confronting the enemy beneath a jaunty floral hat.

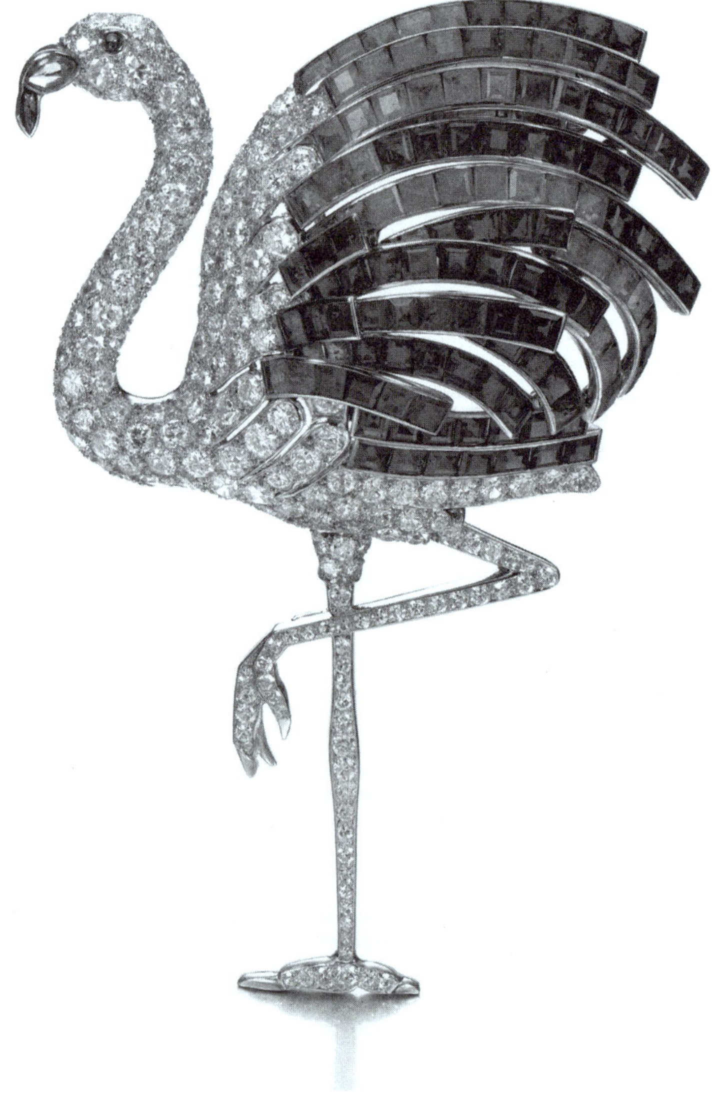

The jewelled flamingo brooch, commissioned by the Duke of Windsor from Cartier in Paris, as a birthday gift for his wife in 1940.

THE MENAGERIE

In May 1940, as German troops stormed through the Low Countries and France, millions of refugees fled from the invasion, desperately trying to escape in a panic-stricken period known as *l'Exode*, or the Exodus. The main roads were soon blocked by cars and lorries that had broken down or run out of petrol, and traffic ground to a halt, but many people continued on foot, pushing prams, carrying exhausted children, dragging their luggage on heavily laden handcarts or wheelbarrows. Families became separated; food and water were in short supply; the sick and elderly collapsed, and fear spread due to the constant danger of attack by Luftwaffe planes strafing the slow-moving columns of refugees. On 16 May, the Windsors left Paris for Biarritz, but once Wallis was safely installed in a luxury hotel there, the Duke somehow travelled back to the French capital. Amidst all the chaos and confusion as the Nazis advanced towards Paris, the Duke of Windsor made his way to the Cartier boutique on Rue de la Paix to collect a brooch in the shape of a flamingo that he had commissioned as a birthday present for Wallis (she would be forty-four on 19 June).

The exotic flamingo would come to be regarded as a highlight of her legendary jewellery collection – it sold for close to £500,000 at the Sotheby's sale in Geneva in 1987, and when it returned to the market in 2010, Cartier bought it for more than £1.7 million. It remains closely guarded within the vaults of the Cartier archives as one of the most iconic brooches in the world; although I was fortunate to see it in London at the V&A Cartier exhibition, alongside Wallis's bold 'big cat' designs that seemed to express her defiance, and what her in-laws regarded as her predatory behaviour. Wallis's feline jewels are remarkable: a panther clip brooch, also ordered by the Duke of Windsor from Cartier in Paris, the lithe creature fashioned out of diamonds and poised – ready to pounce – atop a monumental 152-carat cabochon sapphire; her tiger lorgnette in gold and black enamel, with its gleaming emerald eyes, and a tiger bracelet and brooch of onyx, emeralds and diamonds. Scrutinising these big cats, I am reminded of George V's tiger tattoo, etched on his forearm – along with a dragon on the other arm – when he visited Japan as a sixteen-year-old naval midshipman in 1881. Unlike Wallis, however, King George always kept his fantastical beasts covered up and hidden from view.

Even in such dramatic company, the four-inch flamingo looks extraordinarily flamboyant, and especially so in the context of wartime: a baffling purchase as the storm clouds gathered over Europe. True, flamingos had not yet become associated with the American kitsch of 1950s plastic garden ornaments or cocktail bars. And it is possible that the Duke remembered a distinctive Cartier flamingo bibelot, carved from rose quartz and adorned with diamond eyes, which was part of his grandmother's menagerie of figurines at Sandringham. (This had been a gift to Queen Alexandra in 1908, from the wife of the then US ambassador to London, a similarly keen collector of the carved creatures that were made fashionable by Fabergé and Cartier.) So the Windsor flamingo is not entirely without precedent, but it still seems anomalous in the circumstances. Unfortunately, there is no record of what prompted the Duke's choice, but the meticulously kept Cartier ledger does reveal that his commission was dated 4 March 1940; that he had supplied the firm with the original gemstones, in the form of an existing necklace and four bracelets; and that the designer was able to reuse forty-two calibré-cut rubies, forty-two sapphires, forty-two emeralds, and 102 diamonds. These colourful jewels created the flamingo's iridescent tail-feathers; the beak was set with a cabochon citrine and

The Duchess of Windsor (top) wearing her flamingo brooch in Bermuda, August 1940; and (above) in Madrid, June 1940.

sapphire, the eye with another sapphire; and one of the bird's elegant diamond legs was hinged to allow for movement.

The first time that Wallis was seen in public wearing the flamingo was on her husband's forty-sixth birthday, 23 June 1940, at the Ritz Hotel in Madrid; the couple were photographed there together, and even though the surviving images are black-and-white, the large brooch looks so striking that it is impossible to miss. Four days previously – on Wallis's own birthday – the Windsors had left their home on the French Riviera in a convoy of cars carrying a quantity of their possessions, to drive to Spain (a neutral country that was nevertheless under the control of the fascist dictator General Franco, who maintained close links with the Nazi regime). By then, the Duke had already jettisoned his friend Fruity Metcalfe – abandoning his steadfast aide in Paris on 27 May without any warning or form of transport – in order to pick up Wallis in Biarritz. 'Re my late Master, he has run like two rabbits,' wrote Fruity to his wife, furiously. 'He never made one single mention of what was to happen to me . . . He has taken all cars and left not even a bicycle! . . . He has denuded the [Paris] house of all articles of clothing and all his clothes, etc. After twenty years I am through – utterly I despise him, I've fought and backed him up (knowing what a swine he was for 20 years), but now it is finished . . . The man is not worth doing anything for. He deserted his job in 1936. Well, he's deserted his country now . . . It is the end.'

It was not, however, the end of the spy conspiracies that would surround the Windsors in the following weeks, in the febrile period when Hitler prepared to launch an invasion of England under the code name Operation Sea Lion. Some of the conversations that purportedly took place between the Windsors and various Nazi spies, diplomats and emissaries are as outlandish as the flamingo brooch. And it remains impossible to prove, conclusively, whether or not the Windsors actively colluded with German plots to make them king and queen following Hitler's planned conquest of Britain. Yet even at the time, stories of their treachery reached London, as Chips Channon recorded in his diary on 1 July 1940: 'Rumours are over-ripe and rife. Diana C[ooper] told me today that the

Windsors genuinely believe that they will be restored to the throne under German influence: he will become a sort of Gauleiter and Wallis a queen. Perhaps!' Two days later, Channon heard the same story via his friend the Duke of Kent, who had returned the previous day from Portugal, where the Windsors were then on their way from Madrid. Channon quoted Kent as saying, 'My brother wants to be a Gauleiter!' (This position was the third-highest rank in the Nazi leadership; Goebbels, for example, was the Gauleiter of Berlin.)

The foreign diplomats who encountered the Windsors during their stays in Madrid and Lisbon came away with similar impressions; for example, the Spanish foreign minister reported to General Franco that the Duke of Windsor was entirely opposed to the war: 'He throws all the blame on the Jews and the Reds and [Anthony] Eden with his people in the Foreign Office and other politicians, all of whom he would have liked to put up against a wall . . . If [the Germans] bombed England effectively this could bring peace. He [the Duke of Windsor] seemed very much to hope this would occur.' Meanwhile, the US ambassador to Spain, Alexander Weddell, told the Secretary of State in Washington that Wallis was even more direct in expressing her pro-German views than her husband, citing her startling declaration that 'France had lost because it was internally diseased'.

Baron Oswald von Hoyningen-Huene, the German ambassador to Portugal, wrote in comparable terms to Ribbentrop on 10 July, soon after Churchill had asked the Duke of Windsor to leave Europe and become Governor of the Bahamas. According to the well-connected ambassador, 'the appointment of the Duke as Governor of the Bahamas is for the purpose of keeping him away from England . . . He is convinced that had he remained on the throne, war could have been avoided . . . The Duke believes with certainty that continued heavy bombing will make England ready for peace.'

By this point, British intelligence sources were sending equally alarming testimony to London. On 7 July, Sir Alexander Cadogan, Permanent Under-Secretary for Foreign Affairs, was informed that 'Germans expect assistance from Duke and Duchess of Windsor, the latter desiring at any price to become Queen. Germans have been negotiating with her since 27 June . . . Germans think King George will abdicate during the attack on London.' The monarch was presumably briefed on this espionage report, because three days later Cadogan noted in his diary that he had lunched with the King, who was aware of the 'quisling activities' of his brother. The news was all the more shocking given that the Battle of Britain had just commenced, with the Luftwaffe launching multiple bombing raids on ports, coastal radar stations, and shipping convoys in the English Channel.

Meanwhile, the Windsors had requested, via diplomatic intermediaries, that the German authorities protect their French properties; and that Wallis's maid should be given safe passage to travel back to their home in Paris to collect various belongings for them, including bed linen. Ribbentrop immediately agreed; and perhaps emboldened by this development, came up with a plan to detain the Windsors in Europe, either through a large cash bribe of 50 million Swiss francs, or via more coercive means. The latter would only be necessary, according to Ribbentrop, if the Duke was hesitant about collaborating with the Nazis; any such qualms, believed Ribbentrop, would suggest 'a fear-psychosis that forceful action on our part would help him to overcome'. Nothing came of this plot (known as Operation Willi), and on 1 August the Windsors set sail from Lisbon for the Bahamas. Eight days later, they docked at Bermuda, where Wallis appeared wearing her flamingo brooch, and the couple eventually arrived at Nassau on 17 August.

There, they were regarded with such suspicion that the FBI prepared a surveillance report for President Roosevelt. This claimed that 'the Duchess had recently been in direct contact with von Ribbentrop and was maintaining constant contact and communication with him'. Noting that Wallis was sending her clothes to New York for dry-cleaning, the FBI speculated that 'the transferring of messages through the clothes may be taking place'.

In truth, Wallis appears to have been genuinely concerned about her wardrobe; indeed, she had even persuaded US consular staff to retrieve her favourite Nile-green swimsuit from La Croë (the Windsors' villa on Cap d'Antibes), so that she could take it with her to the Bahamas. This unlikely yet successful mission was christened Operation Cleopatra Whim by the Americans; and Wallis's continuing sartorial whims generated disapproving publicity in the US press. One piece, published in the *American Mercury* in June 1944, reported: 'Her purchases, since she moved to Nassau, have averaged a hundred dresses a year.' Despite the Nazi occupation of Paris, Wallis was still able to order Mainbocher, after the Chicago-born couturier moved his business to New York in 1940. According to Helen Worden, the *American Mercury* journalist, 'Mainbocher's black afternoon dresses are now $500.' The Duchess 'is proud to be called the best dressed woman in the world', wrote Worden. 'It is a profession with her.' More harmful was the claim that Wallis kept a signed photograph of Ribbentrop on her dressing table; Worden's anonymous source was a house guest who had stayed with the couple at their home in the Bahamas: 'When this friend commented on the picture, the Duchess said she had known and liked von Ribbentrop before the war.' The Windsors were so enraged by the article that the Duke demanded that the FBI should investigate whether the *American Mercury* was part of a wider conspiracy against Wallis, on the curious grounds that he believed Worden to be Jewish. She was not, and when the Foreign Office became involved, it simply stated in a memo: 'Miss Helen Worden makes her case well and it is a damaging one.'

The Windsors, for their part, detested living in the Bahamas, which they believed to be a banishment brought about by what the Duke called 'the vindictive jealousy' of his family. Whenever possible, they escaped to shop and socialise in Miami, Palm Beach and New York, and Wallis also busied herself renovating and redecorating their official residence. This expenditure in turn caused ill feeling towards the Windsors; the Nassau House of Assembly had reluctantly voted a sum of £4,000 for the refurbishment, prompting a local newspaper, the *Daily Tribune*, to comment that the money would have been better spent on buying an extra fighter aircraft to defend Buckingham Palace, which had just been bombed. For her part,

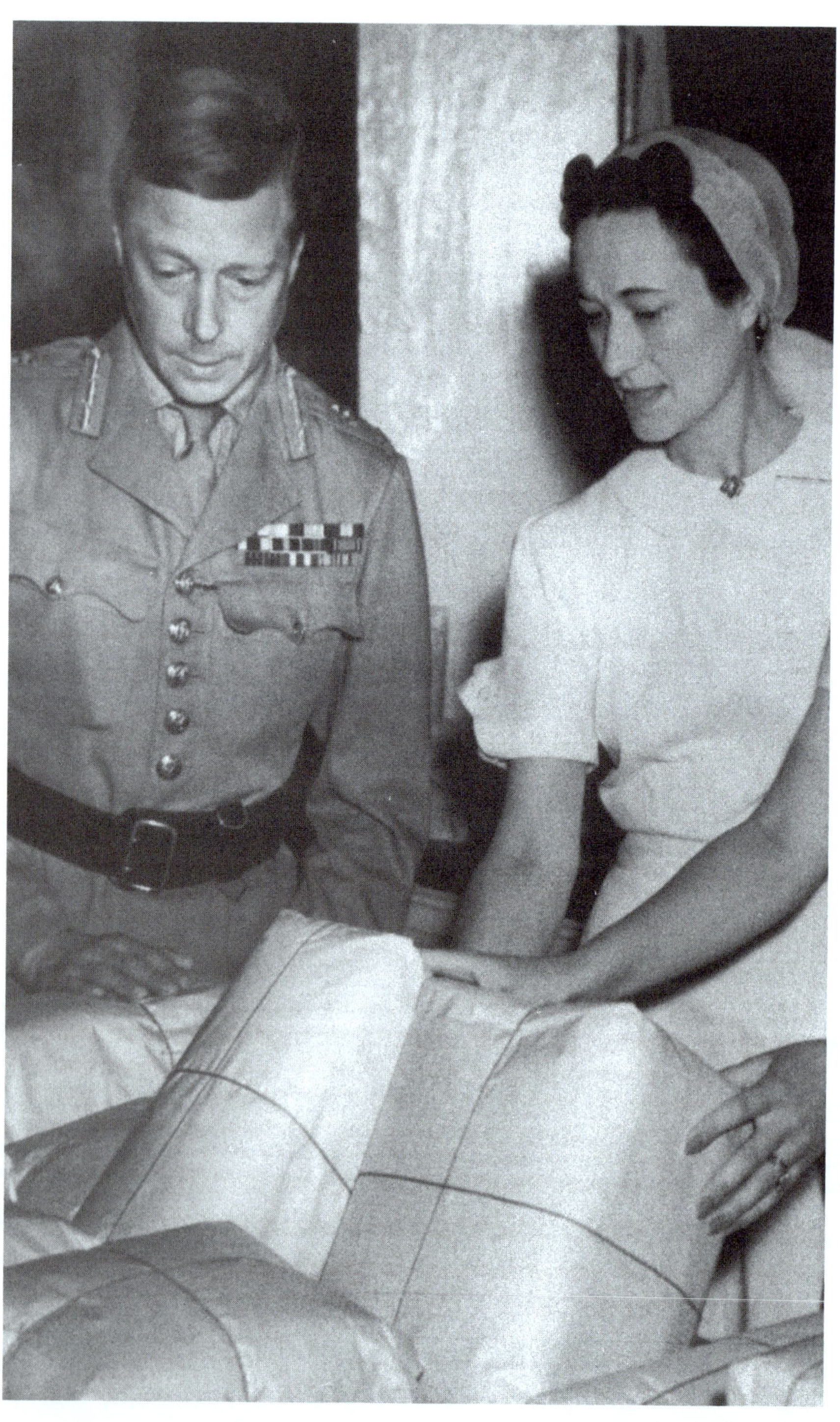

The Duke and Duchess of Windsor at the Red Cross in the Bahamas, November 1940.

Wallis said that she would prefer the Blitz to the boredom of the Bahamas. 'One might as well be in London with all the bombs and excitement and not buried alive here,' she wrote to her aunt on 25 October 1940; and followed this up with another letter in November: 'We both hate it and the locals are petty-minded, the visitors common and uninteresting.'

Nevertheless, just as in Paris, the Duchess did involve herself in the activities of worthy local charities, including the Red Cross. When she appeared in the July 1943 issue of American *Vogue*, Wallis looked like a demure angel of mercy in a pristine Red Cross uniform (which had, coincidentally, been redesigned for the US service by Mainbocher). The photographs were accompanied by the Duchess's account of their lives in the Bahamas: 'Like everyone else, we live from hand to mouth,' she said. 'Government House at Nassau is on a completely wartime schedule . . . Food rationing is stringent in Nassau, and grumbling about war's adjustments, any kind of rationing, bores me, infuriates me.' As always, Wallis's vigilance about weight was evident: 'The Duke has for his luncheon, all year round, a hot green vegetable, fruit compote and maté . . . I keep my weight at around 112 [pounds], just by being careful.'

The Duchess's apparently casual remarks in American *Vogue* also betrayed her insecurity and capacity for self-deception (or possibly deceit). 'In wartime, especially, my clothes philosophy . . . is simply to look neat, appropriate, and inconspicuous. I don't give much time to clothes, as mine are just correct, well-cut and of good materials. Since I can't be pretty, I try to look sophisticated, but unfortunately, I always want to be dressed like everybody else. When I am out I always feel dowdy, and wish that I had thought of getting THAT dress, and wearing it THAT way.'

In reality, the wartime photographs of Wallis reveal her to be anything but inconspicuous, and certainly never dowdy. But whenever she appeared in public flaunting the flamingo brooch (for instance, during a high-profile visit to Miami in December 1940), this did not look inappropriate, given that it was the national bird of the Bahamas. However, the link between the flamingo and the islands cannot explain why the Duke chose the brooch for his wife, since at the time he commissioned it from Cartier, he had no idea that they would be dispatched there. After all, Churchill only came up with the idea of the appointment in early July, having failed to induce the Duke to return to England from Lisbon.

I have never found a conclusive explanation for the flamingo – despite going down endless rabbit holes of research – but it nevertheless seems somehow fitting for a woman who had once described herself as 'Wallis in Wonderland'. In Lewis Carroll's original story, Alice struggles to play croquet with a live flamingo as a mallet: 'She succeeded in getting its body tucked away, comfortably enough, under her arm, with its legs hanging down, but generally, just as she had got its neck nicely straightened out . . . it *would* twist itself round and look up in her face, with such a puzzled expression that she could not help bursting out laughing.' At least Wallis could keep her palm-sized flamingo firmly pinned to her lapel; and much as she protested about the dreariness of the Bahamas, it gave her some distance from her husband's disapproving family. Nor would she be confronted there by an angry queen shouting 'Off with her head!', unlike poor Alice; although Wallis certainly complained about Winston Churchill in similar terms. 'Of course one must obey the dictate of this Churchill or be beheaded,' she wrote to a friend in October 1940.

Alongside the puzzle of the flamingo is that of the arcane Cartier snake necklace that Wallis wore on a trip to New York in 1943. On this occasion, she posed for a portrait with her husband by Dorothy Wilding (a favoured royal photographer who had studios in Mayfair and Manhattan). It was not the first time that Wilding had photographed the Windsors, nor would it be the last. But for me, it is the most memorable of her portraits of the couple: the Duke looking winsome, a toy soldier dressed up in his Welsh Guards uniform, while Wallis is in a sleeveless Mainbocher gown, her gloved arms firmly folded, her right wrist displaying the ruby and diamond Cartier bracelet that her husband had given her for their first wedding anniversary in June 1938. As always, it is hard to read the look on her face – which has been skilfully retouched to smooth away any flaws or wrinkles. Is there a hint of defiance in her determined gaze? Or is it resignation? Her Cartier necklace sends a similarly ambivalent message:

The Duke and Duchess of Windsor in New York, 1943. She is wearing her Cartier snake necklace and ruby bracelet. Photograph by Dorothy Wilding.

The TATLER

Vol. CLI. No. 1964. London, February 15, 1939 | POSTAGE: Inland 2d.; Canada and Newfoundland 1½d., Foreign, 3½d. | Price One Shilling

Photo: Cecil Beaton

THE DUCHESS OF WINDSOR—A New Portrait

This portrait of the beautiful wife of H.R.H. the Duke of Windsor, with whom she is also seen in a photograph on the succeeding page, has only just been taken. The Duke and Duchess have spent much time recently at their villa at Cap d'Antibes and are moving into their new house in the Avenue Sauchet in Paris very shortly. The Duchess has the well-deserved reputation of being one of the best dressed women in the world. The Duke, as every one knows, is an ardent golfer and is rapidly becoming first class at the game it is tightly coiled around her neck, like a dangerous serpent, yet its scales seem to turn, at each end, into feathery tips, rather than anything more venomous. Is she feeling suffocated or empowered by this token of her husband's love? Is she in control of the snake, even if it kills her, reflecting the legend of Cleopatra committing suicide by allowing a venomous asp to bite her?

There are precedents for royal women wearing snakes; including the majestic portrait of Queen Elizabeth I, painted towards the end of her life, in which a jewelled serpent is embroidered on the left sleeve of her ornate dress, representing her wisdom and cunning. (Intriguingly, Elizabeth I's gown in the painting is also embellished with eyes and ears, as if to suggest her omniscient intelligence – both her own, and that of her all-seeing, all-hearing spies – which enabled her to triumph over the conspiracies and plots against her.) Legend has it that Queen Victoria was buried with a snake ring given to her by Prince Albert, and while there is no evidence for this, she certainly possessed mourning jewellery that incorporated the mythic symbol of the ouroboros, a serpent that devours its own tail, denoting immortality or everlasting love. When Queen Victoria's oldest son, the future Edward VII, married Princess Alexandra in 1863, he presented her with a brooch made from an ancient Egyptian scarab, mounted in a pair of gold cobras. Alexandra wore a serpent bracelet, as well, which remained part of the private collection of Elizabeth II (although the latter reputedly never liked it, believing it to be ill-omened). The errant Edward VII was too prone to adultery to be associated with eternal love; but he was given a Fabergé cigarette case by his favourite mistress, Alice Keppel, which was encircled by a sinuous snake made of diamonds. Following her husband's death in 1910, Alexandra returned the case to Mrs Keppel, who eventually gave it to Queen Mary in 1936. And in yet another historical twist, Alice Keppel's great granddaughter, now Queen Camilla, inherited an Edwardian family heirloom in the form of a diamond snake necklace that she continues to wear to this day.

As for the Windsor snake: the Duke originally purchased the choker in Paris in 1937, when it was described by Cartier as a '*Collier Torque*

Double Serpent En Diamants'. This might seem to be a perverse choice of gift for his wife, given that their beloved pet dog – a Cairn terrier named Slipper – died after being bitten by a snake in the grounds of the Château de Candé in April that year. Nevertheless, it is clearly visible, along with her ruby bracelet and emerald engagement ring, in Cecil Beaton's portraits of Wallis in Paris in 1939. On this occasion, she chose to wear it with a far more elaborate Mainbocher gown than in the subsequent Wilding sitting: a dramatic dress embellished with sequined embroidery. I have studied the Beaton images, alongside those by Dorothy Wilding, and I keep coming back to the necklace. Late at night, my eyes growing tired from staring at these seductive pictures, my mind wanders from the myth of Cleopatra's death to the biblical scene of Eve succumbing to the temptation of the snake. Thus follows the Fall, the exile from Eden, and the punishment of Adam and Eve.

But how much did Wallis remember from her religious education as a child? In her autobiography, she writes about attending church with her grandmother, who would read to her from a family Bible, and recalled her daily prayers at school. Did she feel that Eve had been more sinned against than sinning? Or had she cast off Christian doctrine, as a snake sheds its skin? These are my circular thoughts, and yet it is hard to reach a conclusion about the impenetrable Wallis, or her true motives. Like a serpent, she slithers away from me, and although she might, after all, be harmless rather than poisonous, perhaps one should keep a safe distance.

There is, however, an unlikely postscript to this chapter. Not long ago, I visited Bonhams in London, to view some papers and photographs relating to the Duke and Duchess of Windsor before these were auctioned. One of the lots included a manuscript by the American gossip columnist and socialite Elsa Maxwell, whose tumultuous relationship with Wallis veered between close friendship and passionate enmity. This particular document, written in 1956, evidently coincided with their period of feuding, for she portrayed Wallis as 'the Iron Duchess', possessed of a sinister ability to mesmerise the Duke, and thereby make him 'her creature'. Broadening her animalistic theme, Maxwell described Wallis treating her husband like a puppy, at best, or if she was in a more contemptuous mood, telling him to 'buzz off, mosquito'.

Anyway, as I was crossing the road just outside the auction house, still preoccupied by Wallis, I was involved in a traffic accident, which left me badly bruised, cut and shaken. Back at home the following day in the Norfolk countryside, I was startled to see a black snake in our kitchen, with white markings around its neck that looked like a string of pearls. It was a warm afternoon in midsummer, and the snake slipped out the same way it had come in – through an open door. My husband had gone for a walk with our dog, and no one else witnessed the episode. But despite the blow to my head, I was sure that the snake was not a hallucination. When I told my husband, who is perfectly rational but familiar with my propensity for magical thinking, he remarked that it must have been a visitation from Wallis; and perhaps, for good measure, she had knocked me down the previous morning. I laughed, but felt the hairs rise on the back of my neck. As it happens, the date was 19 June – her birthday.

'FASHION IS INDESTRUCTIBLE'

On 7 September 1940, the Battle of Britain entered a new phase, as the Luftwaffe began a campaign of relentless aerial attack that would become known as the Blitz (from the German word 'Blitzkrieg', or 'lightning attack'). That afternoon, hundreds of enemy aircraft appeared in the clear skies over the Kent countryside, flying in formation towards London's East End, where they began by dropping incendiary bombs onto the Ford motor plant at Dagenham and the Beckton gasworks. As these exploded into flames, the German pilots were already reaching their next targets: the Docklands, where warehouses and factories were surrounded by narrow streets of housing. Within minutes, there were raging fires spreading for miles along both sides of the River Thames, from North Woolwich to Tower Bridge, while choking fumes and cinder-laden smoke made it difficult to breathe or see clearly. After a brief lull, the Luftwaffe returned with raids that lasted until dawn, guided by the blazes of the earlier attacks, unleashing high-explosive bombs to wreak further havoc. Water mains were damaged, so hydrants ran dry as firemen struggled to contain the raging infernos; telephone and electricity cables were destroyed, adding to the chaos and panic. On that first night alone, 436 people were killed, including seven firemen, and at least 1,600 were seriously injured. The remorseless bombing campaign against London would continue unabated for the next eight months, and there

The King and Queen at the bomb-damaged Buckingham Palace, September 1940.

were further raids on towns and cities across the country, resulting in the deaths of more than 43,500 civilians.

The royal family were at Windsor Castle during the first weekend of the Blitz, while Queen Mary had already been evacuated to stay with her niece, the Duchess of Beaufort, at Badminton House in Gloucestershire. But on Monday 9 September, the King and Queen returned to London, to embark upon the first of what would be many tours of devastated neighbourhoods. In the early hours of the following morning, a delayed action bomb exploded in Buckingham Palace, destroying the swimming pool that had been installed two years previously, and shattering most of the windows – including those in the King's study. 'I had been sitting in my room the day before without knowing that it was a time bomb,' he wrote in his diary; and although he and his wife had already returned to Windsor Castle by the time of the explosion (and usually slept there with their daughters), a daytime raid on Buckingham Palace, on the morning of Friday 13 September, came close to killing them both.

The direct hit was clearly deliberate – a German plane had emerged out of the clouds and flown straight up the Mall – and as Elizabeth explained in a letter to her mother-in-law, it was too sudden to allow them to reach an air-raid shelter. They heard 'the noise of an aircraft diving at great speed, and then the scream of a bomb. It all happened so quickly that we had only time to look foolishly at each other, when the scream hurtled past us, and exploded with a tremendous crash in the quadrangle. I saw a great column of smoke & earth thrown up into the air, and then we all ducked like lightning into the corridor.' Six bombs were dropped, two of which had fallen just yards from where they had been standing in the King's study, creating immense craters in the ground. Three workmen were wounded – one later died of his injuries – but the royal couple kept to their planned timetable, returning to the East End that afternoon.

'The damage there is ghastly,' wrote Elizabeth to Queen Mary in the same letter. 'I really felt as if I was walking in a dead city . . . through the broken windows one saw all the poor little possessions, photographs, beds, just as they were left. At the end of the street was a school which was hit, and collapsed on top of 500 people waiting to be evacuated – about 200 are still under the ruins. It does affect me seeing this terrible and senseless destruction. I think that really I mind it much more than being bombed myself . . . One could not imagine that life could become so terrible. We must win in the end.'

The school that she referred to was in Canning Town, and had been a temporary shelter for hundreds of men, women and children who were sent there after their homes were destroyed on the first night of the Blitz. But it offered no proper protection against the continuing onslaught, and despite repeated pleas for the occupants to be moved to a safer location, they were still there when the school was hit by a bomb in the early hours of Tuesday 10 September. So appalling was the death toll that the censors refused to allow any detailed reports or photographs of the tragedy to appear in the press, in order not to undermine public morale.

Harold Nicolson, who was aware of the true horror of this and other disasters, thanks to his job at the Ministry of Information, was rightly concerned about the consequences. 'There is much bitterness,' he wrote in his diary on 17 September. 'It is said that even the King and Queen were booed the other day when they visited the destroyed areas . . . Clem [Clement Davies, a Welsh MP] says that if the Germans had had the sense not to bomb west of London Bridge there might have been a revolution in this country.' As it was, the Luftwaffe had 'smashed about Bond Street and Park Lane and readjusted the balance'. In all, there would be nine such raids on Buckingham Palace during the Blitz, and when word spread that the royal residence was a prime target, as Nicolson noted in his diary on 18 September, the 'East End people now refuse to be sent to the West End, especially anywhere near Buckingham Palace'.

These were the circumstances that prompted the Queen to say, famously, that she was glad the palace had been bombed because it meant that she could 'look the East End in the face'. The King expressed a similar view in a letter to his mother, writing on 14 October about their visits to see people 'who had lost their relations and homes, & we have both found a new bond with them as Buckingham Palace has been bombed as well as their homes, and nobody is immune'.

In this context – and in marked contrast to the censorship surrounding the bombed school in Canning Town – it was important for the public to know that the palace had been attacked. Hence the swift response of the Ministry of Information to invite forty or so journalists and photographers (including Cecil Beaton) to see the damage for themselves, and share it with as wide an audience as possible. Beaton duly portrayed the King and Queen looking resolute beside the bomb-damaged palace; George standing proud in his military uniform, Elizabeth poised in a Hartnell ensemble and carrying a handbag. 'It is the genius of the Queen that has caused the Palace to be bombed so that the East Enders should not feel that they are alone in their misery,' wrote Beaton in his diary, mischievously. 'What a *wonderful* person that Queen is, just by being so nice and so good.'

The Queen's ability to appear sympathetic and reassuring (whatever she was feeling inside) would prove to be as essential as her Hartnell outfits. Her skill in doing so was witnessed by Lord Woolton, the Minister of Food, as he escorted the royal couple on a visit to the bomb sites of South East London. At one community centre, he recorded in his diary on 11 October 1940, 'a very dirty child' in its mother's arms reached out for the Queen's pearl necklace. Seeing that a photographer had just missed capturing the moment, Woolton whispered to her, 'Your Majesty, you've broken a pressman's heart.' 'Without showing the slightest sign that she had heard,' continued Woolton, 'she moved back into position so that the pressman could take his photograph. The incident was, in fact, the only thing recorded in the press!'

Meanwhile, the ever-attentive Norman Hartnell continued to be an expert ally in shaping the Queen's wartime image. 'What could she wear when visiting bombed sites and the devastated areas all over the country?' he asked in his memoir. 'How should she appear before the distressed women and children whose own kingdoms, their small homes, had been shattered and lay crumbled at her feet?' Some answers can be found

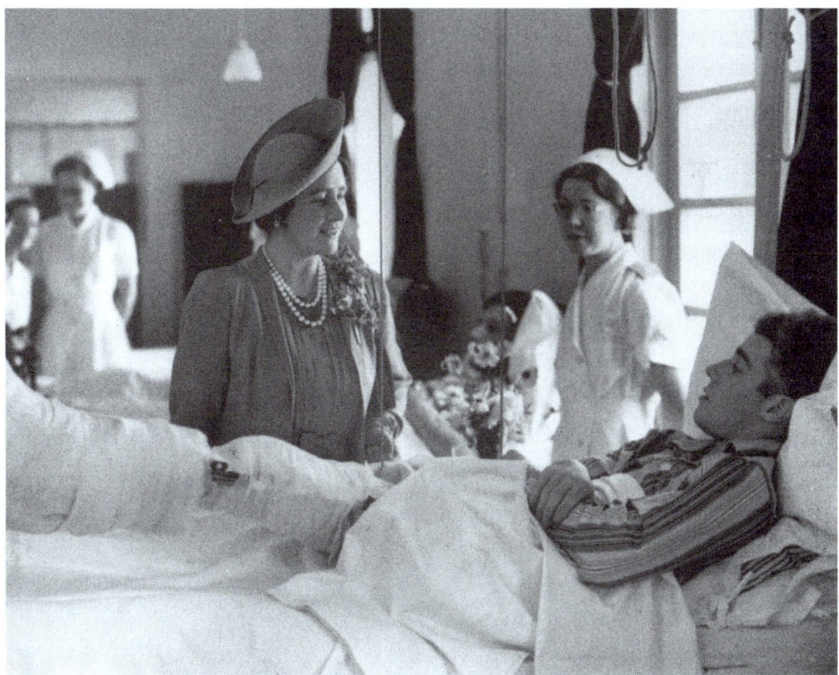

Queen Elizabeth (top) talking to the residents of a bombed area of London, September 1940; and (below) with an injured soldier during her tour of a hospital, June 1940.

within the Royal Archives at Windsor Castle, where Hartnell's original accounts for Queen Elizabeth's purchases are carefully stored in a file. As one might expect, the beginning of the new reign, leading up to the coronation, had required a more regal wardrobe for Elizabeth: hence a total bill of £1,040 for the six months to June 1937. (This included ten evening gowns, several dresses and coats for Royal Ascot, numerous hats, and an ermine-trimmed silver fox cape.) After the outbreak of war, the focus shifted to patriotic colours: a blue and red tweed suit and cape ordered in September 1939, for example, at a cost of £23. In November 1939 – still during the Phoney War – Hartnell provided 'a black velvet gas-mask case'; but surprisingly, Elizabeth had not yet stopped ordering her signature Fairy Queen dresses. The accounts for the autumn of 1939 reveal that she bought a hand-embroidered 'white slipper satin crinoline gown' in September, and another 'white tinsel lace evening gown and coatee' in November. The following spring and summer, she purchased three similarly romantic evening dresses, although the majority of her bill of £1,160 that year was for daywear, in pink, pale blue and grey crêpe with matching tweeds. And it was in these Hartnell day dresses that she undertook her Blitz outings.

According to William Shawcross, her official biographer, 'she certainly stood out in the bombed streets. Her gentle ostentation was deliberate and it seems to have been effective. It was encouraging for people who had lost everything to see that the Queen still had her style.' In retrospect, this might have been a risky strategy – how could 'style' be anything other than irrelevant, when 27,500 high-explosive bombs were dropped on London in the first two months of the Blitz, turning large parts of the city into an apocalyptic wasteland? The royal family's former home at 145 Piccadilly was destroyed on 7 October 1940 – just one of more than a million houses that were left in ruins during the Blitz. As Cecil Beaton admitted in his diary on 10 October, 'One still feels a sinking of the heart at the sight of ever more bomb damage: windows blown in and tumbled wreckage of rubble in the road.' And yet his eye for detail – and for the human stories that would shape his wartime photography

– was still attuned: 'A small dwelling – its front cut away – gives a doll's house effect, with the parlour, where the evening meal was being eaten on the cloth-covered table, a teapot and bowl of tomatoes exposed to passers-by . . . and the staircase leads to an upper floor that no longer exists.'

Nor was the Queen alone in the propaganda strategy of putting on a brave face along with her Hartnell hats. When the staff of *Vogue* were forced by air raids to work in the basement of their Bond Street offices, the editor, Audrey Withers, continued to sport a fashionable hat in these cramped surroundings. One member of the *Vogue* staff was killed in the Blitz, and others were bombed out of their homes, losing all their possessions, yet the magazine did not stop publishing fashion shoots. 'Fashion is Indestructible' proclaimed *Vogue* in September 1941, beside a photograph by Cecil Beaton of a young woman – Elizabeth Cowell, an announcer for the BBC – wearing a smart black-and-white herringbone suit designed by Digby Morton. She is looking away from the camera, an upright figure surveying the ruins of the Temple Church in London's Inns of Court; a stoic embodiment of the wartime slogan to 'Keep Calm and Carry On'.

The claim that fashion is indestructible could easily be mocked as wilfully wrongheaded or wishful thinking. After all, its own most brilliant advocates have acknowledged that it is inherently ephemeral; none more so than Coco Chanel, with her declaration, 'Fashion fades, style is eternal.' Yet while its products may be evanescent, those who still believe in the possibilities of fashion – whether for reasons of business or pleasure or vocation – are capable of unwavering commitment to the craft, even in wartime. Consider, for example, the story of the man who created the suit featured in the *Vogue* photograph: Henry Digby Morton, a Dublin-born couturier who embodied the resilience of the fashion business, having survived the sinking of a transatlantic ocean liner on 17 September 1940. Digby Morton and his wife Phyllis (the editor of *Woman and Beauty* magazine) were on their way from England to North America to promote British fashion exports as a means of raising funds for the war effort, when their ship was torpedoed by a German submarine 600 miles from land. Among the passengers on the SS *City of Benares* were ninety

Opposite: Paternoster Row in London, reduced to rubble by the Blitz. Above: The Hon Mrs Reginald Fellowes, President of the Incorporated Society of London Fashion Designers, wearing a Molyneux jacket and a hat by Aage Thaarup. Photographs for *Vogue* (1941) by Cecil Beaton.

evacuees being sent to Canada; the majority of the children on board were killed in the attack.

Digby Morton and his wife somehow managed to swim through the darkness to a lifeboat, and then spent twenty hours in the stormy seas of the North Atlantic, waiting to be rescued, by which point half of those in the vessel with them had died of exposure. Shortly after returning to England, Phyllis described (to the *Daily Mirror*) how she had held a fourteen-year-old girl in her arms, trying to comfort her after her mother had drowned; the girl survived, but Phyllis found it almost impossible to talk or write about the tragedy. Digby Morton, meanwhile, went straight back to work at his Mayfair premises on Grosvenor Street, where he and Phyllis lived in a small flat on the top floor. He had already revealed his practical approach by designing a uniform for the Women's Volunteer Service (WVS) and ingenious overalls for female factory workers; and although he remained committed to the decorative art of couture, he also contributed to the Utility collections commissioned by the Board of Trade, which offered well-made, inexpensive garments after the introduction of clothes rationing.

On 12 February 1941, Digby Morton's designs formed part of the first ever fashion show staged at Buckingham Palace, where the King and Queen watched nine models presenting fifty-four couture outfits that were to be exported to South America, again for the specific purpose of fundraising for the war effort. In the press coverage, the King was said to have noticed 'the glamorous' evening gowns, but thought the coats and suits were 'rather plain'. The Queen, however, remarked that they were very wearable, and commented, 'I could see myself in them.' A second show took place at the palace later that month – on this occasion to display children's clothes in the presence of the Queen, who ordered several dresses for her daughters. According to a report in *The Times*, the event was organised by the Manchester Cotton Board to encourage exports to

Austerity dress designed by Norman Hartnell, c.1943. Official photograph for the Ministry of Information (whose London headquarters at Senate House are visible behind the model).

the US, citing 'the British children who are refugees in America' as 'the inspiration for the parade of Lancashire cotton frocks'.

Quite aside from the practical need to generate much-needed revenue from exports, these unprecedented (and never to be repeated) fashion shows at the palace had a polemical motive, indicating that the royal couple were calm, confident and well-dressed, even as the Luftwaffe resumed its attacks on British cities. (Indeed, Buckingham Palace itself would be struck again on 8 March 1941.) The emphasis lent by the King and Queen to fashion exports also represented a symbolic show of strength during the Battle of the Atlantic, when Royal Navy warships and merchant vessels were regularly attacked and sunk by the Germans. On 12 February alone – the same day as the first couture presentation – seven merchant ships in a British convoy were destroyed at sea.

The designers involved in the events at the palace – most notably Hardy Amies, Norman Hartnell, Edward Molyneux and Henry Digby Morton – continued to exemplify the ways in which fashion was regarded as a patriotic wartime activity. Hartnell related in his autobiography that he and his fellow couturiers 'occupied a dual position in those war years. As far as exports were concerned, we were very important; but, on the home front, clothing manufacturers became servants of the Board of Trade.' The rationing of garments, textiles and footwear had been instituted by the Board of Trade in June 1941, and Hartnell and his colleagues were drafted to work on Utility clothing from 1942 onwards, all of them following strict guidelines on the limited amount of fabric and buttons that could be used. In Hartnell's case, mindful of his position as a royal dressmaker, he had first asked Queen Elizabeth's permission to take part in the Utility scheme. She encouraged him to go ahead, saying (as Hartnell recounted): 'You have made so many charming things for me that if you can do likewise for my countrywomen, I think it would be an excellent thing to do.' If the Queen could be seen to wear couture during the Blitz, then the government hoped that making affordable versions of Hartnell's designs available to the public might help to maintain morale and a shared sense of unity on the Home Front.

In the cases of Molyneux and Amies, their wartime roles had an added dimension. The former had remained in Paris until just two days before the Nazis occupied the city, and on the day that France surrendered, he crossed the Channel on a coal barge, accompanied by his butler; apparently both men stepped off the grimy boat looking unruffled and still immaculately groomed. Molyneux then moved into Claridge's, which was conveniently close to his Mayfair couture house on Grosvenor Street, and devoted himself to supporting the war effort in every possible way. Not only did he donate the profits from his business to the British government to buy munitions, he was an energetic propagandist. One of his export designs in 1941, for instance, featured 'Blitz debris buttons', reminding North American buyers of the battle still being waged over the skies of Britain.

Captain Molyneux's keen understanding of dress codes extended far beyond sartorial proselytising; as befits a former member of a cryptanalysis intelligence unit during the First World War, he set about renewing and extending his espionage contacts. His nephew, Peter Hope Lumley, whose mother worked for the London branch of the company, joined the British Army Intelligence Corps, as did Molyneux's talented assistant, John Cavanagh, and another protégé, Hardy Amies. At the same time, Molyneux kept open his Paris couture house on Rue Royale, which could be used as a secret meeting point for members of the Special Operations Executive. One of the youngest SOE agents, twenty-two-year-old Violette Szabo, arrived there in April 1944 and chose three Molyneux dresses for herself; tragically she was arrested on her next mission to France, in June 1944, and deported to Ravensbrück concentration camp in Germany, where she was murdered in January 1945. Another SOE agent, Wing-Commander F. F. E. Yeo-Thomas, had been the general manager of Molyneux's Paris couture business until the outbreak of war, and remained in touch with the staff there, as well as liaising with Captain Molyneux in London. Like Violette Szabo, Yeo-Thomas was arrested and brutally tortured by the Gestapo, and transported to Germany on the same train as her. Unlike Szabo, he survived his time at Buchenwald concentration camp, and returned to his job at Molyneux in Paris. He was subsequently a key prosecution witness both at the Nuremberg trials, where he was able to identify Buchenwald officials, and at the war crimes trial held by a US military tribunal at Dachau. In March 1946, the King presented Yeo-Thomas with the George Cross in a ceremony at Buckingham Palace; the citation praised his 'courage and initiative' displayed on three separate missions to France, and his 'amazing fortitude and devotion to duty throughout his service abroad, during which he was under the constant threat of death'.

After these harrowing experiences, Yeo-Thomas found it understandably difficult to readjust to civilian life, and he left Molyneux in 1948; his physical and mental health deteriorated in the subsequent years, and he died at the age of sixty-two in 1964. He was by no means alone in suffering grievous and long-lasting harm from the trauma of his imprisonment. Yet there were a few survivors who found different ways in which to re-engage with the outside world. Amongst the most unusual was Brian Stonehouse, an SOE agent in France who never lost his love of fashion, and became a highly regarded illustrator for *Vogue* in New York in the 1950s. One of his drawings from that era hangs in our home, portraying a female figure of such evocative elegance that she and her clothes achieve a timeless quality that transcends the fashions of the period. Stonehouse was undoubtedly a talented artist, but for me, the beautiful surfaces of his work have an added dimension, given the barbarity of his wartime saga. Having been arrested by the Gestapo near Lyon at the end of October 1942, he endured solitary confinement and incarceration in five different Nazi concentration camps, ending up in Dachau in September 1944. When the camp was finally liberated on 29 April 1945, Stonehouse forced himself to sketch the corpses piled up in the crematorium the following day, as evidence for future war crimes trials. He also helped in the search for four missing SOE agents, whose fate remained unknown at the end of the war, by drawing the women he had seen arriving at Natzweiler-Struthof concentration camp in July 1944. Brian had never met them before (although one, Vera Leigh, shared his interest in fashion, having founded her own millinery business in Paris), and he did not know their names. But he remembered that one of the women had tied her hair with 'a piece of Scottish tartan silk ribbon, wearing a light grey flannel suit – the coat a shortish swagger model – obviously English'. He recalled that the ribbon looked 'like a gesture of defiance': a heartbreaking detail that identified the wearer as Diana Rowden, who was brutally murdered alongside Vera Leigh and their two companions, Sonia Olschanezky and Andrée Borrel, by being injected with poison and then burned alive on their first night at Natzweiler.

The Imperial War Museum in London contains the recording of an interview with Stonehouse, made in 1987 as part of an oral history project: 150 minutes of him telling his story, his voice steady, even as he outlines the horrors of the camps. He had just graduated from Ipswich Art School when war broke out, a few days after his twenty-first birthday, and had already signed up for military service earlier that year. After serving as a gunner in the Royal Artillery, he transferred to SOE in 1942, and was parachuted into France that summer, with the cover story that he was an art student who had worked for *Vogue* in Paris before the war. His clandestine role as a wireless operator was as dangerous as it was daring, and the threat of betrayal and death was constant: a quarter of the male SOE agents posted to France did not survive the war, and more than a third of the forty-one female agents were killed. Yet somehow, Stonehouse – whose identity as a gay man he kept hidden – did not lose his faith in fighting for freedom, nor in fashion. After he arrived in France, he tells the interviewer, he bought a bottle of Schiaparelli perfume (annoyingly, the man conducting the interview does not ask why, or for whom). He explains that he also purchased a pair of 'raffia' shoes, because his English shoes were leather, and they made him look conspicuous in occupied France, where leather was no longer available for civilian footwear. When he and his friend and fellow SOE agent Bob Sheppard were liberated from Dachau, they wrapped scarves around their necks made of blue polka-dot silk, which they had found in one of the camp's workshops. There are no photographs of that moment – but the image has remained in my mind, the fluttering silk transformed into a symbol of liberation, seized from a place that reduced people into numbers, then ground them into dust.

Stonehouse remained in Germany until September 1946, testifying at war crimes trials, and questioning a number of Nazi prisoners. On one occasion, he found himself looking into the face of a former Gestapo officer called Arnold Schneider, whom he had encountered during his own imprisonment and interrogations in Paris; at the time, Schneider had informed him that he was about to be shot as a spy. When Stonehouse was offered the opportunity to retaliate, by beating or shooting Schneider, he refused, saying that he would not behave in the same way as his former tormentors had treated him; that he would not be reduced to their level of inhumanity.

In 1979, after living in the US for more than three decades, where he illustrated the beau monde at play in New York and Palm Beach, as well as working on advertising campaigns for Elizabeth Arden, Stonehouse returned to England. Two years later, he was commissioned to paint a portrait of Queen Elizabeth the Queen Mother, for the Special Forces Club in London, which had been founded in 1945 by veterans of SOE. Over the course of several months, during their sittings at Clarence House, the two became friends, and Brian continued to be invited as a guest to the Queen Mother's lunch parties until his death in 1998.

His portrait of her still hangs in the Special Forces Club, a suitably discreet building with an unmarked front door on a side street in Knightsbridge. I have been there just once – to give a talk about Catherine Dior, her work for the French Resistance, and her imprisonment alongside female SOE agents in Ravensbrück. As one would expect, the Club has always been private, and it continues to have the air of a safe house for its current members, many of whom work in the intelligence services; hence no details are available about its links with the royal family, other than the fact that Princess Anne is the longstanding Patron of the Club, as was her grandmother before her. During my visit, I admired Stonehouse's painting of the Queen Mother, alongside a collection of photographs of the SOE operatives who served in the Second World War (those who were killed in action have their pictures framed in black). The Queen Mother is depicted in a white and gold embroidered gown, that surely must have been made for her by Norman Hartnell, her blue sash of the Order of the Garter, two cameo brooches pinned to the riband (one of her husband, another of her daughter Elizabeth), and a diamond tiara, necklace, bracelet and earrings. The regal magnificence is softened by the way in which she is tilting her head to one side, facing the artist with a sympathetic, searching look in her eyes; as if she is as intent on knowing him as he is to capture her true likeness. Her gaze lingers in this secretive setting, suggesting a mutual understanding with the artist; a shared belief, perhaps, that a sense of style need not be altogether extinguished by the ugliness of war.

Not far from the royal portrait is another of Stonehouse's artworks: a poignant watercolour that he presented to the Special Forces Club in 1985, to commemorate the four female agents he had seen at Natzweiler. Here they remain, forever young, dressed in their own clothes, still defiant; the summer sky is blue above them, the soft contours of green hills are just beyond them; the unimaginable darkness of their fate kept at bay by the artist's delicate, gentle brushstrokes.

QUEEN, COUTURIER, SOLDIER, SPY

I do not know if Brian Stonehouse ever worked alongside Hardy Amies during their SOE missions, but I like to think of them enjoying a companionable drink together at some point, perhaps when they were both undergoing training at a secret location in Britain during the war, or afterwards, in a quiet corner of the fashion world. Stonehouse drew men as well as women – his portrait of his friend Bob Sheppard is in the Imperial War Museum, and his illustrations of dashing chaps in debonair suits would have appealed to Hardy Amies. The nonchalant figures in these pictures seem to epitomise the advice contained in Amies's book, the *ABC of Men's Fashion* (published in 1964): 'A man should look as if he had bought his clothes with intelligence, put them on with care, and then forgotten all about them.'

I met Amies when I was working at *Vogue* in the 1990s, and Sir Hardy, who had been knighted by the Queen in 1989, was photographed for the magazine's Millennium issue. He was walking with a stick, and suffering from the frailties of age, yet still looked admirably dapper in his bespoke tailored suit and well-polished gentlemen's shoes. I had heard his nickname, 'Hardly Amiable', which derived from a reputation for being waspish, snobbish and irascible; but I approached him with the respect that he deserved, and found him to be surprisingly cordial during the time that we spent together. By this point, his fame had been eclipsed

Hardy Amies, *c.*1953. Photograph by Baron.

by a new generation of London designers, such as John Galliano and Alexander McQueen – both of whom he abhorred as provocative showmen. But *Vogue* acknowledged Sir Hardy as the elder statesman of British fashion, even if he was no longer at its forefront. I was of course aware that Amies had designed for the Queen, but rather than answering my polite questions about his own role as a royal dressmaker, he steered our conversation towards Norman Hartnell and Cecil Beaton. 'I'm a clever old queen,' he remarked, 'but Norman was a silly old queen, and Cecil was an unhappy old queen.' I also knew that he had served in some covert capacity during the war; but I was too young to appreciate quite how much of his life he had kept concealed – both his sexuality, and his role as a spy who had twice signed the Official Secrets Act. When I did ask him about his wartime memories, he simply shrugged, and said he chose not to remember. Given that he was ninety years old by then, his right to forget seemed unarguable.

As it is, some of Amies's war record still remains mysterious. A large proportion of SOE's files were destroyed after 1945 – its official historian M. R. D. Foot, who had himself been an intelligence officer during the war, estimated that only 'one-eighth of what was committed to paper' survives. I have studied Amies's military personnel file in the National Archives; but as Foot commented in his authoritative volume, *SOE in the Low Countries*, the papers that were released after Amies's death in 2003 would, like everything else related to British intelligence, have first been subject to 'laundry'. Amies gave a very brief autobiographical account of the war in his memoirs (*Just So Far*, published in 1954, and its updated edition, *Still Here*, in 1984). But as Foot observed, these pages were 'modest and discreet'.

Even so, what emerges is an extraordinary story, in which Amies juggled his commitment to couture with his dedication to his country, and found ways to balance the clandestine demands of espionage with the more open displays of fashion. The thread that ran through all of his activities was a patriotic loyalty to the monarchy, which he expressed through royal dressmaking, as well as military service. The former he

I acknowledge the receipt of this Identity Card and will comply with the General Conditions of Issue.

Hardy Amies

Signature of Holder

Date

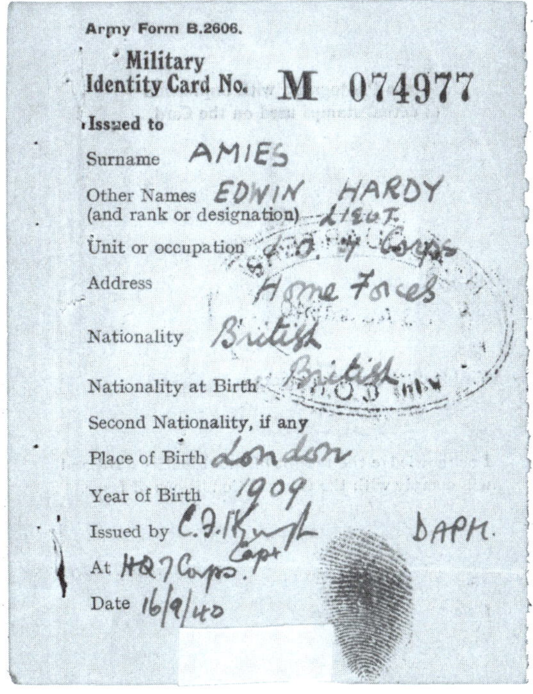

Army Form B.2606.

Military Identity Card No. M 074977

Issued to

Surname AMIES

Other Names EDWIN HARDY
(and rank or designation) LIEUT.

Unit or occupation H.Q. 7 Corps

Address Home Forces

Nationality British

Nationality at Birth British

Second Nationality, if any

Place of Birth London

Year of Birth 1909

Issued by C. J. Knight Capt DAPM.

At HQ 7 Corps.

Date 16/9/40

Hardy Amies's military identity card, during his training as an intelligence officer.

traced back to his mother, Mary, who had started her career as a seamstress for a court dressmaking establishment in Mayfair. There she rose to become a saleswoman, or *vendeuse*, continuing to work after her marriage in 1906 to an architect, and throughout her first pregnancy. Mary's first child, christened Edwin after his paternal grandfather, and Hardy after her maiden name, was born on 17 July 1909 at his parents' flat in a Maida Vale mansion block. In his teens the young Amies adopted Hardy as his preferred forename, dropping Edwin without any regret. And his keen sense of attachment to his mother's workplace, and to her profession, is apparent in his memoir: 'I like to think that I was almost born on the steps of a court dressmaker,' he wrote in *Still Here*, by which point he was already famous as a couturier to Queen Elizabeth II.

As a 'great treat' on a Saturday morning his mother would take him with her to work, where he enjoyed playing with pieces of fabric in the stockroom. 'I was outrageously spoiled by the staff, many of whom I clearly remember, and indeed some of whom I still see,' he recalled. 'I am intensely proud of this connection of mine with the pre-war Court dress-making world.' Indeed, one of his mother's colleagues, Maud Beard, became a fitter for Amies after he set up his own couture house in 1946, and worked on the first outfits that he designed for Princess Elizabeth, before she became queen.

Although Queen Mary was never a client of Hardy's mother, there was much excitement about the opportunity to see her on her occasional visits to Becontree on the outskirts of East London, where the family lived. They had moved there when Hardy's father, Captain Herbert Amies, was appointed the Resident Agent for London County Council soon after the end of the First World War. Herbert Amies had proved his capability and determination as a soldier, rising to become adjutant of his regiment; and having returned home to London, he became responsible for the large public housing estate that was being built at Becontree. It was in this capacity that Captain Amies was chosen to accompany Queen Mary and King George V on two separate occasions, when they toured the expanding project. Hardy recalled the Queen's 'magnificent presence', and described the astonishing effect that her appearance had on him as a teenager, when he saw her 'driving through the East End of London in the morning in pale-green lamé, wearing emeralds'.

His support for the monarchy was passionate, visceral and life-long. 'I would die for it,' he declared, in an interview at the age of eighty-three. 'I really would take out a gun and go and shoot people if they ever threatened it. It's one of our most precious assets. To destroy it would be the most wicked thing. I say this not just because I admire the present queen. I would still support the monarchy even if we had a bad queen, heaven forfend that we did. It's the idea that I defend; primogeniture is order – it's God.'

Yet for all his devotion to the stability represented by the monarchy, Amies was not altogether conformist, particularly given his identity as a gay man in an era when homosexuality was illegal. He was already in his late fifties at the time of the 1967 Sexual Offences Act, which decriminalised private sexual acts between men over the age of twenty-one in most of the UK, while also imposing heavier penalties on what were termed 'street offences' (leading to the arrest of men who were accused of being involved in homosexual activities in public places). It was not until 1994 that the age of consent for homosexual men was lowered from twenty-one to eighteen.

This may explain why Amies chose to escape to Europe when he left school, rather than studying at university in England (as his father had hoped). He had already shown the versatility that would define his career: as a schoolboy at Brentwood in Essex, Amies enjoyed amateur dramatics, playing female leads in productions of Shakespeare and Sheridan, and joining the school's Officer Training Corps, which gave him his first opportunity to travel abroad, to a military camp in Belgium. In 1927, at the age of eighteen, he journeyed to the South of France to take up a teaching post at an English school in Antibes, and then moved to Paris, working for a carriers and customs agency, arranging the delivery of French silks to London dressmakers. Early the following year, having become fluent in French, Amies set off to Bendorf, a small town on the banks of the Rhine, where he would learn German while staying as a paying guest at the family home of the local Protestant pastor, Ernst von Claer. In his autobiography, Amies describes his destination as 'the Pfarrhaus' (the parsonage), a 'large eighteenth-century house in an ugly little village on a dull stretch of the Rhine between Coblenz and Bonn'; yet it would prove to be the springboard for his sexual education, as well as an introduction to German culture. For it was here that Amies met a friend of the von Claers, Johann Witte (known as 'Jonny'), the manager of a local ceramic tile factory, who offered him a job as a salesman. Witte was in his early thirties, and the pair embarked on an intense relationship. In the ensuing two years, Amies travelled throughout Germany, and was introduced by Witte to the country's literature, politics and classical music. At this point, the nearest large town, Coblenz, was still occupied by French troops, to the bitter chagrin of its German population, under the terms of the Armistice that marked the end of the First World War. 'I regret to say that in spite of the kindness I had received in France I became completely pro-German in my way of thinking,' confessed Amies in his memoir. 'Certainly living in Germany one had the feeling of living in the middle of Europe, although I never went further east than Berlin.'

With hindsight, wrote Amies, his time in Germany in the late 1920s was as influential as it was immersive: 'I had seen that Germany felt strongly . . . that she ought to dominate with her culture and her industry the Balkans and Slav countries on her borders; that she felt she was as worthy of being considered a great Power as France, whom she admired for her artistic and cultural attainments but despised for her corruption [and] egotism.'

He had also experienced the freedoms of the final years before the Nazi dictatorship, referring in his memoir to discovering 'the curious nightlife of Berlin and the more virile and vigorous junketing in the dives off the Reeperbahn in Hamburg'. Yet amidst the decadence of the Weimar Republic, this was a period that saw the rise of National Socialism; and several of his friends in Germany declared themselves to be impressed by Hitler. When Amies was interviewed (by the publisher

Naim Attallah), he said: 'The family with whom I stayed welcomed Hitler as a saviour of the middle classes and the aristocracy, and I simply went along with them and didn't question their judgement. A much greater influence in my life at that time was the manager of the local factory, a north German, an extremely orderly man, who, I now realise, was very attracted to me. He was an intelligent, politically clear-thinking man, who favoured the Nazis to begin with, but changed in the course of events, and by the time I left he was very disillusioned.' Amies did not name Witte, and nor did he go into the details of their relationship – having told Attallah in the previous sentence that 'we're in danger of getting on to sex, which I said we weren't going to talk about'. (The interview took place in 1992, when Amies still seemed unwilling to be entirely open about his sexuality.)

In 1930, as the political and economic situation deteriorated in Germany, Hardy returned to England, and worked as a salesman for a weighing machine company in Birmingham, in the hope that he would soon be posted abroad. In fact, he was dispatched back to London, where he proved himself to be a success in this not altogether congenial employment. He maintained his links with Germany, in part through his beloved younger sister Rosemary, who followed in his footsteps first to Bendorf, to lodge with the von Claer family, and then to Berlin, where she lived with a Jewish family until 1937. Hardy visited Rosemary on holiday every summer, and was able to observe what he later described as 'the Nazification of the Pfarrhaus'. The pastor had two sons and a daughter, and Amies reported that the youngest boy, 'with whom I had been such good friends, was by now an ardent young Nazi officer in the Army'. Other members of the von Claer family were similarly enthusiastic about Hitler, having become what Amies described as 'easy prey to the outward attractions of the Nazi creed . . . Like so many others, they felt a joy and pride in the recrudescence of a national spirit. Even Jonny . . . was not untainted. He liked the apparent fairness and order of the new regime.' This may explain why both Jonny and his tile factory, which he bought in 1941, survived the war.

Meanwhile, thanks in part to his mother's contacts, Amies found himself a new role at a Mayfair dressmaker, Lachasse, where he began work as a manager in February 1934. Founded in 1928, Lachasse had thrived under the creative direction of its original designer, the talented Henry Digby Morton, who specialised in making innovative yet elegant women's suits. Amies, writing in his memoir, observed that 'Morton's philosophy was to transform the suit from the strict *tailleur*, or the ordinary country tweed with its straight up and down lines, uncompromising and fit only for the moors, into an intricately cut and carefully designed garment that was so fashionable that it could have been worn with confidence at the Ritz'.

Digby Morton had already left Lachasse to set up his own couture house, and Amies was asked to step in as a replacement designer just six months after he had joined the firm. He relished the new opportunity, while discovering that his childhood familiarity with his mother's work stood him in good stead. 'I started straight away by talking to customers: this was literally how I learned my business,' he recalled. 'The general machinery of the house, the functioning of the stock-room, the way materials were sent from here to the workrooms, the hierarchy of the workrooms, the positions of fitters, seconds, first hands, all seemed to me as simple and as natural as if I had known them all my life. As, of course, I had.'

Amies was also fortunate to have the services of an excellent head tailor at Lachasse, known as Mr Ernest, who, like many of the most skilled staff working for Mayfair dressmakers, had moved to London from Europe. 'Mr Ernest was of German extraction, and his training had been in tailoring of a slightly more continental trend than English.' Yet for all these advantageous circumstances, Amies needed to develop his own style as a designer, and he did so by a process of trial and error, combined with an innate talent. 'A great many of the thousand designs I made were extravagant and hideous,' he wrote, when recounting his early years at Lachasse; 'but all the time I was experimenting and all the time I was learning something. Then suddenly something began to emerge from all this.' By

1936, his originality was manifested in the shape of a newly proportioned suit, with a longer jacket than had been available before, and a flattering, lower waistline. 'This gives you much more room to move when in action and makes the jacket lie almost peacefully on its own when you are still,' he explained, in contrast to 'the high-waisted effect' that produced 'a buttoned up and restricted look'.

Amies had already added dresses and coats to the Lachasse collection, and was searching for the most attractive fabrics: 'I went on a tour of the tweed mills in Cumberland. At first, tweeds I was shown seemed no different from those in London: then suddenly something caught my eye in a pile of scraps of old material lying abandoned in the corner. It was a soft tweed made in a mixture of dark plum sprinkled with specks of vivid cerise and then criss-crossed with a fairly large overcheck in emerald green. I know it sounds awful, but the whole tweed glowed.' He chose the fabric for a tweed skirt suit that he named, whimsically, 'Panic', which was greatly admired in the spring couture collection of 1937. Was it co-incidence or playfulness that this particular suit appeared in the season before the coronation of George VI? At any rate, it secured him his first full page in *Vogue*, when the outfit was photographed by Cecil Beaton and published in the April 1937 edition.

By then, Amies was in a relationship with Alexis ffrench, an urbane interior designer and expert on antiques. Alexis's wife Anne had been a customer of Digby Morton at Lachasse, and continued to shop there when Amies took over. Alexis and Anne remained married, and were apparently very fond of one another, but maintained separate homes in London and the country. Hardy moved into Alexis's flat in Belgravia, as well as spending weekends with him at his house in Essex, Messing Park. There, they occasionally socialised with their neighbour Chips Channon and his boyfriend, Peter Coats; as Channon noted in his diary, on 23 May 1949, they lunched together at Messing Park, 'an enchanting house most exquisitely arranged'. He went on to describe Hardy as 'a *charmeur*', and the pair as 'a quaint couple who have lived together for about twenty years' (in reality, their relationship had begun in the mid-1930s, and would last until Alexis's death of cancer in 1956). Another entry, for 16 May 1949, describes Channon and Coats having dinner with the pair at their London flat: 'It is one of those curious *collages* that has lasted more than fifteen years. They are charming together.'

Amies simply described Alexis as a 'friend' in *Just So Far*, but went a little further in *Still Here*, writing that he 'and his wife Anne gave me a family life'. Both had daughters from previous marriages, and according to Amies, 'Anne adopted me into the family. It was useful to have a brother to the girls, especially when the time came to "give them a season". It was wonderful for me to go to debutante balls in Belgrave Square and Pont Street.' Amies also became close to Alexis's sister Yvonne, but it was their older brother, Conrad, who was to influence the next episode of his life. Conrad O'Brien ffrench (who inherited the title of Marquess de Castelthomond from his father) was a daring British intelligence officer who had joined MI6 after the First World War, and later established a network of spies in Austria in the 1930s, to monitor the rise of Nazism and the build-up of German forces.

It was almost certainly on Conrad's recommendation that Hardy was considered for intelligence work at the outbreak of war, although the official version is that he answered an advertisement in *The Times* calling for linguists with knowledge of at least two European languages to sign up for the Corps of Military Police. He was interviewed and accepted for the Intelligence Corps, but after several weeks training at Aldershot, he was sent back to London to await instructions, pending his transfer to an Officers Training Unit.

In December 1939, Amies designed a new collection for Lachasse, and was photographed at work in the couture salon wearing his military uniform and hob-nailed army boots. At the time, he described the collection as having an 'easy silhouette', with 'padded but not unnatural shoulders to accentuate a narrow waist', 'fullish' skirts, and a palette of 'soothing pastels and HOME BROWNS'. Early in 1940, Amies returned to Aldershot for five months of officer training, which he described in his memoir as 'the greatest possible fun. It was exactly like going back to

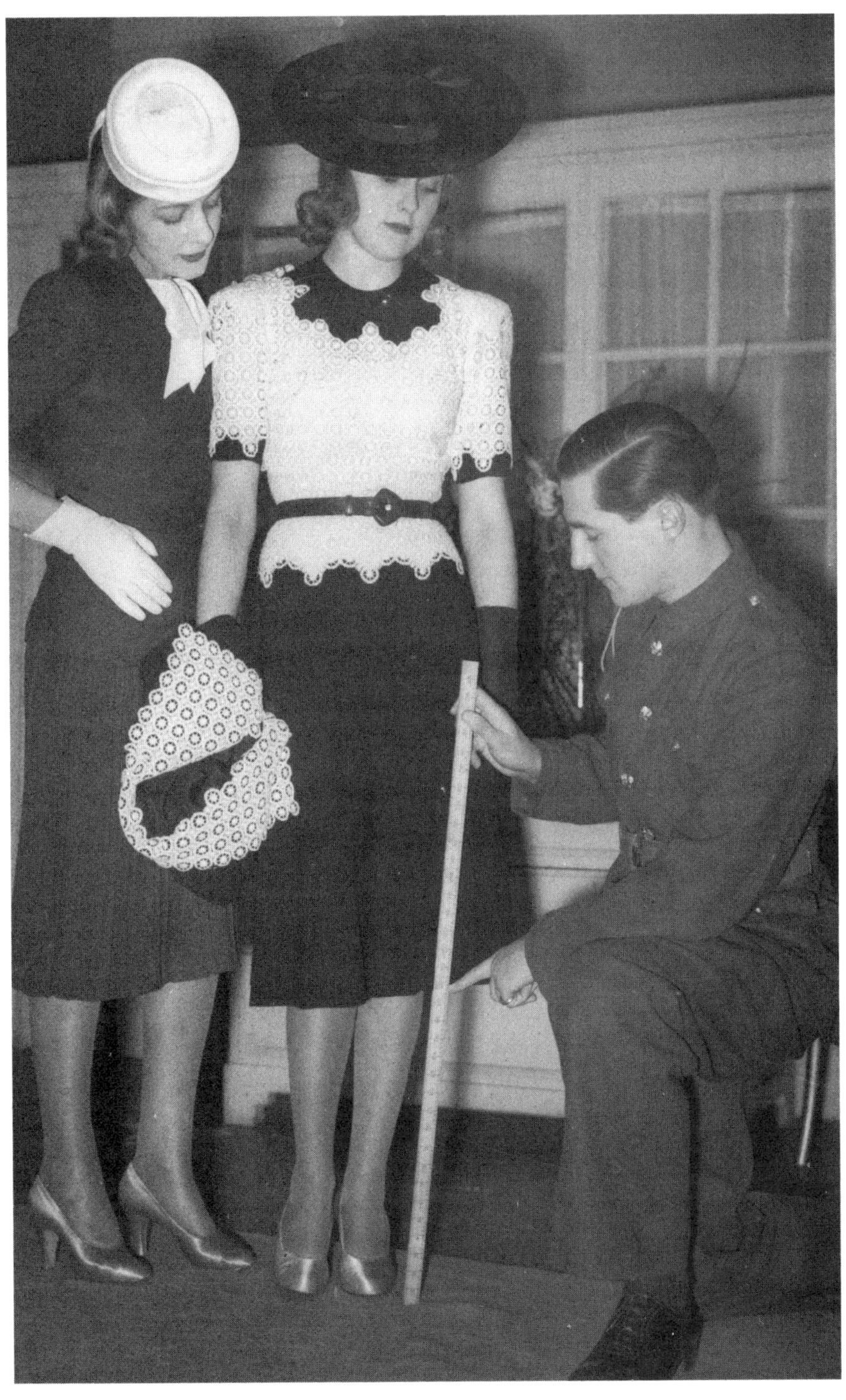

Hardy Amies preparing a new Lachasse collection, during a break from his military training in 1939. Photograph by Fred Ramage.

Utility suit designed by Hardy Amies, February 1945.

school.' This was followed by further training for the Intelligence Corps, and in October 1940 he was posted to the Canadian Corps Headquarters near Leatherhead, where he reported to the Senior Intelligence Officer Lord Tweedsmuir (son of John Buchan, the late Governor General of Canada, and author of *The Thirty-Nine Steps*). Amies described him as 'a shining example of a really good man'; but was surprised to discover the nature of his first mission, when Tweedsmuir sent for him just before Christmas 1940. '"Your country needs you at last," he said, and solemnly pushed an official-looking letter across to me. "You are to help open up another front for us in South America."' As Amies related in his memoir, the letter was from the Board of Trade, requesting his participation in the couture collection that was scheduled to be sent to South America. The success of his contribution gave him the impetus to leave Lachasse, and design ready-to-wear clothing for Bourne & Hollingsworth (a department store on Oxford Street where the new head of fashion was Madge Garland, a former fashion editor of *Vogue* who had encouraged Amies for some time). He also continued to create couture outfits that were sold at the House of Worth in Mayfair; and he was befriended and mentored by Captain Molyneux, whose premises were almost next door to Worth's. 'Molyneux was my god,' he wrote in his memoir. 'I admired tremendously the cool chic of his clothes. Sometimes they might appear heartless, but then he would tuck into the belt of a most severe navy blue woollen dress a bunch of pristine white lilies of the valley.' Speaking to Naim Attallah, Amies returned to the subject of Molyneux's influence on him: 'He believed in simplicity, as I do. All good clothes are totally unfussy. The first dress I ever saw of his was the simplest possible garment that just buttoned up the front, but it was absolutely impeccably made in beige linen with black buttons. And I learned that lesson and I follow it to this day.'

Amies somehow combined his development as a designer with his continuing full-time work as a military intelligence officer. His responsibilities increased in the spring of 1942, when he became a founder member, alongside Hartnell, Molyneux and Digby Morton, of the Incorporated

Society of London Fashion Designers (known as INSOC), in which role he was asked to contribute designs that would meet the Board of Trade's new guidelines for Utility clothing. A year previously, in April 1941, Amies had been recruited by SOE, which involved training at Beaulieu Abbey in Hampshire, where one of the instructors was the spy Kim Philby. Amies's memoir briefly mentions Philby by name, but gives no further information about this treacherous double agent for the Soviet Union. Decades later, when one of Hardy's friends, the author Selina Hastings, discovered that he had overlapped at Beaulieu with Philby, she tried to discover more. His response, as she recalled in her eulogy at Hardy's memorial service in 2003, was to deflect her questioning with wit. When she asked what Philby was like, Amies replied, 'Oh, always trying to get information out of *me*, darling.' What sort of information, she enquired? 'Why, the name of my tailor, of course.'

Thanks to M. R. D. Foot, we do know some details of SOE training, which was intended to create spies and saboteurs who would – in the famous words of Winston Churchill – 'set Europe ablaze'. Part of the instruction took place in what Foot described as a fierce paramilitary school at Arisaig, in the western Highlands of Scotland: 'There, beyond stiff military training, they learned silent killing, living off the country, rock climbing, the use of small boats, and how to use plastic explosive and small arms.' Amies revealed none of this in his memoir, referring simply to cooking buckets of *moules marinière* over open fires. According to Foot, only those students who had already proved their worth in Scotland were sent to Beaulieu; and once there, the instructors' 'most difficult and important task lay in character training: turning civilians and ordinary soldiers alike, inspired by the aggression they had learned at Arisaig, into devoted calculating saboteurs and killers. This cannot have been easy.'

Clearly, Amies proved himself to be capable, as confirmed by a confidential, undated report in his SOE file in the National Archives: 'This officer has done very well on the course. He is far tougher both physically and mentally than his rather precious appearance would suggest. He has displayed great keenness on all subjects and has learnt a great deal. He is always cheerful and ready to take part in any activity. He possesses a keen brain and an abundance of shrewd sense. He could be employed either in a country section or as a staff officer with a formation and should do well in either role. His only handicap is his precious appearance and manner, and these are tending to decrease.' Similarly, a report on Major Amies's progress in June 1943 noted that his 'agreeable manner does not prevent this officer from doing an efficient job in his branch . . . More of a soldier in his performance than his looks.'

By then, Amies had embarked on parachute training near Manchester, and having completed this course successfully, he returned to SOE's London headquarters on Baker Street where he rose through the hierarchy to lead the Belgian section. But if one is to believe his memoir, he was not as confident as might have been expected: 'During most of the time I was working in SOE, I was conscious of having an inferiority complex about the whole thing.' These doubts may have arisen in part because of his sexuality – the references in his file to his 'precious' appearance suggest that Amies was under close scrutiny. Presumably it was a continual strain for him to hide his private life with Alexis, at the same time as having to maintain the secrecy of his espionage activities; for in both these respects Amies was living undercover.

Quite aside from any homophobic prejudice that he might have faced was his sense of guilt about the fate of a number of Belgian agents and members of the Resistance who had relied on him. For, as was the case with all SOE operations, many courageous participants were captured by the Nazis, having been betrayed by collaborators or tracked down by German counter-intelligence forces. 'Grim moments were experienced', he wrote, 'when we had news of people we had recruited, trained and grown to like, being tortured and shot . . . Time and again we had seen organisations, little nests of workers with a small network of communications within Belgium . . . discovered and broken up by the Germans. Or, worse still, we had had cases where a captured wireless operator had been forced to send back messages to us. No one will know what damage was caused through such penetration.' Amies gave no further information in his memoirs, but he was certainly aware of the fatal consequences caused by Prosper Dezitter, a notorious Belgian traitor who posed as a resistant, and was paid by the Germans for every downed Allied airman that he helped capture.

The infiltration of SOE networks was the impetus for Operation Ratweek, a co-ordinated plan to kill Nazi officials and collaborators in 1944. Amies never spoke about it, despite being named in a television documentary as having helped organise the operation; but he did confide in a close friend later in life, and confirmed his active involvement in the retributive plot. His confidential records in the National Archives refer only to him arriving in Brussels with others in September 1944 to provide 'short-term agents for infiltrations through the lines' and 'liquidating affairs relating to SOE operations in Belgium during the Occupation'. Given the late Queen's remark to me about Amies having been 'very good at garrotting Nazis', and the fact that he was trained to undertake silent killing, as well as shooting the enemy, it seems plausible that the word 'liquidating' could be construed to include his involvement in the assassination of collaborators as the German forces retreated to the Belgian border. Even after the liberation of Brussels, more remote areas of the country, such as the Ardennes, remained shrouded in the fog of war, and fierce fighting continued during the Battle of the Bulge until the end of January 1945.

For the official version, however, one must rely on M. R. D. Foot, whose summary and assessment of Amies is as follows: 'He joined T-section in November 1941, to look after training and recruiting. He came to know so much about the section's problems and methods, and was so calm in manner and so quick to take points in', that he was 'eminently suitable' to lead it. Amies became acting head of T-section in August 1943, and was confirmed in this position in February 1944. His successes included funding, sustaining and arming the Belgian Resistance; supporting an escape line that ensured fifty-two SOE agents and eight Allied aircrew evaded capture and reached safety in the first eight months of 1944; sabotaging German transport systems; and securing Antwerp's vital docks against destruction by the retreating German forces in September 1944.

When Amies arrived in Brussels, as he wrote in his autobiography, he was 'caught up at first in the liberation excitement'. But over the course of the subsequent eight months that he worked in Belgium, he found himself confronted by the dire reality of the Nazi occupation, when he 'visited relatives of captured and killed agents, or more often the homes of people who had given them refuge and who had suffered accordingly. Sometimes there would be a reburial service or a Requiem Mass. Always we had to be ready to answer questions . . . "Why were you such a long time coming?"' He also had to deal with 'an unending stream of visitors claiming praise or compensation, or both, for the work they had done . . . It was so difficult to think of patriotism and self-effacement in what seemed to end up in skirmishes for rewards and decorations . . . We were very near the fringe of the skin-saving collaborationist circle, not to mention the opportunists.'

After the war, Amies was awarded the Order of the Crown, one of Belgium's highest honours, for his service to the country. But his memoir places far more emphasis on the bravery of the Belgian SOE agents – some of whom 'had been parachuted from England by us as many as three times'. And as he wrote in a letter to his sister, sent from Brussels on Armistice Day in November 1944, he had met young women who spoke to him 'calmly of the hours they have spent completely stripped in a cold bath in front of eight German officers interrogating them . . . Indeed, their only complaint is that they were not able to do more . . . The story of their resistance must be spread abroad so that they may feel proud of themselves, as indeed they should.'

Perhaps this explains why Amies introduced a number of courageous members of the Belgian Resistance to his friend Lee Miller, the American war correspondent and photographer, when she arrived in Brussels on assignment for *Vogue* in November 1944. Amies had not sought her out – in fact, as she reported to Audrey Withers, her editor at British *Vogue*, he was 'so modest and damned secretive that I did not even find out for days that he was in Brussels'. But once he had received clearance from the local military censor to co-operate with Miller, she photographed him on the streets of Brussels, as well as accompanying him to meet some of his friends in the Resistance, including the aristocratic d'Ursel family. As Miller wrote in her draft story for *Vogue*, 'a lovely young girl, Countess Therese, greeted us . . . we chit-chatted and I kept watching her "baby-face" which had been such a perfect passport for her activities in the Resistance movement. She is supposed to have carried millions of francs in her handbag, delivering funds for arms and bribery, for saboteurs and the hidden army. She wouldn't talk about it because she felt that others had done so much more than she had.'

Miller duly delivered her photographs for *Vogue*, to accompany a short article on Brussels after the Liberation. But at some point, Amies seems to have had second thoughts about the story appearing in *Vogue*, even though it had been approved for publication both by the field censor in Brussels, and again by the censor at the Ministry of Information. According to Amies's file in the National Archives, an unnamed officer was therefore sent to meet Audrey Withers at the offices of *Vogue*, in order to double check that Lee Miller's article and photographs were not disclosing sensitive information. The officer's report, dated 9 January 1945, stated: 'Miss Withers was extremely gracious and readily volunteered to withdraw any picture or cut out any part of the edited article that might in any way compromise or cause anxiety to her old personal friend and colleague Hardy Amies.' Having read the article, the officer concluded that 'it can in no way injure SOE or its connections'. Even so, he made his disapproval clear: 'What seems extraordinary to me is that a serving officer should lend himself and his Secret Service background in the interests of his private affairs, to wit, one of England's chief dress designers . . . to a gaudy publicity stunt together with posed photographs . . . no doubt the profile of Lt. Col. Amies in the next issue of the [sic] Vogue will cause a flutter in many feminine hearts when they realise that their handsome couturier is, after all, the "Scarlet Pimpernel" of this war.' Two days later, the unnamed officer returned to *Vogue* and asked Audrey Withers to cut

Lieutenant Colonel Hardy Amies during his time in Brussels, 1944.
Photograph by Lee Miller.

the brief reference to Amies's activities in London as a fashion designer, prior to his deployment to Brussels, which she duly did.

Rereading these pages, eighty-five years later, I cannot help but feel outraged and hurt on Amies's behalf. After all, he had been asked by the Board of Trade to contribute to the war effort by designing clothes for the Utility collections, and to support overseas fashion exports, for the purposes of both propaganda and fundraising – and to do so at the same time as diligently serving his country as an SOE officer. None of this episode appears in his memoirs, but it might give some context to the following passage about his time in Belgium: 'I must confess that I left Brussels with a tiny touch of bitterness in my heart. I did not think that I had made a success of any of my work there. Seeing sometimes both the British and the Belgian point of view, I had failed to please either.'

Amies did, however, remain intensely curious about the shifts in fashion that he saw in Brussels; for as he wrote to his sister in November 1944, the flamboyant 'Resistance hats' that were prevalent in Paris had reached Belgium: 'they are truly large, that is to say, large crowns rather than brims and decorated with great complications of brightly coloured silks. Tall and complicatedly draped turbans are also seen. They were worn with deliberate bravado throughout the occupation to cause the maximum of annoyance to the German and his dowdy wife; this object achieved, they are now being modified to suit our more austere eyes.'

In the same letter, he gave an equally vivid description of the distinctive 'Zazou' style that had been adopted by 'the younger generation': 'I do not know where this term comes from, but it is Parisian and means roughly "pansy ruffian". You only see the female variety here. It is a sort of romantic, unbalanced, jazz demonstration. The zazou shoe has a high wide heel . . . and is nearly always made in coloured cloth as leather is scarce; the zazou stocking is made of white cotton, thickly knitted and coming only to the knee, the exact equivalent of the Austrian variety; the zazou skirt is full and unaesthetically short, displaying too much bare knee; the zazou jacket is too long for the short skirt and is sometimes cut like a box jacket; zazou hair is just an untidy, long bob, crowned with an enormous hat made of cheap felt . . . The true zazou always carries a tightly rolled umbrella. You can imagine how incongruous the whole effect is, but it is worn quite seriously on the streets . . . I think I am right in saying that it is jazz romanticism.'

To his relief, Amies managed to avoid being posted to Germany at the end of the war – despite the fact that as a bilingual intelligence officer, he would have been useful there. 'I felt mentally exhausted by the struggles at SOE,' he admitted in his memoir, 'and I had a shrewd idea that the administration of the Army of Occupation in Germany was going to be pretty chaotic.' Fortunately for him, 'the powers that be at home' were already making plans for the further promotion of fashion exports that would be vital for Britain's economic recovery, and he was officially discharged from his military duties in September 1945. Soon afterwards, he was presented with his demob outfit, including 'a cavalry mackintosh of excellent cut which I still cherish'. So ended the war for Amies, and he returned to London, determined to use 'the severe lessons in diplomacy' that he had learned during his espionage career to build a couture house of his own. And nowhere would diplomacy – and complete discretion – prove to be more important than in his future role as a royal dressmaker.

Princess Elizabeth and her sister Margaret, delivering a BBC radio broadcast, October 1940.

THEATRE OF WAR

On 13 October 1940, Princess Elizabeth gave her first radio address: a carefully scripted speech for *Children's Hour* on the BBC, broadcast from Windsor Castle, to the evacuees who had been displaced from their homes and sent to the countryside or far away overseas. The fourteen-year-old princess spoke in a high, clear voice, with the clipped upper-class vowels of her mother, but none of the hesitancy of her father; and although her pronunciation now sounds dated, the tender poignancy of her words is still touching if you listen to the recording today: 'Thousands of you in this country have had to leave your homes and be separated from your fathers and mothers. My sister Margaret Rose and I feel so much for you as we know from experience what it means to be away from those we love most of all.'

She did not allude to the carnage of the Blitz; but on the very same evening of her broadcast, an air raid hit a block of flats on Coronation Avenue in Stoke Newington, causing what the *Daily Express* would call 'the greatest bombing tragedy of the whole of London'. The bomb penetrated through all five floors of the building, and detonated in the basement shelter, killing the majority of those who were taking cover there. Four days later, when the King and Queen went to visit the site of the disaster, the rescuers were still digging out bodies. As Queen Elizabeth wrote to her mother-in-law, 'They fear two hundred dead, owing to the fact that the water main burst, & drowned many . . . I do hate these visits so desperately Mama. I feel quite exhausted after seeing & hearing so much sadness, sorrow, heroism and magnificent spirit. The destruction is so awful, & the people too wonderful – they deserve a better world.'

It was against this continuing backdrop of death and devastation that Princess Elizabeth's voice was heard, conveying optimism, and a sense of kinship created by the national ordeal. The speech would have been written for her, but according to Miss Crawford, 'Lilibet herself put in several phrases that were quite her own'. The governess did not give specific details about which those were, but overall – following in the tradition set by George V's reassuring radio broadcasts – there was an emphasis on family and faith: 'We know, every one of us, that in the end all will be well; for God will care for us and give us victory and peace . . . My sister is by my side and we are both going to say goodnight to you. Come on, Margaret.' 'Good night, children,' chimed in Margaret, before her sister's encouraging closing line: 'Good night, and good luck to you all.'

Jock Colville, private secretary to Winston Churchill (and subsequently to Princess Elizabeth), wrote in his diary that he had listened to the broadcast and was 'embarrassed by the sloppy sentiment she was made to express, but her voice was most impressive and if the Monarchy survives, Queen Elizabeth II should be a most successful radio Queen'. The speech may have been sentimental, but it was deemed a propaganda triumph, and was widely covered in the US press as well as in the UK, illustrated by photographs of the sisters sitting together at the microphone, modestly dressed in matching tweed jackets and striped jerseys. The message was one of unity, solidarity and courage, and highlighted that the royal family had not fled their country; for in the oft-quoted words of Queen Elizabeth, 'The children could not go without me, I could not possibly leave the King, and the King would never go.'

There were, in fact, contingency plans in the event of a Nazi invasion, to spirit the royals away to a remote and hidden location, and from there, if need be, to a port that would allow their escape to Canada, where the King could reign in exile. Madresfield, the Worcestershire home of the Earl of Beauchamp, was given the code name Harbour, and identified as a refuge in the west of England, offering a getaway route into Wales. An alternative sanctuary was planned at Newby Hall in Yorkshire, code-named Security, as a staging post if they were fleeing to Scotland. Lilibet's cousin Margaret Rhodes (née Elphinstone), who spent time at Windsor Castle during the war, recalled in her autobiography: 'A hand-picked body of officers and men from the Brigade of Guards and the Household Cavalry, equipped with armoured cars, was on twenty-four-hour call to take the King and Queen and their daughters to a safe house in the country . . . It was a comforting thought that they were around, until I learned that although the operation probably included the corgis, it did not include me.'

Plans were also made to secure the Crown Jewels, whose symbolic value as the talismans of a thousand years of royal history was as great as their monetary worth. Just before the outbreak of war, the coronation regalia had been transferred from the Tower of London to a secret strongroom in Windsor Castle, in a vault beneath the office of the Royal Librarian, Sir Owen Morshead. He wrote to Queen Mary on 28 August 1939 to assure her that the precious jewels, along with other valuables (including paintings) were being protected: 'Here we are busy sandbagging the windows on the ground-floor along the North Terrace, and timbering them inside, and fitting gas-proof doors. The frames of certain of the more valuable pictures hang empty, their canvases having been removed into safe custody. The Crown Jewels came down from the Tower on Saturday evening.'

When Queen Mary's London home, Marlborough House, was bombed on 16 October 1940, she arranged for her cherished collections of paintings and porcelain to be sent to join her at Badminton. 'What a lot of trouble & expense that hateful fiend has put us to!' she wrote to Morshead; 'how I hate the Germans!' She vented her fury with Hitler in an ongoing private battle against ivy; for as James Pope-Hennessy observed in his official biography, 'Queen Mary's enmity towards ivy had long been proverbial at Sandringham, and she had never missed an opportunity to attack it wherever it appeared within the grounds'. Badminton offered her a wider scope; and there she extended her horticultural combat, much to the distress of her niece, the Duchess of Beaufort, whose home Queen Mary had taken over with more than fifty members of her own household. After interviewing the Duchess, Pope-Hennessy noted that Queen Mary was 'fundamentally very very German – the two things she liked most were destruction and order. When left to herself for the day she would have trees cut down right and left in the garden until the Beauforts diverted her into the woods.' He also recorded the Duchess's description of encountering her aunt during an air raid: 'Well there I was in the middle of the night, with my hair all anyhow and in a filthy old dressing gown; and there in the shelter sat Queen Mary, perfectly dressed with her pearls, doing a crossword puzzle.' On one side was her dazed lady-in-waiting, who had taken a sleeping pill and kept flopping over; on the other side was her maid, 'gripping two jewel cases grimly'.

Meanwhile, Sir Owen Morshead remained in charge of the Crown Jewels, as he revealed to Lilibet and her governess. 'One day,' wrote Miss Crawford in her memoir, 'he took us right down to the vaults under the Castle. "Would you like to see something interesting?" he asked us. We said we would. He showed us a lot of rather ordinary-looking leather hatboxes which seemed at first sight just to be all stuffed up with old newspapers. But when we examined these, we discovered the Crown Jewels were hidden in them!'

In January 1941, Morshead sent another letter to Queen Mary, describing the construction of a new secret facility to provide 'greater safety' for 'the most valuable treasures'. This involved descending through a trap door hidden away in one of the castle's maze of rooms, climbing down a ladder into a long underground passageway, to reach two chambers that were being tunnelled out of the rock, and reinforced with concrete and steel. Six months later, Morshead gave a further update to Queen Mary, explaining that the Crown Jewels were now installed in this subterranean bunker, 'but some of the leather cases are showing signs of mildew'. He informed her, too, of his 'bold step' in regard to the state crowns worn by the King and Queen for their coronation in 1937. In accordance with George VI's 'personal wish', Morshead 'took out perhaps a dozen of the most important jewels – the Cullinan [diamonds], the Koh-i-noor, the Black Prince's ruby; and some others, to which the Queen added that fat ruby, the size of a frog, which is mounted in a necklace . . . These stones I wrapped in cotton wool and placed inside a tall glass preserving-jar with a screw top & rubber washer . . . I then packed the glass jar inside a Bath Oliver biscuit tin, which fitted it to perfection.' The biscuit tin, he continued, was a 'sensible' precaution in case of invasion, when 'the roads might become congested: the Crown Jewels are bulky and heavy, and the lorry containing them might not be able to get along. This tin is easily portable; betrays no indication of its contents; is easily disposed of at the shortest notice – even buried or sunk. And it contains the nucleus for a new set of Crown Jewels if the worst should come to the worst. Which God forbid – as I hope he will.'

At the same time as those covert measures were underway, the public propaganda was emphasising that the royal family were like all other British families, suffering similar privations and following the same rules of austerity. Hence the press reporting that Princess Elizabeth's fourteenth birthday in April 1940 had been celebrated with a 'plain' sponge cake, rather than anything more extravagant; and the King's command that a black line was painted on each of the baths in the castle and the palace, to ensure that no more than three inches of hot water should be used, in strict accordance with fuel economy.

However, when bombs exploded in Windsor Great Park, the news was suppressed; as was the fact that the princesses had moved into the castle in May 1940. Instead, they were described as living in 'a house in the country'. Writing from Windsor Castle on 25 October 1940, the Queen told her sister, May Elphinstone: 'We have been attacked here 2 nights running, but don't say a word will you, as we don't want the Germans to know anything that might help them aim!, and it was the first time that the children had actually heard the whistle and scream of bombs. They were wonderful, & when I went to say good-night to Margaret in her bed, I said I hoped she wasn't frightened etc, & she said, "Mummy, it was just like when you take a photograph that doesn't come out – all grey &

blurred, & you see several hands and arms instead of one", & it is so true, really very much what one feels like.'

Of course, the photographs that did appear of the royal family continued to show them looking calm, clear-headed and dutiful: Lilibet in her Girl Guide's uniform, for example; or hard at work in her vegetable garden; or practising with an ARP stirrup pump alongside her father. When she wasn't pictured in her Guide's uniform, she was usually seen in the drab worsted suit and jersey that she wore for her radio broadcast, complete with sturdy brown brogues. The same sartorial code applied when she and her sister were photographed with their parents at Buckingham Palace in October 1942; a rare trip to London for the princesses, and arranged to coincide with a visit from Eleanor Roosevelt (who assessed Lilibet as 'quite serious and a child with a great deal of character and personality . . . She asked me a number of questions about life in the United States and they were serious questions.'). The photographer on this occasion was Cecil Beaton – by then working almost exclusively for the Ministry of Information – and he was struck by the spartan conditions at the palace. 'The glass cupboards, because of bombing, were bare of china and the fireplace was empty,' he wrote in his diary. 'The palace has conformed to wartime strictures and sets an example in austerity. The temperatures in corridors and many of the rooms was little above freezing. There were no flowers in vases. It very likely *is* true that the King allows himself only a few inches of bath water, but this somewhat dour atmosphere did not make my job of picture-making any the easier.' As usual, the King was in military uniform for the portraits, the Queen donned a day dress and pearls, while Lilibet and Margaret wore the same unassuming jackets and skirts with simple cotton blouses; and despite Beaton's concerns, the sober results were exactly what was required by the Ministry of Information for the press. Given that the royal family was still mourning the death of the Duke of Kent – who had been killed in a plane crash in Scotland just two months previously – their sombre faces were only to be expected. As Chips Channon had observed in his diary on 29 August 1942, after attending the Duke of Kent's funeral at Windsor Castle that day, 'The Court looked old and somewhat moth-eaten . . . it is the end

The princesses at war: (top left) in their Guides uniform; (top right) gardening together; (above left) at Windsor Castle; (above right) Princess Elizabeth with her mother.

Opposite: Princess Elizabeth with her father, 1942. Photograph by Lisa Sheridan.
Above: Queen Elizabeth with her daughters, 1942. Photograph by Cecil Beaton.

of an epoch. All elegances are over. Our royalty will become increasingly civic, duty-doing, dour and glamourless.'

Thanks to the diary of Lilibet's friend Alathea Fitzalan Howard, who lived with her grandfather during the war at Cumberland Lodge in Windsor Great Park, it is clear that the princesses' restrained outfits weren't simply for the benefit of the camera. Alathea was a member of the same Girl Guides company as Lilibet, attended weekly art classes and dancing lessons with the princesses, and often visited them at Windsor Castle; and although she dearly loved their company, she was not at all impressed by their wardrobes. 'They wore their old brown check skirts and red Aertex shirts,' she wrote on 23 October 1941, 'which they ought not to do – their clothes have gone down a lot since the war.' Even before clothes rationing was introduced in June 1941, Alathea was critical of their sensible outfits. In May 1940, for example, she was disappointed to see that the sisters were still wearing the same 'bricky coats and skirts and striped jerseys' from the previous year, and in August she described their bathing suits as 'black and plain – awful things'.

Yet what also emerges from Alathea's diary is the genuine warmth and informality of family life at Windsor Castle (a marked contrast to her chilly, aristocratic upbringing, in which she rarely saw her own parents). Her entry for 9 November 1940 describes a rainy Saturday afternoon playing outside with Lilibet and Margaret: 'The Queen joined us, when we gave some scarves to some soldiers, then unblocked a stream. Q[ueen] sweet and held my hand to balance me on a stepping stone. M[argaret] pushed me into some barbed wire tearing my good stocking!' After tea with the King and Queen, they played card games, and then Alathea spent the night with the princesses and their nanny Allah in the castle bomb shelter, 'which was the greatest fun I've ever known'. As she added the next day, she found 'more happiness and homeliness' there with them than anywhere else. Alathea relished the meals at the castle, too, especially the supplements to food rationing: her diary entry for 22 March 1941 recounts that there was crab for lunch and cream for tea, brought back by the King and Queen after their visit two days previously to the badly bombed city of Plymouth. 'Ate chocolates with the Queen . . . [then] Devonshire cream, which the princesses don't like . . . and the King told the Queen she shouldn't eat so much, when she hadn't been out all the afternoon!'

Aside from enjoying regular film screenings, Lilibet and Margaret devised homemade entertainment, both for themselves and the other children (including evacuees) living in Windsor Great Park. In July 1940, they staged an *Alice in Wonderland* concert at a community hall on the estate, to raise money for a wartime charity. 'Lilibet will tap dance,' wrote Alathea after a rehearsal. 'Margaret is in it too. They both play the piano on stage and then Margaret is the Dormouse in the Mad Hatter's Tea Party. We all come on in the finale . . . It's very good, but everyone I've met says it's making them much too cheap. They really shouldn't do it. They ought to get up little plays of their own with their friends but not dance with all the evacuees like this.' The King, however, was delighted, writing in his diary that his daughters 'both did their parts very well & were not at all self-conscious'. Alathea was less impressed: 'Lilibet played the piano badly and the curtain fell on Margaret's head!'

That Christmas, with the help of Miss Crawford, they put on a Nativity play at St George's Hall in the castle. Margaret took to the stage in a white dress singing 'Gentle Jesus, Meek and Mild', while Lilibet appeared as one of the three kings, wearing a crown and a velvet tunic. This led to more ambitious annual productions of Christmas pantomimes until the end of the war, in aid of the Royal Household Wool Fund (which provided the materials to knit comforters for soldiers). These were directed by Hubert Tannar, the headmaster of the Royal School on the Windsor estate, whose pupils also appeared in the shows. The princesses were closely involved in all aspects of the productions, including the scripts, and took leading parts, with Lilibet appearing as the principal boy, and Margaret the leading lady. From the start, the pantomimes were reported in the press, but although they were photographed by Lisa Sheridan (who had started taking pictures

PROGRAMME

OF

Christmas Pantomime

ALADDIN

IN THE

WATERLOO CHAMBER
WINDSOR CASTLE

DECEMBER 16th, 17th and 18th, 1943

PRICE 1s.

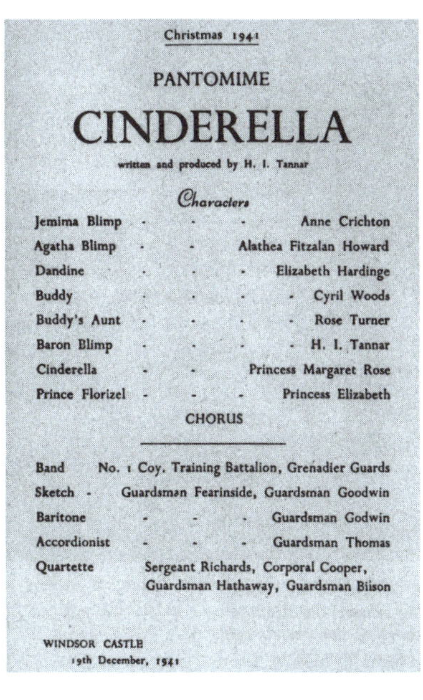

Christmas 1941

PANTOMIME

CINDERELLA

written and produced by H. I. Tannar

Characters

Jemima Blimp	Anne Crichton
Agatha Blimp	Alathea Fitzalan Howard
Dandine	Elizabeth Hardinge
Buddy	Cyril Woods
Buddy's Aunt	Rose Turner
Baron Blimp	H. I. Tannar
Cinderella	Princess Margaret Rose
Prince Florizel	Princess Elizabeth

CHORUS

Band	No. 1 Coy. Training Battalion, Grenadier Guards
Sketch	Guardsman Fearinside, Guardsman Goodwin
Baritone	Guardsman Godwin
Accordionist	Guardsman Thomas
Quartette	Sergeant Richards, Corporal Cooper, Guardsman Hathaway, Guardsman Biison

WINDSOR CASTLE
19th December, 1941

The princesses' wartime Christmas pantomimes. Photographs by Lisa Sheridan.

of the princesses as children in the 1930s), no images were released to the newspapers. Nor were any recordings made public, despite the fact that Robert Wood – the BBC engineer in charge of outside broadcasting who had covered the coronation in 1937, and was now working closely with the likes of Winston Churchill and Charles de Gaulle – had been asked by the princesses to oversee the installation of professional microphones and loudspeakers for their performances. 'So on a number of afternoons I slipped away from my desk,' wrote Wood in his autobiography. 'The pantomimes were a welcome break and cheered everyone up.'

Even so, a number of informal stories about the Christmas shows were shared with journalists, to leaven the news about the slow progress of the war. In December 1941 – the same month that the US joined forces with the Allies, after the Japanese bombing of Pearl Harbor – the *Daily Mirror* informed its readers that Princess Elizabeth had overcome her sore throat in order to appear on stage as Prince Charming opposite her sister Margaret in the title role of *Cinderella*. The *Scotsman* provided additional details, writing that the Queen had supervised the costumes, and 'the coach for Cinderella was a Sedan chair originally the property of Queen Anne'.

The following year, in 1942, Margaret performed as Fairy Thistledown and Lilibet as Prince Salvador in *Sleeping Beauty*, which was covered in *Tatler* (again, without any accompanying images). Instead, a solo portrait of Princess Elizabeth was released that Christmas – taken by Cecil Beaton at the previous sitting at Buckingham Palace in October 1942. Earlier that year, on 24 February, she had been appointed colonel of the Grenadier Guards, and had undertaken her first official public engagement on her sixteenth birthday when she inspected the regiment at Windsor Castle. Her new military role was acknowledged in Beaton's portrait, via the diamond brooch in the form of the regimental cypher that the princess had received as a birthday gift from the Grenadier Guards, and the badge she was wearing on her soldierly cap. 'She had her mother's smile,' wrote Beaton in his diary, 'is extremely well brought up – and has a great knowledge of history.' Other than the addition of the brooch, badge and cap, Lilibet was photographed in the same unpretentious jacket and cotton blouse as she had worn to

Princess Elizabeth wearing the insignia of the Grenadier Guards, 1942.
Photograph by Cecil Beaton.

meet Mrs Roosevelt; and it was this Beaton image that was published on the front cover of *Life* magazine on 15 February 1943. Inside the same issue was another Beaton portrait of Lilibet and her sister in matching dresses; according to the caption, these were made of 'hand-me-down taffeta' that had been turned into 'old-fashioned picture gowns', 'without violating the rationing rules'. (*Life* also reported that Princess Elizabeth was studying American history, and wrote every day to her grandmother Queen Mary.)

By December 1943, the third annual pantomime – starring Lilibet as Aladdin and Margaret as Princess Roxana – was receiving wider coverage in the press; although as always, the location was simply described as an anonymous hall 'somewhere in the country', and there were still no photographs. The war was far from being won: in his Christmas radio broadcast that year, the King spoke of the continuing need for 'hard working and hard fighting – perhaps harder working and harder fighting than ever before'. But despite the requirement for the royal family to be seen as serious-minded, the news of the pantomime spread. A favourable review even appeared in *The Stage*, which informed its readers that the princesses had performed before an audience of several hundred soldiers, 'supported by a vigorous chorus of local schoolchildren' and an orchestra 'provided by the Royal Horse Guards band'. Meanwhile, details about *Aladdin*'s costumes were reported in the *Sunday Post*: 'Princess Elizabeth made her first entrance in traditional pantomime style by popping out of a laundry basket. She wore long trousers of white silk with a Chinese kimono shirt, and later a "utility suit", as she called it, of light blue shorts and top.' And it was the august pages of *The Times* that included the significant news that Prince Philip of Greece was in the audience, alongside the King and Queen and his cousin the Duchess of Kent.

More details about the burgeoning romance feature in Alathea's diary. Lilibet had first told her friend about Prince Philip in April 1941, saying that 'P was her boy'. He crops up again in the diary six months later, on 23 October that year, when Lilibet shares the news that 'Philip, her beau, had been for the weekend . . . She said he's very funny, which doesn't sound my type actually – the only thing that <u>does</u> bore me about the

Royal Family is that they all will tell one jokes that they've heard on [the] wireless, etc. No one else I know is the least interested in these sort of silly jokes, but then the K and Q and the princesses are v. simple people.' On 21 December 1941 – the weekend of the pantomime – Alathea was finally introduced to Prince Philip. 'Lilibet was sweet today – her Philip came and is quite nice but not my type.' Two years later, on 18 December 1943, when Alathea was in the audience for *Aladdin*, she was more impressed, describing him as 'very fair and older-looking than when I saw him last year. He seems so suited to PE [Princess Elizabeth] and I kept wondering today whether he is her future husband. I think it is the most desirable event that could possibly happen.'

'Windsor Castle was a wonderful place on wet days,' wrote Miss Crawford, remembering the five years of war when she lived there with Lilibet and Margaret. 'There was so much of it to be explored, so many odd nooks and corners where we had never been before.' And somewhere in the cupboards or storerooms of that immense fortress, the costumes worn by the princesses in *Aladdin* were preserved, along with several others from the 1944 pantomime (*Old Mother Red Riding Boots*). More than eight decades after they were put away, the flamboyant outfits were unearthed, and displayed to the public in a small exhibition at Windsor Castle in the winter of 2021. This took place in the same room that the pantomimes had been staged, the Waterloo Chamber; and what seemed most striking to me when I visited was the richness of the costumes, in direct contrast to the understated clothes that the princesses had dutifully worn throughout the war. Lilibet's Aladdin 'utility suit' turned out to be made of teal-blue silk, teamed with a handsome gold paisley wool jacket and a jaunty tasselled hat; while Margaret's long gown in which she appeared as Princess Roxana was of scarlet and gold silk damask. Three similarly elaborate Edwardian-style outfits survived from the final pantomime: a white voile and lace-trimmed dress worn by Margaret; and for Lilibet, a patterned chintz bathing suit and a pink silk-satin full-length gown. In her autobiography, Lisa Sheridan remembered that the King 'was particularly enthusiastic' that she should photograph his oldest daughter in her frilly pink dress, which had 'cascades of white lace sewn into formal patterns on [the] bodice and skirt', and was worn with a yellow straw hat, trimmed with 'bright flowers and tilted over the forehead at a fashionable angle'.

At the time, the newspapers reported that the pantomime costumes were 'supervised' by Queen Elizabeth, and Lisa Sheridan described her during a rehearsal, 'thimble on finger, ready to sew, match colours and adjust children's clothing'. But Miss Crawford recalled that although they had found various 'pieces of brocade and tapestry and suitable oddments we could borrow for dressing up', they had hired the princesses' dresses and wigs. And according to the Royal Collection Trust, the costumes were supplied by two theatrical costumiers (H. & M. Rayne and L. & H. Nathan), with some additional outfits from Norman Hartnell. Certainly, the accounts in the Royal Archives show that in 1941 Hartnell adapted a pair of 'white lace and tulle' dresses, one for each of the princesses. In the same year, the designer made another dress for Lilibet, out of her 'own blue acorn printed silk', and altered her 'own worsted flannel jacket'.

The exhibition also revealed the imaginative watercolours of fairy-tale characters that had decorated the walls of the Waterloo Chamber for the pantomimes. These had been painted by Claude Whatham, a teenage evacuee who was studying part-time at the nearby Wycombe School of Art; and they were pasted into the empty frames, to fill the spaces left when the original oil paintings had been removed for safekeeping. Lisa Sheridan remembered, 'The names of the original subjects of the portraits were still on the frames and we laughed together as we read the title of King William IV under the colourful representation of Little Red Riding Hood!' Miss Crawford shared similar memories: 'There was Dick Whittington with his cat gazing down from a frame marked Charles I. Mother Goose appeared as Queen Henrietta Maria, and so on all round the room. I had wondered if the King would object, but I need not have bothered. Not long afterwards I heard His Majesty showing someone round and pointing them out, saying "What do you think of my ancestors?"'

By chance, I had already seen Whatham's fairy-tale pictures when I happened to visit the castle in November 2020; they had been uncovered during the Covid lockdown earlier that year, after the oil paintings in the Waterloo Chamber were removed for restoration and cleaning. I was there to do some filming about a Norman Hartnell dress that belonged to the Queen and had been adapted into a bridal gown for her granddaughter Princess Beatrice to wear at her wedding at Windsor that summer. By the time of the filming, Covid restrictions were in place again, so the castle was closed to the public, and it seemed particularly gloomy in the November twilight. As my guide pointed out the pictures in the Waterloo Chamber, and told me the story of the princesses' pantomimes, I tried to imagine what it must have felt like when the room was filled with the laughter and applause of an appreciative audience, gathered there to enjoy themselves, even amidst the darkness of the war. And I thought, too, of the Queen's speech that she had made from Windsor in April 2020, speaking to her people about the challenges of the Covid pandemic, and offering reassurance: 'We will succeed – and that success belongs to all of us.' She also cited her first broadcast from the castle in 1940 when her sister had been at her side, and the losses and separation that so many had suffered during the war. And yet again, the Queen offered optimism, and the promise that 'better days will return; we will be with our friends again; we will be with our families again; we will meet again.'

On this occasion, she wore a long-sleeved green dress with a turquoise and diamond brooch that had belonged to her grandmother, Queen Mary, and a traditional pearl necklace and earrings of the kind that her mother had worn during the war. About 24 million people watched her speech, and it is impossible to calculate what proportion of those viewers had heard her radio broadcast in 1940. But for many of us – including me – her voice sounded as familiar as if it was our own grandmother speaking. And with that familiarity came an echo of the past that seemed comforting, however troubling the circumstances, and whatever sorrows the unknown future might hold.

IN UNIFORM

On 8 May 1945, when victory in Europe was finally declared, the royal family stepped out onto the balcony of Buckingham Palace to wave to the cheering crowds below. The balcony had been repaired in time for VE Day, but the palace still bore the scars of war: its unglazed windows were boarded up, the glass missing from the repeated bomb damage. The King had donned his uniform of an Admiral of the Fleet; the Queen was in a blue dress and matching coat designed by Norman Hartnell, while Princess Margaret wore a similarly feminine skirt and jacket. In marked contrast to her mother and sister, Lilibet was attired in the military khaki of the Auxiliary Territorial Service, which she had joined as a subaltern shortly before her nineteenth birthday in April.

Thus it was that when the King granted his daughters their wish to leave the palace that night – and the freedom to join the spontaneous celebrations – Lilibet was wearing an anonymous army uniform, just like many other girls of her age. Her cousin Margaret Rhodes (who had been living at the palace after she began working for MI6) was with the royal party, and described the momentous outing in her memoir: 'This sort of freedom was unheard of as far as my cousins were concerned. There must

Princess Elizabeth in her ATS uniform, 1945. Photograph by Paul Popper.
Overleaf: the royal family on the balcony of Buckingham Palace on VE Day, May 1945.

have been about sixteen of us and we had as escort the King's Equerry, a very correct Royal Navy captain in a pin-striped suit, bowler hat and umbrella. No one appeared less celebratory, perhaps because he took his guardian responsibilities too seriously.'

Lilibet, she continued, 'pulled her peaked cap well down over her face to disguise her much photographed image, but a Grenadier among the party positively refused to be seen in the company of another officer, however junior, who was improperly dressed. My cousin didn't want to break King's regulations and so reluctantly she agreed to put her cap on properly, hoping she would not be recognised. Miraculously she got away with it.'

Despite the restraining presence of the King's Equerry, the royal group soon became swept up in the euphoria. 'London had gone mad with joy,' remembered Margaret Rhodes. 'We could scarcely move; people were laughing and crying; screaming and shouting and perfect strangers were kissing and hugging each other. We danced the Conga . . . the Lambeth Walk and the Hokey-Cokey, and at last fought our way back to the Palace, where there was a vast crowd packed to the railings.' The princesses joined in the chorus calling out, 'We want the King; we want the Queen!' Before long, 'the double doors leading onto the balcony were thrown open and the King and Queen came out, to be greeted by a rising crescendo of cheers . . . It was a view of their parents that the Princesses had never before experienced and for all of us young people it was the grand finale to an unforgettable day.' But for Lilibet and Margaret, as their cousin observed, it was also 'a unique burst of personal freedom; a Cinderella moment in reverse, in which they could pretend they were ordinary and unknown'.

Lilibet's own diary was more measured, recording simply that on VE Day, 'PM announced unconditional surrender. Sixteen of us went out in crowd, cheered parents on balcony. Up St J's St [St James's Street], Piccadilly, great fun.' What becomes clear from her diary, too, is that the single night of liberation portrayed in popular culture actually took place on four separate occasions. On 9 May, she wrote: 'Out in crowd again – Trafalgar Square, Piccadilly, Pall Mall, walked simply miles. Saw parents on balcony at 12.30am – ate, partied, bed 3am!' Three months later, on

Crowds at Buckingham Palace, VE Day, 1945.

Princess Elizabeth changing a tyre during her ATS training, April 1945.

15 August, following the final surrender of Japan: 'Out in crowd, Whitehall, Mall, St J St, Piccadilly, Park Lane, Constitution Hill, ran through Ritz. Walked miles, drank in Dorchester, saw parents twice, miles away, so many people.' Finally, on 16 August: 'Out in crowd again. Embankment, Piccadilly. Rained, so fewer people. Congered [sic] into house [Buckingham Palace] . . . sang till 2am. Bed at 3am!'

Although the princesses were spotted amidst the multitude during the night of 15 August, Lilibet was recognised only once on VE Day, according to another member of their party, by a Dutch serviceman (and he withdrew discreetly, saying simply that it was a great honour). If she was Cinderella 'in reverse', then it was her ATS uniform that allowed her to hide in plain sight in the crowds.

Conscription for single women between the ages of twenty and thirty had been introduced in December 1941, and by the end of the war, the ATS numbered 200,000 personnel. But unlike the Wrens or the WVS, with their smart uniforms designed by Molyneux and Digby Morton respectively, the ATS was regarded as the Cinderella of the women's military services, with its drab khakis and bulky jackets. Hence the attempt to make it look more desirable, with a recruiting poster commissioned from the talented graphic designer Abram Games, who created a striking image of a glamorous woman in profile, wearing red lipstick, her blonde hair visible beneath her ATS cap. The poster was issued in the autumn of 1941, and swiftly nicknamed the 'Blonde Bombshell'; but Jean Knox, the director of the ATS, complained that it looked like a lipstick advertisement, and objections were also raised by the Conservative MP Thelma Cazalet-Keir. 'Our girls should be attracted into the Army through patriotism and not glamour,' she argued. 'It is not the kind of poster that would encourage mothers to send their girls into the Auxiliary Territorial Service.' After several weeks of lively debate in the press, the poster was withdrawn, and replaced with a less controversial design, featuring a black-and-white photograph of a sensible-looking young woman named Private Mary Roberts. 'Private Mary – In. Glamour Girl – Out' announced a headline in the *Sunday Express*.

Princess Elizabeth, however, needed no such encouragement to volunteer for the ATS. According to Miss Crawford, Lilibet had 'agitated' to join up from the age of sixteen; but even when she turned eighteen, her father was 'very reluctant' to allow this, fearing that she would face 'a certain amount of danger and hazard'. By 1943, about 56,000 ATS women – including Churchill's youngest daughter, Mary – were serving with anti-aircraft units; 335 were killed by enemy action, and many more injured. Even in the final months of the war, German ballistic rockets were continuing to strike targets in England; one of the last V-2 flying bombs destroyed a block of flats in East London on 27 March 1945, killing 134 people. Eventually, Lilibet persuaded her father, and she embarked on training at an ATS centre near Camberley in Surrey, where she learned to drive army trucks, as well as vehicle maintenance and engine mechanics. Unlike the other recruits, she did not move into barracks – instead travelling to and from Windsor Castle every day – but her khakis were the same as those of her peers. 'There was great excitement when her uniform came,' wrote Miss Crawford. 'She was very proud of it, and I think the King in his own heart was very proud of his daughter for having taken this stand.' Margaret, meanwhile, overcame her annoyance at being left out 'when she saw how very unbecoming khaki was'.

Alathea Fitzalan Howard, however, remained dubious about her royal friend's military service, even though she herself had already signed up to work as a nurse. 'Went out with the princesses and Crawfie,' she noted in her diary on 15 March 1945. 'PE was wearing her ATS battle dress, which consists of trousers and I thought she looked awful and that it is shockingly bad for her to be seen about in them. She now drives all over the place, even halfway to London – I really cannot understand them allowing her to do it . . . It <u>may</u> be a good thing for the post-war world, but in my opinion to preserve her dignity should be the first consideration.' Alathea also disapproved of Lilibet's new hairstyle, which was not at all becoming, in her view: 'She has had her hair done shorter, which does not suit her as it broadens her face so.'

Three weeks later, she reported that Lilibet 'appears to be enjoying her course at Camberley v. much . . . passing her day in such new and unaccustomed surroundings . . . must be an exciting and not unpleasant experience.' Nevertheless, Alathea's choice of a birthday present for her friend suggests that she was still trying to persuade her of the appeal of a more imaginative wardrobe: 'I chose an old volume, bound in white vellum, of fancy dresses – beautifully illustrated.' Much to Alathea's relief, when she was a guest at a dance held at Buckingham Palace on 20 June 1945, Lilibet looked suitably romantic in a 'pale pink' evening gown, 'easily the prettiest dress in the room'.

Given that clothes rationing was still in place – as it would be until 1949 – Lilibet could not be seen to be wearing extravagant new dresses. When she had been photographed by Cecil Beaton to mark her eighteenth birthday in April 1944, she wore what he described as a 'nondescript' day dress, and appeared not to have 'freshly washed' hair. He was, however, pleased to see that 'when her face lights into a smile she is delightful'. In March 1945, Beaton returned to photograph her again, this time in evening dress, although the resulting pictures were not released in the UK until February 1946.

By this point, the radical reforms introduced by Attlee's Labour government, which had won a landslide victory in July 1945, were underway, leading to the creation of the National Health Service, the establishment of the welfare state, and the nationalisation of key industries. In these circumstances, the royal family had to be seen to evolve from their wartime role, as a symbol of a united, brave and embattled Britain, to one that befitted a post-war era of sweeping social change. In reality, as Attlee himself would write in 1959, neither he, nor the Labour party, were republicans, 'even in theory and certainly not in practice'. Thus George VI was able to follow his father's example in establishing a cordial relationship with a Labour prime minister; and Attlee came to admire the King not only for his 'great sense of duty' and 'moral courage', but also his 'high degree of adaptability, tolerance and historical insight'.

Even so, it helped that the exhortation to 'Make do and mend', during a time of continuing austerity, was implicit in Beaton's images of Princess Elizabeth, for she was still wearing her mother's hand-me-down Hartnell gowns that had been adjusted for her. Beaton subsequently wrote in his memoir *Photobiography* (published in 1951): 'Of all that we photographed that afternoon, by far the most successful was the pink spangled crinoline which was one of her mother's pre-war dresses, now altered to fit the daughter. These sunny, smiling photographs, taken against my old Fragonard background, had an enormous success, and were quite the most charming that I had yet seen of the Princess.'

The only jewellery she wore in the Beaton portrait was a simple pearl necklace: there are no diamond earrings, no sparkling bracelets, and certainly no rings. And despite the suggestive ebullience of the Fragonard backdrop – the same one that Beaton had used for her mother six years previously, in July 1939 – the princess has a calm, serene look on her face. She transcends the borrowed dress and the rococo scene; she is not a fairy-tale Cinderella on her way to the ball, but a young woman who might be on the verge of discovering an identity of her own.

According to Hardy Amies's own account, Princess Elizabeth did not become his leading couture client until 1950, when she approached him to design clothes for her forthcoming tour of Canada. By then, Amies was already making suits for her lady-in-waiting, Lady Alice Egerton, which the princess had admired; and he had built a reputation for the excellence of his tailoring. Indeed, by setting up his premises on Savile Row – the traditional home of gentlemen's tailoring – Amies was signalling to the world that he was proposing something very different to Norman Hartnell's sequined crinolines. Thus, he offered women the sartorial dignity that was previously associated with menswear – an approach that could be seen in his work as a royal couturier. This becomes evident in his updated autobiography, *Still Here*: 'Above all I have felt from the beginning that the Queen needs clothes that help her in what I can only describe as her work. The Queen once spoke of this to me as "going about my business".' In turn, the Queen's handwritten letters to Amies reveal

Princess Elizabeth wearing one of her mother's pre-war Hartnell evening gowns, March 1945. Photograph by Cecil Beaton.

that she was remarkably businesslike in her dealings with him: making her own appointments for fittings and keeping track of her expenditure. On 5 May 1963, for example, she wrote to him from Windsor Castle in the following terms: 'Thank you for your note with the account, warning me to beware of the cost of the pink embroidered evening dress before I actually read it – it is quite a shock! I fear, that in future, I shall be unable to order dresses which are so expensive which is a great pity, as the pink one is so pretty, but I am sure you will understand!'

It would be misleading to suggest that Amies simply made tailored suits and coats for his royal client (although those he did create were superbly cut). Indeed, the clothing archives at Windsor contain several beautiful evening gowns that he designed for the young queen in the 1950s. She wore one of these – a majestic full-skirted grey satin dress, embellished with pearls and embroidered in a pattern of golden leaves – to dinner with President Eisenhower during the state visit to the United States in 1957. Another equally romantic gown was made for her 1959 tour of Canada, and features layers of embroidered grey voile, gathered at the back with pink ribbons. But in general, his work tended to be more restrained than that of Hartnell, with a discipline that extended to colour as well as cut. In contrast to her mother's pastel Hartnell ensembles, Amies suggested subtle alternatives. 'I wanted to get away from the cliché of the pale-blue dress,' he wrote, describing his earliest designs for Princess Elizabeth, while acknowledging that 'blue was obviously going to be the Princess's great colour, dictated by those oversized blue eyes. So our first success with Her Royal Highness was a dress and coat in heavy silk . . . The colour was truly thunder-blue . . . and the coat was cut on what is appropriately known as a "princess" line: that is to say, there is no seam at the waist, the seams flowing from the shoulder to the bottom of the skirt . . . which then moved exceptionally gracefully.' Another memorable success was an elegantly cut white lace day dress, the soft femininity of the fabric offset by the precise tailoring, with a narrow belt emphasising the slim silhouette, and the geometric neckline providing a discreet frame to display Elizabeth's favoured choice of a pearl necklace.

Perhaps what is most significant about her relationship with Hardy Amies is that she chose him herself: not to replace Norman Hartnell, who continued in his role as the pre-eminent royal couturier, but to add another dimension to her sartorial arsenal. Amies's wartime experience had not only taught him about the vital attention to detail that allowed a secret agent to operate undercover in enemy territory, but it also educated him in the subtle yet significant variations of uniforms. After all, he had chosen to have his own army uniform tailored on Savile Row, to ensure that it met his exacting standards; and he was alert to the visual effects of military emblems. As he disclosed in his memoir, having successfully completed his parachutist training in 1943, he was entitled to wear a parachute badge on his left sleeve: 'This I did with some pride, feeling, I suppose, that it counteracted the "softness" of my green Intelligence Corps cap, or better still nullified the effect of the Intelligence Corps badge, of which the rather badly drawn Tudor Rose motif was described by a wag as a "pansy resting on its laurels".' (In other accounts, the wag was Amies himself.)

Accordingly, he grasped from the beginning of his professional association with Princess Elizabeth that she would need a working wardrobe in which every feature, however minute, had been considered in advance, so that nothing looked incongruous or ill-judged. 'How proud I am that I have been and still am able to serve the Queen by making dresses for her,' he declared in 1954, observing that 'she is prepared to take every care to appear beautifully and appropriately dressed', but having done so, was free to get on with her job. 'The elegance achieved is therefore quite effortless.'

Alongside Amies's rigorous tailoring, one of the most memorable outfits worn by the princess in the post-war era was the military uniform in which she accompanied her father to the King's Birthday Parade, or Trooping the Colour, in June 1947. This annual ceremony had been suspended throughout the war, and in 1946 as well, but finally returned the following year, with the guardsmen parading in battledress. Both the King and Princess Elizabeth were on horseback; she rode sidesaddle, in a bespoke dark blue uniform that signified her role as colonel of the Grenadier Guards.

And it was in this outfit that she appeared in a full-page photograph on the front cover of the *Sphere*. An accompanying article reported that 'the Princess's militarised riding habit aroused considerable interest, and it was revealed after the ceremony that her cap, with the Guards' peak and the insignia of the regiment, was of the King's designing'.

In the years to come, as sovereign, she would until 1986 continue to ride in the procession from Buckingham Palace to Horse Guards Parade, escorted by troops of the Household Cavalry. Her distinctive uniform was a scarlet tunic made by the equestrian tailors Bernard Weatherill, and a plumed bearskin tricorn hat designed by the Danish-born milliner Aage Thaarup. No ballgown could ever outshine the strength, confidence and patriotism conveyed by that uniform; and as the Queen once told my husband's father, the occasion that gave her most pride was riding back down the Mall after Trooping the Colour at the head of her Guards.

Princess Elizabeth in her uniform as the Colonel of Grenadier Guards, Trooping the Colour, June 1947.

PRINCESS BRIDE

From childhood onwards, Princess Elizabeth had proved herself integral to what her father dubbed 'The Firm' – building the business of the royal family. But when it came to her choice of husband, she showed a streak of independence, for Prince Philip was by no means regarded as an ideal suitor, either by her parents or their advisers. Three of his sisters had married Nazis, and joined the Nazi party themselves; and his background was an unwelcome reminder of the Windsors' own Germanic heritage. Certainly, Lilibet's mother is said to have referred to Philip as 'the Hun', even though he and her daughter were already related through the intricate tapestry of Queen Victoria's European dynasty, with its myriad threads and links to Germany.

Indeed, Philip's mother, Princess Alice of Battenberg, had been born in the Tapestry Room at Windsor Castle in 1885, in the presence of her great-grandmother Queen Victoria. So, too, had Alice's mother, Princess Victoria of Hesse and by Rhine, who grew up to marry her cousin, Prince Louis of Battenberg. As a consequence, Prince Philip's family tree – like all those intermarried descendants of Victoria and Albert – is fiendishly complicated. But the key point is that it contains the numerous German relatives that had caused such embarrassment to George V in the First World War, when he felt it necessary to change the family name from Saxe-Coburg-Gotha to Windsor. At the same time, new names were

Princess Elizabeth and her fiancé Lieutenant Philip Mountbatten at Buckingham Palace, July 1947.

found for George V's German relations living in England: hence Philip's maternal grandfather, Prince Louis of Battenberg, became the Marquess of Milford Haven, with the anglicised family name of Mountbatten. But nothing could be done to change the names of the Hesse relatives, who continued to live in Germany (and were, moreover, associated with the dreaded haemophilia that had afflicted the family). Philip was also a living reminder of the fate of the Romanovs, to whom he was closely related through both of his parents, and whose murder cast such a long shadow over their British cousins.

Born in a royal summer residence on the island of Corfu in June 1921, Philip was the youngest of five children and the only son of Prince Andrew of Greece and Denmark. As with the majority of European princelings in an era of uprisings and insurrection, his early life was one of exile, after his family was forced to flee Greece in 1922, when Prince Andrew was banished by a revolutionary government. George V sent a British naval ship to evacuate them (perhaps haunted by his failure to rescue the Romanovs four years previously; for like both the Tsar and Tsarina, Prince Andrew was another first cousin of the King). But rather than joining their Mountbatten relatives in England, they lived in a modest house on the outskirts of Paris, where Princess Alice's behaviour became increasingly erratic and delusional. In February 1930, she was sent to a psychoanalytic sanatorium near Berlin, where she was diagnosed as a 'paranoid schizophrenic' by the doctor in charge of the clinic, who consulted his friend and colleague Sigmund Freud for advice on how to treat Alice. There is no evidence that Freud actually met Alice, nor that psychoanalysis proved entirely helpful; she was profoundly deaf, which appears not to have been taken into account during her treatment. But after her doctor concluded that Alice was suffering from a 'neurotic-pre-psychotic libidinous condition', Freud advised 'an exposure of the gonads [ovaries] to X-rays, in order to accelerate the menopause'. Inevitably, this remedy did not cure her mental anguish (which seems more likely to have been caused by the unhappy fate of so many members of her family) – and Alice was subsequently dispatched to a Swiss sanatorium where she remained for two and a half years. Meanwhile, her estranged husband moved to the Riviera, drifting between Cannes and Monte Carlo.

From this point onwards, Philip's upbringing became even more itinerant. His maternal grandmother, Princess Victoria, was still alive and living in a grace-and-favour apartment at Kensington Palace, so the decision was made to send the nine-year-old Philip to an English prep school, Cheam. After three years there, he was moved to a boarding school at Salem in southern Germany, run by a zealous headmaster named Kurt Hahn, who advocated a spartan philosophy emphasising physical fitness, self-discipline and resilience. Were it not for the fact that Hahn was Jewish, and an outspoken critic of Hitler, Philip might well have completed his education in Germany; but as it was, when Hahn moved to Scotland, and founded Gordonstoun in 1934 along similar principles, Philip enrolled as a pupil at the new school.

His four older sisters, however, remained in Germany with their husbands, where their paths soon crossed with the Nazi regime. Philip's sister Sophie married her kinsman Prince Christoph of Hesse (a nephew of Kaiser Wilhelm II), who joined the Nazi party in 1931 and the SS the following year. The couple were friends with Hermann Göring, and among the guests of honour at his wedding in 1935; and Sophie herself entered the women's wing of the Nazi party in 1938. Prince Christoph rose to become an SS *Oberführer* and head of the intelligence branch of the Air Ministry; he also served in the Luftwaffe and was killed on active duty in October 1943. Two of Philip's sisters, Margarita and Cecile, became members of the Nazi party in May 1937, alongside their respective spouses. In November that year, Cecile and her husband, the Grand Duke of Hesse, died in a plane crash; Philip attended their funeral in Germany as a sixteen-year-old schoolboy, surrounded by relatives wearing Nazi uniforms, and crowds giving the Hitler salute.

While there could be no doubt of Philip's own loyalty to his adopted country, given his distinguished naval career during the Second World War, his sisters' affiliations were troubling. After all, when Buckingham Palace was bombed during the Blitz, there was speculation that Christoph of Hesse might have been involved in the planning; unfounded rumours even had Christoph as the navigator of the bomber that flew down the Mall in September 1940 in an attempt to kill the royal couple. Such was the King's sensitivity to his own family's links with Germany – including those of his older brother – that in August 1945, he ordered a secret mission to retrieve various papers. This mysterious operation was carried out by Sir Owen Morshead and Anthony Blunt, the Surveyor of the King's Pictures (and an agent for MI5 during the war; in later years he would be unmasked as a Soviet spy). Officially, the pair were tasked with recovering the correspondence between Queen Victoria and her oldest daughter Vicky, the wife of the German Emperor Frederick III and mother of Kaiser Wilhelm II. These letters were kept by the Hesse family – specifically, Vicky and Frederick's daughter Princess Margaret – at Schloss Friedrichhof, just outside Frankfurt. It had also become the wartime home of Prince Philip's sister Sophie, the widow of Margaret's son Christoph. According to Morshead, Princess Margaret, who had lost three sons during the two world wars, was filled with 'rancorous hatred' towards England; but he managed to coax her into handing over the letters, with the promise that they would be better protected at Windsor Castle. In the following eighteen months, Blunt made three subsequent trips to Germany on behalf of the King, to recover further papers and possessions. That the expeditions were carried out at the same time as attempts were being made by the King to suppress a file of documents relating to the Duke of Windsor's dealings with the Nazis (including with Christoph's brother, Philipp of Hesse) has led to a variety of theories about the motives of all concerned. These are as arcane as the genealogy that binds the Hesses and the Windsors – and indeed Philip and Lilibet. Suffice to say, George VI was extremely worried; leading Sir Alexander Cadogan (the senior official at the Foreign Office) to note in his diary on 25 October 1945, after a meeting at Buckingham Palace: 'King fussed about the Duke of Windsor File and Captured German Documents.'

All of which may explain why Lilibet's parents remained uncertain about their daughter's romance with Philip. According to the official royal

Philip with his three surviving sisters (from left), Margarita, Sophie and Theodora, October 1947.

biographer William Shawcross, they felt that an aristocratic Englishman might be a better choice; he writes that Hugh Euston, son and heir to the Duke of Grafton, and an officer in the Grenadier Guards who had been stationed at Windsor Castle during the war, 'was high on the list of suitable young men'. At the time, Alathea Fitzalan Howard – who was herself dazzled by Hugh Euston – was disappointed to discover that he was being lined up for Lilibet. In May 1942, after a dance at Windsor Castle, she wrote in her diary that 'everyone's talking of the way in which the Royal Family single him out – he's staying the night there and he sat by the princess at supper'. The gossip had reached Chips Channon by May 1943, when he attended a service at St Paul's Cathedral where the royal family were present. Channon noted in his diary that Elizabeth and Margaret were 'dressed alike in blue which made them seem like little girls . . . I was struck by how plain and unattractive the princesses looked and how shy and stiff they seemed. Shocking. I trust that Hugh Euston will be a salutary influence.'

Yet Channon, with his voracious appetite for royal tittle-tattle, had already pounced on the rumours about Philip when he happened to meet him in Athens in January 1941: 'He is extraordinarily handsome and I at once recalled my afternoon's conversation with Princess Nicholas [Philip's aunt and the mother of Princess Marina] – so he is to be the Prince Consort and it is for that he is serving in our Navy!!!? He is here on leave for a few days with his more than mad mother. He is a *charmeur*; but I should deplore such a marriage: he and Princess Elizabeth are too inter-related and the Mountbatten-Hesse family are famous for their ill-luck and madness. Disaster pursues them.'

Certainly, Philip's family had suffered a number of tragedies. His paternal grandfather, King George of Greece, was assassinated by an anarchist in 1913; five years later came the murder of his mother's aunt and uncle, the Tsar and Tsarina, along with their children. The plane crash that had killed Philip's sister Cecile and her husband also took the lives of their two eldest children and unborn child. Their only surviving daughter died of meningitis less than two years afterwards. Philip's uncle and mentor,

George Mountbatten, second Marquess of Milford Haven, succumbed to cancer at the age of forty-five in 1938; while his stateless and impecunious father died of a heart attack in Monte Carlo in 1944.

Despite all these challenges, not to mention a childhood so nomadic as to unsettle even the most confident boy, Philip had thrived both at school and in the Royal Navy. He had benefited, too, from the guidance of his surviving uncle, Lord Louis (or 'Dickie') Mountbatten, who was as ambitious for his nephew as he was in his own, glittering career as a naval commander and future Viceroy of India. Not only was Philip attractive, he was enterprising, resourceful and possessed of a keen intellectual curiosity. And to those who knew her best, it appeared as if Lilibet had set her heart on Philip from the start, despite her parents' efforts to introduce her to more conventional suitors. According to her cousin Margaret Rhodes, 'Princess Elizabeth dutifully waltzed, foxtrotted and quickstepped, and engaged her partners in small talk, but she was waiting for one man to come home from the war. She had been enamoured of Prince Philip of Greece from an early age . . . She never looked at anyone else. She was truly in love from the very beginning.'

It is a measure of her determination that she overcame not only her parents' doubts, but those of influential members of the inner royal circle, including the Queen's younger brother, David Bowes-Lyon, who was vehemently opposed to the match. 'Some of the King's advisers did not think him good enough for her,' wrote Miss Crawford. And Jock Colville, who was appointed Princess Elizabeth's private secretary in the summer of 1947, became aware of a cloud of disapproval at Balmoral that August, as he recorded in his diary: 'Lords Salisbury, Eldon and Stanley think him no gentleman, and in a sense they are right. They also profess to see in him a Teutonic strain.' Harold Nicolson was briefed by Tommy Lascelles in similar terms: 'The family were at first horrified when they saw that Prince Philip was making up to Princess Elizabeth. They felt he was rough, ill mannered, uneducated and would probably not be faithful.'

Queen Mary, however, who was well versed in Philip's royal lineage, was not altogether opposed to the idea of the marriage. According to her friend Mabell Airlie, Queen Mary had first met Philip as a small child, when he came to tea at Buckingham Palace, but remembered him only vaguely as 'a nice little boy with very blue eyes'. Later, while he was at Gordonstoun, and visiting his cousin Princess Marina, he made more of an impression on the old queen, who told Lady Airlie: 'He's inherited the good looks of both sides of the family. He seems intelligent too. I should say he has plenty of common sense.'

During the war, Queen Mary knitted several scarves and pullovers for Philip, and 'followed his career in the Navy with interest'. In January 1946, when Mabell joined her at Sandringham, they discussed the romance between Lilibet and Philip: '"They have been in love for the last eighteen months," she said. "In fact longer, I think. I believe she fell in love with him the first time he went down to Windsor, but the King and Queen feel that she is too young to be engaged yet. They want her to see more of the world before committing herself, and meet more men. After all she's only nineteen, and one is very impressionable at that age."'

When Lady Airlie pointed out that she had fallen in love at nineteen, and 'it lasted for ever', Queen Mary agreed: '"Yes, it does happen sometimes, and Elizabeth seems to me that kind of girl. She would always know her own mind. There's something very steadfast and determined in her – like her father. She won't give her heart lightly, but when she does it will be for always."'

In September 1946, while Philip was staying at Balmoral, the young couple became informally engaged, but no official announcement was made. According to Miss Crawford, the royal household 'were all a little bewildered. I think what it really amounted to was that neither the King nor the Queen could make up their minds what was best for their very dear daughter, and so postponed [the] decision.' When a newspaper reported that the princess was engaged, the Palace issued a statement denying the rumour; and as Miss Crawford recalled, 'On top of this came the announcement that Princess Elizabeth and her sister would accompany the King and Queen on their trip to South Africa early in 1947. Prince Philip, everyone noted, was not to be of the party.' The tour would separate Lilibet and Philip for four months – from the beginning of February until May – and allow the King and Queen to spend an extended period of time together with their daughters. 'It was clear [Lilibet] was not happy about the South African trip,' wrote Crawfie. 'She would have liked to have matters fixed, and to be properly engaged before she went away, I know.'

Nevertheless, preparations for her first foreign tour went ahead, involving numerous fittings for a new wardrobe. Norman Hartnell designed the majority of the clothes: seventeen dresses for the Queen, fifteen for Elizabeth and ten for Margaret; while additional outfits for the princesses were supplied by Edward Molyneux, with hats for all three created by Aage Thaarup. The trip coincided with a bitterly cold winter in Britain, where fuel shortages and power cuts made the freezing conditions even more difficult to endure. When the time came for their departure, the King worried that he should not be leaving his people during a period of such hardship, but the prime minister, Clement Attlee, advised him that postponing or cutting short the tour would only cause further alarm.

Even though clothes rationing would last for another two years, exemptions were made for the Queen and her daughters on this occasion. 'Everyone was sick of dull wartime austerity,' wrote Aage Thaarup in his autobiography (*Heads and Tales*, published in 1956). 'I wanted to make these hats really gay and charming.' He therefore chose to adorn them with South African ostrich feathers – both as 'a nice compliment' to the country hosting the royal tour, and because he considered the plumes to be 'a milliner's most dramatic and beautiful trimming'.

The royal outfits received widespread and approving coverage in the national press, which described the Queen and her daughters as 'unofficial ambassadresses for British fashion'. As with the Queen's pre-war visits to France, Canada and the United States, 'dress diplomacy' was regarded as key to the success of the tour, which was intended to strengthen the

Princess Elizabeth aboard HMS *Vanguard*, during the royal family's journey to South Africa, 1947.

links with South Africa, at a time when many of its inhabitants regarded the Crown as an unwelcome symbol of British imperialism.

On 17 February – the day of the royal family's arrival at Cape Town – *The Times* reported that South African wool had been used by Norman Hartnell for the Queen's 'soft apricot pink' ensemble, and for several of Princess Elizabeth's coats, dresses and suits. *The Times* also informed its readers that 'South African ostrich feathers' had been used to trim one of the Queen's afternoon dresses 'in mist-blue' with a 'cross-over bodice', and a matching felt hat. The lengthy article was illustrated with drawings of three full-length evening dresses: a Hartnell gown for the Queen, of 'white slipper satin with full crinoline skirt . . . decorated with large motifs in a flower design of gold thread guipure lace, encrusted with gold paillettes, gold pearls, crystals and diamonds'; and for the princesses, two dresses designed by Edward Molyneux: Elizabeth's 'in stiff blue faille with fichu of blue lace, embroidered with paillettes', and Margaret's 'in pale pink silk chiffon'.

This and other articles appeared just days after the well-publicised launch of Christian Dior's debut collection in Paris on 12 February, an extravagantly romantic style that represented the opposite of wartime austerity. Despite being christened the New Look by Carmel Snow, the influential editor of *Harper's Bazaar*, it was as much a nostalgic reimagining of the Belle Époque, the gilded age before the trauma of the Great War. In their own way, Hartnell's corseted crinoline gowns were in line with Dior's feminine silhouettes, and Molyneux's graceful designs represented an equally marked contrast to the war's Utility clothing. At the time, Dior's New Look was castigated by some Labour politicians as being a profligate waste of scarce resources. Ernestine Carter, the fashion editor of the British edition of *Harper's Bazaar*, described being summoned to a meeting with Sir Stafford Cripps, the socialist president of the Board of Trade – and soon to be Chancellor of the Exchequer – where he made it clear that he regarded Dior's New Look as 'the work of the Devil', banging the table and calling for 'a law' against such excess. Another Labour MP, Mabel Ridealgh, denounced the New Look as an 'utterly ridiculous, stupidly exaggerated waste of material and manpower'; and her equally trenchant political colleague, the MP Bessie Braddock, condemned it as the 'whim of idle people'.

But the royal wardrobes were celebrated rather than censured in the press, which highlighted the choices for the South African tour as showing patriotic support for the British textile industries. The *Yorkshire Observer*, for example, announced that 'some of the exquisite fabrics . . . have been woven by workers in the mills of West Riding', including a fine lilac georgette for the Queen and a herringbone tweed for Princess Elizabeth. Elsewhere, the Aberdeen *Press and Journal* hailed the selection of clothes as having been 'chosen with the greatest care in the knowledge that women in all parts of the world are looking to it as a proof that "Britain Can Make It" . . . We Scots can take pride in the fact that our own products figure . . . The Queen specially ordered a length of her favourite powder-blue material from a Scottish mill.' Similarly, the *Essex Chronicle* was delighted that the royal party would be wearing 'pure silk crêpe' made in the local mills; the *Nottingham Journal* emphasised that the city's famous lace was a component of the evening gowns; the *Daily Record* featured the use of Lancashire cotton; and the *Daily Post* declared that these 'real fairy trousseaux' proved that 'the work of British fingers is as exquisite as anything that Paris could produce'.

For most of the tour, Lilibet's main duty was to be silently on show: smiling and waving beside her parents. According to Tommy Lascelles, the King suffered from 'repeated spasms of stage fright, which gave me much trouble'; but he was pleased to see their elder daughter's professionalism on her first trip abroad. 'Princess Elizabeth is delightfully enthusiastic and interested,' he wrote to his wife Joan on 18 February, the day after they had been welcomed to Cape Town with a state banquet; 'she has her grandmother's passion for punctuality, and, to my delight, goes bounding furiously up the stairs to bolt her parents when they are more than usually late.' By the end of the tour, he was even more gratified by her 'solid and enduring qualities', including her ability to 'take on the old bores with much of her mother's skill', and never shirk 'that

Princess Elizabeth prepares to deliver her twenty-first birthday speech, April 1947.

exhausting part of royal duty. For a child of her years, she has an astonishing solicitude for other people's comfort; but what delights me especially is that she has become extremely businesslike . . . She has developed an admirable technique of going up behind her mother and prodding her in the Achilles tendon with the point of her umbrella when time is being wasted in unnecessary conversation. And, when necessary – not infrequently – she tells her father off to rights.'

Perhaps most impressive of all was Princess Elizabeth's landmark speech to mark her twenty-first birthday, an address to the Commonwealth that came to be seen as defining the commitment to duty which shaped her long reign. The original draft had been composed by Dermot Morrah, a leader writer for *The Times*, and then edited by Lascelles, before being carefully rehearsed by the princess with her parents. The final version was pre-recorded on Sunday, 13 April in the garden of the Victoria Falls Hotel (in what was then the British colony of Southern Rhodesia), and broadcast by the BBC from Cape Town on her birthday, 21 April 1947. Nearly eight decades later, her words have lost none of their emotional resonance: a vow that has the solemnity of a nun or a knight promising allegiance unto death: 'I declare before you all that my whole life, whether it be long or short, shall be devoted to your service and the service of our great imperial family to which we all belong.'

The monochrome film footage of Elizabeth recording her speech reveals that she was wearing a modestly cut day dress, a pearl necklace, and low-heeled white shoes. I have searched long and hard in the Royal Archives to identify the designer of this particular dress, but if there is a record, it has so far eluded me. It looks too understated to be by Norman Hartnell, which is why one might assume its elegant restraint is the work of Edward Molyneux; although a now-forgotten court dressmaker named Avis Ford also contributed several outfits for the South African tour. (Miss Ford – as she was known to her loyal clients – began as an apprentice to Madame Handley-Seymour, and rose to become chief fitter to Queen Mary, as well as making children's clothes for the little princesses.) Nor does history relate whether the dress was made of

Lancashire cotton, Essex silk or some other equally patriotic material. All that remains is the evocative film of a young woman in an unadorned white dress, its pristine folds framing her youthful innocence, as well as her sacred promise to her peoples.

The princess's broadcast was widely praised at the time. The *Scotsman* applauded her for 'speaking from her heart', and expressed the hope that her 'pledge of devotion' would 'strike a responsive chord in every generous heart'; *The Times* declared her words would 'long be remembered throughout the Commonwealth'. Meanwhile, the *New York Times* praised her 'humane touch, sincerity and, above all, youthful idealism', and also drew comparisons with Elizabeth I and Queen Victoria, noting that she 'bears the name of one and preserves the regal blood of the other. To this combined magic she adds a magic of her own, a beauty, a grace and graciousness now in full flower.'

But for all the idealistic talk, there was an ugly side to the royal tour, even if it was not reported in the international press. The King was overheard to describe an escort of Afrikaner policemen as 'the Gestapo', because he felt they were preventing him from mixing freely with black South Africans. Yet when the party drove through a gold mining town, and saw the police pursuing a black man sprinting towards the royal car, it was the Queen herself who hit him over the head with her parasol, even though he turned out to be a loyal ex-serviceman who was calling out, 'My King! My King!', and clutching in his hand a ten-shilling note as a birthday present for Princess Elizabeth. The King's equerry, Peter Townsend, recalled in his memoir how 'the Queen, with her parasol, landed several deft blows on the assailant', and saw her parasol, 'broken in two, disappear over the side of the car. Within a second, Her Majesty was waving and smiling, as captivatingly as ever, to the crowds.' Townsend was asked by the King to check that the victim was 'not too badly hurt', but the damage had been done.

Quite aside from the local tensions that were evident during the visit, in the broader context of South African politics the royal trip, and Princess Elizabeth's speech, could be regarded as a failure. One of the principal objectives was to lend support to the beleaguered prime minister, Jan Smuts, who had been a stalwart ally to Britain during the war, but now faced rising Afrikaner nationalism. The following year, however, Smuts was ousted when the Nationalists won the election, introducing the apartheid laws that brought about even stricter racial segregation, as well as laying the groundwork for leaving the Commonwealth and becoming a republic (which took place in 1961). Further afield, the 'great imperial family' was already on the verge of destruction: with the partition of India in August 1947, creating the independent, self-governing countries of India and Pakistan, the nineteenth-century fabric of Empire was tearing at the seams. Princess Elizabeth spoke of unity, peace and love, yet in reality, the fall of the British Empire was marked by as much bloodshed, brutality and violence as had been endemic in its rise. Even so, in voicing her aspiration for a Commonwealth in the future that would be 'more free, more prosperous, more happy, and a more powerful influence for good in the world', Princess Elizabeth displayed the confidence and certainty of the true believer. And there could be no doubting the absolute conviction of her 'act of dedication', with which she echoed the dutiful principles of her father and grandfather, as well as promising that the 'noble motto, "I serve"', would be the fundamental tenet of her own reign, whenever it should begin.

By the time the royal party returned from South Africa, Prince Philip was a naturalised British citizen, having submitted his application (guided by Lord Mountbatten) at the end of the previous year. And rather than assuming his paternal dynastic name – Schleswig-Holstein-Sonderburg-Glücksburg – he took his uncle's anglicised surname, thereby becoming Philip Mountbatten. According to Miss Crawford, the young couple immediately resumed their romance, and on the evening of 9 July 1947, a Court Circular was issued from Buckingham Palace: 'It is with the greatest pleasure that the King and Queen announce the betrothal of their dearly beloved daughter, the Princess Elizabeth, to Lieutenant Mountbatten, RN.' When they made their first public appearance together the next day at a garden party at Buckingham Palace, Lady Airlie was glad to see that Lilibet looked 'flushed and radiant with happiness', and she was 'again reminded of Queen Victoria . . . she had the same air of majesty'. As for Philip: 'I noticed that his uniform was shabby – it had the usual after-the-war look – and I liked him for not having got a new one for the occasion as many men would have done, to make an impression. Observing him I thought that he had far more character than most people would imagine. I wondered whether he would be capable of helping Princess Elizabeth some day as the Prince Consort had helped Queen Victoria. I felt that he would.'

A reminder of their shared family heritage was contained within the engagement ring that Lilibet was wearing, which was made of diamonds from a tiara given to Philip's mother as a wedding present from the late Tsar and Tsarina. Nicholas and Alexandra had been among the innumerable royal guests at the nuptials of Princess Alice and Prince Andrew in 1903, when a great gathering took place at Darmstadt, the capital of the Grand Duchy of Hesse. It would prove to be one of the last occasions when all branches of Queen Victoria's family tree were together – and before so many lost their thrones; but Alice's tiara survived the ensuing wars and revolutions. When her son told her of his plans to propose, Alice set off to Paris to fetch it from the bank vault where her jewels had been deposited in 1930, at the time of her mental breakdown. (Despite Chips Channon's description of Alice as 'more than mad', she had in fact largely recovered by the late 1930s, and subsequently devoted herself to the welfare of others, spending much of the Second World War in Athens, where she worked tirelessly for the Red Cross and sheltered a Jewish family in her home, thereby saving them from arrest by the Gestapo.) Having retrieved her tiara, Alice took it to the London jewellers, Philip Antrobus Ltd, who dismantled it to make an engagement ring of the bridegroom's own design: a large diamond in the middle, surrounded by five smaller stones. The remaining diamonds from the tiara were fashioned into another present for Lilibet: a bracelet that Philip gave her as a wedding gift.

Although his mother's diamonds made it safely to England, none of Philip's sisters were invited to the wedding. Nor were the Duke and Duchess of Windsor. The concern that the union should be perceived as thoroughly 'British' was also reflected in the making of the bridal gown, which was commissioned from Norman Hartnell in mid-August 1947. As the wedding was to take place on 20 November, this gave Hartnell and his seamstresses less than three months to make the dress, as well as those for the bridesmaids, including Princess Margaret, and for Lilibet's mother and grandmother.

Adding to the stress was the urgent question about the exact origins of the materials for the wedding gown and train; for the prime minister himself had asked Tommy Lascelles to ascertain whether or not these were entirely British. Hartnell in turn faced similar queries, as he described in his memoir: 'What was the nationality of the worms that had provided the silk from which the satin was made and with which I intended to make the dress?' The wedding train, he explained, was fashioned from satin woven at Lullingstone Castle in Kent, while the fabric for the dress was ordered from the Scottish firm of Winterthur near Dunfermline: 'And then the trouble started. I was told in confidence that certain circles were trying to stop the use of Scottish satin on the grounds of patriotism; the silk worms, they said, were Italian, and possibly even Japanese! Was I so guilty of treason that I would deliberately use *enemy* silk-worms?' Hartnell immediately telephoned the firm, 'begging them to ascertain the true nationality of the worms.' '"Our worms," came the proud reply, "are Chinese worms – from Nationalist China, of course." After which we were able to get on with the real job with a much easier conscience.'

And the scale of the job was immense, for both the floor-length gown and fifteen-foot train were embroidered with thousands of pearls into intricate garlands of white York roses, blossom and wheat sheaves. 'All these motifs had to be assembled in a design proportioned like a florist's

Princess Elizabeth (above and opposite) in her Hartnell wedding gown with her father, pageboys and bridesmaids at Westminster Abbey, 20 November 1947. Photographs by Bert Hardy.

The wedding day of Princess Elizabeth and Philip Mountbatten, newly created Duke of Edinburgh.

bouquet,' wrote Hartnell. 'Wherever there was space . . . I drew more wheat, more leaves, more blossom of orange, syringa or jasmine.' It took 350 seamstresses, working solidly for seven weeks, to make the wedding dress, with its fitted bodice, long sleeves and full skirt. To ensure secrecy, the workroom windows were whitewashed and curtained with thick white muslin, and Hartnell's manager remained on the premises at night, keeping watch against any potential intruders.

Meanwhile, the bridesmaids' dresses were made of ivory silk tulle, embellished with what Hartnell called 'a milky way of small star-shaped blossoms embroidered with pearl and crystal'. For Queen Elizabeth, Hartnell created a 'dress of apricot and golden brocade, gracefully draped and trailing'; and for Queen Mary, 'a dress and coat of golden tissue embossed with sea-blue chenille'. These highly ornate couture ensembles had to be produced (at least in theory) within the continuing restrictions of rationing. Hundreds of generous women posted coupons from their own ration books to Buckingham Palace, so that the princess could use them for her dress; but as Miss Crawford explained, 'these were always returned by registered post, with a letter of thanks from the Princess. It was not legal to give clothing coupons away.' Like all other brides of the time, continued Miss Crawford, she had 'a small extra allotment of coupons given to her by the Board of Trade. But there was, besides, a great deal of material at the Palace bought at different times and places by the Queen, and Queen Mary, to say nothing of gifts of silk and muslin, and brocades that came from different parts of the Empire. All this helped.'

The wedding also provided an opportunity to reveal jewels that had been hidden away during the war, both at the ceremony itself, and for the preceding celebrations. 'It was a week of gaiety such as the Court had not seen for years,' wrote Lady Airlie. 'There were parties at St James's Palace to view the wedding presents, a Royal dinner party for all the foreign Royalties, and an evening party at Buckingham Palace . . . Most of us were sadly shabby – anyone fortunate enough to have a new dress drew all eyes – but all the famous diamonds came out again, even though most of them had not been cleaned since 1939.'

The bridal diamonds, however, were gleaming, in the form of the Fringe Tiara. This was a family heirloom, originally created for Queen Mary in 1919, out of diamonds taken from a tiara that Queen Victoria had given to her as a wedding present in 1893. Mary had worn the original tiara on her wedding day, and she gave the refashioned tiara to her daughter-in-law Elizabeth in 1936. Lilibet, too, chose to wear the Fringe Tiara as a bride; but on the morning of her wedding, the frame snapped. Fortunately, a representative from Garrard, the jewellers that had made the tiara in 1919, was able to repair it speedily. But then came another mishap, when Lilibet realised that the pearl necklace she had planned to wear – a wedding present from her parents – was on display, alongside the other gifts, at St James's Palace. She summoned her private secretary, Jock Colville, and asked him to retrieve the pearls – and with half an hour to go before the royal procession left for Westminster Abbey, he set off through the crowds. Having persuaded several burly policemen who were guarding the presents that he was not 'a brazen burglar', Colville returned with the pearls in time for the bride's departure. A further misadventure loomed, as Lilibet's bridal bouquet could not be found. 'When the uproar was at its height,' wrote Miss Crawford, 'the footman suddenly remembered he had . . . put it into a cupboard to keep it cool.'

The bouquet included myrtle, taken from a plant in the gardens of Osborne House, Queen Victoria's home on the Isle of Wight. Not long ago, on a sunlit spring morning, I visited Osborne to search for the plant, and the story of its origin; for legend has it that myrtle has been grown there ever since the mid-nineteenth century, when it was propagated from a sprig brought back from Germany by Victoria and Albert as a family memento. Following Queen Victoria's death at Osborne in January 1901, the property was presented to the nation by her son, Edward VII (who preferred his own country estate at Sandringham). Nowadays, Osborne is open to visitors, and retains its confident air of high Victorianism: a grandiloquent mishmash of Italianate splendour and the English seaside, with touches of the Raj in its interiors, including the Durbar Room designed by the Punjabi architect, Bhai Ram Singh. The gardens are similarly ebullient, but amidst all the brightly coloured rhododendrons and camellias, I come across the more modest myrtle bushes, tucked into a sheltered bed along a terraced wall. Hidden behind them is a faded, weathered plaque, which nevertheless retains its emphatic nineteenth-century inscription: 'This MYRTLE was raised from a sprig cut off the Nosegay presented to THE QUEEN on leaving GOTHA Sept. 3rd, 1845, by H.R.H. the DOWAGER DUCHESS of SAXE GOTHA and ALTENBURG (Grandmother to H.R.H. the PRINCE CONSORT).' A conversation with one of the knowledgeable guides confirms that Victoria and Albert's oldest daughter carried sprays of Osborne myrtle in her wedding bouquet in 1858, as did subsequent generations of royal brides, including Princess Diana, and her sons' brides, Catherine and Meghan. Thus the German myrtle has been naturalised in English soil, and the plant's descendants continue to flourish at Osborne, even though the property has long since ceased to be a royal residence.

At the funeral of Queen Elizabeth II, the wreath on her coffin contained myrtle that derived originally from a sprig in the bouquet that she had carried at her wedding in the same abbey, seventy-five years before. Amidst all the pomp and pageantry, these delicate white flowers and small green leaves might have been obscured; but somehow, they remain fresh in my memory, more poignant, and miraculous even, than the most imposing bejewelled regalia.

CONSECRATION

A fairy tale is sometimes told about Lilibet's early married life, in which she and her husband were just like any other young couple; a sentiment that had already been expressed by the Archbishop of York in his sermon at their wedding in Westminster Abbey, when he said that the ceremony was 'exactly the same as it would have been for any cottager who might be married this afternoon in some small country church in a remote village in the Dales'.

In reality, the service was broadcast on the radio to an estimated worldwide audience of 200 million people; and when the bride and groom (who had been created the Duke of Edinburgh, Earl of Merioneth, Baron Greenwich, a knight of the Garter and a Royal Highness) were filmed leaving the Abbey, a commentator for Pathé News declared that this was 'a family wedding for the entire British people'. After appearing on the balcony of Buckingham Palace to smile and wave to the cheering crowds, the newly-weds set off for their honeymoon with the bride's corgi and a retinue of servants: a footman, a valet, a detective and a dresser (Margaret MacDonald, Lilibet's former nursery maid who would continue to serve her until she retired in her eighties). Throughout the first week of their honeymoon – spent at Broadlands, Lord Mountbatten's home in Hampshire – they were besieged by avid sightseers. When they attended a Sunday morning service at nearby Romsey Abbey, hundreds of people rushed into

The newly-wed royal couple leaving Westminster Abbey, 20 November 1947.

the church to stare at them. Others crowded into the churchyard, teetering on ladders and standing on chairs to get a closer view. After the couple left, their more orderly fans queued up to take turns at sitting in the same pew that the royal couple had recently vacated.

The second part of their honeymoon was spent at Birkhall, on the Balmoral estate, but even in these remote Scottish surroundings in mid-winter, they were not alone. Writing to her cousin Margaret Rhodes, Lilibet described the army boots and leather jerkin she had worn on their deer-stalking expeditions, so that she 'looked more in keeping with everyone else' (referring to the Balmoral ghillies that accompanied them). 'I couldn't help wishing that a photographer would come along . . . as he would never have believed what he saw! I imagined that I might be like a female Russian commando leader followed by her faithful cut-throats, all armed to the teeth with rifles.'

Lilibet and Philip returned to Buckingham Palace in December, where they were still living when their first child was born less than a year later, on 14 November 1948. The following month, Cecil Beaton was summoned to the palace to take pictures of the new mother and baby. 'Prince Charles, as he is to be named, was an obedient sitter,' recorded Beaton in his diary on 14 December. 'He interrupted a long, contented sleep to do my bidding and open his blue eyes to stare long and wonderingly into the camera lens, the beginning of a lifetime in the glare of public duty.' The images depicted the baby prince in an elaborately lace-trimmed cradle, his mother sitting beside him, gazing lovingly at her first child; and although the painted backdrop gave a theatrical effect, Beaton also created a sense of emotional intimacy.

It had been the baby's grandmother, Queen Elizabeth, who had prompted the commissioning of these first portraits of Prince Charles; and her shrewd understanding of the importance of Beaton's work was evident in her own sitting with him on the same day. That morning, Beaton photographed Queen Elizabeth in a stately black velvet crinoline gown by Norman Hartnell, especially created for the portrait (at Beaton's prompting), to offset her magnificent diamonds. On her head she wore

Princess Elizabeth and her firstborn son, Prince Charles, December 1948.
Photograph by Cecil Beaton.

Queen Elizabeth wearing a black velvet Hartnell gown, December 1948.
Photograph by Cecil Beaton.

the Oriental circlet tiara, originally made for Queen Victoria by Garrard in 1853; on her bodice, an imposing fringed brooch worn by Victoria in Winterhalter's 1859 portrait. Around her neck were a pair of spectacular diamond necklaces: the first an heirloom from Queen Victoria, the second a coronation gift from George VI. Another of Queen Victoria's most splendid jewels, a large diamond bracelet, glittered on her gloved left wrist.

Thus Beaton immortalised three generations of the house of Windsor in just a few hours; and as he himself would subsequently observe in *Photobiography*, 'the effect was spectacular'. His idealised images of royal motherhood were widely reproduced around the world; and along with his portrait of the resplendent, dignified Queen – officially commissioned to mark her silver wedding anniversary – they served as a way of diverting public attention from the ailing King. By then, George VI was seriously ill, and suffering acute pain in his legs and feet; on 12 November 1948, two days before the birth of his first grandchild, he was examined by a cardiovascular specialist, who diagnosed him with arteriosclerosis (hardening of the arteries). The doctors feared that the King's right leg might have to be amputated, but after enforced bed rest, this drastic action was avoided, although he did undergo an operation in March 1949 in an attempt to clear a blocked artery.

That summer, Lilibet and Philip moved into a home of their own in the grounds of St James's Palace – the freshly refurbished Clarence House, complete with a new nursery. 'It had cream walls and a blue carpet, and enchanting cream-coloured chintz with red nursery-rhyme figures all over it,' wrote Miss Crawford, almost as if she wished her former pupil was still a little girl in her charge. 'It had its own miniature bathroom, with bath, towel-rails, and bath towels all to scale. Lilibet's own nursery-china cupboard was moved over there. It was packed with the small ornaments she had always loved so dearly herself – little soldiers, little mice, little coaches, and whole families of teddy bears.' By then, there was a growing household of staff to serve the young family, including two Scottish nursemaids and a nursery footman for the infant prince.

In October 1949, Philip resumed his naval career when he was appointed second-in-command of HMS *Chequers*, leader of the First Destroyer Flotilla of the Mediterranean Fleet, based on the island of Malta. A week after Charles's first birthday, Lilibet joined her husband, leaving their son in the care of his nannies and grandparents, just as she had so often been left as a baby. 'It was as nearly an ordinary life as she got,' said Margaret Rhodes, in that the princess went out and about by herself in Malta, where the shopkeepers noticed she was unfamiliar with handling her own cash. But unlike an ordinary naval couple, they lived in Lord Mountbatten's spacious villa on the island, which had a staff of nineteen, in addition to her lady-in-waiting and dresser, and Philip's valet and equerry. There they spent the Christmas of 1949, while Charles remained with his grandparents at Sandringham. Lilibet was soon pregnant again, and gave birth to her daughter, Princess Anne, at Clarence House on 15 August 1950. In early September, Philip returned to Malta to take command of the frigate HMS *Magpie*, and shortly after her son turned two in November, Lilibet flew to Malta and stayed on for Christmas, having handed over the children to their grandparents.

This relatively carefree time in the Mediterranean was curtailed by the increasing need for the princess to stand in for her unwell father at important events, such as the Trooping the Colour parade in June 1951. Philip came back to London in July that year, effectively giving up his active naval service, when it became clear that he too would be required to accept more royal responsibilities, including overseas state visits. In September, King George underwent a biopsy that revealed he had lung cancer (although the word was never used: the doctors instead spoke euphemistically of 'structural changes'); and then an operation to remove his left lung. On 24 September, the day after her father's surgery, Lilibet sent a handwritten letter to Hardy Amies: 'I am writing to you in the strictest confidence. In view of the unfortunate turn in the King's health, I have strong reason to believe that he will be unable to undertake the tour of Australia and New Zealand. I would very much like you to prepare some sketches for me to see . . . as a precaution against any sudden decision for us to go in the King's place.'

In the event, the King's tour of Australia and New Zealand was cancelled, but his daughter and son-in-law did go ahead with a long-planned state visit to Canada in October 1951. The diplomatic intention was to demonstrate the strength of the relationship between the two countries, as well as gratitude for its unstinting wartime support, when over a million Canadians had served in active military roles. To prepare for the worst, Margaret MacDonald packed black mourning clothes for the princess, while Martin Charteris – a former military intelligence officer who had replaced Jock Colville as her private secretary – travelled with the documents required for her accession.

The attractive young couple were greeted with large crowds and great excitement, but there was a difference in style between Lilibet and her mother. To begin with, she smiled less easily, and without the famously professional assurance of Queen Elizabeth; and although she did her best to meet the expectations of her public, she complained in private to Charteris that her face 'was aching with smiling'. As she gained in experience on this tour (and those that followed), she learned to balance the combination of remote majesty and human sympathy that was required in her role. So, too, she became ever more skilled in the art of composure, as exemplified by her grandmother Queen Mary, even when surrounded by photographers whose determination to capture her on film meant that splinters of glass from exploding flash bulbs were found scattered over her coats.

The clamour to get closer to the princess was at odds with the need to preserve her dignity and mystique; which may explain why no precise details or drawings of her outfits were released to the press. Again, this was a very different approach to that taken by her mother on previous royal tours, when Norman Hartnell had been permitted to provide previews that drew fulsome coverage in newspapers and magazines. And rather than the feminine, feather-trimmed garments favoured by Queen Elizabeth – in the light pastels that allowed her to be instantly identified by those who had gathered to watch her – Lilibet chose a daytime wardrobe of precisely tailored coats and suits, in more muted shades of green, slate blue, or brown. Just one of her outfits designed by Hardy Amies

Opposite: Princess Elizabeth wearing an evening gown by Hardy Amies at a state banquet in Ottawa, October 1951. Above: Hardy Amies designs for the princess's royal tour of Canada, including (top left) her gown for the Ottawa banquet, made of white lace threaded with gold tissue; and Amies's signature tailoring.

was red – although he also contributed a gold and white lace evening gown that she wore to great effect at a state banquet in Ottawa. Journalists struggled to supply their readers with any further information about Amies's contribution, and he remained discreetly silent on the subject. Hartnell, too, stayed tight-lipped, commenting only in his memoir: 'This was the first occasion upon which I was asked to design clothes of a darker colour. One ensemble was of deep olive green velvet, another of clear slate blue, another of holly berry red cloth with a black velvet collar.' (The bold primary colours – bright as a child's painting box – that she would wear with such aplomb in later life, were only introduced in the 1960s, the second decade of her reign, by which time she had established the seriousness of her purpose, while showing her readiness to adapt to the visual requirements of newly popular colour television broadcasts.)

Amies's tailoring for the 1951 tour tended to look more stylish than Hartnell's slightly clumsy version of New Look daywear that the princess had worn on a short trip to Paris in May 1948. But Hartnell still excelled at creating glittering evening dresses for the princess, which were very much in keeping with those he had made for her mother from the late 1930s onwards. As always, the fairy-tale gowns and diamond tiaras produced the desired effect; hence President Truman's comments when he welcomed the royal couple to Washington on 31 October 1951: 'When I was a little boy I read about a fairy princess, and there she is.'

If these traditional Hartnell crinolines signalled that it was business as usual, there was one unexpected flash of levity when the royal couple donned 'Canadian cowboy costumes' (hurriedly sourced by their dresser and valet) to join an evening of square dancing at Government House in Ottawa. This provided an opportunity, at last, for the special correspondent for *The Times* to write a fulsome description: '[The princess] put on a brown checked blouse with white Peter Pan collar and cuffs, a steel blue flared skirt with appliqué and floral beaded embroidery, and Cuban-heeled black shoes. The Duke of Edinburgh wore a white checkered shirt with a red kerchief round his neck, blue jeans and brown suede "loafers".' Rather to my surprise, the skirt not only returned to England with the princess, but is still stored in the warehouse in Windsor Great Park, where I happened to come across it while examining several neatly fashioned velvet coats from the Canadian tour. A label identifies it as having been made by 'Juli Lynne Charlot, California'; the felt appliqué features a buxom blonde spilling out of her strapless purple dress. It is a marvellously improbable garment; and I like to think that its preservation might reveal a hint of Elizabeth's sense of humour, and the moments when her smile was entirely natural.

No sooner were the royal couple back at home – where Churchill had returned as prime minister after Labour lost power in the general election on 25 October 1951 – than plans were being made for them to undertake a Commonwealth tour of Australia and New Zealand, travelling via Kenya and Ceylon, in place of the King and Queen. They had already missed their son's third birthday, and the itinerary for the new state visit would involve them being away from their children for six months, plying their trade in the royal family firm where statecraft takes precedence over the day-to-day intimacies of parenthood.

The King, his face gaunt in the bitter cold of a winter wind, bid his daughter farewell at London Airport on 31 January 1952, as she and her husband departed for Kenya, on the first stage of their epic journey. Once there, after two days of official engagements, they went to Sagana Lodge, which had been a wedding present from the people of Kenya, and had an overnight stay at Treetops, a renowned wildlife-viewing platform built in a large tree. (The setting may have looked idyllic, but it would soon be associated with one of the most brutal episodes in colonial history: the Mau Mau rebellion against British rule. A state of emergency was declared in Kenya in October 1952, and Treetops was subsequently used as a military lookout for soldiers who were ordered to shoot suspected insurgents on sight. In May 1954, it was burned down by rebels; and by the time it was rebuilt in 1958, the uprising had been violently suppressed.)

On 5 February 1952, the same night that Elizabeth and Philip were at Treetops, the King died peacefully in his sleep at Sandringham; but the news did not reach them until they returned to Sagana Lodge the following day. Martin Charteris would later speak of seeing her there, still wearing jeans from the safari expedition, as she came to terms, simultaneously, with the loss of her beloved father and her new status as sovereign: she was 'sitting erect, no tears, colour up a little, fully accepting her destiny'. He asked her what she wanted to be called as queen. 'My own name, Elizabeth, of course,' she replied.

She was twenty-five years old, the same age as Elizabeth I at her accession to the throne, as Churchill observed in his memorable broadcast on 7 February. 'Famous have been the reigns of our queens,' he declared. 'Now that we have the second Queen Elizabeth . . . our thoughts are carried back nearly 400 years to the magnificent figure who presided over and, in many ways, embodied and inspired the grandeur and genius of the Elizabethan age.' His speech ended with the evocation of a more recent female monarch: 'I, whose youth was passed in the august, unchallenged and tranquil glories of the Victorian era, may well feel a thrill in invoking once more the prayer and the anthem, "God Save the Queen!"'

As soon as the new queen returned to England, descending from the plane in her black mourning garb, the industrious workings of royalty had to continue; like an endlessly spinning machine, a loom that could never be allowed to stop, for fear that it might not start again. The royal family's personal sense of bereavement was intensely painful: despite his prolonged ill health, George VI's death had come as a shock to his wife and daughters; after all, he was only fifty-six. And yet they were expected to play their respective parts to ensure the smooth-running system of succession. So, too, was Queen Mary, who had witnessed five reigns, and knew more than anyone about the etiquette and tactical manoeuvres of monarchy. Thus she did graceful homage to the new sovereign, curtseying and kissing her granddaughter's hand; but also took decisive action, just a few days after the death of the King, when she was informed that Lord Mountbatten had been heard to boast that 'the house of Mountbatten now reigns'. Queen Mary summoned Jock Colville, who had returned to work at 10 Downing Street the previous year. He enlisted Churchill's support, and the royal matriarch's view was upheld, that the house of Windsor, founded by her husband in 1917, should prevail, much to the annoyance of the Duke of Edinburgh, who declared that this decision reduced his status to that of 'a bloody amoeba'. (It was only with the birth of Prince Andrew in 1960 that Mountbatten-Windsor was adopted as the royal family's surname; and the anglicised nomenclature, devised in the First World War as a cover for their German origins, now seems a tattered remnant in the wake of Andrew's disgrace and demotion.)

While these negotiations took place behind the scenes, the ceremonial spectacle continued. The coffin of George VI, like that of his father before him, was brought from Sandringham to London, to lie in state in Westminster Hall. Chips Channon was there to witness the arrival of the cortège, just as he had been sixteen years previously, following the death of George V; and as his diary makes clear, he had lost none of his curious interest in the hosiery of royal women in mourning. On 11 February, he described seeing the three generations of queens, heavily veiled, 'like figures in a Greek tragedy. First walked the young queen, all in black but wearing flesh-coloured stockings . . . Behind her to the right was the Queen Mother – unmistakably her with her curious sideways lilting walk. She was erect in her own special way. With her, on her left, was Queen Mary . . . fragile, I thought, with her veil and her black umbrella and her steel-coloured stockings.'

Queen Mary did not attend the interment at Windsor Castle on 15 February; but instead asked her friend Mabell Airlie to watch the funeral procession with her as it passed Marlborough House. 'We sat alone together at the window, looking out into the murk and gloom,' wrote Lady Airlie. 'As the cortège wound slowly along the Queen whispered to me in a broken voice, "Here *he* is," and I knew that her dry eyes were seeing beyond the coffin a little boy in a sailor suit. She was past weeping, wrapped in the ineffable solitude of grief. I could not speak to comfort her. My tears choked me. The words I wanted to say would not come. We held each other's hands in silence.'

And what of Queen Mary's oldest surviving son, the Duke of Windsor? He had been in New York with Wallis when news reached him of the death of his brother, but he travelled alone to London for the funeral, after it was made clear to him that his wife would not be welcome. Queen Mary had appealed to her daughter-in-law Elizabeth on his behalf, writing on 10 February 'to beg & beseech of you & the girls to see him & to bury the hatchet after 15 whole years . . . I gather [he] is awfully upset as in old days the 2 brothers were devoted to each other before that dreadful rift came. I feel grieved to have to add this extra burden on you 3 just at this moment but . . . I feel that you are so kind hearted that you will help me over what is to me a most worrying moment in the midst of the misery & suffering we are going through.' Her plea worked, to a degree, in that the Queen Mother, together with her daughters, greeted the Duke of Windsor on the day he arrived in England, when he joined them for tea at Buckingham Palace.

Queen Mary therefore felt able to write with some optimism to her brother and sister-in-law, the Earl and Countess of Athlone: 'So that feud is over I hope, a great relief to me.' For her part, she had already given her son a strand of her precious pearls, as a gift for his wife: a jewelled rapprochement that became one of Wallis's favourite necklaces. (It was this same necklace that Wallis, by then increasingly frail, would wear to the Duke of Windsor's funeral in 1972: the first and last occasion that she was invited to stay at Buckingham Palace, and when the visible differences between her and her husband's sister-in-law and niece were laid to rest. All three of the Windsor women were attired in black; all wore their royal pearls.)

But in the immediate aftermath of the King's death, and despite Queen Mary's hopes for an end to hostilities, the correspondence between the Duke and Duchess of Windsor suggests that the family remained divided, rather than united by grief. The Duke was angry to be informed that the annual allowance of £10,000 he had received from George VI would not be continued by the new queen. Wallis was equally furious, writing to her husband on the day of the funeral: 'I can hardly believe this can go on at this time. I hope you have not taken the expensive trip to lose the

The Duke of Windsor with his mother Queen Mary, meeting for the first time since his abdication nine years previously; October 1945. Photograph by Reg Speller.

£10,000 and to be insulted.' The Duke replied that it had been a 'difficult, painful and discouraging trip. Cookie [their name for Queen Elizabeth the Queen Mother] was sugar . . . and other relations and Court officials correct and friendly on the surface. But gee the crust is hard & only granite below.' As for the question of the £10,000 allowance, he added, 'It's hell to be even this much dependent on these ice-veined bitches, important for WE as it is.' His final insult was reserved for Winston Churchill, who he referred to as 'Cry Baby', because the prime minister had shed tears in his presence, 'as usual'.

Neither the Duke nor the Duchess were invited to his niece's coronation, which was planned to take place on 2 June the following year. As the Archbishop of Canterbury noted in his diary after discussing the matter with the new monarch on 6 November 1952: 'The Queen would be less willing than anyone to have him there.' When the Duke of Windsor asked his solicitor, George Allen, to raise the matter with the sovereign's private secretary Tommy Lascelles, the response was brutally uncompromising. Lascelles wrote to Allen on 10 November that the presence of the Duke and Duchess of Windsor at the coronation would be 'condemned . . . as a shocking breach of taste' and would strike a 'distressing and discordant note', which would be upsetting for the Queen. Allen argued that sixteen years had passed since the abdication – surely long enough for the couple to be accepted? – to which Lascelles replied that some events could never be erased. 'Have you or I, for example, forgotten the Somme?'

In March 1953, the Duke of Windsor returned to London to visit his eighty-five-year-old mother, having been informed by her doctors that she was very unwell, and nearing the end of her life. He was reluctant to go back to 'that wretched place', as he wrote to his wife during his journey from New York, especially as 'the bulletins from Marlborough House proclaim the old lady's condition to be slightly improved! Ice in place of blood must be a fine preservative.' When he arrived on 11 March, he was told that she might die at any moment, but that it was impossible to predict when, exactly. 'It's one of the most trying situations I've ever found myself in,' he told Wallis, 'and hanging around someone who has been so mean and vile to you my sweetheart is getting me down.' His reaction to his mother's death, on 24 March, suggests there had been little sense of reconciliation, at least on his part: 'My sadness was mixed with incredulity that any mother could have been so hard and cruel towards her eldest son for so many years and yet so demanding at the end without relenting a scrap. I'm afraid the fluids in her veins have always been as icy cold as they are now in death.' He was no less scathing about the rest of his family, as he made clear in a letter to Wallis on the day of his mother's funeral (which took place at Windsor Castle on 31 March): 'What a smug stinking lot my relations are and you've never seen such a seedy worn-out bunch of old hags most of them have become.'

Queen Mary, punctilious to the last, had left instructions in her will that the coronation should not be delayed because of her death. By this point, the plans had been finalised – including the much-debated question as to whether the ceremony should be filmed for television, as proposed by Prince Philip, his wife's choice as chairman of the Coronation Commission. At first, the Queen and the Archbishop of Canterbury had misgivings about allowing cameras into the Abbey, fearing that it would detract from the dignity of the ceremony. But Philip's bold view prevailed, that everyone should have the opportunity of watching the spectacular drama of their new queen being crowned. Churchill, too, had complete confidence in the ability of the young monarch to rise to the occasion. 'All the film people in the world, if they had scoured the globe, could not have found anyone so suited to the part,' he said to his doctor, Lord Moran, in February 1953.

Chips Channon had predicted in the early days of the new reign that it would have 'a Gotha tinge'; and he was proved correct, in that various ostracised relatives were welcomed back into the family, most notably Prince Philip's three surviving sisters. They attended the coronation with their German husbands, sitting in the royal box alongside their mother, who wore a grey nun's habit of her own design. Princess Alice was not in fact a real nun, despite her intense religiosity and continuing charitable endeavours in Greece. As Prince Philip explained to her biographer,

Hugo Vickers, in 1997, 'wearing the habit meant that she did not have to worry about clothes or getting her hair done'.

But the overall impression created at the coronation was of thoroughly British pageantry, with a powerful sense of history that was heightened, rather than dispelled, by the television broadcast. This was thanks in part to Richard Dimbleby's evocative narration for the BBC from inside the Abbey, and the vivid spectacle itself, which would be watched on television by 27 million people in the UK out of a population of 50 million. At the time, only one in five households owned a television set, the majority of them having been rented or bought especially for the coronation. Millions of others listened on the radio, both at home and abroad, while the BBC's television coverage was picked up by US networks, reaching an estimated audience of 85 million in North America, and transmitted in Australia, Canada and across Europe in the first global broadcast for the British monarchy.

If the filming of the coronation offered a fresh form of inclusiveness to a worldwide audience, who could now see inside the Abbey for the first time, it was nevertheless a highly controlled medium. So, too, were the all-important sartorial manifestations of the Crown, which gave the impression of ancient tradition, stretching back through the centuries, but had in fact been reinvented by Norman Hartnell, in close consultation with the Queen. His designs extended to new robes and coronets for the peeresses, as well as gowns for all the royal women – including the Queen Mother, Princess Margaret and the Duchess of Kent – and the six maids of honour. As a consequence, the effect was of visual cohesion; and at its heart was the Queen's superb coronation gown. This was surely one of the most memorable garments of the last century, and a high point not only in Hartnell's career, but in the history of London couture. Six years after Paris had reasserted its dominance in the world of fashion with Dior's New Look, the dressmakers of Mayfair at last achieved a level of prestige that approached their French counterparts. This rare triumph could only be accomplished with consistent royal patronage, of a kind that is less perceptible today, when there appears to be a greater reluctance on the part of royal women to parade the trappings of privilege in the form of haute couture.

For all the grandeur of the coronation, the Queen approached the matter of her attire with the same briskly conscientious efficiency that she dealt with the paperwork in her red boxes. In his memoir, Norman Hartnell described the original commission, which took place at Buckingham Palace in October 1952: 'In simple conversational tones the Queen went on to express her wishes. Her Majesty required that the dress should conform in line to that of her wedding dress and that the material should be white satin.' Hartnell took a rather more poetic approach, and first immersed himself in historical research, beginning with the splendid coronation attire of Elizabeth I: 'She had worn a tiara-like headdress with flowers and jewels in her hair, a radiating and bejewelled ruff, heavy pearl earrings, a fur-trimmed cloak, puffings studded with more jewels, ruffles at the wrists and a fan of peacock feathers.' This, he accepted, 'seemed a trifle ornate' for the new queen. He then moved on to study Queen Anne, 'who most unhappily was crippled with gout on the day of her Coronation', and Queen Victoria (whose crimson velvet coronation robes remain in the Royal Collection).

Having gathered 'all the factual material' available to him, Hartnell let his imagination roam, summoning up the theatrical fantasies that had inspired his couture from the 1920s onwards. 'My mind was teeming with heraldic and floral ideas,' he recalled. 'I thought of lilies, roses, marguerites and golden corn; I thought of altar cloths and sacred vestments; I thought of the sky, the earth, the moon, the stars and everything heavenly that might be embroidered upon a dress destined to be historic.'

Altogether, Hartnell came up with nine varying designs to present to the Queen, and she chose the one including four British emblems (a Scottish thistle, Tudor rose, Irish shamrock and Welsh daffodil). She also expressed the wish that the floral motifs of the Commonwealth should be added to the embroidery: the Canadian maple leaf, Australian wattle flower, New Zealand fern, South African protea; as well as lotus flowers for India and Ceylon, and wheat, cotton and jute for Pakistan. Much to

Queen Elizabeth II at her coronation, as the canopy is placed over her head before her anointing, June 1953.

Hartnell's dismay, when he requested that the relevant heraldic authority – the Garter King of Arms – should supply decorative examples of the British emblems, he was told that a leek, rather than a daffodil, was the correct symbol for Wales. 'The leek I agreed was a most admirable vegetable,' he observed, 'full of historic significance and doubtless of health-giving properties, but scarcely noted for its beauty. Could he not possibly permit me to use the more graceful daffodil instead? "No, Hartnell. You must have the Leek," said Garter, adamant . . . In the end, by using lovely silks and sprinkling it with the dew of diamonds, we were able to transform the earthy Leek into a vision of Cinderella charm . . . fit to embellish the dress of a queen.'

Hartnell's final design was accepted by the Queen when he presented it to her at Sandringham, along with those for her maids of honour, who would be her trainbearers. As a last, secret embellishment, he added one four-leafed clover for luck, amidst the cluster of shamrocks, hoping that her hand would 'touch this small omen of good fortune. This the Queen did as she finally tried on her sumptuous gown and gently caressed the spreading skirt. Although it is not etiquette for me to quote the exact terms of Her Majesty's verdict, she did use the one word, "Glorious".'

Amidst all the splendour, it was the sight of the Queen being anointed with holy oil, wearing a simple white linen shift, that Hartnell found most moving: the only part of the ceremony that was not filmed by the television cameras, but which he could see from his privileged position in the royal box. In an account of the coronation that he kept private, Hartnell wrote that this, the act of consecration, was 'the loveliest moment'. It was a scene of high drama, with a golden canopy held above the Queen's head, but also the most symbolically sacred, when the Archbishop of Canterbury made the sign of the cross on her hands, chest and head, proclaiming the Queen's divine right to rule: 'Be thy Head anointed with holy Oil: as kings, priests and prophets were anointed. And as Solomon was anointed King by Zadok the priest and Nathan the prophet, so be thou anointed, blessed and consecrated Queen over the Peoples, whom the Lord thy God hath given thee to rule and govern.'

If Hartnell was integral to creating the regal style of the coronation, so too was Cecil Beaton, who had been commissioned to take the official royal portraits (which were staged not at Westminster Abbey, but afterwards at Buckingham Palace). Beaton's schedule began at dawn, as he made his way to find a seat at the Abbey, perched high in the rafters, from where he could produce illustrations and a report for *Vogue*. In his diary, Beaton recorded that he had hidden sandwiches in his grey top hat, to keep his energy up during a long day; and that the vantage point from 'my rook's nest' gave him a clear view of the proceedings. He was well aware of the months of lengthy preparations and meticulous planning that had taken place, and had already attended a dress rehearsal at the Abbey two days previously. 'Yet this spectacle today transcended all preconceived notions,' he wrote. 'The ceremonial seemed to be as fresh and inspiring as some great play or musical event that was being enacted upon a spontaneous impulse of genius . . . a mote of light caught a gold sequin fallen on the carpet, on a jewel in a bishop's ring . . . It was all living and new: it was history, but of today and the future. It was something that is pulsating and vital to us, and an essential part of the life we believe in.' For Beaton, the 'most superbly dramatic' moment was the crowning itself: 'The expression on the small face of the Queen is one of intense expectancy until, with magnificent assurance, the Archbishop thrusts down with speed and force the Crown onto the neat head.'

After the ceremony, Beaton rushed home, 'took a fistful of aspirins', slept for nearly an hour, and then dashed to the palace. By this point, the Queen was only just returning after a two-hour-long procession from Westminster Abbey. As her golden carriage pulled into the courtyard, she appeared to Beaton to be 'somewhat dazed and exhausted'; but when she arrived upstairs in the Green Drawing Room, she had already recovered, ready to be photographed: 'In came the Queen, with her ladies, cool, smiling, sovereign of the situation.' The previous day, Beaton and his assistants had erected a painted backdrop of Westminster Abbey, with draped damask curtains on either side, that highlighted the sense of the monarch appearing on an operatic stage. Like earlier coronation portraits of Elizabeth I, the Queen held the orb and sceptre in her hands; on her head was the Imperial State Crown, containing four pearls believed to have been Elizabeth I's earrings. This was the crown that her father had worn at his coronation in 1937, set with nearly 3,000 diamonds, including the immense Cullinan stone, and the Black Prince's ruby: the same jewels that Owen Morshead had prised from their settings during the war, to hide in a biscuit tin in a vault at Windsor Castle.

Beaton worked fast, having placed the Queen in front of 'my "blow-up" Abbey background. The lighting was not at all as I would have wished, but no time for readjustments: every second of importance.' So stressful were the circumstances, he admitted, 'I had only the foggiest notion of whether I was taking black and white, or colour, or giving the right exposures. The Queen looked extremely minute under her robes and Crown, her nose and hands chilled and her eyes tired. "Yes," in reply to my question, "the Crown does get rather heavy."'

Afterwards, he confided in his diary, 'I felt somewhat dissatisfied; the sensation of achievement had escaped me.' He was anxious about whether he had managed to achieve 'any worthwhile pictures' and worried that he had 'never become airborne . . . Not only was I depressed, but rather alarmed.' When his film was developed the next day, it was with surprise and relief that he realised 'that so many of the pictures were excellent'. Studying Beaton's portraits again now, they still strike me as exceptional, with a glamour and romance that has never been surpassed in subsequent royal imagery. In the words of Sir Roy Strong, the former director both of the National Portrait Gallery and the V&A, 'it is no exaggeration to place his work alongside that of Holbein, Velazquez or Van Dyck, for it offers a similar heady combination of art and propaganda'.

It is not altogether surprising, however, that Beaton felt assailed by doubts on the day of the coronation, as he attempted to capture the image of the Queen. Her style had been shaped by Beaton, and by Hartnell and Amies, too; but her spirit remained sacrosanct, shielded by the inviolability that should always encircle a successful sovereign. For if her uncle, Edward VIII, had taught her anything, it was that outward charm

Above: The Queen's maids of honour in their Hartnell coronation gowns.
Opposite: Queen Elizabeth II on her coronation day, 2 June 1953.
Photographs by Cecil Beaton.

and beauty, however alluring, are not sufficient to sustain a reign. Simply to be seen is not enough to be revered; something more profound is required, to withstand the constant scrutiny that accompanied her role as the most recognised woman on the global stage.

From her parents and grandparents, the young Elizabeth had learned the importance of wholehearted faith and sincerity – unfashionable virtues that cannot be dissembled – and an understanding of the gravity of her vocation. These are the steadfast qualities that gave a sense of integrity to her role, adding substance and meaning to her splendid robes, graceful gowns and sparkling jewels. So, too, was an intangible element of selflessness in her character that allowed her to manifest humility, even as she wore the crown. But she also possessed a streak of the steeliness that her royal grandfather had shown, a certain ruthlessness that must on occasion eclipse personal emotion, when hard choices have to be made to safeguard the monarchy.

Unlike Elizabeth I or Victoria, Elizabeth II was to preside over a nation that was losing its empire, rather than acquiring new dominions, and at a time when many of her subjects were questioning the role of the United Kingdom, and its place in the world. And yet this queen seemed to offer an optimistic idea of Britishness – a semi-imaginary realm drawn together by a shared heritage and subtle affinities; that looked to the future, as well as drawing on the past. All this, she did with imperturbable steadiness and quiet fortitude, showing that soft power need not be inconsequential, as she fashioned her own place in history. Such is the unparalleled achievement of a woman who was not born to ascend the throne, but came to accept that she would be Queen unto death . . . 'Lilibet, By Herself'.

Queen Elizabeth II, 1968. Photograph by Cecil Beaton.

ACKNOWLEDGEMENTS

I am deeply grateful to His Majesty the King for granting access to the Royal Archives, and to Julie Crocker, Senior Archivist at the Royal Archives, whose expertise I was able to rely on. My gratitude extends to all those at the Royal Collection Trust who have provided assistance: Caroline de Guitaut, Surveyor of the King's Works of Art; Beth Jones, Collections Information Manager; Alessandro Nasini, Senior Curator of Photographs; and Cecilia Oliver, Textile Conservator. I have also been guided by Claudia Acott Williams, Curator of Collections at Kensington Palace; Foteini Aravani, Digital Curator at London Museum; and Beatrice Behlen, Senior Curator, Fashion and Decorative Art, at London Museum.

My heartfelt thanks are due to Oriole Cullen, Senior Curator of Fashion at the V&A, for her friendship and thoughtful advice throughout the writing of this book; and to Sonnet Stanfill, Senior Curator of Fashion at the V&A, for her contribution to my understanding of Schiaparelli. I would also like to thank Andrew Riley and his colleagues at the Churchill Archives in Cambridge for their help while I was reading the letters and diaries of Lady Diana Cooper. I am similarly grateful to Dr Adam Crothers, Special Collections Assistant at St John's College, Cambridge, during my time studying Cecil Beaton's diaries. Whenever I have felt particularly baffled by Beaton, I have turned to his authorised biographer, Hugo Vickers, who has been generous in sharing his unrivalled knowledge, both in this regard and other matters. Sally Bedell Smith has been equally thoughtful with her insights and experience as a royal biographer; as have the jewellery expert Geoffrey Munn, and Sarah Lindberg, Manuscript Specialist at Bonhams.

I could not have written this book without the help of David Freeman, loving friend and companion to Hardy Amies; I am truly grateful to him for everything he has so kindly shared with me.

The magnificent team at Faber are a privilege to work with: in particular my brilliant and inspiring editor, Laura Hassan; Kate Ward, a superb designer with an unrivalled commitment to editorial excellence; Pete Adlington, the stellar art director; and Amanda Russell, a patient and meticulous picture researcher. I am also grateful to my US publishers, Claiborne Hancock and Jessica Case at Pegasus Books, who have offered encouragement and enthusiastic support from the start.

My peerless agent, Sarah Chalfant, has offered wise counsel and good judgement, as always; and I have depended on her colleagues at the Wylie Agency, as well, in particular Jessica Bullock.

I owe many thanks, too, to Adam Phillips, for his perceptive suggestions; to my friend Anna Murphy for solidarity; and to Helena Lee and Lydia Slater for their sisterliness at *Harper's Bazaar*.

Last, but certainly not least, to my beloved husband Philip Astor, without whom I would never have met the Queen. A rigorous reader of every sentence of this book, throughout multiple drafts, a challenging critic, and a comforting presence whenever I felt overwhelmed by the scale of the task . . . my constant companion, from Balmoral to Windsor Castle, and forever my strength and stay.

A NOTE ON NAMES

There is a confusing degree of repetition in both the names and titles of members of the royal family in the first half of the twentieth century; and so in the hope of providing some clarity for the reader, here is a brief list of the sovereigns and their consorts who are key figures in this book:

GEORGE V (reigned 1910–36)

BORN Prince George Frederick Ernest Albert (1865)
MARRIED Princess Victoria Mary ('Princess May') of Teck
WHO BECAME Queen Mary (consort 1910–36; dowager 1936–53)

EDWARD VIII (reigned January–December 1936)

BORN Prince Edward Albert Christian George Andrew Patrick David (1894)
KNOWN AS David to his family
BECAME Prince of Wales (1910–36)
AFTER HIS ABDICATION BECAME Duke of Windsor (1936–72)
MARRIED Wallis Simpson
WHO BECAME Duchess of Windsor (1937–86)

GEORGE VI (reigned 1936–52)

BORN Prince Albert Frederick Arthur George (1895)
KNOWN AS Bertie to his family
BECAME Duke of York (1920–36)
MARRIED Lady Elizabeth Bowes-Lyon
WHO BECAME Duchess of York (1923–36)
THEN Queen Elizabeth (1936–52)
THEN Queen Elizabeth the Queen Mother (1952–2002)

ELIZABETH II (reigned 1952–2022)

BORN Princess Elizabeth Alexandra Mary (1926)
KNOWN AS Lilibet to her family
MARRIED Philip Mountbatten, formerly Prince Philip of Greece and Denmark
WHO BECAME Duke of Edinburgh (1947) and a British prince (1957)

A NOTE ON SOURCES

As Margaret Atwood famously observed, writing involves 'negotiating with the dead'; but for those of us attempting to write about royal history, one must also negotiate with the living sentinels who guard the dead, protecting their letters and diaries in secure archives and museum collections. If you do manage to find a way past these gatekeepers, you descend to a place that Atwood names 'the Underworld', where the secrets are kept: 'It's got the skeletons in the closet, and any other skeletons you might wish to get your hands on. It's got the stories, or quite a few of them.' In my case, it tended to be clothes, rather than skeletons that I was searching for; and although I was looking for stories, too, I was aware of the risks of losing my own thread. To quote Atwood again: 'As long as you continue to write, you continue to explore the work of writers who have preceded you; you also feel judged and held to account by them.'

It is with this in mind that I offer the following notes, as a respectful tribute to the writers who have gone before me, and the archivists that have guided me through the labyrinth. To the reader, I should add that any loose ends are inevitable, and perhaps integral to my narrative.

The Royal Archives have been fundamental to my research. The specific files from the Royal Archives that I have drawn on throughout the book, particularly relating to the work of Norman Hartnell and Hardy Amies, are as follows:

QEII/PRIV/PERS: Norman Hartnell's dress designs for Princess Elizabeth.
QEQM/PRIV/DRESS: Letter from Hartnell to Queen Elizabeth, 1947.
AEC/GG/059: Two order books and alteration docket book re: Hardy Amies.
LC/LCO/TRADESWARR/QEII/004: Papers relating to the Warrant of Appointment of Hardy Amies Ltd as dressmaker to Queen Elizabeth II.
PS/PSO/GVI/PS/SV/02718/2: Letter from Norman Hartnell regarding arrangements for him to attend to Queen Elizabeth's dresses during the state visit to Paris in 1938.
QEQMH/PS/GEN: Letter from Hartnell to Queen Elizabeth the Queen Mother, 1968.
QEQMH/PS/GEN: Letter from Long (a Hartnell employee), 1949.
QEQMH/PS/DRESSER/PATTERN: Three boxes of dress designs.
QEQMH/TREAS/CSP: Bills and fabric samples from Norman Hartnell, 1939–75.
LC/LCO/TRADESWARR/QEQM: Trades Warrants file re: Norman Hartnell.

QEQMH/TREAS/CSP: Norman Hartnell bills and samples, 1937–75.
QEQM/PRIV/HAR: Cards from Hartnell.

The Royal Collection Trust has been an equally important resource, for it contains many of the garments, photographs, paintings, jewels and other objects that feature in my book. I have conducted further research in the Royal Ceremonial Dress Collection at Historic Royal Palaces.

For additional material relating to Norman Hartnell, Hardy Amies and Edward Molyneux, I have drawn on the following collections: the V&A (including fashion drawings by Hartnell, and some of his most significant designs); London Museum (which has preserved the complete oral history of Hardy Amies, with recordings of Amies himself and all of his employees); the Imperial War Museum (for interviews with Amies, and documents and objects relating to wartime clothes rationing and the Utility clothing scheme). The National Archives have provided me with the military records of Edward Molyneux and Hardy Amies. In addition, I have relied on the private papers and correspondence of Hardy Amies, kindly made available to me by his loyal friend and companion, David Freeman, who has shared precious insights and memories during my research. Amies's memoirs, *Just So Far* (Collins, 1954) and *Still Here* (Weidenfeld & Nicolson, 1984), have also been essential; as has Norman Hartnell's autobiography, *Silver and Gold* (Evans, 1955).

I have consulted Cecil Beaton's original diaries at St John's College, Cambridge, alongside those he published, as follows: *The Wandering Years: 1922–1939* (Weidenfeld & Nicolson, 1961); *The Years Between:1939–1944* (Weidenfeld & Nicolson, 1965); *The Happy Years: 1944–1948* (Weidenfeld & Nicolson, 1972); *The Strenuous Years: 1948–1955* (Weidenfeld & Nicolson, 1973). I have also relied on Beaton's memoir *Photobiography* (Odhams Press, 1951), and his authorised biography by Hugo Vickers (*Cecil Beaton*, Weidenfeld & Nicolson, 1985). The V&A's collection of Beaton's royal photographs has been equally vital to my research, as has the Imperial War Museum's archive of his work for the Ministry of Information between 1940 and 1945.

Lady Diana Cooper's letters and diaries have been another important source; I have studied her original manuscripts at the Churchill Archives Centre, Cambridge, alongside the second and third volumes of her published memoirs: *The Light of Common Day* (Rupert Hart-Davis, 1959) and *Trumpets from the Steep* (Rupert Hart-Davis, 1960).

The following official royal biographies have been indispensable sources: *King George V: His Life and Reign* by Harold Nicolson (Constable, 1952); *King George VI: His Life and Reign* by John Wheeler-Bennett (Macmillan, 1958); *Queen Mary* by James Pope-Hennessy (George Allen & Unwin, 1959); *Edward VIII* by Philip

Ziegler (Collins, 1990); and *Queen Elizabeth the Queen Mother* by William Shawcross (Macmillan, 2009). All of the above were authorised by the royal family and their advisers, which means that I have relied on these books for accurate dates and original quotations from diaries, correspondence, memorandums and other documents. However, the authors were restricted in certain respects. As Harold Nicolson reported in a letter to his wife, Vita Sackville-West, he was allowed a 'free run' of the Royal Archives, but would be expected 'to omit things and incidents which were discreditable'. At times, Nicolson found these restrictions frustrating, but his own lively letters and diaries provide a vivid counterpoint to his respectful biography of George V. For example, as he wrote to Vita on 17 August 1949, he was feeling 'rather down' about tackling the period before his subject became 'a wise old King', because it seemed to him that before George came to the throne, he did 'nothing at all but kill animals and stick in stamps'. These letters and diaries were skilfully edited by his son Nigel Nicolson, and I have consulted the three volumes that cover the period after 1930: *Harold Nicolson: Diaries and Letters 1930–1939* (William Collins, 1966); *Harold Nicolson: Diaries and Letters 1939–1945* (William Collins, 1967); *Harold Nicolson: Diaries and Letters 1945–1962* (William Collins, 1967). For earlier letters and diaries, I have referred to *The Harold Nicolson Diaries 1907–1964* (edited by Nigel Nicolson, Weidenfeld & Nicolson, 2004).

Similarly, I studied James Pope-Hennessy's official biography of Queen Mary in conjunction with his delightfully uncensored and often hilarious interview notes, edited by Hugo Vickers and published as *The Quest for Queen Mary* (Hodder & Stoughton, 2018). An added dimension is provided by the diaries and letters of Sir Alan 'Tommy' Lascelles, deftly edited by Duff Hart-Davis: *In Royal Service: Letters and Journals of Sir Alan Lascelles, 1920–1936* (Hamish Hamilton, 1989), and the updated edition of *King's Counsellor: Abdication and War* (Weidenfeld & Nicolson, 2020). A consummate private secretary who served four monarchs, Tommy Lascelles steered John Wheeler-Bennett, Harold Nicolson and James Pope-Hennessy through the process of writing their respective royal biographies. According to the royal biographer Sally Bedell Smith, Lascelles had romantic relationships with both Nicolson – at Oxford – and Pope-Hennessy, while he was writing the book. For good measure, Nicolson and Pope-Hennessy also had an affair with each other. She alluded to these intimacies in her own exceptionally well-researched book, *George VI and Elizabeth* (Michael Joseph, 2023).

As for the Duke and Duchess of Windsor, both published their autobiographies: *A King's Story* by the Duke of Windsor (Cassell, 1951); and *The Heart Has Its Reasons* by the Duchess of Windsor (Michael Joseph, 1956). Their ghostwriter, Charles V. Murphy, who worked on these memoirs, subsequently made his exasperation clear in his book,

The Windsor Story (co-written with J. Bryan III, William Morrow, 1979). But perhaps the most intriguing of all – for me, at least – are the Duke of Windsor's reminiscences in *A Family Album* (Cassell, 1960), in which he shares his thoughts on fashion.

Further insights into the Windsors come from Michael Bloch, who in 1979 began working for their lawyer, Suzanne Blum, giving him unique access to their personal papers and correspondence. Hence his books are invaluable sources: *The Duke of Windsor's War* (Weidenfeld & Nicolson, 1982); *Operation Willi* (Weidenfeld & Nicolson, 1984); *Wallis and Edward: Letters 1931–1937* (Weidenfeld & Nicolson, 1986); *The Secret File of the Duke of Windsor* (Bantam, 1988); *The Reign and Abdication of Edward VIII* (Bantam, 1990); *Ribbentrop* (Bantam, 1992); *The Duchess of Windsor* (Weidenfeld & Nicolson, 1996).

Throughout my research and writing of this book, I have been accompanied by the inimitable voice of Henry 'Chips' Channon, whose unexpurgated journals were superbly edited by Simon Heffer and published in three volumes, as follows: *Henry 'Chips' Channon: The Diaries 1918–1938* (Hutchinson, 2021); *Henry 'Chips' Channon: The Diaries 1938–1943* (Hutchinson, 2021); *Henry 'Chips' Channon: The Diaries 1943–1957* (Hutchinson, 2022).

'I HAVE TO BE SEEN TO BE BELIEVED'

The quote that forms the title of this chapter was attributed to Queen Elizabeth II by Jonny Dymond, the BBC's royal correspondent, in his report on the day of her death, 8 September 2022. Aside from my personal encounters with the late Queen, and her family, friends and members of her household, I have drawn on Marion Crawford's memoir of her life as a royal governess: *The Little Princesses* (Cassell, 1950). Walter Bagehot's *The English Constitution* was essential reading (edited with an introduction and notes by Miles Taylor, Oxford University Press, 2009). I have also been influenced by David Cannadine's essay, 'The Context, Performance and Meaning of Ritual: The British Monarchy and the "Invention of Tradition", *c.*1820–1977', published in *The Invention of Tradition* (edited by Eric Hobsbawm and Terence Ranger, Cambridge University Press, 1983).

THE HOUSE OF WINDSOR

As cited in the text, I have conducted my own original research at Windsor Castle. Secondary source material comes from Marion Crawford's memoir; and that of Mabell, Countess of Airlie, a lifelong friend of Queen Mary, and her lady-in-waiting for fifty years (*Thatched with Gold*, Hutchinson, 1962).

I have also consulted Kenneth Rose's excellent biography of George V, which includes Queen Elizabeth the Queen Mother's memorable recollections of her royal father-in-law (Weidenfeld & Nicolson, 1983); Jane Ridley's equally insightful biographies of Edward VII (Chatto & Windus, 2012) and George V (Chatto & Windus, 2021); and *The Three Emperors* by Miranda Carter (Fig Tree, 2009), a riveting study of that dysfunctional trio of royal cousins, George V, Kaiser Wilhelm II and Tsar Nicholas II.

'SHE HAS SET THE BABE FASHION FOR YELLOW'

I have derived source material from *Counting One's Blessings: The Selected Letters of Queen Elizabeth the Queen Mother* (edited by William Shawcross, Macmillan, 2012). Secondary sources include these particularly illuminating biographies: *Elizabeth, the Queen Mother* by Hugo Vickers (Hutchinson, 2005); *George VI* by Sarah Bradford (Weidenfeld & Nicolson, 1989); *George VI and Elizabeth* by Sally Bedell Smith (Michael Joseph, 2023); and *The Queen* by Ben Pimlott (HarperCollins, 1996).

Harold Nicolson's letter to his wife Vita, in which he tells her about his 'new friend' Edward Molyneux, is dated 15 September 1919, and appears in *The Letters of Vita Sackville-West and Harold Nicolson: 1910–1962* (edited by Nigel Nicolson, Weidenfeld & Nicolson, 1992). A little more detail regarding Nicolson's relationship with Molyneux is derived from James Lees-Milne's biography, *Harold Nicolson: Volume One 1886–1929* (Chatto & Windus, 1980).

George V's remarks about Ramsay MacDonald and his colleagues were recorded in the memoir of Lady Cynthia Colville, *Crowded Life* (Evans, 1963). Additional details regarding Britain's first Labour government came from *The Wild Men* by David Torrance (Bloomsbury Continuum, 2024).

Alongside Norman Hartnell's own memoir, I have drawn on his detailed biography by Michael Pick (Zuleika, 2019), and the museum catalogue that accompanied two exhibitions of Hartnell's designs staged in 1985 at the Museum of Costume in Bath and the Brighton Museum (*Norman Hartnell*, published by the Royal Pavilion, Art Gallery and Museums, Brighton/Bath City Council, 1985).

The reference to Noël Coward's relationship with Prince George, the Duke of Kent, comes from Philip Hoare's absorbing biography of Coward (Sinclair-Stevenson, 1993). The rumour that Kent was blackmailed appears in the diary of Robert Bruce Lockhart on 28 April 1932: 'There has been a scandal about Prince George – letters to a young man in Paris. A large sum had to be paid for their recovery.' (*The Diaries of Sir Robert Bruce Lockhart 1915–1938*, edited by Kenneth Young, Macmillan, 1973.)

I am also indebted to D. J. Taylor's panoramic social history, *Bright Young People*

(Vintage, 2008); Paula Byrne's perceptive study of Evelyn Waugh and the Lygon family, *Mad World* (HarperPress, 2010); and Beverley Nichols's nostalgic memoir *The Sweet and Twenties* (Weidenfeld & Nicolson, 1958).

As noted in the text, Janet Flanner's detailed profile of Queen Mary appeared in the *New Yorker* in May 1935.

'THAT WOMAN IN MY OWN HOUSE!'

As is evident, from this chapter onwards, there are repeated references to the relationship between Wallis Simpson (the future Duchess of Windsor) and the Prince of Wales (the future Edward VIII and Duke of Windsor) in the lively letters, diaries and memoirs of Cecil Beaton, Chips Channon, Diana Cooper, Tommy Lascelles, Harold Nicolson, James Pope-Hennessy, and Queen Elizabeth the Queen Mother. Another insider's view is provided by Robert Bruce Lockhart, whose first mention of meeting Wallis Simpson appeared in his diary on 24 October 1934, and whose well-informed commentary continues throughout the ensuing years. I have sourced his quotes from *The Diaries of Sir Robert Bruce Lockhart 1915–1938*. A similarly important source, as cited in the text, is the author Marie Belloc Lowndes, whose diaries and letters were edited and published by her daughter, Susan Lowndes (*Diaries and Letters of Marie Belloc Lowndes*, Chatto & Windus, 1971). Marie Belloc Lowndes's journal is notable in that it records her impressions of meeting Ernest Simpson, as well as his wife Wallis, and she also took the time to write a lengthy analysis of the events leading up to the abdication in her diary entry of 20 January 1937. I have also quoted from the Windsors' own memoirs (*The Heart Has Its Reasons*, *A King's Story* and *A Family Album*); and the volume of their correspondence edited by Michael Bloch (*Wallis and Edward: Letters 1931–1937*).

George V's fury at the presence of Wallis Simpson in Buckingham Palace – 'That woman in my own house!' – is sourced from his biography by Kenneth Rose (and Rose himself cites the papers of Count Mensdorff, from the State Archives in Vienna). Quotes from the diary of John Aird, equerry to the Prince of Wales, are taken from Philip Ziegler's official biography of Edward VIII. So, too, is the memorable response by Tommy Lascelles to the Prince's claim that Wallis was not his mistress ('as credible as . . . a herd of unicorns grazing in Hyde Park and a shoal of mermaids swimming in the Serpentine'; this comment also appears in *King's Counsellor*); and the disapproving views expressed by Cynthia Colville and Clive Wigram. Ziegler notes George V's concern about his son's refusal to eat (including the King's letter sent to Edward on 20 April 1913, begging him to '*eat more*'). Edward himself quoted the same letter in *A Family Album*, and from the letter from his father admonishing him for losing weight. In the chapter about his father, Edward recalled: 'Rather as he kept a game book, he kept also a weighing book, in which family weights were recorded at intervals.' The Duchess of Devonshire's letter to her husband about Edward's refusal to eat – 'The poor boy is evidently suffering from hysteria . . . [He was] threatened with a rest cure and forcible feeding' – was written on 20 May 1913, and cited by Jane Ridley in her enlightening biography of George V. Lascelles reported Clive Wigram's expostulation that Edward was 'mad' in his diary (*King's Counsellor*); and admitted that 'the same thought . . . was in the minds of many of us during those sombre months'.

Edward's letters to his former mistress, Freda Dudley Ward, were published in *Letters from a Prince*, edited by Rupert Godfrey (Little Brown, 1998). His subsequent affair with Thelma Furness – and her account of being usurped by Wallis Simpson – is described in Lady Furness's joint autobiography with her twin sister, Gloria Vanderbilt (*Double Exposure*, Frederick Muller, 1959). Further details are derived from Frances Donaldson's impressive biography of Edward VIII (Weidenfeld & Nicolson, 1974); Anne Sebba's perceptive biography of the Duchess of Windsor (*That Woman*, Weidenfeld & Nicolson, 2011); and *The Windsor Story* by Charles V. Murphy and J. Bryan III, which includes the vivid quotes about Wallis's 'bite' and Lilli Palmer's description of her 'voracious vitality'. Lilli Palmer also recalled the Windsors in an article published in *Esquire* magazine, in September 1975. The question of Wallis's 'intersexuality' is raised by Anne Sebba and Michael Bloch in their respective biographies, while James Pope-Hennessy's speculation 'that she is not a woman at all' appears in *The Quest for Queen Mary*.

The strange case of Guy Trundle, and his alleged affair with Wallis, is sourced from the Metropolitan Police files in the National Archives (MEPO 10/35). The Special Branch surveillance (and future intelligence operations regarding the Windsors) is analysed in forensic detail by Richard J. Aldrich and Rory Cormac in *Spying and the Crown* (Atlantic Books, 2022).

Edward's pro-Nazi sympathies, as revealed in his conversation with the Austrian diplomat Count Mensdorff, are quoted in Kenneth Rose's biography of George V. Edward's admiring view of Hitler is noted in the diaries of Robert Bruce Lockhart, who recorded his conversation with the Kaiser's grandson, Prince Louis Ferdinand of Prussia, on 13 July 1933: 'The Prince [of Wales] was quite pro-Hitler, said it was no business of ours to interfere in Germany's internal affairs either *re* Jews or *re* anything else, and added that dictators were very popular these days and that we might want one in England before long.'

Damning evidence about the Windsors' fascist affiliations has been meticulously documented in *The Crown in Crisis* by Alexander Larman (Weidenfeld & Nicolson,

2020) and *Traitor King* by Andrew Lownie (Blink, 2021). Andrew Morton has also made a thorough investigation of the stories regarding Wallis's relationships with Ribbentrop, Guy Trundle, et al., in *17 Carnations: The Windsors, the Nazis, and the Biggest Cover-Up in History* (Michael O'Mara, 2015); and *Wallis in Love* (Michael O'Mara Books, 2021). I was particularly interested in Morton's use of the papers of Cleveland Amory, who was commissioned as a ghostwriter for the Duchess of Windsor, but then fired.

Another intriguing viewpoint was provided by Jane Marguerite Tippett, who discovered some of the Windsors' original interviews in the papers of Charles Murphy, along with Murphy's diary entries, and several of the Duke of Windsor's handwritten drafts of autobiographical material; all of which she has woven together to form *The Lost Memoir of Edward VIII* (Hodder & Stoughton, 2023).

The most scurrilous narrative is supplied in Charles Higham's biography, *Mrs Simpson: Secret Lives of the Duchess of Windsor* (Pan, 2005); this contains a great quantity of entertaining gossip. As one might expect, a far more sympathetic portrait is offered by Wallis's loyal friend – and impenitent fascist – Diana Mosley (*The Duchess of Windsor*, Sidgwick & Jackson, 1980).

SANDRINGHAM TIME

The dismaying story of Prince Eddy – the wayward oldest son of Edward VII and Queen Alexandra, who was engaged to Princess May of Teck before his death at Sandringham in January 1892 – was conveyed in tactful terms by James Pope-Hennessy in his biography of Queen Mary. The rumours about Prince Eddy having syphilis and being a client of a homosexual brothel emerged in Pope-Hennessy's lively interviews contained in *The Quest for Queen Mary*, most openly in his conversations with the Duke of Gloucester.

Lord Dawson's controversial decision to hasten George V's death with a lethal injection of morphine and cocaine was revealed in 1986 (in an article for *History Today*) by the royal doctor's biographer, Francis Watson. In his secret notes of the King's death, Dawson recorded: 'At about 11 o'clock it was evident that the last stage might endure for many hours.' In order to ensure 'a brief final scene . . . I therefore decided to determine the end, and injected (myself) morphia gr.3/4 & shortly afterwards cocaine gr.1 into the distended jugular vein.'

Virginia Woolf's letter to her nephew Julian Bell about the death of the King, and Edward VIII's decision to change the clocks at Sandringham, written on 30 January 1936, is included in Woolf's *Selected Letters* (edited by Joanne Trautmann Banks, Vintage, 2008).

The misgivings about Edward VIII's fitness to be king, as expressed by his own advisers and senior political figures, have been thoroughly documented by his authorised biographer, Philip Ziegler, as well as by Frances Donaldson and Alexander Larman in their respective books. Alec Hardinge's concerns are evident in his papers from the period in the Royal Archives, as are those of Tommy Lascelles and Harold Nicolson in their diaries. Frances Donaldson records the observations of Walter Elliot and Robert Boothby, when they witnessed the Maltese cross falling off the crown at George V's funeral.

'MY STRIPTEASE ACT'

Wallis's letters to her aunt are published in Michael Bloch's edited correspondence of the Duke and Duchess of Windsor. Duff Cooper noted his conversation with Wallis in his diary on 27 January 1936, when he observed 'she is hard as nails and doesn't love him' (*The Duff Cooper Diaries*, edited by John Julius Norwich, Weidenfeld & Nicolson, 2005).

Clive Wigram's memo about his meeting with high-ranking civil servants and Foreign Office officials, when they shared their concerns about Wallis's access to confidential documents, and her links with the German ambassador, is included in his papers in the Royal Archives, and quoted in Philip Ziegler's biography of Edward VIII.

The details of Anna Wolkoff's role in the Right Club, her pro-Nazi activities and espionage, are contained in her file in the National Archives (KV2/840-843). Additional context is derived from *Patriotism Perverted: Captain Ramsay, the Right Club, and British Anti-Semitism, 1939–1940* by Richard Griffiths (Constable, 1998); and *The Defence of the Realm: The Authorised History of MI5* by Christopher Andrew (Penguin, 2010).

The Duke of Saxe-Coburg and Gotha's memorandum to Hitler about his conversations with Edward VIII is sourced from a British government collection of documents found in the archives of the German Foreign Ministry, focusing on the period of the Third Reich between April 1935 to March 1936 (*Documents on German Foreign Policy*, series C, vol. 4, HMSO, 1962). Further details concerning the meetings between Edward VIII and the Duke of Saxe-Coburg and Gotha are derived from *Go Betweens for Hitler* by Karina Urbach (Oxford University Press, 2015). Urbach's painstaking academic research has also shed light on Edward's pro-German sympathies as Prince of Wales, and his subsequent dealings with the Nazis as the Duke of Windsor.

For Diana Cooper's descriptions of her various visits to Fort Belvedere and holidays with Edward and Wallis, I have relied on her original letters and diaries in the Churchill Archives to supplement the recollections published in the second volume of her autobiography, *The Light of Common Day*. Additional details come from Philip Ziegler's biography, *Diana Cooper* (Hamish Hamilton, 1981). Helen Hardinge's description of the naked king in Vienna is published in her memoir of her husband Alec Hardinge, *Loyal to Three Kings* (William Kimber, 1967). Marie Belloc Lowndes's account of Wallis and Edward wearing shorts at Balmoral features in her diary entry for 20 January 1937 (*Diaries and Letters of Marie Belloc Lowndes*). Cecil Beaton was shown a home movie of the Balmoral episode by Wallis herself, when he visited her in France in May 1937. Beaton's description of the film as 'obscenely intimate' was recorded in his manuscript diary for this period.

Robert Egerton's private account of Wallis Simpson's divorce proceedings was covered in the *Guardian* newspaper in December 2019, with additional material revealed in 2020 by Alexander Larman in his book, *The Crown in Crisis*. Both here and elsewhere in the narrative, I have relied on the diaries of the Reverend Alan Don (*Faithful Witness: The Confidential Diaries of Alan Don, Chaplain to the King, the Archbishop and the Speaker, 1931–1946*, edited by Robert Beaken, SPCK Publishing, 2020).

Evidence relating to the phone-tapping of Edward VIII is contained in Cabinet Office files in the National Archives (CAB 301/101). Richard J. Aldrich and Rory Cormac describe this intelligence operation in *Spying and the Crown*, and I am also grateful to Professor Aldrich for clarifying further details in answer to my questions. Oswald Mosley's support for Edward VIII, backed by his followers in the British Union of Fascists, is documented by Stephen Dorril in *Blackshirt: Sir Oswald Mosley and British Fascism* (Viking, 2006).

Tommy Lascelles' compelling first-hand account of the abdication is contained in his published diaries: *King's Counsellor: Abdication and War: The Diaries of Sir Alan 'Tommy' Lascelles*, edited by Duff Hart-Davis. Wallis's letter to Ernest Simpson, written in February 1937, appears in Anne Sebba's biography. Janet Flanner's essay about Wallis Simpson's wax effigy at Madame Tussaud's was published in the *New Yorker* on 10 February 1937. This essay, along with her profiles of Queen Mary and Wallis Simpson, and her reporting on the abdication and its aftermath, were reprinted in *London Was Yesterday: 1934–1939* (Michael Joseph, 1975).

HARD CHIC

I have relied on my own research in the archives of Schiaparelli and *Harper's Bazaar*; as well as my essay previously published in *Schiaparelli and the Artists* (Rizzoli, 2017); and Elsa Schiaparelli's vivid autobiography, *Shocking Life* (V&A Publications, 2007).

Additional sources include Janet Flanner's profile of Elsa Schiaparelli in the *New Yorker* (June 1932); Bettina Ballard's memoir, *In My Fashion* (Secker & Warburg,

1960); and Cecil Beaton's *The Glass of Fashion* (Weidenfeld & Nicolson, 1954).

I have quoted from Cecil Beaton's original manuscript diaries in this chapter; his published versions tend to be less harsh in their judgement of Wallis. Wallis's letter to Edward (written on 14 December 1936), complaining about being denied 'the extra chic of creating me HRH', is included in *Wallis and Edward: Letters 1931–1937* (edited by Michael Bloch). Lady Alexandra 'Baba' Metcalfe's diary entries describing the Windsors' melancholy wedding are sourced from Frances Donaldson's biography of Edward VIII.

Emmy Göring's observation that Wallis 'would certainly have cut a good figure on the throne of England' is from her memoir, *My Life with Göring* (David Bruce and Watson, 1972). The Windsors' tour of Nazi Germany was well documented at the time, with eyewitness reporting by the *New York Times*, and filmed for newsreels.

The Duke of Windsor's remark that he 'never thought Hitler was such a bad chap' was recalled by Lord Kinross (his collaborator on *A Family Album*) in Kinross's article, 'Love Conquers All', published in *Books and Bookmen* (vol. 20, 1974). Windsor's unrepentant belief that 'it was the Jews who brought us into the war' was shared by Sir Oswald Mosley in a conversation with Kenneth Rose, who recorded it in his diary after meeting Mosley on 1 November 1970 (*The Journals of Kenneth Rose: Volume 1: 1944–1979*, edited by D. R. Thorpe, Weidenfeld & Nicolson, 2018). There is also a reference in Sir Roy Strong's diary to the Duke of Windsor's continuing admiration for Hitler: following a conversation with one of the Windsors' friends (Diana Phipps, on 15 February 1984), Strong noted that the Duke 'eulogised Hitler. It confirmed all one feared.' (*The Roy Strong Diaries, 1967–1987*, Weidenfeld & Nicolson, 2017.)

Paul Schmidt's recollections of the meeting between the Windsors and Hitler are contained in his memoir, *Hitler's Interpreter* (William Heinemann, 1951). Further details about Philip Attfield, one of the Duke of Windsor's personal protection officers who was also reporting to British Intelligence, were published in Andrew Lownie's *Traitor King*.

Susan Sontag's essay, 'Fascinating Fascism', was included in her collection *Under the Sign of Saturn* (Penguin Classics, 2009).

ROYAL COMMAND PERFORMANCE

There are full accounts of the abdication and the accession of George VI and Queen Elizabeth in their authorised biographies by John Wheeler-Bennett and William Shawcross respectively, who had access to diaries and correspondence in the Royal Archives. Hence, for example, the words of the future George VI, in the days leading up to his brother's abdication – 'If the worst happens & I have to take over, you can rest assured that I will do my best to clear up the inevitable mess, if the whole fabric does not crumble under the shock and strain of it' – are quoted verbatim from John Wheeler-Bennett's official biography. The same quote – taken from a letter written by the future king, on 25 November 1936, to Edward VIII's assistant private secretary Godfrey Thomas – is also included in William Shawcross's biography. Queen Elizabeth's letters on the subject were published in *Counting One's Blessings: The Selected Letters of Queen Elizabeth the Queen Mother.*

Owen Morshead's description of 'the two darling little Princesses in their full kit' at the coronation, written in a letter to his aunt, is in the Royal Archives, and quoted in Shawcross's official biography. Additional details are sourced from the diaries, letters and memoirs already cited (including those by Mabell Airlie, Cecil Beaton, Chips Channon, Diana Cooper, Duff Cooper, Marion Crawford, Alan Don, Tommy Lascelles and Harold Nicolson).

Janet Flanner's series of reports on the coronation and the early reign of George VI were published in the *New Yorker* during the spring and summer of 1937 (10 March, 28 April, 5 May, 16 May, 26 May, 2 June, 23 June, 7 July 1937); and subsequently reprinted in her collection of essays, *London Was Yesterday.*

Aside from my own visits to Buckingham Palace, I have also drawn on Edna Healey's social history of the Palace, *The Queen's House* (Michael Joseph, 1997).

Princess Elizabeth's handwritten essay about her parents' coronation is part of the Royal Collection Trust (RCIN 1080431), and has previously been published in Ben Pimlott's biography of the Queen. Norman Hartnell's descriptions come from his autobiography, *Silver and Gold.* Hartnell's private record of his encounter with Queen Mary was published in Michael Pick's biography. Winston Churchill's remark to his wife during the coronation ('You were right. I see now the "other one" wouldn't have done') is recorded in his daughter's biography of her mother (*Clementine Churchill* by Mary Soames, Doubleday, 2003). Robert Wood's detailed description of the coronation, as well as his experiences as a BBC sound engineer supervising royal broadcasts, appear in his memoir *A World in Your Ear* (Macmillan, 1979).

The infamous history of the Koh-i-Noor diamond is told in *Koh-i-Noor* by William Dalrymple and Anita Anand (Bloomsbury, 2017).

John Updike's moving account of stammering is from his memoir, *Self-consciousness* (Alfred Knopf, 1989).

THE WHITE WARDROBE

Norman Hartnell's creation of the 'white wardrobe' is outlined in his autobiography. Queen Elizabeth's letter to her mother-in-law, Queen Mary, describing herself as 'nearly demented' during the preparations and fittings, is included in William Shawcross's biography. Shawcross provides a full account of the state visit to Paris, as does Sarah Bradford in her biography of George VI. It was Bradford's research in the French government archives that revealed the suspected assassination plots to kill the King and Queen.

William Bullitt's report to President Roosevelt was originally published in *For the President, Personal and Secret: Correspondence between Franklin D. Roosevelt and William C. Bullitt* (Houghton Mifflin, 1972). Janet Flanner's account of the royal visit to France appeared in her July 1938 'Letter from Paris' in the *New Yorker*. Diana Cooper's letter to Conrad Russell, cited in this chapter, is in the Churchill Archives; and I have also drawn on her description of the scene at Versailles from her memoir, *The Light of Common Day*.

Eva Braun's predilection for Ferragamo shoes was revealed by Salvatore Ferragamo himself in his autobiography, *Shoemaker of Dreams* (Harrap, 1968). Hitler's description of Queen Elizabeth as 'the most dangerous woman in Europe', after he watched the newsreel of her appearance at the war memorial at Villers-Bretonneux, is reported in David Duff's *George and Elizabeth: A Royal Marriage* (Collins, 1983) and Michael Thornton's *Royal Feud* (Michael Joseph, 1985).

THE DOLLS

A key resource for this chapter has been Faith Eaton's *Dolls for the Princesses* (Royal Collection, 2002), which includes Princess Elizabeth's letter describing the dolls, written to her French tutor Georgina Guerin. Eaton was involved in the conservation and display of Marianne and France at Windsor Castle, and her archive is held at the V&A Museum of Childhood. As is clear in the text, I have also drawn on Sigmund Freud's essay 'The Uncanny' (Penguin Classics, 2003), and E. T. A. Hoffmann's story, 'The Sandman' (Penguin Classics, 2016).

Martin Gilbert displayed impeccable scholarship in tracing the path from Kristallnacht to the Holocaust, in *Kristallnacht: Prelude to Destruction* (HarperPress, 2006). Alongside the official royal biographies, and Sarah Bradford's authoritative biography of George VI, I have consulted the following sources on Neville Chamberlain's policy of appeasement and the royal family's attitude to the coming war: *Appeasing Hitler* by Tim Bouverie (Bodley Head, 2019); *Munich* by David Faber (Simon & Schuster, 2008); *The Windsors at War* by Alexander Larman (Weidenfeld & Nicolson, 2023); and *Munich: Prologue to Tragedy* by John Wheeler-Bennett (Macmillan, 1963).

Diana Cooper's description of working for the WVS is in her memoir, *The Light of Common Day*. Hilary Mantel's 'Royal Bodies' was originally delivered as a lecture for a *London Review of Books* event at the British Museum on 4 February 2013. It was also published in the *London Review of Books* on 21 February 2013, and subsequently included in her collection *Mantel Pieces* (4th Estate, 2020).

FAIRY QUEEN

Queen Elizabeth's reference to reading the unexpurgated version of Hitler's *Mein Kampf* was published in the collection of her correspondence edited by William Shawcross. Her lively descriptions of the state visit to Canada and North America, expressed in her many letters to Queen Mary and to her daughter Lilibet, are also drawn from the same source (*Counting One's Blessings: The Selected Letters of Queen Elizabeth the Queen Mother*).

Tommy Lascelles accompanied the King and Queen on this tour, and his letters to his wife about the trip are included alongside his diaries in *King's Counsellor*. Sally Bedell Smith provides a detailed report of the tour in her book, *George VI and Elizabeth*, including the fact that more than 3 million people gathered to watch the progress of the royal couple through the streets of New York. Eleanor Roosevelt's impressions of the royal couple were originally recorded in her book, *This I Remember* (Harper, 1949).

As cited in the text to this chapter, I have returned to Marion Crawford's memoir, and the diaries of Harold Nicolson and Cecil Beaton. Hugo Vickers gives a full account of why the photographer was fired by Condé Nast in his biography of Cecil Beaton. Queen Elizabeth's awareness of Beaton's spite is revealed by Vickers in *Malice in Wonderland: My Adventures in the World of Cecil Beaton* (Hodder & Stoughton, 2021). I have also relied on Beaton's memoir, *Photobiography*; and compared notes on Beaton's handwritten diaries with Claudia Acott Williams, Curator of Collections at Kensington Palace, and herself the author of *Cecil Beaton: The Royal Portraits* (Thames & Hudson, 2023).

BATTLE CAMP

Aside from Norman Hartnell's own wartime recollections of dressing Queen Elizabeth, contained in *Silver and Gold*, and the official royal biographies previously cited, I have drawn on Theo Aronson's *The Royal Family at War* (John Murray, 1993); Deborah Cadbury's *Princes at War* (Bloomsbury, 2015); and Alexander Larman's *The Windsors at War*.

As always, Queen Elizabeth's own letters, expertly edited by William Shawcross, are a crucial resource; as are the diaries of Cecil Beaton, the Reverend Alan Don, and

Harold Nicolson. Hugo Vickers' authorised biography of Cecil Beaton describes the staging of *Heil Cinderella*, Beaton's dealings with Queen Elizabeth, and his subsequent wartime activities working for the Ministry of Information. The Duke of Buccleuch's pro-German sympathies are confirmed in Tim Bouverie's *Appeasing Hitler*; Tim Tate's *Hitler's British Traitors* (Icon, 2018); and *Fellow Travellers of the Right* by Richard Griffiths (Constable, 1980).

Susan Sontag's 'Notes on Camp' was first published as an essay in *Partisan Review* in 1964; and subsequently republished in book form by Penguin Classics (2018).

THE MENAGERIE

Key pieces from Wallis Simpson's collection of Cartier jewellery were displayed at the V&A's Cartier exhibition in 2025, including the Flamingo brooch, and I was able to study archival material relating to its creation in 1939. I also drew on *Cartier*, the book that accompanied the V&A exhibition, edited by the co-curators Helen Molesworth and Rachel Garrahan (V&A Publishing, 2025).

I derived further context from Francesca Cartier Brickell's book about her grandfather's family empire, *The Cartiers* (Ballantine, 2019).

My research was immeasurably assisted by the advice and expertise of Geoffrey Munn, as well as his definitive book, *Tiaras: A History of Splendour* (ACC Art Books, 2023). In addition, I consulted two notable books by Suzy Menkes: *The Windsor Style* (Grafton, 1987) and *The Royal Jewels* (Grafton, 1985).

The report by Alexander Weddell, the US ambassador to Spain, to the US Secretary of State, quoting Wallis's view that 'France had lost because it was internally diseased', was dispatched from Madrid on 2 July 1940, and is sourced from documents in the Office of the Historian in the US Department of State (Foreign Relations of the United States Diplomatic Papers, 1940, vol. 3, US GPO, 1958).

Fruity Metcalfe's letters to his wife were included in Frances Donaldson's biography of Edward VIII. Donaldson provides a scrupulously researched account of the Windsors' dealings with the Nazis after the German invasion of France, and their wartime activities generally. Similarly damning material is provided by Deborah Cadbury (*Princes at War*); Alexander Larman (*The Windsors at War*); and Andrew Lownie (*Traitor King*). Michael Bloch supplies further telling evidence in *The Secret File of the Duke of Windsor*, *Operation Willi* and *Ribbentrop*; as does Jonathan Petropoulos in *Royals and the Reich* (Oxford University Press, 2006).

'FASHION IS INDESTRUCTIBLE'

My description of the bombing of Britain in the Second World War owes much to Juliet Gardiner's impressive book, *The Blitz* (HarperPress, 2010).

George VI's wartime diaries are held in the Royal Archives, and extracts have been quoted by his biographers, John Wheeler-Bennett and Sarah Bradford. Queen Elizabeth's wartime letters are drawn from William Shawcross's edited volume of her correspondence and official biography. The first authorised source for her famous quote that she was glad that Buckingham Palace had been bombed, as she could now 'look the East End in the face', is Sir John Wheeler-Bennett's official biography of George VI. Wheeler-Bennett cites an earlier biography, *Queen Elizabeth the Queen Mother*, by an official royal correspondent, Betty Spencer Shew (Hodder & Stoughton, 1955); in turn, Shawcross cites Wheeler-Bennett and Spencer Shew.

Harold Nicolson's wartime observations are sourced from his *Diaries and Letters, 1939–1945*. As previously noted, I have quoted from Cecil Beaton's handwritten diaries, held at St John's College, Cambridge. Lord Woolton's diary entry for 11 October 1940, describing Queen Elizabeth's alertness to the press when he accompanied the royal couple on a visit to a bomb site, is cited by Sally Bedell Smith in her book, *George VI and Elizabeth*; Woolton's original diaries are at the Bodleian Library in Oxford.

The relevant files concerning Queen Elizabeth's purchases from Norman Hartnell are in the Royal Archives (QEQMH/TREAS/CSP).

Aside from my own original research into London's couturiers, I have also drawn on the significant studies published in *London Couture: 1923–1975*, edited by Amy de la Haye and Edwina Ehrman (V&A Publishing, 2015). This includes essays on Edward Molyneux (by Neil Taylor), Henry Digby Morton (by Edwina Ehrman), Hardy Amies (by Ben Whyman) and Norman Hartnell (by Jane Hattrick). I have been influenced, too, by the scholarship of Michelle Jones, who has written an erudite account of the British fashion industry in the 1930s and 1940s in *London Couture and the Making of a Fashion Centre* (MIT Press, 2022).

The role of the SOE agent Violette Szabo, and the wartime activities of Paris couturiers, is covered in greater detail in my book *Miss Dior* (Faber, 2021). I have also drawn on two biographies of Wing-Commander F. F. E. Yeo-Thomas: *The White Rabbit* by Bruce Marshall (Evans, 1952), and *Bravest of the Brave* by Mark Seaman (Michael O'Mara Books, 1997).

The recorded interviews with Brian Stonehouse (along with a number of his wartime drawings, including those documenting concentration camps) are in the collection of the Imperial War Museum. So, too, is the oral history of his friend and fellow SOE agent Bob Sheppard. A collection of his fashion illustrations was exhibited at the Abbott and Holder gallery in London, accompanied by a book (*Brian Stonehouse: Artist, Soldier, War Hero, Fashion Illustrator* by Frederic A. Sharf, 2014).

QUEEN, COUTURIER, SOLDIER, SPY

Aside from my encounters with Hardy Amies, his own memoirs and correspondence, and my conversations with his trusted companion David Freeman, my primary source for this chapter has been Amies's military files in the National Archives (HS 9/29/2). I have also relied on *SOE in the Low Countries* by M. R. D. Foot (St Erwin's Press, 2001). As noted in the text, Foot was himself an intelligence agent, and in the post-war period became the pre-eminent authority on the Special Operations Executive.

Amies's interview with Naim Attallah was published in *No Longer With Us: Encounters with Naim Attallah* (Quartet Books, 2018). I have also been aided by Michael Pick's beautifully illustrated book, *Hardy Amies* (ACC Editions, 2012). Further context comes from *Delicate Mission: Autobiography of a Secret Agent* by Conrad O'Brien-ffrench (Skilton & Shaw, 1979).

Although the following books do not cover the period that Amies spent with Lee Miller in Brussels in 1944, or the incident with Audrey Withers, they nevertheless provided helpful background to my research: *Lee Miller: Fashion in Wartime Britain* by Ami Bouhassane, Robin Muir and Amber Butchart (Lee Miller Archives Publishing, 2021); *Lee Miller's War: Beyond D-Day*, edited by Antony Penrose (Thames & Hudson, 2020); *Dressed for War* by Julie Summers (Simon & Schuster, 2020).

THEATRE OF WAR

Queen Elizabeth's letter to her mother-in-law, Queen Mary, describing the destruction caused by the bombing in Stoke Newington, was written on 19 October 1940, and is included in her collection of letters edited by William Shawcross. I have also drawn on her wartime correspondence throughout this chapter, all from the books by Shawcross already referred to.

Jock Colville's description of listening to Princess Elizabeth's radio broadcast on 13 October 1940 appears in his diary: *The Fringes of Power: 10 Downing Street Diaries 1939–1955* (Hodder & Stoughton, 1985).

Queen Elizabeth's declaration that she would remain in England during the war – 'The children could not go without me, I could not possibly leave the King, and the King would never go' – is quoted in William Shawcross's official biography. However, he also notes that 'the precise moment [for her declaration] is obscure'.

A thorough study of the royal family's wartime security has been made by the military academic Andrew Stewart in his book *The King's Private Army: Protecting the British Royal Family during the Second World War* (Helion, 2015). Margaret Rhodes' wry comment about being left out of these security arrangements features in her memoir *The Final Curtsey* (Umbria Press, 2012).

Owen Morshead's correspondence with Queen Mary about safeguarding the Crown Jewels and other priceless possessions is in the Royal Archives. A delightful account of Morshead's efforts is included in Caroline Shenton's book, *National Treasures: Saving the Nation's Art in World War II* (John Murray, 2021). An equally engaging description of Queen Mary's wartime activities – including her vigorous assault on ivy at Badminton – appears in James Pope-Hennessy's *The Quest for Queen Mary*.

Marion Crawford's memoir provides further colour, as do the diaries of Cecil Beaton and Chips Channon. Eleanor Roosevelt noted the strict adherence to rationing of heating, food and water when she visited Buckingham Palace in 1942 (*This I Remember*). Another precious source has been *The Windsor Diaries: 1940–1945* by Alathea Fitzalan Howard (Hodder & Stoughton, 2020), which offers a remarkably candid, touching and evocative description of wartime life at Windsor. I have also drawn on Lisa Sheridan's autobiography, *From Cabbages to Kings* (Odhams, 1955); she devotes considerable space to her memories of photographing the royal family, including during the war. Robert Wood's reference to providing technical assistance for the wartime pantomimes at Windsor Castle is taken from his memoir, *A World in Your Ear*. Some of the pantomime costumes, and Claude Whatham's paintings, can be viewed online at the Royal Collection Trust (www.rct.uk).

IN UNIFORM

As noted in the text, Margaret Rhodes recounted the story of her outing with the princesses during the celebrations of VE Day (*The Final Curtsey*). Her memoir also includes the diary entries for the period written by her cousin Princess Elizabeth, 6–9 May 1945, and then for 14–15 August (covering the VJ Day celebrations); Rhodes was given permission by the Queen to publish these in her book. The Queen herself recorded her memories of VE Day for the BBC, broadcast on Radio 4 on 8 May 1985. (She was speaking to Godfrey Talbot, a BBC veteran who had been a frontline correspondent with Allied troops during the Second World War, and was appointed as the BBC's first officially accredited court correspondent in 1948.) More recently, King Charles III read aloud these passages from his mother's diaries at a VE Day celebration on 8 May 2025, broadcast around the world by the BBC.

The National Army Museum in London contains informative material on the wartime graphic designs of Abram Games, including his ATS poster, and the reactions that it provoked.

As cited in this chapter, I have quoted from Marion Crawford's memoir and the diaries of Alathea Fitzalan Howard and Cecil Beaton. Clement Attlee expressed his admiration and affection for George VI in a tribute written after the King's death, published by the *Observer* on 10 February 1952. He subsequently wrote about his support for the monarchy in another article for the *Observer*, published on 23 August 1959. Both of these essays have been republished in *Attlee's Great Contemporaries* (Continuum, 2009).

Aside from relying on Hardy Amies's published memoirs, I have also drawn on his private correspondence with the Queen.

PRINCESS BRIDE

The extraordinary story of Prince Philip's mother is brilliantly told by Hugo Vickers in his biography, *Alice, Princess Andrew of Greece* (Hamish Hamilton, 2000). I have derived further information from the following biographies: *Prince Philip: A Family Portrait* by Queen Alexandra of Yugoslavia (Hodder & Stoughton, 1960); *Philip* by Basil Boothroyd (Longman, 1971); *Young Prince Philip* by Philip Eade (HarperPress, 2011); *The Duke: A Portrait of Prince Philip* by Tim Heald (Hodder & Stoughton, 1991); *The Duke* by Ian Lloyd (History Press, 2021). The details of his family's connections with the Nazis were gleaned in part from *Royals and the Reich* by Jonathan Petropoulos (Oxford University Press, 2006). Petropoulos also provides a thorough investigation of the mission in Germany undertaken by Owen Morshead and Anthony Blunt. So, too, does Miranda Carter in her fascinating biography, *Anthony Blunt: His Lives* (Macmillan, 2001).

Ben Pimlott's biography of the Queen provides a detailed account of the concerns raised about Prince Philip, including the quote from the unpublished diaries of Jock Colville regarding Philip's 'Teutonic strain'. Harold Nicolson's diary entry about the royal family's misgivings concerning Prince Philip as a potential husband is quoted by Sarah Bradford in her biography of George VI, and Philip Eade in his biography of Prince Philip. Further details come from the memoirs of Lady Airlie and Marion Crawford.

As cited in this chapter, detailed reports of the royal wardrobes designed by Hartnell and Molyneux for the royal tour of South Africa were published in *The Times* on 17 February 1947. Aage Thaarup, the royal hatmaker, also described his designs in his autobiography, *Heads and Tales* (Cassell, 1956).

Ernestine Carter's account of her dealings with Stafford Cripps, and his disapproval of the New Look, is contained in her memoir, *With Tongue in Chic* (Michael Joseph, 1974). The denunciations of the New Look made by Bessie Braddock and Mabel Ridealgh are drawn from *Austerity Britain: 1945–1951* by David Kynaston (Bloomsbury, 2008).

Queen Elizabeth's letters describing the 1947 tour of South Africa are included in William Shawcross's edition of her selected correspondence. Tommy Lascelles also wrote a series of letters to his wife Joan, and one to his son, describing both the long journey to South Africa, and the tour itself. These were published alongside Lascelles' diaries in *King's Counsellor*. Peter Townsend's lengthy account of the tour was published in his autobiography, *Time and Chance* (Collins, 1978), including a description of the incident when the Queen hit a former serviceman over the head with her parasol.

For a broader understanding of the political context to Princess Elizabeth's twenty-first birthday speech, I relied in part on John Bew's outstanding biography of Clement Attlee, *Citizen Clem* (Riverrun, 2017); and the compelling, landmark study of the British Empire by Caroline Elkins, *Legacy of Violence* (Bodley Head, 2022). I was also influenced by Ben Pimlott's thoughtful analysis of both the speech and the South African tour in his biography of the Queen.

Norman Hartnell gives a detailed description of the creation of Princess Elizabeth's wedding dress in his memoir, *Silver and Gold*.

Jock Colville's retrieval of Princess Elizabeth's pearl necklace is related in his memoir *Footprints in Time* (William Collins, 1976). I derived further details of the royal wedding from the memoirs of Marion Crawford and Margaret Rhodes; the latter was a bridesmaid at the wedding, and described the last-minute dramas of the misplaced bridal bouquet and broken tiara.

CONSECRATION

The description of the crowds that assembled at Romsey Abbey, attempting to catch a glimpse of the royal couple during their honeymoon, is drawn from newspaper reports at the time, as well as Ben Pimlott's biography, *The Queen*. Elizabeth's letter to her cousin, written from Birkhall in Scotland, is sourced from *The Final Curtsey* by Margaret Rhodes. So, too, is the description of Princess Elizabeth's life in Malta. Additional material is drawn from Marion Crawford's memoir.

Cecil Beaton's diaries have again been a vital source, as has his memoir, *Photobiography*; the latter provides the details of his momentous day at Buckingham Palace photographing Queen Elizabeth in her black velvet dress, followed by Princess Elizabeth with her firstborn son, Charles.

The details of Princess Elizabeth's clothes for her royal tour of Canada and the USA are drawn from contemporaneous newspaper reports, as well as the memoirs of Norman Hartnell and Hardy Amies. I have also consulted the private correspondence and papers of Hardy Amies. The letter written to Amies by Princess Elizabeth on 24 September 1951 has previously been published in Ben Pimlott's biography of the Queen.

The fullest account of Elizabeth's reaction to news of her father's death, while she was in Kenya, is in Ben Pimlott's biography. Pimlott interviewed Martin Charteris, who provided him with the details that I have relied on in this chapter. As cited in the text, I have quoted from the diaries of Chips Channon, and Lady Airlie's memoir. William Shawcross's official biography of Queen Elizabeth the Queen Mother is another important source: it contains the letter from Queen Mary (dated 10 February 1952), asking her daughter-in-law to meet with the Duke of Windsor on his trip to England for George VI's funeral, and Queen Mary's subsequent letter to the Athlones (23 February 1952).

The correspondence quoted in this chapter between the Windsors was published in *The Secret File of the Duke of Windsor* by Michael Bloch. So, too, was the bitter exchange between the Windsors' solicitor, George Allen, and Tommy Lascelles.

Norman Hartnell's memoir provides a detailed account of his designs for the coronation. Hartnell's private account of the coronation is quoted in full in Michael Pick's biography of the designer.

Cecil Beaton's memorable description of the coronation, and the subsequent photographic session at Buckingham Palace, is recorded in his diaries.

BIBLIOGRAPHY

Acott Williams, Claudia, *Cecil Beaton: The Royal Portraits* (Thames & Hudson, V&A, 2023)

Airlie, Mabell, Countess of, *Thatched with Gold*, ed. Jennifer Ellis (Hutchinson, 1962)

Aldrich, Richard J., and Rory Cormac, *Spying and the Crown: The Secret Relationship Between British Intelligence and the Royals* (Atlantic Books, 2022)

Amies, Hardy, *Just So Far* (Collins, 1954)

———, *Still Here* (Weidenfeld & Nicolson, 1984)

Andrew, Christopher, *The Defence of the Realm: The Authorised History of MI5* (Penguin, 2010)

Aronson, Theo, *The Royal Family at War* (John Murray, 1993)

Attlee, Clement, *Attlee's Great Contemporaries*, ed. Frank Field (Continuum, 2009)

Bagehot, Walter, *The English Constitution* (Oxford University Press, 2009)

Ballard, Bettina, *In My Fashion* (Secker & Warburg, 1960)

Beaton, Cecil, *Photobiography* (Odhams Press, 1951)

———, *The Glass of Fashion* (Weidenfeld & Nicolson, 1954)

———, *The Wandering Years: 1922–1939* (Weidenfeld & Nicolson, 1961)

———, *The Years Between: 1939–1944* (Weidenfeld & Nicolson, 1965)

———, *The Happy Years: 1944–1948* (Weidenfeld & Nicolson, 1972)

———, *The Strenuous Years: 1948–1955* (Weidenfeld & Nicolson, 1973)

———, *Cecil Beaton, Theatre of War* (Jonathan Cape, 2012)

Bedell Smith, Sally, *George VI and Elizabeth* (Michael Joseph, 2023)

Beesly, Patrick, *Room 40: British Naval Intelligence, 1940–1918* (Hamish Hamilton, 1982)

Bew, John, *Citizen Clem: A Biography of Attlee* (Riverrun, 2017)

Bloch, Michael, *The Duke of Windsor's War* (Weidenfeld & Nicolson, 1982)

———, *Operation Willi: The Nazi Plot to Kidnap the Duke of Windsor, July 1940* (Weidenfeld & Nicolson, 1984)

———, *Wallis and Edward: Letters 1931–1937: The Intimate Correspondence of the Duke and Duchess of Windsor* (Weidenfeld & Nicolson, 1986)

———, *The Secret File of the Duke of Windsor* (Bantam, 1988)

———, *The Reign and Abdication of Edward VIII* (Bantam, 1990)

———, *Ribbentrop* (Bantam, 1992)

———, *The Duchess of Windsor* (Weidenfeld & Nicolson, 1996)

Boothroyd, Basil, *Philip: An Informal Biography* (Longman, 1971)

Bouhassane, Ami, Robin Muir and Amber Butchart, *Lee Miller: Fashion in Wartime Britain* (Lee Miller Archives, 2021)

Bouverie, Tim, *Appeasing Hitler: Chamberlain, Churchill and the Road to War* (Bodley Head, 2019)

Bradford, Sarah, *George VI* (Weidenfeld & Nicolson, 1989)

Bryan III, J., and Charles J. V. Murphy, *The Windsor Story* (William Morrow, 1979)

Byrne, Paula, *Mad World: Evelyn Waugh and the Secrets of Brideshead* (HarperPress, 2010)

Cadbury, Deborah, *Princes at War: The British Royal Family's Private Battle in the Second World War* (Bloomsbury, 2015)

———, *Queen Victoria's Matchmaking: The Royal Marriages that Shaped Europe* (Bloomsbury, 2017)

Carter, Ernestine, *With Tongue in Chic* (Michael Joseph, 1974)

Carter, Miranda, *Anthony Blunt: His Lives* (Macmillan, 2001)

———, *The Three Emperors: Three Cousins, Three Empires and the Road to World War One* (Fig Tree, 2009)

Henry 'Chips' Channon: The Diaries 1918–1938, ed. Simon Heffer (Hutchinson, 2021)

Henry 'Chips' Channon: The Diaries 1938–1943, ed. Simon Heffer (Hutchinson, 2021)

Henry 'Chips' Channon: The Diaries 1943–1957, ed. Simon Heffer (Hutchinson, 2022)

Cohen, Lisa, *All We Know: Three Lives* (Farrar, Straus & Giroux, 2012)

Colville, Lady Cynthia, *Crowded Life* (Evans, 1963)

Colville, Jock, *Footprints in Time* (William Collins, 1976)

———, *The Fringes of Power: 10 Downing Street Diaries 1939–1955* (Hodder & Stoughton, 1985)

Cooper, Lady Diana, *The Light of Common Day* (Rupert Hart-Davis, 1959)

———, *Trumpets from the Steep* (Rupert Hart-Davis, 1960)

The Duff Cooper Diaries, ed. John Julius Norwich (Weidenfeld & Nicolson, 2005)

The Letters of Noël Coward, ed. Barry Day (Methuen, 2007)

Crawford, Marion, *The Little Princesses* (Cassell, 1950)

Dalrymple, William, and Anita Anand, *Koh-i-Noor: The History of the World's Most Infamous Diamond* (Bloomsbury, 2017)

Don, Alan, *Faithful Witness: The Confidential Diaries of Alan Don, Chaplain to the King, the Archbishop and the Speaker, 1931–1946,* ed. Robert Beaken (SPCK Publishing, 2020)

Donaldson, Frances, *Edward VIII* (Weidenfeld & Nicolson, 1974)

———, *A Twentieth-Century Life* (Weidenfeld & Nicolson, 1992)

Dorril, Stephen, *Blackshirt: Sir Oswald Mosley and British Fascism* (Viking, 2006)

Duff-Gordon, Lucy, *Discretions and Indiscretions* (Jarrolds, 1932)

Eade, Philip, *Young Prince Philip: His Turbulent Early Life* (HarperPress, 2011)

Eaton, Faith, *Dolls for the Princesses: The Story of France and Marianne* (Royal Collection, 2002)

Elkins, Caroline, *Legacy of Violence: A History of the British Empire* (Bodley Head, 2022)

Evans, Richard J., *Hitler's People: The Faces of the Third Reich* (Allen Lane, 2024)
Faber, David, *Munich: The 1938 Appeasement Crisis* (Simon & Schuster, 2008)
Fitzalan Howard, Alathea, *The Windsor Diaries: 1940–1945*, ed. Celestria Noel (Hodder & Stoughton, 2020)
Flanner, Janet, *London Was Yesterday: 1934–1939*, ed. Irving Drutman (Michael Joseph, 1975)
Foot, M. R. D., *SOE in the Low Countries* (St Ermin's Press, 2001)
———, *SOE in France: An Account of the Work of the British Special Operations Executive in France, 1940–1944* (Frank Cass, 2004)
Gardiner, Juliet, *The Blitz: The British Under Attack* (HarperPress, 2010)
Gilbert, Martin, *Kristallnacht: Prelude to Destruction* (HarperPress, 2006)
Griffiths, Richard, *Fellow Travellers of the Right: British Enthusiasts for Nazi Germany 1933–1939* (Constable, 1980)
———, *Patriotism Perverted: Captain Ramsay, The Right Club and British Anti-Semitism 1939–40* (Constable, 1998)
Guenther, Irene, *Nazi Chic?: Fashioning Women in the Third Reich* (Berg, 2004)
Hardinge, Helen, *Loyal to Three Kings* (William Kimber, 1967)
Hardman, Robert, *Queen of Our Times: The Life of Elizabeth II* (Macmillan, 2022)
Hartnell, Norman, *Silver and Gold* (Evans, 1955)
Haye, Amy de la, and Edwina Ehrman (eds), *London Couture: British Luxury 1923–1975* (V&A, 2015)
Heald, Tim, *The Duke: A Portrait of Prince Philip* (Hodder & Stoughton, 1991)
Healey, Edna, *The Queen's House: A Social History of Buckingham Palace* (Michael Joseph, 1997)
Higham, Charles, *Mrs Simpson: Secret Lives of the Duchess of Windsor* (Pan, 2005)
Hoare, Philip, *Noël Coward: A Biography* (Sinclair-Stevenson, 1995)
Jones, Michelle, *London Couture and the Making of a Fashion Centre* (MIT, 2022)
King, Stella, *Princess Marina* (Cassell, 1969)
Kinross, Lord, *The Windsor Years* (William Collins, 1967)
Kynaston, David, *Austerity Britain: 1945–1951* (Bloomsbury, 2008)
Larman, Alexander, *The Crown in Crisis: Countdown to the Abdication* (Weidenfeld & Nicolson, 2020)
———, *The Windsors at War: The Royals and the Nazis* (Weidenfeld & Nicolson, 2023)
———, *Power and Glory: Elizabeth II and the Rebirth of Royalty* (Weidenfeld & Nicolson, 2024)
In Royal Service: Letters and Journals of Sir Alan Lascelles, 1920–1936, ed. Duff Hart-Davis (Hamish Hamilton, 1989)
———, *King's Counsellor: Abdication and War: The Diaries of Sir Alan 'Tommy' Lascelles*, ed. Duff Hart-Davis (Weidenfeld & Nicolson, 2020)
Lees-Milne, James, *Harold Nicolson: A Biography: Volume One, 1886–1929* (Chatto & Windus, 1980)

Lloyd, Ian, *The Duke: 100 chapters in the Life of Prince Philip* (History Press, 2021)
The Diaries of Sir Robert Bruce Lockhart 1915–1938, ed. Kenneth Young (Macmillan, 1973)
Longford, Elizabeth, *Elizabeth R: A Biography* (Weidenfeld & Nicolson, 1983)
Diaries and Letters of Marie Belloc Lowndes, 1911–1947, ed. Susan Lowndes (Chatto & Windus, 1971)
Lownie, Andrew, *Traitor King: The Scandalous Exile of the Duke and Duchess of Windsor* (Blink, 2021)
Mantel, Hilary, *Mantel Pieces: Royal Bodies and Other Writing from the 'London Review of Books'* (4th Estate, 2020)
Marks, Leo, *Between Silk and Cyanide: A Codemaker's War 1941–1945* (History Press, 2008)
Marshall, Bruce, *The White Rabbit* (Evans, 1952)
Maxwell, Elsa, *I Married the World* (Heinemann, 1955)
McDowell, Colin, *Forties Fashion and the New Look* (Bloomsbury, 1997)
Menkes, Suzy, *The Royal Jewels* (Grafton, 1985)
———, *The Windsor Style* (Grafton, 1987)
Lee Miller's War: Beyond D-Day, ed. Antony Penrose (Thames & Hudson, 2020)
Lee Miller: Fashion in Wartime Britain (Lee Miller Archives Publishing, 2021)
Molesworth, Helen, and Rachel Garrahan (eds), *Cartier* (V&A, 2025)
Mortimer, Penelope, *Queen Mother: An Alternative Portrait of Her Life and Times* (Andre Deutsch, 1995)
Morton, Andrew, *17 Carnations: The Windsors, the Nazis and the Cover-up* (Michael O'Mara, 2015)
———, *Wallis in Love: The Untold True Passion of the Duchess of Windsor* (Michael O'Mara, 2021)
Mosley, Diana, *The Duchess of Windsor* (Sidgwick & Jackson, 1980)
Muir, Robin, and Josephine Ross, *The Crown in 'Vogue'* (Conran Octopus, 2022)
Munn, Geoffrey C., *Tiaras: A History of Splendour* (ACC, 2023)
Nichols, Beverley, *The Sweet and Twenties* (Weidenfeld & Nicolson, 1958)
Nicolson, Harold, *King George V: His Life and Reign* (Constable, 1952)
———, *Diaries and Letters 1930–1939*, ed. Nigel Nicolson (William Collins, 1966)
———, *Diaries and Letters 1939–1945*, ed. Nigel Nicolson (William Collins, 1967)
———, *Diaries and Letters 1945–1962*, ed. Nigel Nicolson (William Collins, 1968)
———, *The Harold Nicolson Diaries 1907–1964*, ed. Nigel Nicolson (Weidenfeld & Nicolson, 2004)
O'Brien-ffrench, Conrad, *Delicate Mission: Autobiography of a Secret Agent* (Skilton & Shaw, 1979)
Petropoulos, Jonathan, *Royals and the Reich: The Princes von Hessen in Nazi Germany* (Oxford University Press, 2006)
Pick, Michael, *Hardy Amies* (ACC Editions, 2012)
———, *Norman Hartnell: The Biography* (Zuleika, 2019)

Pimlott, Ben, *The Queen: Elizabeth II and the Monarchy* (HarperCollins, 1996)
Pope-Hennessy, James, *Queen Mary:1867–1953* (George Allen & Unwin, 1959)
———, *The Quest for Queen Mary*, ed. Hugo Vickers (Hodder & Stoughton, 2018)
Rappaport, Helen, *Ekaterinburg: The Last Days of the Romanovs* (Hutchinson, 2009)
———, *The Race to Save the Romanovs: The Truth Behind the Secret Plans to Rescue Russia's Imperial Family* (Hutchinson, 2018)
Rhodes, Margaret, *The Final Curtsey: A Royal Memoir by the Queen's Cousin* (Umbria, 2012)
Ridley, Jane, *Bertie, A Life of Edward VII* (Chatto & Windus, 2012)
———, *George V: Never a Dull Moment* (Chatto & Windus, 2021)
Roberts, Hugh, *The Queen's Diamonds* (Royal Collection, 2011)
Rose, Kenneth, *King George V* (Weidenfeld & Nicolson, 1983)
———, *Who's In, Who's Out: The Journals of Kenneth Rose, Volume One: 1944–1979*, ed. D. R. Thorpe (Weidenfeld & Nicolson, 2018)
Sackville-West, Vita, and Harold Nicolson, *Vita and Harold: The Letters of Vita Sackville-West and Harold Nicolson 1910–1962*, ed. Nigel Nicolson (Weidenfeld & Nicolson, 1992)
Schiaparelli, Elsa, *Shocking Life* (V&A Publications, 2007)
Seaman, Mark, *Bravest of the Brave: The True Story of Wing Commander Tommy Yeo-Thomas, SOE Secret Agent, Codename 'the White Rabbit'* (Michael O'Mara, 1997)
Sebba, Anne, *That Woman: The Life of Wallis Simpson, Duchess of Windsor* (Weidenfeld & Nicolson, 2011)
Secrest, Meryle, *Elsa Schiaparelli: A Biography* (Fig Tree, 2014)
Sharf, Frederic A., *Brian Stonehouse, MBE, 1918–1988: Artist, Soldier, War Hero, Fashion Illustrator* (2014)
Shawcross, William, *Queen Elizabeth the Queen Mother: The Official Biography* (Macmillan, 2009)
———, *Counting One's Blessings: The Selected Letters of Queen Elizabeth the Queen Mother*, ed. William Shawcross (Macmillan, 2012)
Shenton, Caroline, *National Treasures: Saving the Nation's Art in World War II* (John Murray, 2021)
Sheridan, Lisa, *From Cabbages to Kings* (Odhams, 1955)
Sontag, Susan, *Under the Sign of Saturn* (Penguin Classics, 2009)
———, *Notes on Camp* (Penguin Classics, 2018)
Spicer, Charles, *Coffee with Hitler: The British Amateurs Who Tried to Civilise the Nazis* (Oneworld, 2022)
Stewart, Andrew, *The King's Private Army: Protecting the British Royal Family during the Second World War* (Helion, 2015)
Strong, Roy, *Cecil Beaton: The Royal Portraits* (Thames & Hudson, 1988)
———, *The Roy Strong Diaries, 1967–1987* (Weidenfeld & Nicolson, 2017)
Summers, Julie, *Dressed for War: The Story of 'Vogue' Editor Audrey Withers, from the Blitz to the Swinging Sixties* (Simon & Schuster, 2020)

Tate, Tim, *Hitler's British Traitors: The Secret History of Spies, Saboteurs and Fifth Columnists* (Icon, 2018)
Taylor, D. J., *Bright Young People: The Rise and Fall of a Generation, 1918–1939* (Vintage, 2008)
Thaarup, Aage, with Dora Shackell, *Heads and Tales* (Cassell, 1956)
Thornton, Michael, *Royal Feud: The Queen Mother and the Duchess of Windsor* (Michael Joseph, 1985)
Tippett, Jane Marguerite, *Once a King: The Lost Memoir of Edward VIII* (Hodder & Stoughton, 2023)
Torrance, David, *The Wild Men: The Remarkable Story of Britain's First Labour Government* (Bloomsbury Continuum, 2024)
Townsend, Peter, *Time and Chance: An Autobiography* (Collins, 1978)
Urbach, Karina, *Go Betweens for Hitler* (Oxford University Press, 2015)
Vanderbilt, Gloria, and Thelma, Lady Furness, *Double Exposure: A Twin Autobiography* (Frederick Muller, 1959)
Vickers, Hugo, *Cecil Beaton* (Weidenfeld & Nicolson, 1985)
———, *Alice, Princess Andrew of Greece* (Hamish Hamilton, 2000)
———, *Elizabeth the Queen Mother* (Hutchinson, 2005)
———, *Behind Closed Doors: The Tragic, Untold Story of the Duchess of Windsor* (Hutchinson, 2011)
———, *Malice in Wonderland: My Adventures in the World of Cecil Beaton* (Hodder & Stoughton, 2021)
Wheeler-Bennett, John, *King George VI: His Life and Reign* (Macmillan, 1958)
Willetts, Paul, *Rendezvous at the Russian Tea Rooms: The Spyhunter, the Fashion Designer and the Man From Moscow* (Constable, 2015)
Williams, Kate, *Young Elizabeth: The Making of Our Queen* (Weidenfeld & Nicolson, 2012)
Williams, Susan, *The People's King: The True Story of the Abdication* (Allen Lane, 2003)
Windsor, the Duchess of, *The Heart Has Its Reasons* (Michael Joseph, 1956)
Windsor, the Duke of, *A King's Story* (Cassell, 1951)
———, *A Family Album* (Cassell, 1960)
[———], *Letters from a Prince: Edward, Prince of Wales to Mrs Freda Dudley Ward,* ed. Rupert Godfrey (Little, Brown and Co., 1998)
Wood, Robert, *A World in Your Ear: The Broadcasting of an Era, 1923–1964* (Macmillan, 1979)
Woolf, Virginia, *Selected Letters*, ed. Joanne Trautmann Banks (Vintage, 2008)
Ziegler, Philip, *Crown and People* (Collins, 1978)
———, *Diana Cooper* (Hamish Hamilton, 1981)
———, *King Edward VIII* (Collins, 1990)

PICTURE CREDITS

p. ii Popperfoto via Getty Images.
vi Yousuf Karsh, Camera Press London.
3 © Hulton-Deutsch Collection/Corbis via Getty Images.
9 © Hulton-Deutsch Collection/Corbis via Getty Images.
14 PNA Rota/Getty Images.
19 Hulton Archive/Getty Images.
20 Hardy Amies/Mary Evans Picture Library.
27 © Hulton-Deutsch Collection/Corbis via Getty Images.
31 © Illustrated London News Ltd/Mary Evans Picture Library.
35 (*above*) Ann Ronan Pictures/Getty Images.
35 (*below*) Bettmann/Getty Images.
36 Popperfoto via Getty Images.
38 Alamy.
41 Culture Club/Getty Images.
42 Topical Press Agency/Getty Images.
50 (*above*) Hulton Archive/Getty Images.
50 (*below left*) Keystone/Getty Images.
50 (*below right*) The Print Collector/Heritage Images via Getty Images.
51 Marcus Adams/Paul Popper/Popperfoto via Getty Images.
59 (*above*) Daily Mirror via Getty Images.
59 (*below*) Lisa Sheridan/Studio Lisa/Hulton Archive/Getty Images.
63 Felix Man/Picture Post/Hulton Archive/Getty Images.
64 Sasha/Hulton Archive/Getty Images.
70 Hulton Archive/Getty Images.
77 © 2025 Man Ray 2015 Trust/DACS, London. Photo Allen Memorial Art Museum.
80 Horst P. Horst/Condé Nast via Getty Images.
81 Horst P. Horst/Condé Nast via Getty Images.
84 (*above left*) © Hulton-Deutsch Collection/Corbis via Getty Images.
84 (*above right*) Keystone/Hulton Archive/Getty Images.
84 (*below left*) Bettmann/Getty Images.
84 (*below right*) © Illustrated London News Ltd/Mary Evans Picture Library.
92 PA Images/Alamy.
95 Popperfoto via Getty Images.
106 De Luan/Alamy.
110 © Hulton-Deutsch Collection/Corbis via Getty Images.

115 Everett Collection Inc/Alamy.
118 Popperfoto via Getty Images.
127 W. & D. Downey/Hulton Archive/Getty Images.
128 Universal History Archive/Universal Images Group via Getty Images.
133 Popperfoto via Getty Images.
141 Bob Thomas/Popperfoto via Getty Images.
146 Cecil Beaton/Condé Nast via Getty Images.
151 Cecil Beaton/Condé Nast via Getty Images.
154 Cecil Beaton/Condé Nast via Getty Images.
155 Popperfoto via Getty Images/Getty Images.
162 (*above*) Daily Herald Archive/National Science & Media Museum/SSPL via Getty Images.
162 (*below*) Popperfoto via Getty Images.
166 FPG/Archive Photos/Getty Images.
168 The Print Collector/Getty Images.
176 (*above*) Fox Photos/Getty Images.
176 (*below*) Hulton Archive/Getty Images.
177 Popperfoto via Getty Images.
182 Popperfoto via Getty Images.
189 Central Press/Hulton Archive/Getty Images.
190 Mary Evans Picture Library/SZ Photo/Scherl.
197 Paul Popper/Popperfoto via Getty Images.
198 Mary Evans Picture Library/Hardy Amies London.
202 Fox Photos/Hulton Archive/Getty Images.
204 Sueddeutsche Zeitung Photo/Alamy.
209 (*above*) © Illustrated London News Ltd/Mary Evans Picture Library.
209 (*below*) Keystone-France/Gamma-Rapho via Getty Images.
217 (*above*) Central Press/Hulton Archive/Getty Images.
217 (*below*) Central Press/Hulton Archive/Getty Images.
220 Bettmann/Getty Images.
226 Bettmann/Getty Images.
232 © Cecil Beaton/Victoria & Albert Museum, London.
233 © Cecil Beaton/Victoria & Albert Museum, London.
236 © Cecil Beaton/Victoria & Albert Museum, London.
239 © Cecil Beaton/Victoria & Albert Museum, London.
240 Popperfoto via Getty Images.
242 Popperfoto via Getty Images.
243 James Jarche/Popperfoto via Getty Images.
251 AFP via Getty Images.
256 Bridgeman Images.
259 (*above*) Bettmann/Getty Images.

259 (*below*) Topical Press Agency/Getty Images.
264 AP Photo/Alamy.
267 © National Portrait Gallery, London.
268 © Illustrated London News Ltd/Mary Evans Picture Library.
272 Fox Photos/Getty Images.
277 (*above*) Topical Press Agency/Getty Images.
277 (*below*) Keystone/Getty Images.
280 Cecil Beaton/Condé Nast via Getty Images.
281 Cecil Beaton/Condé Nast via Getty Images.
283 Creative Commons CC0 License.
290 © Hulton-Deutsch Collection/Corbis via Getty Images.
293 The National Archives.
301 Fred Ramage/Getty Images.
302 Ministry of Information Photo Division Photographer/ Imperial War Museums via Getty Images.
309 © Lee Miller Archives.
312 Popperfoto via Getty Images.
319 (*above left*) Topical Press Agency/Hulton Archive/Getty Images.
319 (*above right*) Lisa Sheridan/Studio Lisa/Hulton Archive/Getty Images.
319 (*below left*) Lisa Sheridan/Studio Lisa/Hulton Archive/Getty Images.
319 (*below right*) © Hulton-Deutsch Collection/Corbis via Getty Images.
320 Lisa Sheridan/Studio Lisa/Hulton Archive/Getty Images.
321 © Cecil Beaton/Victoria & Albert Museum, London.
324 (*both*) Lisa Sheridan/Studio Lisa/Hulton Archive/Getty Images.
325 (*above left, above right, below left*) Lisa Sheridan/Studio Lisa/Hulton Archive/Getty Images.
325 (*below right*) The Print Collector/Heritage Images via Getty Images.
327 © Cecil Beaton/Victoria & Albert Museum, London.
332 Paul Popper/Popperfoto via Getty Images.
334–5 Nixon & Greaves/Mirrorpix/Getty Images.
337 Popperfoto via Getty Images/Getty Images.
338 Popperfoto/Getty Images.
343 © Cecil Beaton/Victoria & Albert Museum, London.
346 Central Press/Getty Images.
348 Bettmann/Getty Images.
353 Paul Popper/Popperfoto/Getty Images.
358 Paul Popper/Popperfoto/Getty Images.
359 Universal History Archive/Universal Images Group via Getty Images.
362 Topical Press Agency/Hulton Archive/Getty Images.
368 Bert Hardy/Picture Post/Hulton Archive/Getty Images.
369 Bert Hardy/Picture Post/Hulton Archive/Getty Images.

370 (*above left*) Topical Press Agency/Hulton Archive/Getty Images.
370 (*both*) Popperfoto via Getty Images/Getty Images.
374 Keystone/Getty Images.
377 © Cecil Beaton/Victoria & Albert Museum, London.
378 © Cecil Beaton/Victoria & Albert Museum, London.
382 Fox Photos/Getty Images.
383 (*all*) Hardy Amies/Mary Evans Picture Library.
389 Reg Speller/Fox Photos/Getty Images.
394 Daily Herald Archive/National Science & Media Museum/SSPL via Getty Images.
398 © Cecil Beaton/Victoria & Albert Museum, London.
399 © Cecil Beaton/Victoria & Albert Museum, London.
401 © Cecil Beaton/Victoria & Albert Museum, London.
402 AFP via Getty Images.

INDEX

Note: References in italics denote photographs. The following abbreviations are used for members of the royal family; different titles for the same person are also indicated using '='. KGV (King George V); KGVI (King George VI); PW (Prince of Wales)=KEVIII (King Edward VIII)=DkW (Duke of Windsor); PP (Prince Philip); QM (Queen Mary); QE (Queen Elizabeth)=QEQM (Queen Elizabeth, the Queen Mother); PE (Princess Elizabeth)=QEII (Queen Elizabeth II); PM (Princess Margaret); WS (Wallis Simpson)=DchW (Duchess of Windsor)